Front endpaper:

LONDON, c. 1600 (?). *This oil painting, measuring 86 by 56 cm., hangs in the Tower Hamlets Central Library, Bancroft Road, Stepney, London E1. The view has been assigned to Claude de Jongh, on evidence I have not seen either questioned or demonstrated, and dated c. 1627 (?) on the basis of a pen and bistre (dark-brown pigment used in water colour) drawing in the Print Room of the British Library; this drawing, tentatively identified as of Winchester House, and attributed (although not with certainty) to de Jongh, bears the inscription April 1627. The dating of the painting could hardly be more speculative: de Jongh also visited England, apparently for short sketching expeditions, in 1615, 1625, and 1627, and could have made the painting at a later date in Holland.*

In Irene Scouloudi's opinion the evidence suggests that the panorama represents London around 1600 (Panoramic Views of London, 1600–1666 *(1953), pp. 43–5). De Jongh—if indeed he executed the painting—does not show Salisbury House and Little Salisbury House, construction of which was well underway by 1602, with completion taking place in 1610. The four Bankside amphitheatres depicted must be the Swan, Bear Garden (rebuilt, 1614, as the Hope), Rose, and Globe. Scouloudi states that the Rose 'was gone by 1606', but it was still in occasional use as late as 1622. She classifies the Tower Hamlets panorama with the numerous derivatives—over thirty variants, falling into four sub-groups—stemming from the engraving presumably by Matthaeus, or Matthew, Merian the elder, published in Gottfried's* Neuwe archologia cosmica *in Frankfurt in 1638. The compendium includes a number of views of European cities. That of London is unsigned, but others bear his name; hence the attribution. C. Walter Hodges thinks that 'Merian himself probably took most of his material from Visscher'* (The Globe Restored: A Study of the Elizabethan Theatre *(2nd ed., 1968), p. 111). Probably so; but the interconnections among the Visscher, Merian, de Jongh, and other related views, including that doubtfully ascribed to Thomas Wyck in the Devonshire collection, deserve fuller study than they have yet received. In this context it may be noted that the Tower Hamlets painting seems to resemble most closely the engraved 'View of London & Westminster from Southwark', presumably itself deriving from Visscher and Merian, 'Gedruckt t'Amsterd, by Rombout vanden Hoeÿe', in the Prints and Drawings Department of the British Museum (Crace Views I, Sheet 16, no. 20). The date 1630 inscribed under the engraving probably represents Crace's guess.*

Recorded as a master of the painters' guild at Utrecht in 1627, de Jongh was born around 1600 and died in 1663. Although he lived mainly in Utrecht, his work, at least until the mid 1630s, places him with the Haarlem school. He seems never to have resided in London. For an authoritative brief study, summarising what is known of his life and analysing his work, see John Hayes, 'Claude de Jongh', The Burlington Magazine, *xcviii (1956), 3–11. To Hayes 'de Jongh emerges as an interesting and sometimes very attractive little master, a refined draughtsman, at his best an artist with a lively feeling for paint, and a figure who achieves a place in the history both of English topographical art and of Utrecht painting' (p. 11).*

However refined his draughtsmanship, de Jongh was not much for topographical accuracy. Hayes is apparently unaware of the Tower Hamlets panorama, which he neither reproduces nor mentions, but he notes the inaccuracies of the artist's best known work, the View of Old London Bridge *in the Iveagh Bequest at Kenwood. Scouloudi points to a number of peculiarities—her word—in the panorama: the pronounced, and fictitious, northward curve of the Thames by the Tower, the exaggerated towers, cupolas, and weather vanes of the Tower itself, the curious three-storied pagoda-like structure to the west of Bankside.*

Whatever topographical liberties the artist has allowed himself, however, his picture is exceptionally handsome and in a beautiful state of preservation. Oddly, it is scarcely known, never having been (so far as I can determine) reproduced. A partial explanation, at least, may be found in the fact that Scouloudi's Panoramic Views, *the only monograph to describe the painting in detail, is hard to come by. Published from typescript in an edition limited to one hundred copies, it is available in the Map Room of the British Library but not, for example, in the Folger Shakespeare Library or the Library of Congress as late as 1979.*

The painting came to the Tower Hamlets Central Library as the gift of Samuel Montagu, M.P., who had bought it at Earl Granville's sale in July 1892.

WILLIAM SHAKESPEARE
Records and Images

Frontispiece:

THE CHANDOS PORTRAIT: OZIAS HUMPHRY'S VERSION. *Folger Shakespeare Library Art Inv. 323. Persuaded that this anonymous portrait was an authentic likeness of Shakespeare, Edmond Malone arranged for a copy to be made at Chandos House in August 1883 by his acquaintance Ozias Humphry (1742–1810), a leading portrait artist of the day, especially noted for his miniatures and later for his work in crayon. In a letter to Humphry on 17 August, Malone expressed his gratitude, at the same time mildly complaining that perhaps too much of the white showed in one of the eyes, making Shakespeare appear to squint (Folger Shakespeare Library MS. C.b.7). Such qualms were passing; Malone treasured the crayon drawing. On 29 June 1784 he noted on the back, 'The original having been painted by a very ordinary hand, having been at some subsequent period painted over, and being now in a state of decay, this copy, which is a very faithful one, is, in my opinion, invaluable.' A vapid engraving of Humphry's drawing by Charles Knight provided the frontispiece to the first volume of Malone's 1790* Shakespeare. *James Boswell, Jr., the biographer's son, used another engraving of the same drawing for the 1821 Third Variorum, which he saw through the press after Malone's death. The eminent portrait-engraver Edward Scriven (1775–1841) executed the most admired version of Humphry's version of Chandos; it appears in James Boaden's* Inquiry into the Authenticity of Various Pictures and Prints . . . of Shakspeare, *facing p. 39, and elsewhere. The original drawing is, to my best knowledge, here reproduced for the first time. On the Chandos portrait, see pp. 175–80.*

WILLIAM SHAKESPEARE

Records and Images

S. SCHOENBAUM

OXFORD UNIVERSITY PRESS
New York

First published 1981 by Scolar Press

Published in the United States
by Oxford University Press, New York

LIBRARY OF CONGRESS CATALOGING IN PUBLICATION DATA
Schoenbaum, Samuel, 1927–
William Shakespeare: records and images.
Includes index.
1. Shakespeare, William, 1564–1616 – Biography – Sources.
2. Shakespeare, William 1564–1616 – Biography.
3. Dramatists, English – Early modern, 1500–1700 – Biography.
PR2893.S32 1981 822.3'3 80–24538
ISBN 0–19–520234–1

Printed in Great Britain by
The Scolar Press, Ilkley, West Yorkshire

To O. B. Hardison, Jr.

Contents

Preface

This book honours an undertaking made, perhaps rashly, six years back. In the Preface to my *William Shakespeare: A Documentary Life* I lamented that the imperatives of narrative design, no less than space limitations, prevented me from admitting a number of facsimiles I would otherwise have very much liked to reproduce. These included the complete run of Stationers' Register entries of Shakespeare's plays and poems, specimens of the forgeries of William-Henry Ireland and J. Payne Collier, as well as (among other curiosities) the purported Shakespeare signature in William Lambarde's *Archaionomia*, an item which had lately attracted considerable press notice. This material I volunteered to present, in due course, in a supplementary volume.

The present work furnishes chapters on Shakespeare's stationers (with the Register entries) and Shakespeare forgeries. Along with other Shakespeare signatures—authentic, spurious, or in varying degrees questionable—and the three pages of *Sir Thomas More* in hand D, the *Archaionomia* item finds a place in a chapter on Shakespeare's handwriting.

I have broadened the scope of my earlier intention by reviewing the history of the principal Shakespeare portraits, genuine or doubtful (mostly the latter), and reproduced them in my pages. These are the main images of my title. A section on Shakespeare in London reproduces in facsimile the whole of Simon Forman's 'Book of Plays', with its descriptions of four plays, including *Macbeth* and *The Winter's Tale*, witnessed by the physician–astrologer before Shakespeare had retired from the stage; also the principal proceedings in the Belott–Mountjoy suit into which Shakespeare was innocently drawn as a witness in 1612, and the purchaser's counterpart—that is, Shakespeare's own copy—of the conveyance for the Blackfriars gate-house he purchased the next year. The chapter on Shakespeare in Stratford gives, along with other items, all seven records in the action brought by Shakespeare, for non-payment of debt, against one John Addenbrooke, and a key extract from Roland Wheler's deposition describing, ostensibly from first-hand knowledge, William Bott's alleged murder of his own daughter Isabella in the great five-gabled house the dramatist later bought in Chapel Street. The existence of the Wheler deposition was unknown to me, and to the public at large, when I wrote my *Documentary Life*.

It is not, I dare say, all that unusual for a sequel to surpass in scale the parent work. One thing leads to another. The chapter on the stationers seemed to call for some preliminary account of the origin and development of the Worshipful Company, its *modus operandi*, and the more teasingly problematic Register entries. Having thus applied myself, I thought that a useful purpose might be served by the inclusion of a dictionary of printers and booksellers, based largely on the wonderfully useful, but not always conveniently available, reference guides of E. Gordon Duff, R. B. McKerrow, and Henry R. Plomer, and supplementing these tools—now more than half a century old—with information provided by more recent studies. Similarly, my account of the debated Shakespeare signatures naturally invited a review of the characteristics of his hand. In surveying the various Shakespeare icons, I thought it might be interesting, and not wholly uninstructive, to include an Ages of Shakespeare postscript drawing upon the rich later tradition, Continental as well as English, of biographical illustration to show the poet from infancy to death.

A decision had early to be reached on whether to include scattered items which had already found a place in the earlier work: Forman's description of *Cymbeline* in performance, for example, or the four Stationers' Register entries, out of sixty-three all told. Repetition has self-evident disadvantages for both author and reader; it can be tiresome. But in the end I opted for overlap. There is something to be said for the ease of consultation allowed by a book that is self-contained, especially if it happens to be of very large format. And why assume that all readers have had the good judgement to equip themselves with the earlier book? That way lies authorial *hubris*. As things worked out, I welcomed the opportunity to review issues, some of them complex, I had previously struggled with. I can fairly say that I have recapitulated nothing by rote, although, by the same token, I have not changed anything simply for the sake of being different.

Of the 165 records and images included in this book, a very large number have never previously been reproduced, as endpapers and frontispiece signal. The front endpaper, a perfectly preserved early oil painting by a Dutch master, shows four playhouses, including the Globe, on Shakespeare's Bankside. The other endpaper, a watercolour view of the Avon, derives from a Warwickshire artist's sketchbook, probably of early nineteenth-century vintage, in the Bedfordshire County Record Office. It is not as early as one would wish, but, then, few earlier views have come down. The frontispiece crayon drawing of Shakespeare by the accomplished Ozias Humphry is familiar enough from subsequent engravings, but the drawing itself is a novelty. Other items reproduced for the first time include Ireland forgeries from private collections and the Folger Shakespeare Library, and a tiny, sensitively executed miniature of Shakespeare, part of a gold cravat pin, in the possession of Mrs. Helen Forsyth of Hampstead. Most of the numerous Stationers' Register entries have not formerly been made available in facsimile.

In seeking, in the pages which follow, to present and assess my materials, I am only too conscious of having wandered afield from the areas of any special expertise I may legitimately claim. I am not a trained palaeographer or art historian, nor an authority on the evolution of English publishing, although that subject is not, I like to think, an entirely closed book to me. Under the circumstances, I have thought it well not to emulate Lord Foppington. In Vanbrugh's *The Relapse*, it will be recalled, this coxcomb finds delight in contemplating the books and gilded looking-glasses of his private gallery. 'Far to mind the inside of a book', he boasts to Amanda in his inimitable accent, 'is to entertain one's self with the forced product of another man's brain. Naw I think a man of quality and breeding may be much better diverted with the natural sprouts of his own.' For present purposes—whatever it may say about my breeding—I have preferred to trust to other men's labours rather than to my own natural sprouts.

The principal sources of my researches are documented in captions and notes, and sometimes directly in the text, as in the 'Note on Authorities' (below, pp. 207–8) in the chapter on Shakespeare's stationers. Where, however, so many have gone before, I am only too conscious of the inadequacy of customary acknowledgement. Who knows what inadvertent omissions will belatedly come to mind after publication? To supplement documentation, I have supplied a Works Cited list bringing together the sources referred to not only in this book but also in the antecedent *Documentary Life*. Such a compendium, besides recapitulating my own obligations, might (I thought) usefully serve students with a special interest in the problems of Shakespearian biography.

But when all is said, the principal *raison d'être* of this book, as of the previous, is not the contextual material but the facsimile illustrations. They represent a priceless and exceedingly vulnerable part of our heritage. So experience has continually brought home to me. Take Shakespeare's will, for example. Comparison of the testator's three signatures as they appeared early in this century with their present condition (see p. 95, below) reveals evident deterioration. Time, that insatiable mouse, has been nibbling. In 1885 C. M. Ingleby published facsimiles of the eight pages of Thomas Greene's jottings, with their references to his cousin Shakespeare, in the Shakespeare Birthplace Trust Records Office in Stratford. The hand—difficult at any time—is fainter now than it was then, as comparison with proof copies based on new photographs made clear. What to do? Should we reproduce Ingleby or the photographs showing the present state of the manuscript? After considerable deliberation, we chose the latter course—although we took the precaution of photographing the Greene diary yet again at the last moment, after page proofs had been corrected. After all, Ingleby's *Shakespeare and the Enclosure of Common Fields at Welcombe* is still available, even if in an edition limited to a mere fifty copies.

In seeing this book through the press, I have, as my last remarks may suggest, followed the routine established for the *Documentary Life*. The Scolar Press supplied proof copies of all items, and I made pilgrimages to the various repositories, which are widely scattered in this country and in England, for on-the-spot comparison with the originals. I was not invariably successful. When, for example, I arrived at the Royal Shakespeare Portrait Gallery in Stratford, proof of the

Flower painting in hand, I found that the Gallery was closed for refurbishing and that the pictures had been taken down for storage. Miss Margaret Jackson and other members of the Royal Shakespeare Company staff strove, beyond the call of duty, to enable me to accomplish my mission; but to no avail. Such experiences were, however, few, and most kindnesses—which were numerous—bore fruit. At Stationers' Hall the archivist, Miss Robin Myers, allowed me and my editor to carry off four stout volumes of the Register for eventual transport by security van to Yorkshire for last-minute rephotographing of a few scattered items. The procedures, however cumbersome and costly, turned out to be well advised. Generally the proof copies *looked* fine, and most of them were; but only comparison with the originals *in situ* could detect failures on the part of either the photographer or the printers. For the author of a book featuring facsimile reproduction, this is no less necessary a step than checking his quotations.

If scholarship is a mostly solitary endeavour, just one inquirer communing with his impersonal sources, it has also its lively communal aspect, and the willingness of friends and colleagues—and mere strangers—to give of their time and knowledge surely constitutes a special glory of this curious way of life. So, too, acknowledgement has its own special pleasure. For their generous willingness to read parts of this book in typescript or proof, I must thank Mr. Robert Bearman, Professor Mark Eccles, Mr. David Piper, Professor Robert K. Turner, Jr., Dr. Stanley Wells, Professor George Walton Williams, and Mrs. Laetitia Yeandle. Mr. Piper I had never met before dropping in on him one day at the Ashmolean Museum to ask if he would read my chapter on Shakespeare portraits: a request to which he at once acceded. I remain startled by my own audacity—but who else could have advised me with like authority? Mrs. Yeandle, the Curator of Manuscripts at Folger, not only read the chapter on Shakespeare's handwriting, but also painstakingly checked my transcriptions from sixteenth- and seventeenth-century documents. My work would certainly have been less accurate without such favours, but of course these well-wishers are in no way responsible for whatever lapses remain.

Although I spent periods at a number of libraries and manuscript repositories, most of the day-to-day work on this book was done at Folger, which comes closer than any temporal institution I know of to fulfilling a scholar's vision of the New Jerusalem. Surely no library anywhere ministers more solicitously to the needs of its readers. I have already mentioned Mrs. Yeandle. Others who catered for my not invariably reasonable demands include Dr. Philip A. Knachel, the Associate Director; Mrs. Nati Krivatsy, the Reference Librarian; Mrs. Lilly Stone Lievsay, the Curator of Books; Mrs. Patricia Senia and Miss Elizabeth Walsh in the Reading Room; Miss Jean Miller in Art Reference; and Mr. Horace Groves, the accomplished Chief of Photoduplication. My dedication to the Folger's Director, a testament of affection, speaks for itself.

I also enjoyed many courtesies at my old haunt, the North Library of the British Museum, and at the Shakespeare Birthplace Trust Records Office. Mr. Ian Willison of the British Library and Dr. Levi Fox and Miss Shirley Watkins in Stratford helped smooth my way. The Library of Congress, to which I had occasional recourse, proved highly instructive in the workings of bureaucracy.

For information and personal kindnesses I am obliged to Mrs. Helen Forsyth, Mr. Sebastian Gaeta, Asher and Julie Sarna, Professor Arthur Sherbo, Professor Brian Vickers, and Professor Franklin B. Williams, Jr. That sceptical philosopher Mr. Oscar Commander, whose wisdom I have had occasion to commend before, demonstrated once again that benign indifference—however anathema to social planners—may in the field of letters be no less wholesome in its effect than catnip to a pampered feline.

The Works Cited section owes a great deal to the cataloguing skills of Dr. Sheila Spector, who for a time assisted me, and Miss Jean Dunnington. Mr. Richard Ansell checked quotations from printed sources, as did Dr. Spector at a later stage. Mrs. Rona Bateman typed the manuscript, and Mr. W. C. Lyles is responsible for the Index. My editor, Mr. Sean Magee, was tireless through a production schedule which went on for almost three years. Yvonne Skargon, who designed the *Documentary Life*, performed with like wonderful skill on *Records and Images*. My amiably uncomplaining secretary, Mrs. Diane Clark, coped with the numerous late additions to typescript and proofs, and was a keen-eyed proof-reader. My amiably uncomplaining wife put up with much.

The University of Maryland generously looked after miscellaneous expenses, such as secretarial and other assistance. I am pleased to be able to boast that I neither applied for, nor received, any fellowship in connection with this project, nor did I request any special academic leave.

So much by way of Preface. It remains to say that with this volume I bid a long goodbye to the Shakespeare documents. They have occupied most of my energies over the past decade, and became familiar companions. Still, I cherish no illusions that I have said the last, or even the penultimate, word on the subject. Scholarship is, after all, process; there will always be additions to knowledge, and reinterpretations of what is already known. The Postscript which follows testifies as much. One would not wish it otherwise. I like to think, though, that it will be a long while before the same records have to be reproduced again.

Washington, D.C.
September 1980

S.S.

POSTSCRIPT. This recourse, which I gladly embrace, enables me to take note of various bits and pieces of information which came my way too late to find a place in my text. Mr. Piper has very kindly passed along to me a Xerox of his photograph of the drawing used as the basis for the engraving of the Holy Trinity 'monument fixed for William Shakespeare the famous poet', as it appears in Sir William Dugdale's *Antiquities of Warwickshire* in 1656. The drawing does not significantly differ from the published engraving which, however, improves upon the subject's proportions. Mr. Piper plans to reproduce the drawing in his Clark Lectures, which Oxford University Press will publish. A report that W. H. Spielmann's exhaustive unpublished monograph—a lifetime work—on the portraits of Shakespeare (see p. 156 below) had found its way to Harvard led me to make enquiries there. Miss Jeanne T. Newlin, the Curator of the Harvard Theatre Collection, wrote to me on 27 December 1979: 'A number of boxes of prints, photos, articles and, in fact, Spielmann's extensive notebooks in manuscript [a form of catalogue or research volumes] are extant here in the Theatre Collection. . . . The earliest correspondence between the dealer in New York and Spielmann in England indicates that there was a manuscript separate from the notebooks prepared by Spielmann for possible publication. In the original shipment to the USA, the manuscript was shipped separately to the dealer and the other crates were shipped to Harvard. . . . I do not have any evidence so far that the manuscript joined the other materials except for casual reference to it. Even so, this may be unofficially based on expectation rather than reality.' Spielmann also figures largely in Paul Bertram's 'What Shakespeare Looked Like: The Spielmann Position and the Alternatives', in *The Journal of the Rutgers University Libraries*, xli, 1 (1979), 1–17. Bertram challenges Spielmann's arguments about the priority of the Droeshout engraving to the Flower portrait (see below, p. 173): 'The assumption that the engraver copied from the "Flower" painting, erring from incapacity rather than conscious intent, and revising his plate to bring it into closer correspondence with the painting, is in any case no less possible than the Spielmann alternative. . . . Since the relatively well painted head and poorly painted body are both drawn worse in the engraving, if we assume the painting was copied from the engraving we must imagine a painter who removed all the defective drawing in the face but only slightly amended the drawing in the body (perhaps an artist with a dual master/apprentice nature)' (pp. 15–16). Bertram draws attention to a presentation copy, with the author's marginal corrections and revisions, of Spielmann's *The Title-Page of the First Folio of Shakespeare's Plays* (referred to in the chapter on portraits) in the Alexander Library at Rutgers.

Carol A. Chillington of the University of Warwick has been good enough to furnish me with the typescript of her long essay, 'Henslowe's, Not Shakespeare's, *Book of Sir Thomas More*'. As the title suggests, she does not accept the Shakespearian authorship of the three pages in hand D. These she would assign to the young John Webster, for whom no manuscript remains have come down (not even a signature), as Dr. Chillington is well aware. She usefully considers the play—

which she postulates was drafted for Worcester's Men at the Rose early in 1603, and revised in March, just as plague was shutting down the theatres—in the context of the working habits of dramatists involved in Philip Henslowe's playhouse operation. Dr. Chillington's speculations reached me barely in time to be noted in this postscript, much less evaluated; interested readers may refer to *English Literary Renaissance*, where it will in due course be printed.

Anthony G. Petti's *English Literary Hands from Chaucer to Dryden* (1977), with a helpful introduction on terminology, abbreviations, punctuation, and numerals, manuscript correction, scribal errors and textual evaluation, and other topics, also reached me late; too late to be commended, along with other guides, in my text—but not too late for me to profit from it.

A Note on Procedures

In quoting from manuscript and printed sources I have, in general, followed the procedures as set forth in my *William Shakespeare: A Documentary Life* (p. xvi). Long *s* and final *j* are normalized, as are the *i–j* and *u–v* equations (e.g. *Mountjoye* rather than *Mountioye*, *unto* for *vnto*, and *abovesaid* for *abouesaid*). I have also extended abbreviations, although not for such common and untroublesome forms as *y^e^*, *&*, *W^m^*, and *M^r^* (for 'Master'), and I have introduced expansions silently. Because of the exceptional interest attaching to the Belott–Mountjoy action, I have (as is customary) included passages scored through in the documents; normally I would pass over in silence passages deleted by the court scrivenor rapidly setting down testimony. With punctuation, or its absence, I have meddled as little as possible. Thus I preserve Simon Forman's use of the full stop where modern usage favours the comma. I have, however, made an exception for the jury list in the Addenbrooke suit, where, following my predecessors' convenient practice, I have modernized punctuation to get round having a vertical column of names. In quoting from the Ireland and Collier forgeries, I have followed the vagaries of their own transcriptions, by which they imposed upon a gullible public in *Miscellaneous Papers and Legal Instruments* and *New Facts regarding the Life of Shakespeare*. Their renderings, after all, belong to the history being recounted in that chapter. The documents, as the facsimiles reveal, differ in many accidentals from their inventors' transcriptions. After his exposure and disgrace, Ireland made numerous copies of his forgeries for the delectation of dilletante collectors, and it is not surprising that they should differ in small details. Collier is another matter. He seems to have been a careless recorder even of his own impostures.

As previously, I have endeavoured to make the facsimiles the same size as the original documents, but inevitably I have had to reduce some that even the large format of this volume would not accommodate. Reduction is appropriately noted. I have also included some enlargements of signatures in the chapter on Shakespeare's handwriting.

In captions and footnotes the place of publication, unless otherwise specified, is London. I have followed the standard practice, in citing dates, of revising the year (where appropriate), but not tampering with day or month. In this period the year (which in England was still reckoned according to the Julian calendar) began officially on Lady Day, 25 March, although popular—as distinguished from legal and governmental—practice varied. Not until the Calendar Act of 1752 was Gregorian reform instituted: eleven days were dropped from that year to correct the discrepancy that had developed between the two calendars, and 1 January became the official first day of the year.

I have used the following abbreviations:

Arber	*A Transcript of the Registers of the Company of Stationers of London; 1554–1640 A.D.*, ed. Edward Arber (1875–94), 5 vols.
BRL	B. Roland Lewis, *The Shakespeare Documents* (Stanford University, 1940), 2 vols.
DL	S. Schoenbaum, *William Shakespeare: A Documentary Life* (Oxford, 1975).
EKC	E. K. Chambers, *William Shakespeare: A Study of Facts and Problems* (Oxford, 1930), 2 vols.
Eyre	G. E. B. Eyre and C. R. Rivington, *A Transcript of the Registers of the Worshipful Company of Stationers: From 1640–1708 A.D.* (1913–14), 3 vols.
Greg	W. W. Greg, *A Bibliography of the English Printed Drama to the Restoration* (1930–59), 4 vols.
H-P	James Orchard Halliwell-Phillipps.
H-P, *Outlines*	J. O. Halliwell-Phillipps, *Outlines of the Life of Shakespeare* (7th ed., 1887).

MA	*Minutes and Accounts of the Corporation of Stratford-upon-Avon*, ed. Richard Savage and Edgar I. Fripp; Publications of the Dugdale Society, vols. i, iii, v, x (Stratford-upon-Avon, 1921–30).
ME	Mark Eccles, *Shakespeare in Warwickshire* (Madison, Wisc., 1961).
SL	S. Schoenbaum, *Shakespeare's Lives* (Oxford, 1970).
SR	Stationers' Register.
STC	*A Short-Title Catalogue of Books Printed in England, Scotland, & Ireland And of English Books Printed Abroad 1475–1640*, comp. A. W. Pollard and G. R. Redgrave (1926).
TB	C. F. Tucker Brooke, *Shakespeare of Stratford: A Handbook for Students* (The Yale Shakespeare; New Haven, 1926).
Wallace	Charles William Wallace, *Shakespeare and His London Associates as Revealed in Recently Discovered Documents*. Nebraska *University Studies*, vol. x, no. 4, 1910.
Wing	Donald Wing, *Short-Title Catalogue of Books Printed in England, Scotland, Ireland, Wales, and British America, and of English books printed in other countries, 1641–1700* (New York, 1945–51), 3 vols.

Acknowledgements of Facsimiles

Bedfordshire County Record Office: rear endpaper.

Bodleian Library (by permission of the Curators): 2, 3, 5, 6, 7, 19, 21, 47, 63, 73, 78, 79, 80.

British Library (by permission of the British Library Board): 1, 4, 32, 40, 41, 43, 48, 52, 53, 54, 74, 76, 83, 89.

British Museum: 61, 64.

Cambridge University Library (by permission of the Syndics): 86.

Dulwich College: 69.

Folger Shakespeare Library (by permission of the Trustees): frontispiece, 20, 23, 49, 50, 51, 55, 58, 75, 77, 87, 88, 90, 92, 93, 94, 95, 96, 97, 98, 99.

Mrs. Helen Forsyth: 85 (photograph by Canton Studios).

Mrs. Lois Avery Gaeta: 84.

Guildhall Library: 18, 39.

Huntington Library: 24, 65, 66, 67, 68, 70.

Mrs. Donald F. Hyde: 56, 57, 59, 60.

National Portrait Gallery, London: 82.

Public Record Office (by permission of the Controller of Her Majesty's Stationery Office): 8, 9, 10, 11, 12, 13, 14, 15, 16, 17, 22, 42, 44, 45, 46.

John Rylands Library: 91.

Stuart B. Schimmel: 62.

Shakespeare Birthplace Trust Records Office, Stratford-upon-Avon (by permission of Trustees and Guardians of Shakespeare's Birthplace): 25, 26, 27, 28, 29, 30, 31, 33, 34, 35, 36, 37, 71.

Shakespeare Memorial Gallery: 81.

Stationers' Hall (by permission of the Worshipful Company of Stationers and Newspaper Makers): 100–162.

Tower Hamlets Central Library: front endpaper.

WILLIAM SHAKESPEARE
Records and Images

I

Shakespeare in London

In the metropolis, as a member of the Lord Chamberlain's company and later the King's Men, Shakespeare fulfilled his treble role of playwright, actor, and sharer. After acquiring New Place and (in his father's name) a coat of arms, he styled himself William Shakespeare of Stratford-upon-Avon in the county of Warwickshire, gentleman, in official documents; but he still needed lodgings in London. From the enrolled subsidy accounts we gather that, some time before October 1596, he lived in St. Helen's, Bishopsgate. By October 1599 he had apparently removed to the liberty of the Clink on the Surrey Bankside, for (as another roll records) the Bishop of Winchester, who held the Clink liberty, had collected Shakespeare's debt. His migration followed that of the players from the Theatre in Shoreditch to the Globe in Southwark. For a while, somewhat later, he lodged with a Huguenot family in Cripplegate ward, to the north-west. At the twilight of his career, in 1613, Shakespeare made a property investment—his last—in Blackfriars. The documents described and reproduced in this chapter, all dating from 1611–13, touch upon these several facets of a busy professional dramatist's life and evoke, through the persons and places that figure in them, something of the ambience of the London through which he moved.

I. Simon Forman at the Globe, 1611

In 'The Book of Plays and Notes thereof per Forman, for Common Policy', Simon Forman, physician and astrologer, describes four productions of plays he himself attended. Three of these he records as taking place at the Globe playhouse in April and May of 1611. The fourth performance he leaves undated, and without notice of the theatre; but this one too he probably saw at the Globe around the same time. Offering as they do the only eyewitness accounts preserved of Shakespeare on the professional stage in his own lifetime, Forman's memoranda comprise an invaluable document, although they present many problems.

A word first about Forman. His manuscript autobiography, diary, and case-books abundantly chronicle the life and times of an Elizabethan physician–astrologer. He was born on 30 December 1552, in the Wiltshire village of Quidhampton, nestled in a valley between the eastern pale of Wilton Park and the tall spire of Salisbury Cathedral. The fourth son of eight children, Simon first studied his accidence with the local schoolmaster–parson, a former cobbler; then, at the free school in the Close at Salisbury, he received tuition from the 'very furious' Dr. Bowles. As a child, Simon had visions of mighty mountains and raging waters, presaging the troubles he would overcome in his riper years.[1] Troubles came soon enough. When Forman was eleven, his father, in whose favour he basked, died, leaving the family destitute. His mother, who would live to be hale at ninety-seven, never loved him. Forced by poverty to leave school, he apprenticed himself to a Salisbury merchant of cloth, drugs, and sundry small wares. After long hours tending customers in the shop, Simon greedily devoured his books by night and extracted from his schoolboy bedfellow accounts of the day's lessons. When, at the age of seventeen, he quit his master, it was to return to the free school. Soon Forman was himself schoolmastering at the

1 Forman describes his dreams in his manuscript Autobiography, included (with spelling modernised) in A. L. Rowse, *Simon Forman: Sex and Society in Shakespeare's Age* (1974). This, the first extended study of Forman, usefully brings together and augments knowledge of Forman's life, and provides a point of departure for subsequent inquiry. On this busy practitioner's diverse clientele, Rowse is inimitably informative. For the medical side, which interests him less, see Mary Edmond, 'Simon Forman's Vade-Mecum', *The Book Collector*, xxvi (1977), 44–60.

1 LONDON. *From James Howell,* Londinopolis; an Historicall Discourse; or, Perlustration of the City of London *(1657), following sig. b2. From the copy in the British Library; shelfmark: 577.g.27. Wing H3090. This bird's eye view derives, like several others, from Visscher's famous panorama (1616), which in turn follows* Civitas Londini. *Although dated 1657, the* Londinopolis *panorama depicts London not later than the first or second decade of the seventeenth century, before Inigo Jones's alterations to St. Paul's*

and the construction of the new Banqueting House. The engraving has sometimes been attributed to Wenceslaus Hollar, and was included in the Hollar exhibition held in the Thomas Fisher Rare Book Library of the University of Toronto in April 1978; but the ascription is doubtful, and the view declared 'almost certainly' not his by Ida Darlington and James Howgego, Printed Maps of London, circa 1513–1850 *(1964), p. 10. The view is here reduced.*

priory of St. Giles. In 1573 he made his way to Oxford 'for to get more learning', and was admitted, as a poor scholar, at a foundation attached to Magdalen College. Academic appointments, as usher or schoolmaster, followed in the country. Then in 1579, while lodging in Fisherton parsonage, he became conscious of his prophetic powers. 'This year', he wrote in his diary, 'I did prophesy the truth of many things which afterwards came to pass. The very spirits were subject unto me; what I spake was done.'[1]

Thus inspired, Forman took up necromancy and medicine. He suffered hard times: he was imprisoned, eked out a living by carpentry, and found himself, poor and bare, in London. There, as an unlicensed practitioner, he cast horoscopes, invoked spirits, and tested urine (while sneering at 'paltry piss'); he prescribed pills and purges, gave counsel, and cured the sick and lame. Forman knew the goodness of faeces, whether a hot fresh cowpat for a bad knee, or 'lye of ashes burnt of doves dung' for thinning hair. To a sufferer from nosebleed he recommended smelling a hog's turd, in addition to marinading stones and cod (testicles and scrotum) in vinegar. Despite such infallible remedies, Forman ran foul of the authorities, especially the powerful Royal College of Physicians, who despised him as an ignorant impostor. He could, they gravely noted, claim familiarity with only a couple of medical authorities, and for his diagnoses boasted that he trusted wholly to his handy ephemerides, or almanac of signs, forecasts, and health hints. The College fined and imprisoned him. By others he was beaten, robbed, and sued. But the terrible plague year of 1592 proved a happy turning point in Forman's career. While established physicians fled to the country, he worked among the urban poor. He survived his own plague sores, and thereafter prospered. In 1603 the University of Cambridge conferred respectability on Forman by licensing him to practise medicine. By then he was charging 2*s*. for a purge, and 5*s*. for a house visit.

High and low called on him: government officials, divines, Levant merchants, town and country gentry, servants (only a sprinkling; most could not afford his fees), seamen, a naval commander. Especially women came, among them Emilia Lanier—'now very needy', Forman noted in a case-book, 'in debt and it seems for lucre's sake will be a good fellow, for necessity doth compel'.[2] Would her husband win preferment, she wondered, and would she ever have the status of a lady? Dr. Rowse believes that Emilia is 'indubitably' Shakespeare's Dark Lady. Other women came to Forman for philtres to arouse or alienate love, or because they were pregnant or had menstrual problems. Actors visited, including Augustine Phillips, the King's man who remembered Shakespeare in his will; but the poets and playwrights stayed away, as did the lawyers and physicians. Forman, however, received a couple of printers with Shakespearean associations: William Jaggard, in danger of the yellow jaundice, and Richard Field, uncomfortable after having swallowed a coin. For himself, Forman did not much approve the printing of books, 'because it hindereth scholars and writing, and maintaineth vice'.[3]

He kept busy in his spare time, writing unpublished treatises on the plague, alchemy, and medicine. Equipped with furnace and stills, he spent years in futile searching for the philosopher's stone. In other pursuits he had better luck. In 1584, at thirty, he first had *halek*, his code expression (an abbreviation for *halekekeros harescum tauros*) for sexual intercourse. Thereafter he enjoyed *halek* regularly; three times, with different partners, on 9 July 1607, when he was fifty-four. It is not the only instance he records of such athleticism. Dr. Rowse believes Forman was 'abnormally heterosexual', a no doubt worrisome condition, the precise disabilities of which are left unexplained.

He died on 8 September 1611. The previous Sunday his young wife Jane, almost thirty years his junior, had teased him about who would die first. 'Oh Trunco, thou wilt bury me', Forman predicted, 'but thou wilt much repent it.' 'Yea, but how long first?' 'I shall die ere Thursday night.' On Thursday, after dinner, feeling very well, he took a pair of oars at Southwark to cross to Puddle Dock. While rowing in mid-stream he collapsed, crying 'An impost, an impost', and died. In Shakespearian fashion, a 'most sad' wind storm immediately followed the event. So

1 'Forman's Diary', in Rowse, *Simon Forman*, p. 280.
2 Quoted by Rowse, *Simon Forman*, p. 100.
3 Quoted by Rowse, *Simon Forman*, p. 89.

Forman's friend, the astrologer William Lilly, reports.[1] Some have suggested, without any supporting evidence, that Forman committed suicide.

One of his clients was Sir Barrington Molyns, who came to Forman in June 1597 'infected with the melancholy and salt phlegm—breeds worms in his nose of stinking sweet and venomous humour'.[2] Sir Barrington, who sought (and received) medical treatment, was on the look-out for a suitable wife. He recalls Abel Drugger ('A miserable rogue, and lives with cheese, / And has the wormes'), nursing hopes of a match with the rich Widow Pliant. But Forman and his circle—the astrologer in his Stone House in Billingsgate, with his furnace and alembics, his horoscopes and nostrums and necromantic spells, taking time out for his casual sexual encounters, while the credulous beat a path to his door cash in hand—all together evoke the grubby and fantasticated ambience of Jonson's London. Maybe the author of *The Alchemist* had Forman in mind when he created Subtle with his bag of confidence tricks; elsewhere Jonson twice refers to Simon by name, in *Epicoene* and *The Devil is an Ass*. But Forman, no charlatan, believed sincerely in his mumbo-jumbo; he really did leave no philosopher's stone unturned. That he consulted the stars for his clinical diagnoses need raise no eyebrows, for astrology was then a respectable adjunct to medicine. Probably Forman killed no more patients than the Establishment physicians of his day.

Hardly a puritan in his life-style, he was an enthusiast of the stage and extracted moral maxims, the practical wisdom of 'common policy', from what he witnessed. His notes record him at the Rose on 4 March 1604 for *Cox of Collumpton* by Day and Haughton. Like so many Henslowe plays, this one is lost, but Forman gives a clue to its content. Cox shoots an arrow through his uncle's head to get land, but later comes to grief along with his three sons. Violence is followed by appropriate retribution; remember, Forman jotted, how Mr. Hammon's son slew the father begging him for mercy, and afterwards fulfilled the dying man's prediction when he betrayed himself by laughing. As thus summarised, the tragedy has perhaps less than Shakespearian resonance, but Forman came away impressed. Words like 'Remember' and 'Observe' signal his appreciation. At the Rose again, less than a fortnight later on 15 March, he saw *Sir John Oldcastle*, in which a quartet of Henslowe hacks—Drayton, Hathway, Munday, and Wilson—vindicated the honour of the Protestant martyr who served as Falstaff's original; at the same time they cashed in on the success of the *Henry IV* plays. In the last year of his life Forman attended the four performances described in his 'Book of Plays': *Macbeth*, *Cymbeline*, *The Winter's Tale*, and *Richard II*.

If his laconic notes convey a unique insight into how Shakespeare on the stage struck a contemporary, they also puzzle, confuse, and sometimes exasperate. A superstitious astrologer hardly qualifies as representative viewer (if such a being can be said to exist) or objective reporter; the experience of the playhouse and the study, what he had seen and what he had read, merge in Forman's mind, and both subserve the imperatives of interpretation. His memoranda on *Macbeth* illustrate the problem at its most acute:[3]

In Mackbeth at the glod 1610 the 20 of Aprill ♄ ther was to be observed firste howe Mackbeth and Bancko, 2 noble men of Scotland Ridinge thorowe a wod the[r] stode befor them 3 women feiries or Numphes And Saluted Mackbeth sayinge of. 3 tyms unto him haille Mackbeth king of Codon for thou shalt be a kinge but shalt beget No kinges &c then said Bancko What all to mackbeth And nothing to me. yes said the nimphes Haille to thee Banko thou shalt beget kinges yet be no kinge And so they departed & cam to the Courte of Scotland to Dunkin king of Scotes and yt was in the dais of Edward the Confessor. And Dunkin bad them both kindly wellcom. And made Mackbeth forth with Prince of Northumberland. and sent him hom to his own castell and appointed mackbeth to provid for him for he wold Sup with him the next dai at night & did soe. And mackebeth Contrived to kill Dumkin. & thorowe the persuasion of his wife did that night Murder the kinge in his own Castell beinge his guest And ther were many prodigies seen that night & the dai before. And when Mack Beth had murdred the kinge the blod on his handes could not be washed

1 *The Lives of those Eminent Antiquaries Elias Ashmole, Esquire, and Mr. William Lilly, written by themselves* . . . (1774), pp. 22–3.

2 Forman, Case-book, cited by Rowse, *Simon Forman*, p. 193.

3 Leah Scragg offers the fullest analysis, and the one I have found most valuable, in 'Macbeth on Horseback', *Shakespeare Survey 26* (Cambridge, 1973), pp. 81–8. She plausibly concludes that Forman's process of composition, while defying explanation, testifies to 'the haphazard workings of an agglutinative memory'.

of by Any means. nor from his wives handes which handled the bloddi daggers in hiding them By which means they became both moch amazed & Affronted. the murder being knowen Dunkins 2 sonns fled the on to England the [other to] Walles to save them selves. they beinge fled, they were supposed guilty of the murder of their father which was nothinge soe Then was Mackbeth Crowned kinge and then he for feare of Banko his old Companion that he should beget kinges but be no kinge him selfe he contrived the death of Banko and caused him to be Murdred on the way as he Rode The next night beinge at supper with his noble men whom he had bid to a feaste to the which also Banco should have com, he began to speake of Noble Banco and to wish that he wer ther. And as he thus did standing up to drinck a Carouse to him. the ghoste of Banco came and sate down in his cheier behind him. And he turninge About to sit down Again sawe the goste of banco which fronted him so. that he fell into a great passion of fear & fury. utteringe many wordes about his murder by which when they hard that Banco was Murdred they Suspected Mackbet.

Then mack dove fled to England to the kinges sonn And soe they Raised an Army And cam into scotland. and at dunston Anyse overthrue mackbet. In the meantyme whille macdovee Was in England Mackbet slewe mackdoves wife & children. and after in the battelle mackdove slewe mackbet.

Observe Also howe mackbetes quen did Rise in the night in her slepe & walke and talked and confessed all & the docter noted her wordes.

Difficulties begin with the date. The wizard uses astronomical signs for days of the week: ♄ signifies Saturn, or Saturday. But on this occasion Forman's crystal ball was clouded, for 20 April fell on a Friday in 1610, as the young Halliwell, astute in such matters, first noted in 1846.[1] To at least one modern authority 'the error is quite understandable as the New Year began on Lady Day'.[2] But Lady (or Annunciation) Day falls on 25 March, and one would have thought the interval of almost a month sufficient for an astrologer to accommodate himself to the change of year. Anyway, many then followed the modern custom and celebrated the New Year in January. It is not clear why Forman made his mistake.

Having got, not very comfortably, past the date, we find ourselves in deep waters again with Forman's first observation. Take him literally and we must envisage actors on horseback at the Globe. Why not? Dennis Bartholomeusz, finding the possibility intriguing, reminds us that the public playhouses boasted capacious stages. (Although he does not pause to consider whether the massive double doors in the tiring house façade would allow mounted entries, presumably they did.) Such entrances, as Bartholomeusz notes, have a history going back to the Middle Ages. On the Elizabethan stage the Duke of Gloucester, plain Thomas, leads a horse—'a very indifferent beast'—in the anonymous *Woodstock*, a play of the nineties; at the Globe some forty years later, Skimmington and his wife enter 'on a horse' in Heywood and Brome's *Late Lancashire Witches*. But one can point to nothing in between. Generally dramatists avoided the inconvenience of large live beasts. Thus, in *The True Chronicle History of King Leir*, Shakespeare's source play, the kings of Cambria and Cornwall enter booted and spurred, and equipped with riding crops; costumes and properties sufficiently indicated the mode of conveyance. So too with Shakespeare. Nobody takes up Richard's offer of a kingdom at Bosworth Field. In *Richard II* the appellants enter armed for the lists, and receive their lances; but the trumpet never sounds. Neither Falstaff nor the spectators see Hal's and Poins's horses, which are tied in the wood; so too Cloten, in *Cymbeline*, ties up his horse safe. Similar instances of bestial evasion might be cited in *Romeo and Juliet*, *The Taming of the Shrew*, and elsewhere. Chambers thinks that maybe some kind of hobby-horse was used in *Macbeth*, and indeed Henslowe's properties included one 'great horse with his leages' – probably of skin and brown paper. Others have thought the effect would be ridiculous. At Stratford in 1972 I saw a Royal Shakespeare Company production of *Richard II* that made plentiful use of hobby-horses. The effect was ridiculous.

Yet Forman mentions riding. He also sets this scene in a wood rather than on the blasted heath of the text. Moreover, his reference to 'fairies or Nimphes' sorts oddly with the Weird Sisters as Shakespeare describes them; those 'secret, black, and midnight hags' with their beards and choppy

1 In 'Early Illustrations of Shakespeare and the English Drama' appended by J. O. Halliwell to his edition of *The Marriage of Wit and Wisdom* (p. 114n) for the Shakespeare Society. Mark Harvey Liddell, usually credited with first detecting Forman's error, apparently noticed it independently in the Introduction to his Elizabethan Shakspere edition of *Macbeth* (New York, 1903), p. xvii, n. 3.

2 J. M. Nosworthy, *Shakespeare's Occasional Plays: Their Origin and Transmission* (1965), p. 14, n. 8.

The Booke of plaies and
Notes therof per formans
for Common pollicie

200

2 SIMON FORMAN'S 'BOOK OF PLAYS', 1611. *Bodleian Library, MS. Ashmole 208, f. 200. The title-page.*

207

3 MACBETH AT THE GLOBE, 20 APRIL 1611. *Bodleian Library, MS. Ashmole 208, f. 207r–v. Transcript: EKC, ii. 337–8; J. M. Nosworthy,* Shakespeare's Occasional Plays: Their Origin and Transmission *(1965), pp. 14–15.*

wales to saue them selues, they beinge
fled, they were supposed guilty of the murder of their father, which was nothinge so.
Then was Mackbeth crowned kinge,
and then he for feare of Banko his old
companion, that he should beget kinges
but be no kinge him selfe, he contriued
the death of Banko, and caused him
to be Murdred on the way as he Rode.
The next night, beinge at supper with
his noble men whom he had bid to a
feaste to the which also Banco should haue
com, he began to speake of Noble Banco, and to wish that he wer ther. And
as he thus did, standing vp to drincke a
Carouse to him, the ghoste of Banco
came and sate down in his cheier behind him. And he turninge A bout to
sit down Again sawe the goste of banco,
which fronted him so, that he fell into a
great passion of fear and fury, Vtteringe
many wordes about his murder, by which,
when they hard that Banco was Murdred
they Suspected Mackbet.
Then MackDove fled to England to the kinges
sonn, And soe they Raised an Army, And cam
into scotland, and at dunston Anyse overthrue Mackbet. In the meantyme whille
Macdovee was in England, Mackbet slew
Mackdoves wife & children, and after in
the battelle Mackdove slewe Mackbet.
Observe Also howe Mackbetes quen did Rise in
the night in her slepe, & walke and talked and
confessed all, & the docter noted her wordes.

fingers and skinny lips. Did nymphs (as Nosworthy speculates) cavort on the Globe stage in 1611 before revision deglamourised them into hags? If so, we may, with Bartholomeusz, detect in the Forman notes Shakespeare's producing hand, and catch 'glimpses of what possibly was the result of creative collaboration between actor and playwright'.[1]

More likely, however, the collaboration took place between Forman the spectator and Forman the reader. The 1577 edition of Holinshed's *Chronicles* features a woodcut engraving of Macbeth and Banquo on horseback. Three respectable Tudor matrons who might credibly pass for nymphs greet them; a background tree sets the scene in a woodland clearing. Holinshed's narrative has the riders 'passing through the woodes and fieldes', while a marginal gloss draws attention to 'the weird sisters or feiries'.[2] It is simpler and probably more reasonable to credit alterations of the play to Forman than to a reviser. Such an interpretation of the evidence finds support in Forman's subsequent reference to an actor on horseback; for the Macbeth of his account has Banquo 'Murdred on the way as he Rode'. In the play the Third Murderer makes it clear that Banquo, back from riding, has left his horses behind and is walking through the park to the palace gate (III.iii.11–14). Elsewhere Forman follows Holinshed for Banquo's envious response to the witches' prophecy:

> Then Banquho, what maner of women (saith he) are you, that seeme so litle favourable unto me, where as to my fellow here, besides highe offices, yee assigne also the kingdome, appointyng foorth nothing for me at all?[3]

Holinshed also lies behind Peter Heylin's rendering in the second (1625) edition of *Microcosmos*: 'This is unequall dealing said *Banquho*, to give my friend all the honors and none unto me. . . .'[4] Shakespeare's Banquo addresses the sisters with a better grace:

> My noble partner
> You greet with present grace and great prediction
> Of noble having and of royal hope,
> That he seems rapt withal. To me you speak not.
> If you can look into the seeds of time
> And say which grain will grow and which will not,
> Speak then to me, who neither beg nor fear
> Your favours nor your hate.

Other anomalies muddle Forman's account. Some of these, such as Macbeth being made Prince of Northumberland, are minor and probably traceable to confused memories of Holinshed. More intriguing is Forman's report that 'when Mack Beth had murdred the kinge the blod on his handes could not be washed of by Any means. nor from his wives handes'. Authorities since Collier have here seen evidence of an omitted scene, the so-called 'mob-accordant incident'. The brevity of the Folio text has encouraged such hypothetical reconstructions, while the interpolations in the witch scenes show that revision of the play did indeed take place. But the dramatic technique suggests that *Macbeth* must always have been short. Nosworthy finds it 'ludicrously impossible' to imagine Shakespeare undertaking a scene of such literal sensationalism.[5] True; but this own proposal that in Act II, scene ii, a towel and bowl of water stood by while the Macbeths performed pantomime ablutions is not notably more probable. Bartholomeusz, willing to swallow horses, takes the ablutions as metaphor: the symbolic significance of stage events—the terrible understatement of 'A little water clears us of this deed'—metamorphoses in the diarist's imagination into an explicit episode. Some such imaginative process may well have operated in Forman's mind. If so, we elsewhere trust him at our peril.

1 Dennis Bartholomeusz, *Macbeth and the Players* (Cambridge, 1969), p. 3.

2 Raphael Holinshed, *The Firste Volume of the Chronicles of England, Scotlande, and Irelande* (1577), 'The Historie of Scotlande', p. 243.

3 Holinshed, 'Historie of Scotlande', p. 243.

4 Peter Heylin, *Microcosmos: A Little Description of the Great World* (Oxford, 1625), p. 509. I adopt the corrected reading 'unequall' from the third edition of 1627; the Folger copy of the 1625 edition gives 'as equall', which presumably represents an error.

5 Nosworthy, ' "Macbeth" at the Globe', *The Library*, 5th Ser., ii (1947–8), 113.

4 MACBETH AND BANQUO ON HORSEBACK. *Raphael Holinshed,* Chronicles of England, Scotlande, and Irelande *(1577), 'The Historie of Scotland', p. 243. Copy in the British Library; shelfmark: 598.h.3.* STC *13568.*

Forman fails to mention the cavern scene, with its apparitions, Show of eight Kings, and dancing witches, although an astrologer professionally involved in prognostication would (one would have thought) find the content of that episode irresistible. Nor does Birnam Wood march to Dunsinane in his notes. But Banquo's ghost, which put Macbeth into a towering 'passion of fear and fury', made as big an impression as the bloody hands. In his exhaustive study of *Macbeth* as a royal play, Henry N. Paul discerns the workings of conscience in Forman, who becomes, like Claudius at 'The Mousetrap', a guilty person sitting at a play. Forman was, after all, a 'wily and disreputable quack doctor and astrologer', concocter of 'many philters and poisonous potions, the uses of which he hoped would never be known'. *Macbeth* stirred uncomfortable associations in such a viewer. Paul notes with satisfaction that Forman's body was recovered from the Thames a few months after the performance, thus suggesting (at least by implication) that Shakespeare's play was more effective than his creation Hamlet's.[1] The passage nicely illustrates the dangers of facile psycho-biography.

The memoranda of the other performances may be discussed more briefly. Evidently Forman watched attentively as 'the Italian'—Iachimo's name escapes him—emerged from his chest in *Cymbeline* and studied the sleeping girl's body before removing her bracelet: a scene calculated to appeal powerfully to an energetically heterosexual male viewer. In his remarks on *The Winter's Tale* Forman gives weight to the pronouncements of the oracle; but that rogue Autolycus made the deepest impression, giving, besides delight, a useful lesson for the student of common policy:

> Remember also the Rog that cam in all tottered like coll pixci and howe he feyned him sicke & to have bin Robbed of all that he had and howe he cosened the por man of all his money. and after cam to the shep sher with a pedlers packe & ther cosened them Again of all their money And howe he changed apparrell with the kinge of bomia his sonn. and then howe he turned Courtiar &c / beware of trustinge feined beggars or fawninge fellouse.

Richard II furnished Forman with similarly useful examples of conduct to remember or beware, but the play he describes is strangely unfamiliar. The overly bold and impolitic Jack Straw is stabbed, when he least suspects, by the Mayor of London, and his army overthrown. 'Therfore in such a case or the like, never admit any party. without a bar betwen, for A man Cannot be to wise, nor kepe him selfe to safe.' The more politic Richard, privily warned, shuts his castle gates

1 Henry N. Paul, *The Royal Play of* Macbeth (New York, 1950), pp. 409–10.

206

Of Cimbalin king of England

Remember also the storri of Cymbalin king
of England in Lucius tyme. howe Lucius
cam from Octauus Cesar for Tribut and
being denied. after sent Lucius wth a greate
Armi of Souldiars who landed at milford
hauen. and Affter wer vanquished by Cim=
balin and Lucius taken prisoner and all
by means of 3 outlawes of the wch 2 of them
were the sonns of Cimbalim stolen from
him when they were but 2 yers old. by an
old man whom Cymbalin banished. and
he kept them as his own sonns 20 yers wth
him in A caue. And howe of them slewe
Clotan that was the quens sonn goinge
to milford hauen to sek the loue of Innogen
the kinges daughter whom he had banished also
for louinge his daughter. and howe the Italian
that cam from her loue conveied him selfe
into A Cheste. and said yt was a chest of plate
sent from her loue & others to be presented to the
kinge. And in the depest of the night she be
ing aslepe. he opened the cheste & cam forth
of yt. And vewed her in her bed and the
markes of her body. & toke awai her braslet
& after Accused her of adultery to her loue &c
And in thend howe he came wth the Romains into
England & was taken prisoner and after
Reueled to Innogen. who had turned her
self into mans apparrell & fled to mete
her loue at milford hauen. & chanchsed to
fall on the Caue in the wodes wher her 2
brothers were & howe by eatinge a sleping
Dram they thought she had bin deed & laid
her in the wodes & the body of Cloten by her.
in her loues apparrell that he left behind him
& howe she was found by Lucius &c.

5 CYMBELINE AT THE GLOBE. *Bodleian Library, MS. Ashmole 208, f. 206. Transcript: EKC, ii. 338–9.*

In the Winters Talle at the glob
1611 the 15 of maye ♄.

Obserue ther howe Lyontes the Kinge of Cicillia was
overcom wt Jelosy of his wife with the Kinge of Bo
hemia his frind that came to see him. and howe he
contriued his death and wold haue had his cup
berer to haue poisoned. who gaue the King of bohe
mia warning therof & fled with him to bohemia /
Remember also howe he sent to the Orakell of appollo &
the Answer of apollo. that she was giltles. and
that the King was Jelouse &c and howe Except the
child was found Again that was loste the Kinge should
die wt out yssue. for the child was caried into bohemia
& ther laid in a forrest & brought vp by a sheppard
and

202

And the Kinge of bohemia his sonn maried that wentch
& howe they fled into Cicillia to Leontes. and the
sheppard hauing showed the letter of the nobleman
by whom Leontes sent a was that child and the Je
wells found about her. she was knowen to be Leon
tes daughter and was then 16 yers old
Remember also the Rog that cam in all tottered like coll
pixci / and howe he feyned him sicke & to haue bin Robbed
of all that he had and howe he cosened the por man of all
his money. and after cam to the shep sher with a ped
lers packe & ther cosened them Again of all their money
And howe he changed apparrell wt the Kinge of bomia
his sonn. and then howe he turned Courtiar &c /
beware of trustinge feined beggars or fawninge fellouss

6 THE *WINTER'S TALE* AT THE GLOBE, 15 MAY 1611. *Bodleian Library, MS. Ashmole 208, ff. 201v–2. Transcript: EKC, ii. 340–1.*

against the Duke of Ireland, who would surprise him with three hundred men by night. This Richard shows a duplicity worthy of Prince John at Gaultree forest:

> Remember also. when the duke and Arundell cam to London with their Army. king Richard came forth to them and met them and gave them fair wordes. and promised them pardon and that all should be well yf they wold discharge their Army. upon whose promises and faier Speaches they did yt and Affter the king byd them all to A banket and soe betraid them And Cut of their heades &c because they had not his pardon under his hand & sealle be fore but his worde.

Whoever wrote the play Forman saw, one wonders whether *2 Henry IV* influenced it—or the account. Dr. Rowse, assuming that the *Richard II* acted at the Globe on 30 April 1611 was Shakespeare's, remarks:

> It contains a passage which does not now appear in the text—we do not know whether it was subsequently suppressed, or whether alterations were made. We do know that the text when first published had to omit the abdication scene, for political reasons.[1]

But not a single scene described by Forman appears in Shakespeare's play, nor are the characters as Shakespeare drew them. The Gaunt of this *Richard II* is a secret contriver of villainy—'Beware by this Example of noble men / and of their fair wordes & sai lyttell to them, lest they doe the Like by thee for thy good will.' More reasonable, surely, to infer that the King's Men in 1611 had another play on Richard II. After all, the bloom was long since off Shakespeare's—a decade earlier, the company had tried (if unsuccessfully) to resist a revival, 'holdyng that play of Kyng Richard to be so old & so long out of use as that they shold have small or no Company at yt'.[2] So Shakespeare's fellow and well-wisher, Augustine Phillips, deposed on 18 February 1601 in the aftermath of the Essex rebellion. There is nothing unusual about different playwrights drawing inspiration from the same historical or literary sources; more than one drama in this age dealt with Hamlet and with Julius Caesar and with Cleopatra. Two plays on Richard II survive. Forman's jottings testify to the existence of a lost third.

A NOTE ON THE GENUINENESS OF FORMAN'S 'BOOK OF PLAYS'

When Sir Edmund Chambers included the four entries from the 'Book of Plays' among the records of 'Performances of Plays' comprising Appendix D of his *William Shakespeare*, nobody (including Chambers) had yet worried, at least publicly, about their authenticity. Most students have accepted them since too. But, as sceptical voices are every now and then heard, the historian does well to acknowledge their presence.

The unease, such as it is, springs from several sources. Partly it derives from the character of the notes themselves, especially those on *Macbeth*, with their omissions and anomalies. Why should the diarist have more than once echoed Shakespeare's source but never the language of the play he had just witnessed? How can Macbeth stand up to drink a carouse to Banquo, when, according to the text, he has never sat down, the table being—for him—full? It is strange that an astrologer who regulated his affairs by the calendar should err respecting a date. (Forman, of course, *was* strange.) Then, too, April—even late April—seems a trifle early in the season for the King's Men to have transferred from their intimate heated winter playhouse in Blackfriars to the open air of the Globe on Bankside; we know from Malone that Sir Henry Herbert, Master of the Revels in the last decades of the Caroline stage, noted in his Office Book (since lost) that 'the King's Company would usually begin to play at the Globe in the month of May'. But probably no suspicions would ever have arisen had not J. Payne Collier announced the 'Book of Plays' to the world, and in a volume, *New Particulars regarding the Works of Shakespeare*, containing a number of unequivocal forgeries. Nor did the way in which Collier described his discovery disarm doubt. 'Not long since', he reveals, 'a gentleman of my acquaintance, of peculiar acquirements, was employed to make a catalogue of the Ashmolean MSS. only, and he, very unexpectedly, found among them the notes I had anxiously sought in a different direction. He instantly forwarded a

1 Rowse, *Simon Forman*, pp. 13–14.
2 EKC, ii. 325.

copy of them to me.'[1] Who was this mysterious gentleman? Did he truly exist? One accepts at one's peril the testimony of an accomplished liar. The only surprising aspect of this affair is that doubts surfaced so late in the day.

They did so when Joseph Quincy Adams expressed 'some uneasiness as to the genuineness' of the Forman document he reprinted in his 1931 edition of *Macbeth.* What most excites Adams's suspicions is that, of the four plays Forman describes, three are by Shakespeare, and the fourth of special Shakespearian interest: in the light of the Collier connection, almost too good to be true. 'Of course it is impossible to be sure of forgery on internal evidence alone', Adams judiciously concluded, 'but I cannot help feeling that the manuscript should be subjected to the careful scientific scrutiny of some modern expert in handwriting, such as Dr. Samuel A. Tannenbaum.'[2] This public invitation Dr. Tannenbaum, psychiatrist and palaeographer, found irresistible. In his *Shaksperian Scraps* of 1933 he musters for the assault the heavy artillery of 'scientific bibliotics'—what Greg dryly dismisses as 'idiotic bibliotics'. This science (Tannenbaum explains, in a style lending itself to condensation) 'enables the scholar to do either of two things: first, to determine the genuineness or the spuriousness of a literary document, that is, of a document having some literary significance; second, to determine whether a literary manuscript was or was not written by the person alleged, or supposed, to have written it.'[3] How point one differs from point two is perhaps not self-evident, nor does Tannenbaum explain what sets bibliotics apart from other modes of enquiry.

His methods indeed seem conventional enough. He casts doubt on Collier's relation of the discovery of the Forman notes; he takes him to task for failing to provide a detailed description of the 'Book of Plays'; he analyses the content of the manuscript. But his biggest guns are 'graphiologic'. Using Forman's brief memorandum on *Cox of Collumpton* as his control specimen, and armed with a low-power microscope, Tannenbaum sets forth the minute evidences of forgery in the 'Book of Plays': an improperly formed *w*, an unnecessarily elongated *J*, redundant minims, clumsy joints or breaks, faked shading here, bungling and patching there. Everywhere he finds 'abnormal' (a favourite word) formations. In Collier himself, not only his hand; fastening the forger to an imaginary couch, the psychiatrist diagnoses dementia praecox of the paranoid type. Tannenbaum goes on to theorise, somewhat unscientifically, that Collier procured a genuine Forman diary, eradicated the writing by means of a chemical solution, resized the paper, and only then set down the fabricated notes.

To these arguments J. Dover Wilson and R. W. Hunt addressed themselves a quarter of a century later.[4] At the Bodleian a few moments' inspection sufficed to satisfy Wilson that the whole Tannenbaum hypothesis was 'perfectly fantastic', and his theory of erasure by chemical solution 'even more far-fetched' than the rest. Wilson found the hand of the 'Book of Plays' indistinguishable from that of other papers in Ashmole 208: a volume which betrayed no evidence of tampering. He makes an especially telling point respecting 'coll pixci' in Forman's description of tattered Autolycus. What manner of pixy is a 'coll pixci'? The *Oxford English Dictionary* (not available to Collier) gives 'colle-pixci' as one of several established sixteenth-century variants of 'colt-pixie', defined as 'A mischievous sprite or fairy, formerly believed in, in the south and south-west of England'. (Thus Nicholas Udall in 1542: 'I shall be ready at thine elbow to plaie the parte of Hobgoblin or Collepixie.') In *New Particulars* Collier mistranscribes the word as 'Coll Pipci'. He was clever about throwing sceptics off the scent with planted errors, but not so clever as that.

In an afterword to Wilson, the palaeographer R. W. Hunt, Keeper of Western Manuscripts at the Bodleian, offers his judgment that the script of the 'Book of Plays' represents genuine writing of the Jacobean period. In doing so, he makes the point—surely valid—that the strongest evidence in such questions is not the analysis of individual letters (Tannenbaum's ostensible strong suit)

1 J. Payne Collier, *New Particulars regarding the Works of Shakespeare* (1836), p. 6.

2 William Shakespeare, *Macbeth*, ed. Joseph Quincy Adams (Cambridge, Mass., 1931), p. 298.

3 Samuel A. Tannenbaum, *Shaksperian Scraps and Other Elizabethan Fragments* (New York, 1933), pref., p. xv.

4 J. Dover Wilson and R. W. Hunt, 'The Authenticity of Simon Forman's *Bocke of Plaies*', *Review of English Studies*, xxiii (1947), 193–200.

In Richard the 2 at the glob
1611 the 30 of Aprill d

Remember therin howe Jack straw by his overmoch boldnes not beinge pollitick nor suspectinge Anye thinge was soddenly at Smithfeld Bars stabbed by walworth the mayor of London & soe he and his wholle Army was overthrowen therfore in such a case or the like, never admit any party without a bar betwen for A man cannot be to wise, nor kepe him selfe to safe

Also remember howe the duke of gloster The Erll of Arundell oxford and others crossinge the kinge in his humor about the duke of Erland and Bushy wer glad to fly and raise an hoste of men and beinge in his Castell howe the d of Erland cam by nighte to betray him with 300 men but havinge privy warninge ther of kept his gates fast And wold not suffer the Enimie to Enter which went bak again with a flie in his eare and after was slaine by the Erll of Arundell in the battell

Remember also when the duke and Arundell cam to London with their Army king Richard came forth to them and met them and gave them fair wordes and promised them pardon and that all should be well yf they wold discharge their Army upon whose promises and faire Speaches they did yt and Affter the king byd them all to A banket and soe betraid them And Cut of their heades &c because they had not his pardon under his hand & sealle before but his worde

7 THE ANONYMOUS *RICHARD II* AT THE GLOBE, 30 APRIL 1611. *Bodleian Library, MS. Ashmole 208, f. 201*$^{r-v}$*. Transcript: EKC, ii. 339–40.*

but 'the general impression made by the script on an eye accustomed to the study of hands of earlier ages'. As for Tannenbaum's specific objections: these are either incorrect or, having as their control a brief specimen of Forman writing set down a decade before the 'Book of Plays', based on an inadequate and unscientific sampling. Hunt, moreover, verified Collier's account of his discovery. Library records showed that the latter's informant was W. H. Black, who catalogued the Ashmole collection at Bodley. In an interleaved proof copy of his catalogue, Black noted, opposite his entry for Forman's 'Book of Plays', 'I made a transcript of this curious article, in 1832, for my friend J. P. Collier, which he designed to print.'

On the basis of such a demonstration an impartial judge might assume that Wilson and Hunt had settled the question of the genuineness of the 'Book of Plays' once and for all. So Nosworthy and others have concluded. To the suspicious, however, all things are suspect. In an article in *Notes and Queries* in 1958, Sydney Race rehearsed some of the old arguments, and added a few new ones.[1] Forman, he suggests, would not have made the 'serious lapse' of omitting the play-house and date of performance for *Cymbeline*; nor, as an educated auditor, would he have failed

1 Sydney Race, 'Simon Forman's "Bocke of Plaies" Examined', *Notes and Queries*, cciii (1958), 9–14.

to include details—for all the productions—of text, acting, and staging, as well as the names of the clever lads who took the female parts. But of course Forman was writing for 'common policy', not the benefit of twentieth-century theatre historians. Race sagaciously observes that the hand of the accounts is that of a man in vigorous health; it therefore cannot belong to Forman, 'who in 1611 was nearing the end of his life and who was deep in practices which took him far from the study of Shakespeare and left him no time to pass his days idly in theatre going'. But Lilly tells us that Forman enjoyed excellent health until the day of his death, and even busy professionals find time for their pleasures: else the Forman diaries would have fewer *halek* entries.

Race concluded that Collier invented the accounts of all five plays, including *Cox of Collumpton*, but himself forged only the *Cox* notes. The rest were fabricated for him by Peter Cunningham, the maligned Audit Office clerk once accused of having forged the Revels Accounts of 1604–5. But modern scholarship has demonstrated conclusively that the Revels Accounts are genuine; Race is merely dredging up an old canard. The 'Book of Plays' is genuine too. It is not in the laboriously mastered feigned hand of the known Collier forgeries, but (allowing for normal variations in one individual's handwriting over a period of years) is compatible with the hand of the voluminous Forman papers.

II. The Belott–Mountjoy Suit, 1612

A year after Simon Forman saw *Macbeth* and the others at the Globe, their author found himself drawn into a real-life drama, the materials of which resembled less his own plays than the City comedies of love, money, and intrigue of his contemporary Thomas Middleton. A summons issued by the Court of Requests, dated 7 May 1612 and marked returnable immediately ('r Imed'), demanded the presence of William Shakespeare, gent., and others to give evidence in Whitehall in a civil action, Stephen Belott, plaintiff, *versus* Christopher Mountjoy, defendant.[1] Normally this court (which the Civil War swept away, along with other archaic legal machinery) served as 'a kind of relief Court of Chancery, specially devoted to dispensing Equity to poor suitors'.[2] The plaintiff indeed protests that he and his wife had many mouths to feed, with more no doubt on the way, 'so that theire poore trade is not able to give them maintenance'; but he was merely indulging in *pro forma* poor-mouthing. Belott was not hard-pressed, and the summons tersely describes him as *nil pauper*. Nor was his adversary and father-in-law Mountjoy a pauper. Apparently suits respecting dower fell within the jurisdiction of the Court of Requests.

Contested, in this cause, was a marriage settlement negotiated many years earlier. Shakespeare was then lodging with the Mountjoys, and as a sympathetic member of the ménage he found himself involved in the courtship negotiations which ultimately became the object of litigation. In his deposition the dramatist allows that he has known the parties, both plaintiff and defendant, 'as he now remembrethe for the space of tenne yeres or thereabouts'—a time span offered, and to be taken, as approximate. Presumably Shakespeare sojourned with the Mountjoys for some time before, and perhaps after, 1604, when Stephen Belott's wedding took place. For the biographer the Court of Requests documents bring special revelations. They yield our only certain London address for Shakespeare; his address, moreover, during a phase of supreme creativity. They furnish, in his signed testimony, an authentic signature, only the sixth of indisputable authenticity. And, alone among the numerous Shakespeare records, they show the poet of humanity in the midst of human involvement with ordinary folk. The story bears detailed retelling.

Christopher Mountjoy was a French Protestant, born at Crécy, who had fled with other Huguenots to England after the St. Bartholomew Day Massacre of 1572. In London he established himself as a skilled tiremaker, or manufacturer of ladies' wigs and ornamental headgear. (In his chronicles Edward Hall refers to gentlewomen 'with marveylous ryche & Straunge tiers on their heades'.) His adopted country rewarded Mountjoy's material success by placing him on the tax

1 The names, as one expects, are variously spelled; e.g. Bellot, Belot, Bellott, even Plott.

2 Arthur Underhill, one of the Conveyancing Counsel to the High Court of Justice, thus characterises Requests in his article 'Law' in *Shakespeare's England* (Oxford, 1917), i. 388.

rolls. As one of two 'Strangers'—that is, aliens—assessed in the adjoining parishes of St. Alphege's and St. Olave's in 1599, he paid 26*s*. 8*d*. for property valued at the respectable sum of £5. The petty collectors appraised Shakespeare's goods, too, at £5, but foreigners were subject to double taxation. Mountjoy was similarly assessed in the subsidy of 1600, but in 1607 (the Patent Rolls show) he became naturalised by paying an unspecified sum to John Levingston, Esq., who held a royal patent to collect denization fees. Mountjoy could easily afford these expenses. When Peter Courtois, a band-maker in the Blackfriars, died in 1603, his will mentions, without anxiety about collection, the 'fifty shillings and elevenpence Mr. Mongeoy doth ow me for purled work'; the size of the debt suggests that Mountjoy found no difficulty in commanding adequate credit.[1] A witness in 1612 describes him as 'Amongst his Neighboures thought to be a suffitient man in estate and abillitie'.

He held the lease of two houses. One was in Brentford. In the other, a double tenement on the north-east corner of Muggle (later Monkwell) and Silver Streets in Cripplegate ward, Mountjoy carried on his trade, along with his wife Mary, their only daughter, also named Mary, and the apprentices. This was on the ground floor. They lived on the upper floors, where Shakespeare for a time rented rooms as a lodger. Did he, as has been suggested, ponder the tragic mysteries in Mountjoy's 'derke garrett'?

And what drew him to Cripplegate? For one thing, the neighbourhood was solidly respectable, and Shakespeare, well on the way to becoming a man of substantial means, did not disdain respectability. John Stow, in his *Survey of London*, remarks on the 'divers fayre houses' in Silver Street, and conjectures that the road took its name from the silversmiths dwelling there. Old Peni-boy, in *The Staple of News*, was bred '*In* Silver-*streete*, *the* Region *of* money, *a good seat for a Usurer*'.[2] In *The Melancholy Knight* Samuel Rowlands parts company with 'the *Joviall* sort', those

> That have their hundreds yeerely to receive;
> For they and I, I know shall never meete
> In Golding lane, nor yet in Silver streete.[3]

Opposite the Mountjoy premises, at the north end of a garden plot in Muggle Street, stood Neville's Inn, the 'great house builded of stone and timber, now called the Lord Windsors house, of old time belonging to the *Nevels*'.[4] Nearby, in the same street, was another imposing presence: Barber Surgeon's Hall. Here hung Holbein's famous painting—which Shakespeare may have seen—showing Henry VIII granting a new charter to the Barber Surgeons; among the nineteen life-sized figures depicted was Dr. Butts, the King's physician, who figures briefly as the revealer of knavery in Shakespeare's late play on the reign of Henry VIII. At the top of Muggle Street a dozen fortunate needy found entertainment at the almshouses lately founded by a former Lord Mayor, Sir Ambrose Nicholas, in order to provide twelve poor folk with seven pence a week, plus five sacks of coal and a quarter of a hundred faggots each year, all 'of his gift for ever'. (Shakespeare, as we shall see, was acquainted with Sir Ambrose's son.) On the corner, where Muggle Street ran into the ancient Roman wall that still stretched across what was in former days the northern boundary of the city, lay the Hermitage of St. James in the Wall, purchased in the reign of Edward VI by William Lamb for the clothworkers of the city, and so latterly known as Lamb's Chapel. Across from the Mountjoy house, on the south-west corner, where Silver and Noble Streets joined, stood the parish church of St. Olave, 'a small thing, and without any noteworthy monuments'; here Mountjoys were married and buried. At the top of Little Wood Street, the next over on the east from Silver Street, one of the seven city gates, Cripplegate, gave its name to the ward which the wall straddled.

1 J. C. Whitebrook, 'Some Fresh Shakespearean Facts', *Notes and Queries*, clxii (1932), 93. Whitebrook suggests that this Mountjoy might possibly have been Christopher's brother Nowell, also a tiremaker; but although that is conceivable it seems unlikely, as Nowell was only around twenty-one in 1603.

2 Intermean after Act III, in *Ben Jonson*, ed. C. H. Herford and Percy and Evelyn Simpson (Oxford, 1925–52), vi. 343.

3 Samuel Rowlands, *The Melancholie Knight* (1615), sig. B2; cited in *Ben Jonson*, x. 280.

4 John Stow, *A Survey of London* (1603), p. 317. In this paragraph, as below (p. 42), on Blackfriars, I am indebted to Stow for numerous topographical details.

Possibly (and this is merely speculation) Shakespeare met the Mountjoys, and learned of their vacant chambers, through Jacqueline Field, the French wife of his Stratford countryman, Richard Field, who printed *Venus and Adonis* and *The Rape of Lucrece*. Jacqueline would have known the Mountjoys from their common ties with the Huguenot church in London. Moreover, the Fields from around 1600 lived in Wood Street, close to the tiremaker's shop. Shakespeare was not the only prominent playwright to find transient accommodation above a tradesman's premises: Aubrey in his *Brief Lives* reports that for a time Ben Jonson had 'lived without temple Barre at a Combe makers shop about the Elephant & Castle'.[1]

Jonson also resided in the parish of St. Giles, just north of the city wall, in Cripplegate. The district attracted theatre folk: Dekker, Munday, and Nathaniel Field lived in St. Giles, as did William Johnson, an actor with the Queen's Men. One turning east of Silver Street, and Shakespeare would have found himself in St. Mary Aldermanbury. Here, in the little parish church, his beloved fellow John Heminges married and had fourteen children baptised; here, a respected parishioner, he served as churchwarden and sidesman, and here he and his wife Rebecca were buried. The Condells too worshipped in the same local church, and Henry busied himself with parish affairs. He and his wife Elizabeth also lie buried in St. Mary Aldermanbury.

Evidently the location suited theatre folk; certainly it was convenient. A short walk due south along Wood Street, past the Fields' house and the gloomy prison walls of the Counter, past Love Lane ('so called of wantons'), would bring Shakespeare to St. Paul's, where, in the churchyard, he could browse amongst the latest offerings on the booksellers' stalls. If he continued on Wood Street and crossed Cheapside (in the shadow of the Great Cross periodically defaced as a symbol of popish superstition), then strolled down along Bread Street where the Mermaid Tavern beckoned, and past Watling Street, he would find himself at Queenhithe, headquarters of the London watermen who held their sessions informally at a riverside alehouse, the Red Knight. A wherry from the Salt Wharf would waft the playwright across the Thames to the Globe on Bankside. The whole journey, door to door, might occupy less than a half-hour.

In the great metropolis, with its multitudes and sprawling suburbs, paths unexpectedly crossed. The Mountjoys knew Simon Forman.[2] On 16 September 1597, as she was taking the air in Silver Street, Mme Mountjoy lost a French crown and a couple of rings out of her purse. When they failed to turn up, she consulted the magus. That was on 22 November. Forman records the visit in a Case-book, although whether he succeeded in retrieving the missing items by necromancy he does not say. His client was then thirty. Ten days later she returned for medical advice, complaining of sundry pains—in head, side, and stomach—as well as dizziness and a weakness in the legs. The physician diagnosed her as eleven weeks pregnant; a perhaps not totally unexpected consequence of her indiscretions with a local mercer, Henry Wood of Swan Alley, in Coleman Street, a short way (along the City Wall) from the Silver Street shop. In a cryptic marginal comment, Forman wrote, 'Mary Mountjoy alained [i.e. concealed]'. Apparently the liaison, matter for a sequel to *Michaelmas Term*, went undiscovered. In March 1598 Mary asked—with what hopes?—whether her husband would be sick or not. Mr. Wood asked (in his mistress's behalf) 'whether the love she bears will be altered or not'. *His* wife, visiting Forman, asked whether she should keep shop with Mme Mountjoy, and was gravely counselled to proceed, with the commonsense caution that they 'take heed they trust not out their wares much, or they shall have loss'. Christopher Mountjoy asked how his runaway apprentice Ufranke de la Coles would shape up. In the upshot Mme Mountjoy did not bear a child, go into business with Mrs. Wood, or leave her husband. Ufranke, Forman notes, 'was taken and Committed to prison'.[3] Mountjoy engaged a new apprentice. These events occurred in 1598.

The tiremaker's new assistant was Stephen Belott, who was boarding with the Mountjoys. In France four years earlier, his widowed mother had married an Englishman, Humphrey Fludd, who describes himself (in his deposition) as 'one of his Majesties Trumpetores'. Fludd, it appears,

1 Herford and Simpson give the text of Aubrey's Brief Life of Jonson in their edition, i. 178–81, from which I quote.

2 Rowse is to be credited with discovery of this new information, which he gives in *Simon Forman*, pp. 98–9, 183; it was earlier the subject of his article 'Secrets of Shakespeare's Landlady' in *The Times* (23 April 1973), p. 6.

3 See R. E. Alton, review of *The Casebooks of Simon Forman: Sex and Society in Shakespeare's Age*, the paperback edition of Rowse's *Simon Forman*, in *Notes and Queries*, ccxxiii (1978), 457. Alton corrects and supplements Rowse.

persuaded Mountjoy to employ Stephen as an apprentice, and undertook to furnish his stepson with apparel and linen. Years later, after greed and acrimony had poisoned the relationships, Mountjoy swore that Fludd had reneged on his responsibilities and that he, Mountjoy, had for six years 'wholy and solye mayntayned' Belott; a claim his younger brother Nowell Mountjoy, also a tiremaker, confirmed, although even he allowed that Stephen's friends sometimes sent him 'A Cloake or payre of Stockinges or such a thinge'. Fludd, however, insisted that he had given his stepson three suits and a couple of cloaks, as well as (on many occasions) money, and paid 'the Barber for Cuttinge the hayre of his heade'. Nobody denied that Belott, working alongside Mountjoy's daughter in the shop, perfected himself in the art of tiremaking, an art she too had mastered, or that the apprentice (in the words of his own Bill of Complaint) 'did obtayne the good will and affecion of him the saide Christopher'. *Good will and affection*: the phrase recurs. Joan Johnson, trained as a basketmaker but employed as a domestic in the Mountjoy household, testified *ex parte* Belott that 'the defendant seemed to beare greate good will and affection toewardes the plaintiff when he served him, gevinge him reporte to be A verry good servaunte'—despite which, 'shee never herd the defendant confesse and saye that he had greate proffitt and Commoddytie by the plaintiffes service'. Others had similar recollections.

Keen to see something of the world after completing his term in 1604, Stephen travelled into Spain, furnished by his master 'with mony and other necessaryes for the Jorney to the vallue of six poundes or thereaboutes'. So Mountjoy alleged, but Belott scornfully denied that the old man had given him anything. Nevertheless, in late autumn, he returned to his bench in Silver Street, where he won the heart of the tiremaker's daughter. Stephen was a presentable enough suitor, and the girl's mother encouraged the match. As Joan Johnson, sharp-eyed among her dusting pans, puts it, in the passionless locutions of a legal document, 'there was A shewe of goodwill betweene the plaintiff and defendantes daughter Marye which the defendantes wyffe did geve Countenaunce unto and thinke well of. And as shee Rememberith the defendant did send and perswade one mr Shakespeare that Laye in the house to perswade the plaintiff to the same marriadge'.

Her testimony is confirmed by Daniel Nicholas. Sir Ambrose's son, and a resident of Cripplegate for many years, he knew both plaintiff and defendant over a long period, and, it seems (from his frequent references to the name), was on familiar terms with Mr. William Shakespeare. In his two depositions Nicholas twice tells the same tale. He heard

> one William Shakespeare saye that the defendant did beare A good opinnion of the plaintiff and affected him well when he served him, And did move the plaintiff by him the said Shakespeare to have [a] marriadge betweene his daughter Marye Mountjoye [and] the plaintiff. And for that purpose sent him the said Sh[akespeare] to the plaintiff to perswade the plaintiff to the same, as Shakespere tould him this deponent which was effected and Solempnized uppon promise of A porcon with her.

Thus Nicholas deposed on 11 May 1612. On 19 June he testified that Mountjoy had never invited him to talk with Belott about marrying Mary,

> but M[r]: William Shakespeare tould him this deponent that the defendant sent him the said M[r] Shakespeare to the plaintiff about suche A marriadge to be hadd betweene them, And Shakespeare tould this deponent that the defendant tould him that yf the plaintiff would Marrye the said Marye his daughter he would geve him the plaintiff A some of monney with her for A porcion in Marriadge with her. / And that yf he the plaintiff did not marry with her the said Marye and shee with the plaintiff shee should never coste him the defendant her ffather A groat whereuppon, And in Regard M[r] Shakespeare hadd tould them that they should have A some of monney for A porcion from the father they weare made suer by m[r] Shakespeare by gevinge there Consent, and agreed to Marrye, ~~gevinge each others hand to the hande~~ And did Marrye.

Such a ceremony in Shakespeare's presence constituted troth-plight. The marriage register of St. Olave records the wedding, on 19 November 1604, of 'Stephen Plott, and Mary Montjoye'. Whether the playwright who brought the principals together witnessed the ceremony along with other friends of the two families, the records do not disclose.

For a time Mary and Stephen lived under the paternal roof and, employing their highly developed skills, lent Mountjoy a hand with his tiremaking. That was the agreement, and what he had counted upon. But he and his son-in-law did not get along. After six months, rather than the stipulated two years, the Belotts moved out to set up in business on their own. George Wilkins, a victualler and reputed whoremaster of St. Sepulchre's parish, relates how

> after the plaintiff was married with Marye the defendantes daughter he the plaintiff and his wyffe came to dwell in this deponentes house in one of his Chambers. And brought with them A ffewe goodes or houshould stuffe which by Reporte the defendant her father gave them, ffor which this deponent would not have geven Above ffyve poundes yf he had bene to have bought the same.

In St. Sepulchre this Wilkins was landlord of a tavern in Cow Cross, or Turnmill Street, notorious as a resort of thieves and whores. He had underworld connections, may have kept a brothel, and was often in trouble with the law respecting felonies of one sort or another. Curiously, he had a Shakespeare connection. The same Wilkins was a minor littérateur who over a brief period—from 1606 to 1608—published a number of miscellaneous works, including a play, *The Miseries of Enforced Marriage*, and a novella, *The Painful Adventures of Pericles, Prince of Tyre*. Shakespeare used the latter as the source for his own *Pericles*, of which, quite possibly, Wilkins was responsible for all or part of the first two acts.

The St. Olave register lists the burial of 'Mary, wife of Christofer Montjoy' on 30 October 1606. She had tried to make peace between her husband and Stephen—'he hath often herd Marye the defendantes wyffe', deposed Thomas Flower, a Merchant Taylor in Wood Street, '. . . in her lyffe tyme urdge her husbond the defendant to geve somthynge more unto the plaintiff and his wyffe then he had donne before whereunto the defendant Mountjoye would commonlye answeare her that he would not promise them any thinge because he knewe not what he should neede him selfe'. After Mary's death the Belotts returned to Silver Street, where hostilities resumed. Quarrels erupted over a loan by Stephen to his father-in-law, over expenses they had agreed to share for silver wire and other commodities, and over a brewer's bill run up by Stephen. Most important, the young man claimed the promised portion of £60, none of it received, and assurance of £200 more when Mountjoy died. The latter insisted that he had given the Belotts household stuff worth £20, and £10 besides 'to put into theire pursse'. As for the rest, he said (in the hearing of Christopher Weaver, a Silver Street mercer) 'he would Rather Rott in prison then geve them any thinge more then he had geven them before'. Stephen and Mary moved out, this time for good. The stage was set for litigation.

The Bill of Complaint drawn up by Belott's solicitor (Ralph Wormlaighton) and Mountjoy's Answer composed by his (George Hartoppe), followed by Belott's Replication and Mountjoy's Rejoinder, set forth the issues of contention. On 7 May 1612 the court summoned the witnesses, and four days later they deposed. The questions went as follows:

> Interrogatories to bee mynistred to Wittnesses to bee produced on the parte and behalf of Stephen Belott Complainant againste Christopher Mountjoye Defendant.
>
> 1 Inprimis whether doe you knowe the parties plaintiff and defendant and howe longe have you knowne them and either of them.
> 2 Item whether did you knowe the Complainant when he was servaunt with the said defendant howe and in what sort did he behave himself in the service of the said defendant and whether did not the said defendant Confesse that hee had got great profitt and Comodytie by the service of the said Complainant.
> 3 Item whether did not the said defendant seeme to beare great good will and affeccone towardes the said Complainant during the time of his said service and what report did he then give of the said Complainant toucheing his said service and whether did not the said defendant make a mocion unto the said Complainant of marriage with the said Mary in the Bill menconed being the said defendantes sole Child and daughter and willingly offer to performe the same yf the said Complainant should seeme to be content and well lyke therof. and whether did not hee lykewise send anie person or noe to perswade the said Complainant to the same. declare the truthe of your knowledg herin.
> 4 Item what some or somes of moneye did the said defendant promise to give the said Complainant for a porcon in marriage with the said Marye his daughter whether the some of threscore poundes or what other somme as you knowe or have hard and when was the same to bee paied whether at the daie of Mariage of the said Complainant and the said Marye or whath other tyme and what further porcion did the said defendant promise to give unto the said Complainant with the said Marye at the tyme of his decease whether the some twoe hundred poundes or what other somes and whether uppon the said perswacones and promisses of the said defendant did not the said Complainant shortly after marrye with her the said Marye declare the truthe herin as you knowe verylie beleve or have Credybly hard.

5./ Item what parcells of goodes or houshold stuffe did the defendant promise to geve unto the complainant in Marriadge with his said wiefe And what parcells of goodes did he geve him in Marriage with his said wyffe. did he not geve them these parcels (vizt.) One ould ffetherbed, one oulde ffether boulster, A flocke boulster, a thine greene Rugg, two ordanarie blanckettes woven, two paire of sheetes, A dozine of napkines of Course Dyaper, twoe short table Clothes, six short Towelles & one longe one, An ould drawinge table, two ould Joyned stooles, one Wainscott Cubberd, one Twistinge wheele of woode, twoe paire of litle Scyssers, one ould Truncke and a like ould Truncke/ One Bobbine box: And what doe youe thincke in your Conscyence all these said parcelles might be woorthe at the tyme when they weare delivered by the defendauntes appoyntment, unto the plaintiffes declare the truthe hearein at lardge.

'In such cases', as Wallace observes, 'the complainant always, in both bill and interrogatories, makes the defendant appear hardhearted or even villainous, and his own abused condition as most pitiable. We may depend upon it that, if the goods mentioned in the last interrogatory were not rich and elegant, they are at least made to appear as poor and beggarly as possible. Mountjoy and Bellott were both more prosperous than here suggested'.[1]

In Whitehall the examiner interrogated the witnesses while his clerk set down their answers. The deponents then signed their testimony. Joan Johnson gave evidence first, and affixed her mark, then Daniel Nicholas testified, and finally William Shakespeare. Both parties must have looked forward with mingled feelings of hope and trepidation to Shakespeare's testimony; for, of all those involved, he alone was a disinterested witness of what had taken place almost a decade earlier in Silver Street—a witness, moreover, whom the contestants had fully trusted and fully informed. Shakespeare deposed as follows:

William Shakespeare of Stratford upon Avon in the Countye of Warwicke gentleman of the age of xlviii yeres or thereaboutes sworne and examined the daye and yere abovesaid deposethe & sayethe

1. To the first Interrogatory this deponent sayethe he knowethe the partyes plaintiff and deffendant and hathe know[ne] them bothe as he now remembrethe for the space of tenne yeres or thereabouts./

2. To the second Interrogatory this deponent sayeth he did know the complainant when he was servant with the deffendant, and that duringe the tyme of his the complainantes service with the said deffendant he the said Complainant to this deponents knowledge did well and honestly behave himselfe, but to this deponentes remembrance he hath not heard the deffendant confesse that he had gott any great proffitt and comodytye by the said service of the said complainant, but this deponent saithe he verely thinckethe that the said complainant was A very good and industrious servant in the said service And more he canott depose to the said Interrogatory/

3. To the third Interrogatory this deponent sayethe that it did evydentlye appeare that the said deffendant did all the tyme of the said complainantes service with him beare and shew great good will and affecceon towardes the said complainant, And that he hathe hard the deffendant and his wyefe diverse and sundry tymes saye and reporte that the said complainant was a very honest fellowe: And this deponent sayethe that the said deffendant did make A mocion unto the complainant of marriadge with the said Mary in the bill mencioned beinge the said deffendantes sole chyld and daughter and willinglye offerred to performe the same yf the said Complainant shold seeme to be content and well like thereof: And further this deponent sayethe that the said deffendantes wyeffe did sollicitt and entreat this deponent to move and perswade the said Complainant to effect the said marriadge and accordingly this deponent did move and perswade the complainant thereunto: And more to this Interrogatye he cannott depose:/

4. To the ffourth Interrogatory this deponent sayth that the defendant promissed to give the said Complainant A porcion ~~of money and goodes~~ in marriad[ge] with Marye his daughter:/but what certayne porcion some he Rememberithe not / nor when to be payed ~~yf any some weare promissed~~, nor knoweth that the defendant promissed the ~~defendant w~~ plaintiff twoe hundered poundes with his daughter Marye at the tyme of his decease./ But sayth that the plaintiff was dwellinge with the defendant in his house And they had Amongeste them selves manye Conferences about there marriadge which [afterwardes(?)] was Consumated and Solempnized. And more he cann[ott depose]

5. To the vth Interrogatory this Deponent sayth he can saye noth[ing] touchinge any parte or poynte of the same Interrogatory for he knoweth not what Implementes and necessaries of houshould stuffe the defendant gave the plaintiff in marriadge with his daughter Marye./

William Shakper

As may be seen, on the crucial fourth interrogatory—concerning the amount of the bride's portion and when it was to be paid—Shakespeare's memory faltered.

1 Charles William Wallace, 'New Shakespeare Discoveries: Shakespeare as a Man among Men', *Harper's Monthly Magazine*, cxx (1910), 496.

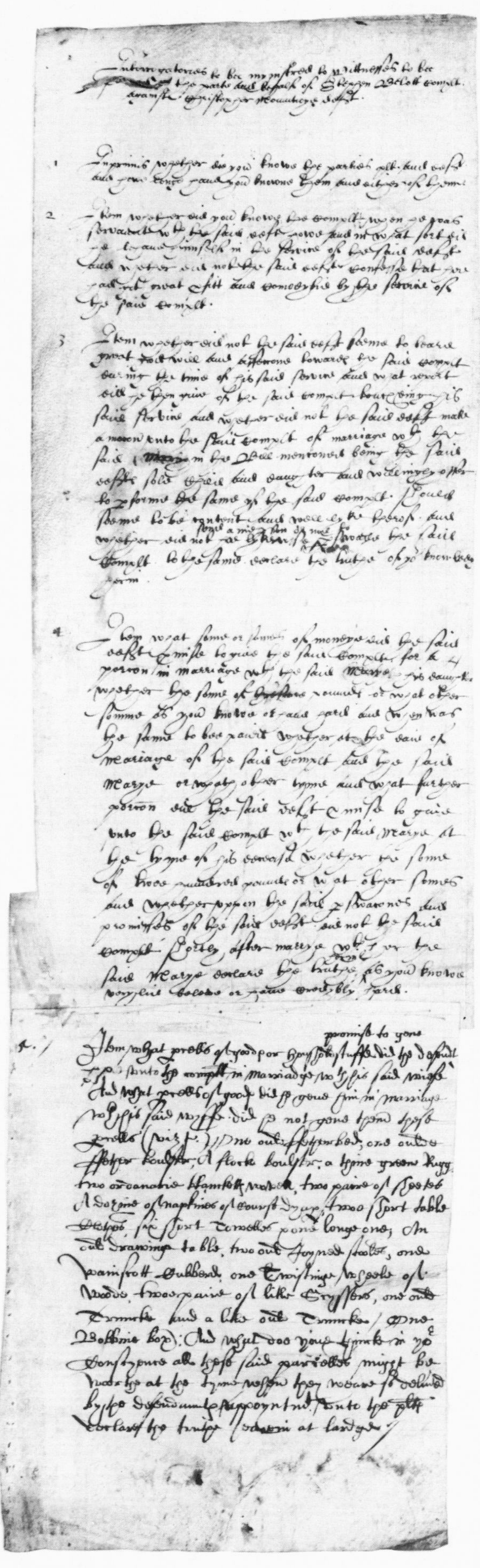

8 THE BELOTT–MOUNTJOY SUIT: THE FIRST SET OF INTERROGATORIES, 11 MAY 1612. *Public Record Office, Court of Requests, Documents of Shakespearian Interest, Req. 4/1. Transcript: Wallace, pp. 278–9; BRL, ii. 428–9. For an account of the discovery of the Belott–Mountjoy suit by Charles William Wallace and his wife Hulda in the Public Record Office in 1909, see* SL, *649–51. Wallace announced and analysed his findings in an essay, 'New Shakespeare Discoveries: Shakespeare as a Man among Men', in* Harper's Monthly Magazine, *cxx (1910), 489–510.* Harper's *announced the article as the first in a series, but no sequel instalments followed. Later in the same year Wallace brought together, without interpretative comment, the twenty-six documents of the actions, plus thirteen others of related interest, in his Nebraska* University Studies *monograph. The document is here reduced by about half.*

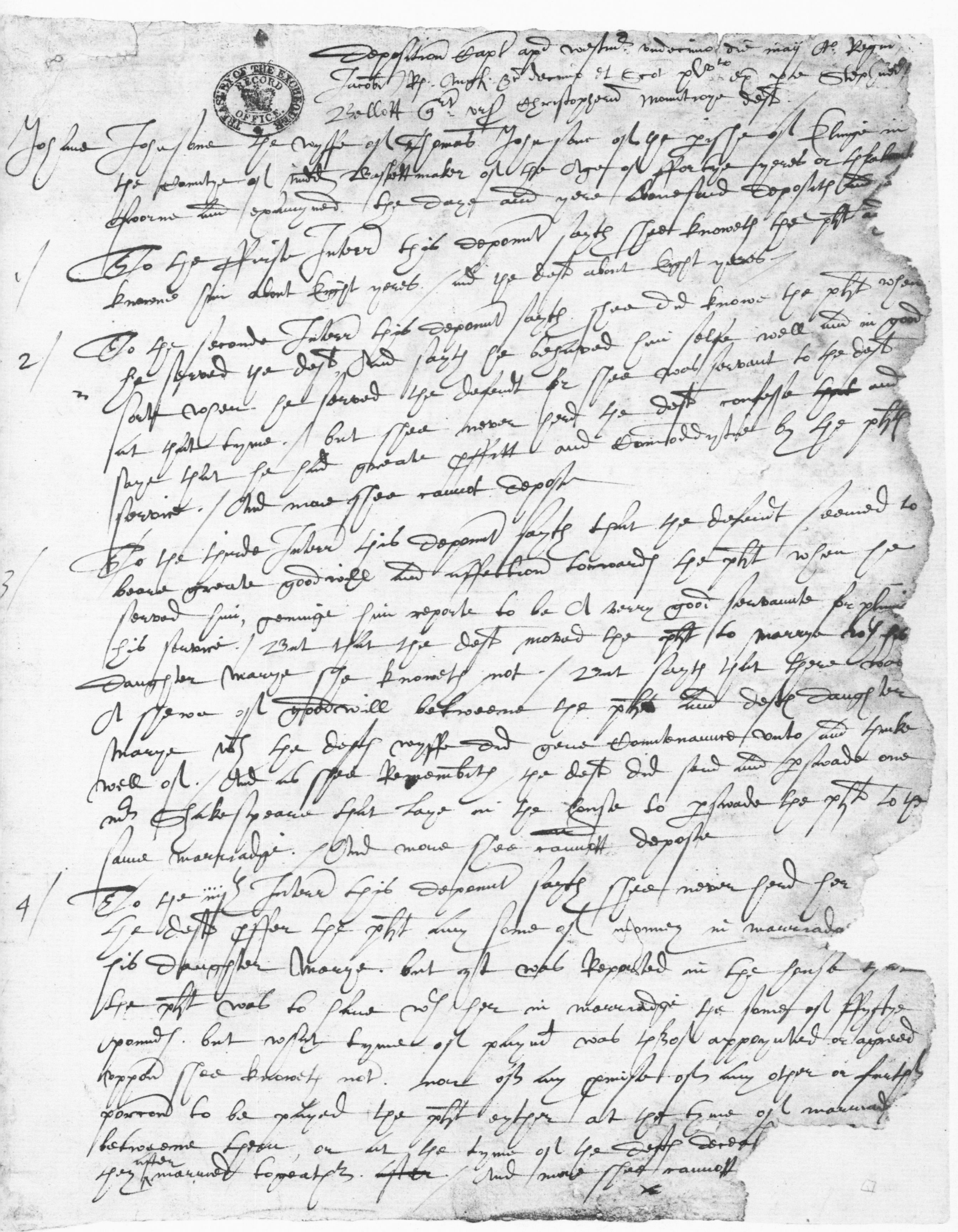

9 JOAN JOHNSON'S DEPOSITION, 11 MAY 1612. *Public Record Office, Court of Requests, Documents of Shakespearian Interest, Req. 4/1. Transcript: Wallace, pp. 279–80; EKC, ii. 90 (third interrogatory only); BRL, ii. 430 (third interrogatory only). It is here reduced by approximately one quarter.*

5/ To the vth Interr this deponent sayth shee ~~knoweth not what~~ ~~some of money~~ Trelles of goods and houshold stuff the defendt promised to geve vnto the plt in marriadge wth his wyffe. But sayth the deft gave in marriadge wth her to the deft the smalle parcells goods in the Interr mentioned but the valewe of them ~~deponent~~ certaynlie knoweth not but thinketh they were worth some eight pounds or thereaboutes. And more shee cannott depose

Daniell Nicholas of the parishe of St. Olphadge within Creplegate London gent of the age of ffyftye two yeres or thereaboutes sworne and examined the daye and yere abovesaid deposeth and sayth

1/ To the ffyrste Interr this deponent sayth he hath knowne the plt about twenty yeres and deft about twelve yeres

2/ To the seconde Interr this deponent sayth he knewe the plt servaunte vnto the deft who behaved him selfe very well in the defendts service he never herd to the contrary And they said that the deft thrived well by the plts service wth him. And more he cannott depose

3 To the thirde Interr this deponent sayth he herd one Wm: Shakespeare saye that the deft did beare a good opinion of the plt and affected him well when he served him, And did move the plt by him the said Shakespeare to have a marriadge betweene his daughter Marye Mountioye [and] the plt. And for that purpose sent him the said Shakespeare to the plt to perswade the plt to the same, as Shakespeare tould him this deponent wch was effected and solempnized uppon promise of a porcion wth her. And more he cannott depose.

4 To the iiijth Interr this deponent sayth ~~[struck through]~~ that the plt did Requeste him this deponent to goe wth his wyffe to Shakespe[are]

Daniell Nicholas

10 DANIEL NICHOLAS'S DEPOSITION, 11 MAY 1612. *Public Record Office, Court of Requests, Documents of Shakespearian Interest, Req. 4/1. Transcript: Wallace, pp. 281–2; EKC, ii. 90–1 (third and fourth interrogatories only); BRL, ii. 431 (third and fourth interrogatories only). The deposition is here reduced by approximately one third.*

to vnderstande the truthe howe muche and what the deft did promise

bestowe on his daughter in marriadge wth him the plt, who

And askinge Shakespeare therof, he Answered

that he promissed yf he the plt would marrye wth Marye his

the deftes onlye daughter, he the defendt would by his

promise as he Remembered geue the plt wth her in marriadge about the some of

ffyftye poundes in money and certayne househould stuffe /

And more he cannott depose touchinge the said Inter

to his Remembraunce for he remembereth not any some

sett downe for payment of the porcon or deliuerye of the househould

stuffe. but only that he would geue her som what at

the tyme of her marriadge /

5/ To the vth Interr his deponent Can saye nothinge more

then he hathe alreadye deposed.

Danell Nicholas

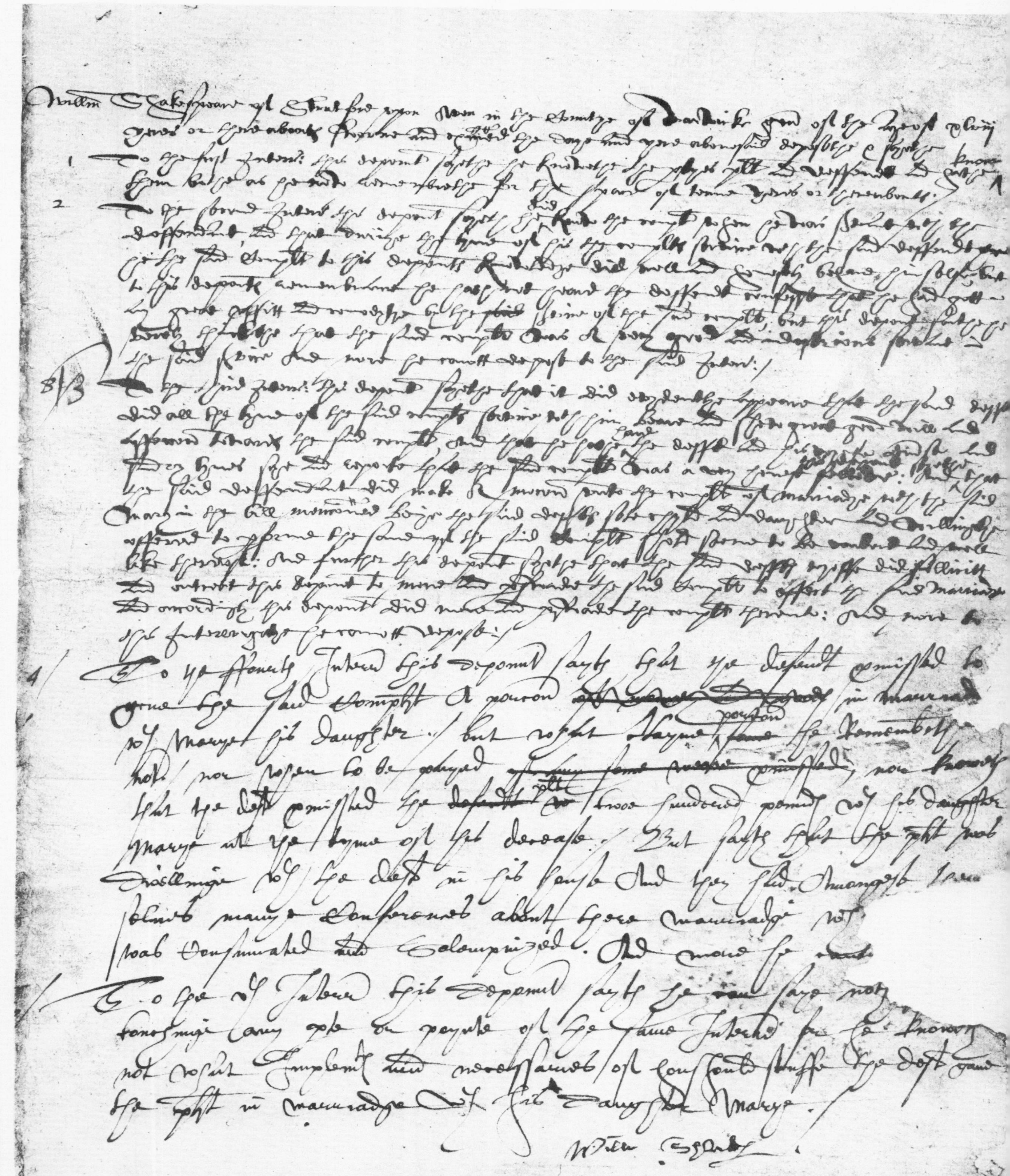

11 SHAKESPEARE'S DEPOSITION, 11 MAY 1612. *Public Record Office, Court of Requests, Documents of Shakespearian Interest, Req. 4/1. Transcript: Wallace, pp. 282–3; EKC, ii. 91–2; BRL, ii. 429–30;* Shakespeare Survey 3 *(Cambridge, 1950), p. 13. The deposition is here reduced by approximately one third.*

12 THE SECOND SET OF INTERROGATORIES, 19 JUNE 1612. *Public Record Office, Court of Requests, Documents of Shakespearian Interest, Req. 4/1. Transcript: Wallace, pp. 285–6. Reduced by approximately one third.*

Deposition capt apud Westm decimo nono die Junij Ao
Regni Jacobi Re: Angl: &c decimo et Scot xlvto: ex pte
Stephani Bellott vs Christopherum Mountioye deft

Daniell Nicholas of the parishe of St. Alphadge within Criplegate London
gent of the Age of threescore and two yeares or thereabouts
sworne and examined the daye and yeare abovesaid deposeth and
sayeth

1/ To the ffirst Interr this depont sayth he hath knowne the
pl about twelue yeares, and the defendt about twentye yeares.

2/ To the seconde Interr this depont sayth that the defendt
is Amongeste his neighboures in thought to be A sufficient
man in estate and abillitie, and Reporte is amongst the neighboures
that he hath divers leases [illegible] about where he dwelleth
and at [illegible] worthe by reporte thirtye pound p Ann:
or thereabouts: And by reporte he hath latelie taken newe leases
of them: but what yeares are yett to come in them his leases this
depont knoweth not / And sayth he thinketh in his Conscyence
the defendt receiveth about thirtye pound yearly Rent de claro for the
same houses / And sayth he heard one Christopher Weaver saye
that [illegible] the defendt ~~sayd that the estate of his est~~ hadd
A good estate to give anye man his owne and to give the pl
his daughter yf he pleased / but the defendt hadd made an othe
that Although the same came then the pl his daughter, he the deft
would sitt in prison before he would give the ~~[illegible]~~ pl
any one groate [illegible]
And more he cannott depose

3/ To the thirde Interr this depont sayth that ~~the reporte of the~~
pl [illegible] Humphrey ffludd reported in this depont
presence [illegible] that [illegible] the pl was often
and [illegible] tymes [illegible] by him the said Humphrey ffludd
and the wyfe mother and others of the pltes ffrendes, [illegible]
most parte of the [illegible]

Daniell Nicholas

13 DANIEL NICHOLAS'S DEPOSITION, 19 JUNE 1612. *Public Record Office, Court of Requests, Documents of Shakespearian Interest, Req. 4/1. Transcript: Wallace, pp. 286–8; EKC, ii. 92–3 (fourth interrogatory only); BRL, ii. 432 (fourth interrogatory only). Reduced by approximately one third.*

hym out of his house wth the defendt/ And more he cannott depose touchinge the same Interr/

4 To the iiijth Interr this deponent sayeth that the defendt did never send him this deponent vnto the Complt to make mocion of marriadge betweene the Complt and the said Marye Mountioye beinge the defendts sole daughter and Childe: but Mr William Shakespeare tould him this deponent that the defendt sent him the said Mr Shakespeare to the plt about suche A marriadge to be hadd betweene them, And Shakespeare tould this deponent that the defendt tould him that yf the plt would marrye the said Marye his daughter he would geve him the plt A some of money wth her for A porcion in marriadge wth her. And that yf he the plt did not marry wth her the said Marye and shee wth the plt shee should never coste him the defendt her ffather A groat, wherevppon And in regard Mr Shakespeare hadd tould them that they should haue A some of money for A porcion from the father they weare made sure by Mr Shakespeare by gevinge their Consent, and agreed to marrye And did marrye. But what some yt was that Mr Mountioye promissed to geve them he the said Mr Shakespeare could not remember, but said yt was ffyftye powndes or theraboute to his beste Remembrance: And as he remembreth Mr Shakespeare said he promissed to geve them A porcion of his goodes: but what, or to what valewe he remembreth not/ And more he cannott depose.

5 To the vth Interr this deponent sayeth that after the marriadge solempnized betweene the plt and Marye, one George Wilkins tould him this deponent that the defendt gave them some Implementes belonginge to houshould, wch goodes weare in the said Wilkins his Custodye, wch goodes the said Wilkins

Daniell Nicholas

reported he would not geve them ffyve poundes for/ And more he cannott depose

Daniell Nicholas

[illegible]

William Eaton apprentice wth the complt of the Age of nynetene yeres or therabouts sworne and examyned the daye and yere aforesaid deposeth and sayth

1/ To the first Inter this deponent sayth he hath knowne the plt three yeres or therabouts And the deft about seven yeares and a halfe.

2/ To the seconde Inter this deponent sayth he cannot certainly depose any thinge touchinge the defts estate or habillitie. only sayth he knoweth the deft hath a howse in Mugwell streete in Silver streete London and another att Brainforde, but what they are worth by the yeare he knoweth not / nor hath heard the deft speake any thinge thereof as in the Inter is supposed / And more he cannot depose

3 To the thirde Inter this deponent can saye nothinge

4 To the iiijth Inter this deponent sayth he hath heard mr Shakespeare saye that he was sent by the defendt to the plt to move the plt to haue a marriadge betweene them the plt and the defendts daughter Marye Mountioye. And herd mr Shakespeare saye that he was wished by the deft to make offer of a certayne some that the defendt said he would giue the plt wth his daughter Marye Mountioye in marriadge, but he hath forgott the same / And more he cannot depose touchinge the same Inter.

5/ To the vth Inter this deponent can saye nothinge but of his owne knowledge nor by credible report

william Eaton

3.

14 WILLIAM EATON'S DEPOSITION, 19 JUNE 1612. *Public Record Office, Court of Requests, Documents of Shakespearian Interest, Req. 4/1. Transcript: Wallace, pp. 288–9; EKC, ii. 93 (fourth interrogatory only); BRL, ii. 432 (fourth interrogatory only). Reduced by approximately one third.*

George Wilkins of the parishe of St Sepulchers London Victualer of the
Age of thirtye Syxe yeres or thereaboutes sworne and examyned
the daye and yeare abovesaid deposethe and sayethe

1 To the first Interr this deponent sayethe he hath knowne the
plt about seaven yeres and the deft as longe. /

2.3.4 To the second, third and fowerth Interr this deponent is not examyned
at the request of the plt /

5 To the vth Interr this deponent sayethe that after the plt was
married wth Marye the deft daughter the plt and his
wyffe came to dwell in this deponents house in one of his
Chambers. And brought wth them A ffewe goods or householdstuffe
wch by reporte the defendt her father gave them after wch
this deponent would not have geven above ffyve poundes yf he had bene
to have bought the same / And more he cannott depose
touchinge the same Interr

Georg: Wilkins

15 GEORGE WILKINS'S DEPOSITION, 19 JUNE 1612. *Public Record Office, Court of Requests, Documents of Shakespearian Interest, Req. 4/1. Transcript: Wallace, p. 289. Reduced by approximately one third.*

Humfrey ffludd of the parishe of St. Giles without Cripplegate ~~london~~ one of his Mats. Trumpetors of the age of ffyftye three yeres or thereabouts sworne and examined the daye and yere abouesaid deposethe and saythe

1/ To the ffirste Interr this deponent saythe he hathe knowne the plt about eighteene yeares for he maried his mother in ffraunce And the defendt he hathe knowne about eighteene yeres for he put the plt to be the defendts apprentice /

2/ To the seconde Interr this deponent is not examined at the Requeste of the plt. / Humfrey fludd

4

·3/ To the thirde Interr this deponent saythe that whileste the plt was in service wth the defendt, this deponent gaue the plt three suits of apparrell for twoe cloaks, And three suits of ~~apparell~~ And his mother gaue him good store of lynnen ^apparrell and lynnen^ wch coulde not ~~for~~ serve him lesse then three yeres, besides the defts wife so stoode unto him that he this deponent and the plt mother weare fayne to geue theire monny and to manye tymes to paye the Barber for cuttinge the hayre of his heade / And more he cannott depose /

4·5/ To the iiijth and vth Interr this deponent is not examined at the Requeste of the plt. / Humfrey fludd

16 HUMPHREY FLUDD'S DEPOSITION, 19 JUNE 1612. *Public Record Office, Court of Requests, Documents of Shakespearian Interest, Req. 4/1. Transcript: Wallace, pp. 289–90. Reduced by approximately one third.*

Nowell Mountioye of the parishe ~~of the parishe~~ of St. Olaves in Sylver Streete
London Tyremaker of the Age of thirtye yeares or thereaboutes sworne and
examined the daye and yeare abovesaid deposeth and sayeth./

1/ To the ffirste Interr this depont sayeth he hath knowne the plt
about ffowerteene yeares and the deft ~~ffowerteene yeares or~~ longer
for he is this depontes brother./

2/ To the seconde Interr this depont sayeth that his brother the defts
estate is not much, ffor he hath but the lease of twoe houses
one lease of the house wherein he dwelleth devided into twoe tenementes
and A lease of A house in Braineford by wch leases he gayneth
an overplus of Rent more then he payeth to the valewe of aboute
nyneteene or seaventeene poundes p Ann. / And hath A lease tyme in the
of the house wherein he dwelleth of some thirty yeares to come
wch he receaved but latelie, but howe longe tyme he hath to
come in the house he hath at Braineford he knoweth not./
Albeit the deft is much in debte, And soulde or pawned his
plate A greate weighte [illegible] so that his estate cannot be very
greate./ And sayeth that he hard his brother the deft saye that
yf he weare condempned in this suite vndeserved he would
lye in prison before he would geve the plt any thinge. / And
more he cannott depose./

3/ To the thirde Interr this depont sayeth that ~~after~~ the plt
was A yeare A boarder in the defts house before he became the
defts Apprentice dureinge wch tyme he beleveth the deft did
not mispende the plt: but after the plt became the defts
Albeit his ffrinds might send him sometymes A cloake or paire of stockings or such lyke thinge
servant the deft mispended him ~~A~~ wch he knoweth to be true
for that he and the deft when the plt served him. And
knowe the truthe thereof. And more he cannott depose./

7

nouel montioi

17 NOWELL MOUNTJOY'S DEPOSITION, 19 JUNE 1612. *Public Record Office, Court of Requests, Documents of Shakespearian Interest, Req. 4/1. Transcript: Wallace, pp. 291–3; EKC, ii. 93–4 (extract from fourth interrogatory); BRL, ii. 433 (extract from fourth interrogatory). Reduced by approximately one third. The deposition is concluded overleaf.*

4 To the iiijth Interr this depont sayth he was never sent by the deft
unto the Complt to make a motion to him of a marriadge to be
had betweene the Complt and Mary Mountioy the defts sole
child and daughter, nor knoweth of any other that was by the
defendt sent unto the complt uppon that message: but the complt
tolde this depont that one Mr Shakespeare was imployed by the
deft about that busines: in what manner or to what effecte
he knoweth not: And sayth he never heard the deft saye that
yf his daughter Mary marryed not wth the complt shee should not
have a groate from him / nor knoweth that the deft promissed to
geve the complt any porcion of money wth his daughter Mary in marriad
nor howe muche he promissed yf he promissed any, nor knoweth
uppon what promise the Complt contracted him selfe wth
the said Marye / And more he cannott depose /

5 To the ffyfte Interr this depont sayth that after the complt
marriadge wth the said Marye, he this depont went to see
them, And the complt uppon some speeches betweene this depont
and the complt the complt tolde him that the deft did geve
him wth his daughter in marriadge the some of ten pounde
and certayne houshold stuffe, but the valewe of the houshold stuffe he knoweth
not / And more he cannott depose /

noel montioe

That was on 11 May. On the 15th the court ordered publication of the depositions the following Wednesday, and set a hearing for the second day of the next term. But a month later, on 15 June, the court postponed publication and hearing, and gave the parties another opportunity to examine witnesses, with the hearing deferred until the last Saturday of term. In the second set of interrogatories *ex parte* Belott, Shakespeare's name appears in the margin alongside the lengthy fourth question, which more or less repeats the matter of the same interrogatory in the first set:

> 4. Item whether did not the said defendant or some other by his appointment send you or any other
> person to your knowledge unto the said Complainant to make a mocion of marriadge betwixt the said
> Complainant and the said Mary Mountjoy beinge the defendantes sole Childe and daughter, and what
> William wordes did the said defendant use unto you or to any other to your knowledge touchinge the marryage of the
> Shake- 4 said Complainant with the said Mary, whether did not the defendant then say that yf shee the said Mary
> speare did not Marry with the said Complainant, that shee the said Mary should not Coste him nor have a groate
> from him, and whether did not the said defendant likewise promise that yf the Complainant and the said
> Mary did marry together that then hee would give a porcion with the said Mary unto the said Complainant;
> howe muche was the said porcion that hee then promised, whether not the somme of threescore pounds or
> what other somme as you thinke in your Conscience to bee true? and before whome did the said defendant
> soe promise the same, whether before you or any other to your knowledge, and whether uppon the said
> promisses and perswacions did not the said Complainant Contracte himselfe with the said Mary?

Evidently attorney Wormlaighton still nursed hopes that Shakespeare might produce the needed facts; but although on 19 June the appointed examiner interviewed eight witnesses—among them Humphrey Fludd, George Wilkins, and Nowell Mountjoy—Shakespeare did not a second time give evidence.

There was a third set of interrogatories and depositions, these on behalf of Mountjoy, on 23 June. All through the testimony the witnesses fail to recall the amount of the portion, or they recollect it as fifty pounds rather than the sixty alleged by Belott; about an additional portion payable on Christopher Mountjoy's death they remember nothing. The court, petitioned to render a verdict on vaguely recalled hearsay evidence, washed its hands of the case, referring the final determination to 'the Reverend & grave overseers and Elders of the french Church in London'. The elders found for Belott, and ordered Mountjoy to pay him twenty nobles, which, equivalent to £6. 13*s*. 4*d*., fell far short of the £250 and more he sought. A year later the fine remained delinquent. Later the church chastised Mountjoy for his profligate way of life with one Michel Art, by whom he allegedly had two bastards,[1] which the putative parents denied. On 24 February 1614 he was excommunicated for 'sa vie desreglée & desbordée'. Remarried, he died in 1620 after having devised a will in which he endeavoured to defraud his only legitimate offspring of her share in his estate.

The Great Fire of 1666 obliterated the house in Silver Street where Shakespeare had once lodged. Early in the present century a brick structure on the same site was leased by the landlord, New College of Oxford University, to the United Kingdom Temperance and General Provident Institution, which in turn sub-leased the property for use as a public house and inn called the Cooper's Arms. Enemy air action during World War II destroyed this establishment, along with much of the surrounding neighbourhood. St. Olave's church, where the Belotts married, is gone, and the London *A to Z* street map lists no Monkwell Street, although a St. Olave Court remains.

III. Shakespeare's Blackfriars Investment, 1613

Although Shakespeare made a number of shrewd investments, some of them substantial, in land, houses, and tithes, these mostly took place in Stratford and its environs rather than in London. Only once, and then late in his career, did he buy a property in the metropolis which provided him with the means for his investments, and where for over two decades he spent most of his days. On 10 March 1613, describing himself as 'William Shakespeare of Stratford upon Avon in the Countie of Warwick gentleman', he agreed to pay Henry Walker, a citizen and minstrel of

1 BRL gives the name incorrectly as Mabel (ii. 431).

18 BLACKFRIARS AND BANKSIDE. *From Wenceslaus Hollar, 'Long View' of London from Bankside, 1647. Guildhall Library; shelfmark: Large Bound Views, Box 1. For an account of this panorama see* DL, *caption to item 78, p. 90. This detail is reduced.*

S. Pauwls Church
5. ÿ Waterhouse
S. Andre in Holborne
Heygat
Paulus wharfe
Queene hythe
The 3. Cranes
the Eel Ships
T H A M E
Winchester house

London, £140 for a house in Blackfriars.

This is a district of the capital rich in Shakespearian associations. Thanks to Wenceslaus Hollar's marvellously detailed 'Long View' of London, we can visualise the Blackfriars precinct as it would have appeared in Shakespeare's day to a visitor strategically positioned on the south bank of the great tidal river. The Globe playhouse stood directly in view on Bankside. On the opposite side of the Thames fashionable Blackfriars residences crowded almost to the water's edge. To the east the river laved the stone walls of Baynard's Castle, a gloomy fortress with a dozen towers with turrets and eaves, and a central arched water-gate that gave access *via* river-steps. There Richard of Gloucester, flanked aloft by two well learned bishops while citizens crowded the courtyard, put by and then accepted with feigned humility 'the golden yoke of sovereignty'. Baynard's Castle was now owned by the Earl of Pembroke, who looked upon Shakespeare's plays and their author, while he lived, with so much favour. To the west stood the Temple, built by the Knights Templars 'after the forme of the temple nere to the sepulchre of our Lord at Jerusalem' in the twelfth century, and more than once re-edified. Here in the Temple's pleasant garden grew the red roses and white that the dramatist, in a brilliant scene in *1 Henry VI*, imagined Suffolk and Richard Plantagenet plucking to set in motion a fateful sequence of events. Between Castle and Temple stretched the nine acres of the Dominican priory complex which before the Dissolution comprised a self-contained religious community with church and chapter house, kitchens, library, stables, lodgings, and sundry out-buildings. The Thames bounded the Blackfriars precinct on the south, Ludgate Hill on the north. Thick walls, each with a gate, surrounded the domain on all four sides. The tenement that Shakespeare bought was erected partially above the gate in the eastern wall leading to the 'Capital Mesuag' occupied by Henry, ninth Earl of Northumberland.

Shakespeare's gate-house was situated on St. Andrew's Hill, once called Puddle Hill or Puddle Dock Hill, and 'right against the Kinges Majesties Wardrobe'. A short walk away at the bottom of the street, where the Thames flowed, lay the wharf still called Puddle Dock. 'Water gates on the bankes of the River Thames have beene many', Stow observes in his *Survey*, 'which beeing purchased by private men, are also put to private use, and the olde names of them forgotten.' Among these, lovingly enumerated, is a 'water gate at Puddle wharfe, of one Puddle that kept a wharfe on the West side therof, and now of Puddle water, by meanes of many horses watred there'.[1] Thus happily did name and nature coincide at Puddle Dock, where the Thames ran into a narrow creek which at low tide became little more than a mud flat.

The premises that Shakespeare acquired included (according to the indenture) 'also all that plott of ground on the west side of the same Tenement which was lately inclosed with boordes on two sides thereof by Anne Bacon widowe, soe farre and in such sorte as the same was inclosed by the said Anne Bacon, and not otherwise, and being on the third side inclosed with an olde Brick wall; Which said plott of ground was sometyme parcell and taken out of a great peece of voyde ground lately used for a garden'. The terms of the agreement assured the purchaser free ingress and egress 'by and through the said greate gate and yarde there unto the usuall dore of the said Tenement'. This yard came to be known as Ireland Yard, after a tenant, William Ireland, who paid Henry Walker £7 a year rent for his haberdashery over the gate. Shakespeare may well have known the haberdasher, although the latter seems to have surrendered his lease while the transfer of the property was being worked out. (In the eighteenth century, when the Blackfriars gate-house title-deeds surfaced, young William-Henry Ireland found it to his purpose to claim kinship with his early namesake.)

Joining with Shakespeare in the conveyance were William Johnson, John Jackson, and John Hemmyng. The last must have been (despite a few biographers' doubts)[2] the colleague who was unwilling to let the memory of so worthy a friend die. Johnson's participation furnishes such factual basis as we have for the romantic legend of Shakespeare's membership of the Mermaid club, for this 'Citizein and Vintener of London' was the genial landlord of the celebrated Cheapside tavern where on the first Friday of each month poets, wits, and witlings gathered to quaff

1 Stow, *Survay*, p. 41.
2 See, for example, H-P, *Outlines*, i. 239.

Mermaid ale and feast on words nimble and full of subtle flame. Jackson was possibly the Hull magnate who married the sister-in-law of Elias James, the godly brewer of Puddle Dock memorialised in a manuscript epitaph ascribed, around 1640, to 'Wm: Shakespeare'.[1] The name Jackson is too commonplace, however, for the identification to amount to more than a plausible guess.

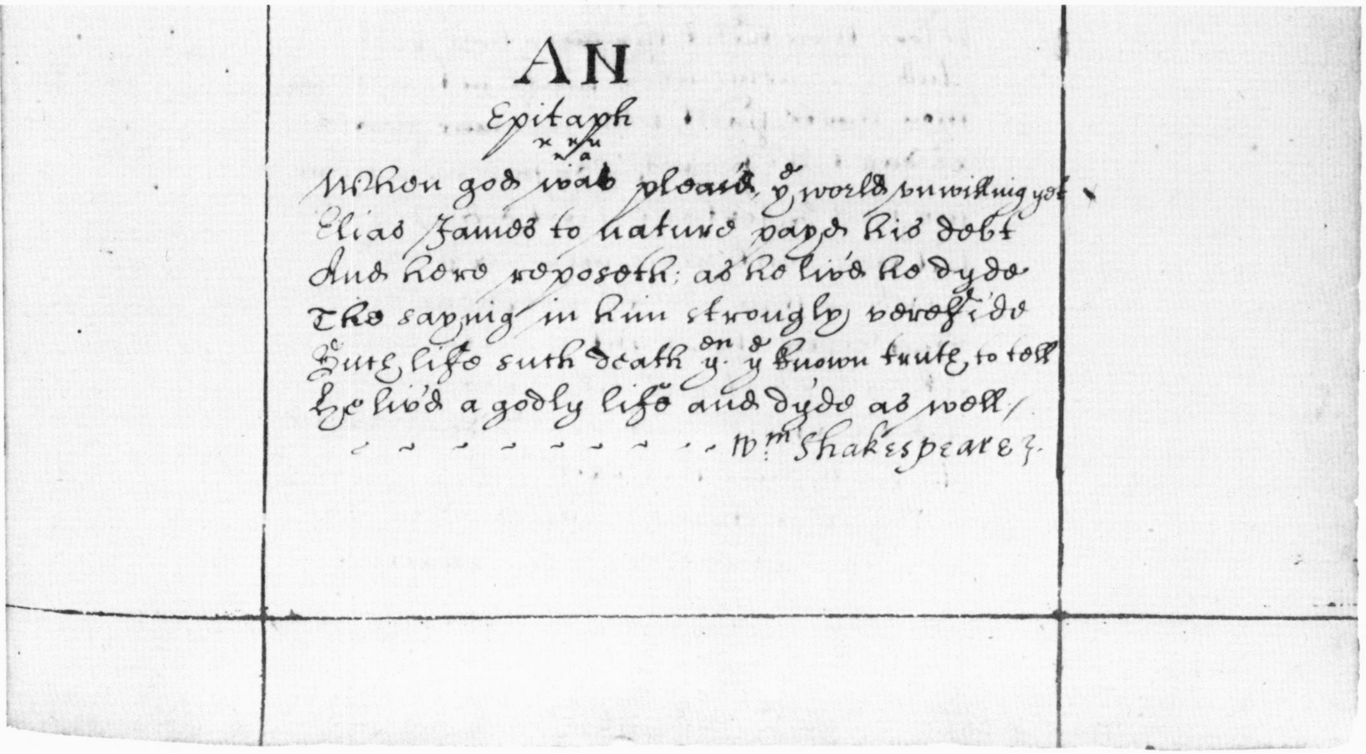
AN
Epitaph
When god was pleasd, ye world unwilling yet
Elias James to nature payd his debt
And here reposeth: as he livd he dyde
The saying in him strongly verefide
Such life such death: then ye known truth to tell
he livd a godly life and dyde as well.
Wm: Shakespeare.

19 THE ELIAS JAMES EPITAPH *Bodleian Library, MS. Rawlinson Poet. 160, f. 41. Transcript: EKC, i.551. As EKC notes, the Bodleian* Summary Catalogue of Western Manuscripts *(iii.315) states that the collection was 'written in about 1640'.*

Technically these three associates enjoyed the status of co-purchasers, but they acted merely as trustees: Shakespeare alone put up the purchase money, for which the gate-house was assured to him, 'his heires, and assignes for ever'. When it came time for him to draw up his will, he bequeathed to his daughter Susanna 'All that Messuage or tenemente with thappurtenaunces . . . in the blackfriers nere the Wardrobe'. An agreement involving co-purchasers had the practical effect of denying Anne a dower right in the estate, for English common law barred a widow's claim on property of which her husband did not hold sole proprietorship. 'Such porcedure', Sir Sidney Lee argues, 'is pretty conclusive proof that he had the intention of excluding her from the enjoyment of his possessions after his death.'[2] Others have discerned a similar suggestiveness about the gate-house conveyance. Maybe they are right; maybe the arrangement indeed implies connubial disaffection. But Shakespeare did not establish conditions that would negate his widow's interest in his other possessions, some of which were more valuable than the Blackfriars lodging. Perhaps prosaic business motives impelled him. Whatever his reasoning, we cannot at this remove of time safely reconstruct it from the available evidence.

Shakespeare, Johnson, and Jackson—but not Heminges—signed the vendor's copy of the conveyance, but only Walker's signature was required for the counterpart held by the purchaser. William Atkinson, the Clerk of the Brewers' Company, served as an independent witness; also

1 Leslie Hotson makes the suggestion and assembles the evidence in 'Shakespeare Mourns a Godly Brewer', *Shakespeare's Sonnets Dated and Other Essays* (1949), pp. 111–24. Joseph Quincy Adams earlier guessed that Elias, although not mentioned in the local registers, came of the numerous Jameses of Stratford ('Shakespeare as a Writer of Epitaphs', *The Manly Anniversary Studies in Language and Literature* (Chicago, 1923), pp. 88–9).

2 Sidney Lee, *A Life of William Shakespeare* (4th ed. of revised version; 1925), pp. 488–9.

the scrivener, Robert Andrewes, and his assistant Henry Lawrence. It was Lawrence who lent his seal ring, with the initials 'HL', used to impress the wax in the tags of the vendor's copy. That these formalities took place in London is confirmed by the fact that on the day of the signing Walker hastened to the Court of Chancery to deposit the conveyance as required by the Bargain and Sale procedure being followed. The enrolment on the Chancery Close Roll now rests in the Public Record Office (Chancery, Close Rolls, c.54/2184, no. 45), where it is listed in the contemporary index to grantees ('Rot. Claus., II Jac I, pars 31'). The document repeats the language of the original indenture, with this notation appended: 'et memorandum quod undecimo die Marcii, anno suprascripto, prefatus Henricus Walker venit coram dicto domino rege in Cancellaria sue, et recognovit indenturam predictam, ac omnia et singula in eadem contenta et specificata, in forma supradicta'.

The Blackfriars estate cost Shakespeare more than twice the *sexaginta libras sterlingorum* which, according to the foot of fine, he laid out for New Place; but the latter figure need not be taken at face value. However that may be, London property fetched higher prices than Stratford, although Walker paid only £100 for the gate-house in 1604. Lodgings in Blackfriars were becoming desirable, with a consequent inflation of property values. Shakespeare did not, as with his previous investments, put down the whole sum. On 11 March, the day after witnessing the conveyance, he executed another deed stipulating that £60 of the purchase price was to remain on mortgage until paid, 'at one entier payment without delaie', on 29 September next (Michaelmas), in Henry Walker's house in St. Martin's parish, near Ludgate. As was customary in mortgage agreements of this period, the document does not specify the rate of interest nor make provision for a possible extension of the term of the loan. When Shakespeare died it was still outstanding.

Presumably the Halls liquidated the mortgage before 10 February 1618. On that date a deed was executed by which Johnson, Jackson, and Heminges, 'in performance of the confidence and trust in them reposed by William Shakespeare, deceased', transferred the estate to new trustees, John Greene of Clement's Inn and Matthew Morrys of Stratford. Both were long-standing and trusted friends of the family: Greene, the Town Clerk's brother, had (as the latter's diary records) discussed the Welcombe enclosures with Shakespeare; Morrys, warmly remembered in the will of John Hall's father, named children Susanna and John. Now Greene and Morrys acted in 'the use and behoofe of . . . Susanna Hall', and of her lawful issue. The effect of the transfer of trusteeship was to keep the Blackfriars gate-house in the entail of Shakespeare's family.

The gate-house had earlier, before Shakespeare died, figured in a Chancery suit (Bendishe, *et al. versus* Bacon, 26 April–22 May 1615). The poet joined with others to recover the title-deeds, evidences, etc., of the Blackfriars tenement and the larger estate to which it had belonged, these legal papers then being in the possession of a former owner, Mathias Bacon. Charles William Wallace, who discovered the relevant documents—the Bill of Complaint, Answer, and Decree—in the Public Record Office, thought he had unearthed a buried quarrel. More likely the action merely represented friendly litigation on the part of new owners to invest Bacon with the authority of the court of Chancery before he surrendered documents to which they were legally entitled.

If the history of the gate-house is not comparably lurid with that of New Place, it too has its moments, although these are associated with intrigue rather than murder.[1] Situated a stone's throw from the Thames, the house had 'many places of secret conveyance in it', linking up (it seems) with 'secret passages towards the water'. A pair of oars at Puddle Wharf could whisk away or deposit a fugitive Catholic; more than once the priest-hunters came and searched. A long history of recusant association invited suspicion. In 1554 the lodging was in the occupation of Thomas Thirlby, Bishop of Ely, who bought some additional lands and buildings before conveying his holdings to William Blackwell, the Town Clerk of London. This Blackwell had married Margaret Campion, a relative of the Jesuit martyr. Blackwell, who died around 1569, left the gate-house to his widow. After Thirlby, at heart a Catholic, was deprived and committed to Lambeth Palace, Archbishop Parker—his gaoler—graciously allowed him to lodge for a time with

1 EKC (ii. 165–9) summarises the history of the gate-house. On the melodramatic associations of New Place, see below, pp. 51–3.

Mrs. Blackwell in the gate-house. There, 'in Bishop Thirlby's chamber', as Lord Burghley was informed in 1577, Katheryn Carus, a justice's wife, died 'with all her pryde and popery'.

Around 1586 a property-holder in the precinct, Richard Frith, performed the office of a good citizen by reporting to his alderman his dark misgivings about 'One great howse in or adjoyning to the Blackfreres, wherein Mr. Blackwell, the towne clerke, sometyme dwelt'. He goes on:

> Nowe there dwelleth in it one that is a very incomformable man to her Majestie's proceedings. It hath sundry back-dores and bye-wayes, and many secret vaults and corners. It hath bene in tyme past suspected, and searched for papists but no good done for want of good knowledge of the back-dores and bye-wayes, and of the dark corners. I thynke it were better a convenient serche of it were made in the morning, or daytyme, then in the night, because of the dark corners, leaving the consideration thereof of your Worship's better discretion.[1]

In 1590 the gate-house passed to Mathias Bacon, Margaret's grandson. One of his tenants, John Fortescue (nephew of Sir John Fortescue, the Master of the Wardrobe whose official residence stood on the other side of St. Andrew's Hill), hid priests in the house and received 'such stuff as they brought from Rome'. The authorities warned Fortescue, and during his absence in the country searched his house. He and his wife Ellen (a kinswoman of Southampton) and their daughters freely admitted their recusancy, but denied concealing priests. Fortescue protested to his cousin the Earl of Essex—no Catholic sympathiser—

> There was nothinge founde within my commande in all my howse, but suche things as my lewde and wretched butler had locked in a desk of his within that office, so farr from my knolledge (on my Salvation) as is heven from yerthe. And nothing, Right honorable, can torment me more, then that her Majesti should think me so undutifull, in whose service I have bine imployed thes 21 yers, and never yet tutched with any blott of suche disorder, and not lickly I would berere my self of that benefytt which hathe maintained my selfe, my wyfe and children thes many yeres.[2]

Such expostulations notwithstanding, Fortescue in the next reign had associations with Catesby and other Gunpowder conspirators. Eventually, with his family, he removed to the more congenial surroundings of St. Omer.

Why did Shakespeare buy this house of interesting heritage? 'What could be more convenient if he wanted a London residence for himself?', Dr. Rowse replies by asking rhetorically, '—on the spot for the Blackfriars theatre, down the street to the wharf and into a wherry across the Thames to the Globe.[3] He is right about proximity: the gate-house stood only a couple of hundred yards from the winter playhouse of the King's Men. But by March 1613, when Shakespeare signed the papers, he had already seen *The Tempest* produced, and was putting the finishing touches to *Henry VIII.* Only (as seems likely) collaboration with John Fletcher on *The Two Noble Kinsmen* remained. Shakespeare's professional career was virtually over; he had but a few years left to tend the Great Garden of New Place. There is no evidence that he ever contemplated using his tenement as a lodging. Indeed, shortly after the purchase, Shakespeare installed a tenant: his will refers to 'one John Robinson' as dwelling in the Blackfriars messuage. (A John Robinson was one of the five witnesses to Shakespeare's will, but he probably was not the dramatist's tenant. Several men of this name resided in Stratford, including John Robinson, labourer, who had a son baptised in 1605.[4] It would be a nice irony if the gate-house tenant were John Robinson, resident of Blackfriars, who joined in 1596 with other inhabitants of the precinct to petition the Privy Council to prevent Burbage from establishing a common playhouse—if that petition, discovered by J. Payne Collier, is genuine.) Another suggestion holds that Shakespeare secured the Blackfriars estate not for himself but to furnish a site for the new Globe playhouse after fire had destroyed the old. But the Globe did not burn down until two months after the conveyance, and, while poets may no doubt justly claim gifts of prophecy, it seems unlikely that Shakespeare ordered his affairs on the basis of clairvoyance. The bargain he sealed on 10 March 1613 was most probably a financial speculation pure and simple. Others in the King's Men were

1 *Queen Elizabeth and Her Times*, ed. Thomas Wright (1838), ii. 249n.

2 EKC, citing Lord Clermont, *Family of Fortescue*, 435, gives the text of Fortescue's letter (ii. 167).

3 Rowse, *William Shakespeare: A Biography* (1963), p. 445.

4 ME, 142.

investing in the Blackfriars. The Burbage brothers, Richard and Cuthbert, had bought properties there in 1601 and 1610, and would do so again in 1614, until they had acquired most of the ground west of the Blackfriars theatre as far as Water Lane.

The Great Fire of 1666 that obliterated most of medieval London raged with special ferocity in the Blackfriars precinct. Only a doorway of the old priory was left standing, to be incorporated in the last century into the outer wall of a parish lumber warehouse adjacent to St. Anne's burial ground. But Ireland Yard, near the Blackfriars underground station, remains as a place name to remind the knowledgeable visitor of the gate-house which Shakespeare once owned.

2

Shakespeare in Stratford

In the end—despite whatever the capital offered in the way of intellectual and imaginative stimulus, professional opportunities, proximity to the Court, and Dark Ladies—he chose Stratford. At the height of his London fame Shakespeare returned each year to his native town, and there he passed his latter days in ease and retirement; so his earliest biographers report. As a prosperous and respected country squire, Shakespeare comported himself in the time-honoured style of prosperous, respected squires. That is, he bought houses and land in the neighbourhood, entered upon litigation to recover bad debts, and mildly interested himself in local affairs. Tradition holds that he cultivated his garden. The materials of the present chapter—New Place, the John Addenbrooke suit, and the Welcombe enclosures imbroglio—illustrate aspects of Shakespeare's life as a Warwickshire man of property.

I. New Place

The imposing house at the angle of Chapel Street and Chapel Lane (also called Dead Lane) had already stood for a century when Shakespeare purchased it in 1597. In his will, drawn up just before he died in 1496, Sir Hugh Clopton, a mercer and prominent citizen (once Lord Mayor) of London, bequeathed to his great-nephew William his 'grete house in Stratford upon Avon', subject only to the life interest of one Roger Paget, Master of the Guild. Paget died in 1504, and the great-nephew in 1521. Around 1540, in his perambulation of England, the King's antiquary John Leland remarked on the 'praty howse of brike and tymbar' by the north side of the 'right goodly chappell'. The pretty house was first called 'the Newe Place' when Adrian Quiney (great-grandfather of the Thomas who married Shakespeare's daughter Judith) lived there in 1532. The word *place* in the name signifies a dwelling or mansion.[1] New Place must have presented a handsome appearance in those days.

(In a book published in 1925, *The Old Houses of Stratford-upon-Avon*, H. E. Forrest muddied the waters by arguing, with some show of evidence, that the great house built by Clopton must have been the nine-gabled structure in Chapel Street now known as the Shakespeare Hotel, and thus to be distinguished from the New Place bought by Shakespeare.[2] The former, 'by far the largest house in Stratford', is appropriately called a Great House, whereas the latter, having a mere five gables, was 'of very modest dimensions'. Before 1567, Forrest believes, no house stood on the ground adjacent to Chapel Lane; the ground where, some time before 1597, New Place was erected. But Forrest has not seen all the evidence, and what he has seen he misconstrues; the best authorities, including Chambers and Eccles, ignore him. Still, as the book exists to mislead the uninitiated, a brief rebuttal is perhaps in order. The line of descent of New Place from Sir Hugh Clopton to Shakespeare may be traced with reasonable confidence. A house with a frontage of over sixty feet and a depth of eighty, or thereabouts, was not by the standards of the time small, and anyway the Shakespeare Hotel consists of two buildings, the northern one (about sixty feet long) dating probably from the early sixteenth century. Hugh Reynolds and his family lived there in Shakespeare's day. The other building, on a half-H plan, and known locally as the 'Five Gables', is most likely of early seventeenth-century origin.[3] It remains for a future investigator

1 *OED*, 'Place', II.4.b.

2 H. E. Forrest, *The Old Houses of Stratford-upon-Avon* (1925), pp. 93–106.

3 Philip Styles, 'The Borough of Stratford-upon-Avon', in *The Victoria History of the County of Warwick* (1904–69), iii. 227.

21 STRATFORD CHURCH, RIVER, AND MILL, C. 1760. *Folger Shakespeare Library: Art Vol. d76, p. 3, item b. This small watercolour painting by an unknown artist is mounted in Vol. XIX of twenty-one numbered volumes of* Artistic Records of the Life of Shakespeare *catalogued in* A Calendar of the Shakespearean Rarities . . . formerly preserved at Hollingbury Copse . . . (*2nd ed. enlarged; ed. Ernest E. Baker, 1891*), *where it appears as item 658, p. 133, with the description: 'Stratford Church, river and mill, from a painting executed about the year 1720. This was the date assigned to it from the costume by the late Mr. Planché.' But the picture cannot be so early. It is a copy of a primitive landscape, painted in oils, which is on display at New Place. This oil, which has since deteriorated, is one of seven eighteenth-century landscape views of Stratford in the possession of the Shakespeare Birthplace Trust. Of these one* (*smaller than the rest*), *of the mill and weir, bears the endorsement 'E. Grubb del. et pinxit, 1762'. As Edward Grubb was born c. 1740, he must have then been around twenty-two. The fact the paintings were preserved locally suggests that the artist too was local, and Grubb is the only possibility for all but one* (Stratford from Cross-o'-the-Hill, *which, unlike the others, was painted after the present stone spire of Holy Trinity replaced the old wooden one in 1763*). *The painting of which the watercolour here reproduced is a copy was purchased by the Trust in 1931. Three others in the same series came to the Trust in 1866 as the gift of Charles Lucy. Of these one,* The River Avon and Holy Trinity Church, *forms the front endpaper to* DL. *All twenty-one of the Halliwell-Phillipps scrapbooks of artistic records are now in the Folger Shakespeare Library.*

to demonstrate that New Place was an earlier name for the Stratford Hilton.)

Like other handsome structures, New Place ran down. In 1543 another William Clopton, the previous owner's son, leased the house along with some lands in the district for £10 a year to Dr. Thomas Bentley, Henry VIII's well-heeled physician and more than once president of the Royal College of Physicians. At his death six years later Bentley—so Clopton avouched in Chancery—'lefte the said manour place in great ruyne and decay and unrepayryd'.[1] When Clopton himself died in 1560, he devised his Stratford estates to his son, also named William. But these were encumbered with legacies, and besides, the young heir felt impelled to travel; so he parted with some of his patrimony, including New Place, and went off to Italy, perhaps for religious reasons: the Cloptons remained staunchly Catholic. A William Bott had been living at New Place as a tenant for several years. He took possession in 1563, and also became Clopton's agent, while the master stayed abroad. In the same year, according to the deposition of a purported eye-witness, Bott poisoned his own daughter. Presumably the crime, if it indeed happened, took place at the Great House which Shakespeare eventually bought.

This Bott hailed from the Wold in Snitterfield, the village three miles north of Stratford where Shakespeare's grandfather farmed. The two men were acquainted; twice, along with others, they appraised the estates of lately deceased villagers. Apparently the first student to show an interest in Bott was the historian of New Place, J. C. M. Bellew, over a century ago. He early smelled a rat, and concluded from the character which oozed out (his phrase) from the records that 'Bott must have been a thoroughly unprincipled, pettifogging attorney, doing all the dirty work of Stratford and its neighbourhood'.[2] Almost everybody has assumed that Bott practised law; but though he willingly gave legal advice when it served his interests to do so, he was not himself a lawyer, if one may accept the testimony of William Conyers. He speaks of 'one William Botte of Stretford upon Aven' as 'being sometyme suspected for felony and burglary and a person who by reason he was sometyme undersheref of the countie of Warwick takethe upon hym knowlege and to give counsell in matters concerninge the lawe and dothe dailie procure and styrre up muche quarreling sedicion and strif'.[3]

Others shared Conyers's unflattering view of Bott. With good cause. Finding Bott an unsatisfactory agent, Clopton complained of withheld rents and a forged deed, and went so far as to bring action in Chancery to recover missing jewellery and legal instruments. The deputy steward of Stratford accused Bott of dishonesty; the latter countered with a slander action, claiming that, because of the charges, he had been deprived of '*magna ineffabilia lucra*'. Bott similarly sued Roland Wheler for denouncing him thus at the Swan: 'Wylliam Bott thou art a false harlott a false vyllayne & a Rebellyon and I wyll make the to be sett on the pyllory.' Another witness confirms this characterisation: 'Lett every man beeware of hyme for he is counted the craftieste marchant in all our contrey . . . and it is said that if botte had hade his Right he had been hanged longe ago'. To such testimony may be added that of John Harper of Henley-in-Arden. He describes Bott as 'a man clearly void of all honesty, fidelity, or fear of God, and openly detected of divers great and notorious crimes, as, namely, felony, adultery, whoredom, falsehood, and forging, a procurer of the disinherison of divers gentlemen your Majesty's subjects, a common barretour, and stirrer of sedition amongst your Majesty's poor subjects'.[4] Harper knew whereof he spoke, for he was Bott's son-in-law. The literally, as well as figuratively, poisonous master of New Place

1 ME, 87. Eccles's authoritative chapter, 'Shakespeare at New Place', pp. 84–110, compendiously summarises the available facts; it has furnished numerous details for this section. Now over a century old, H-P, *An Historical Account of the New Place, Stratford-upon-Avon, the Last Residence of Shakespeare* (1864), remains the fullest treatment, and is still useful.

2 J. C. M. Bellew, *Shakespere's Home at New Place, Stratford-upon-Avon* (1863), p. 341. On Bott see also Edgar I. Fripp, *Shakespeare Studies Biographical and Literary* (1930), pp. 11–12, 53; also ME, 87–8. Bott (the surname only) intriguingly appears in the surviving fragment of a letter beginning 'Good Mrs. Shakespeare'. Neither signed nor dated, the letter was used in the binding of Johann Piscator, *Analysis logica omnium epistolarum Pauli* (3rd ed.; 1608) in Hereford Cathedral Library; see F. C. Morgan, 'Honorificabilitudinatibus', *Notes and Queries*, ccxxiii (1978), 445.

3 Public Record Office, Stac 5 C. 75/34; transcript among the papers of E. Tangye Lean, Shakespeare Birthplace Trust Records Office.

4 Cited by Bellew, p. 342, whose text I follow.

gives a local habitation to a malevolence, sinister in its dimensions, which fascinated Shakespeare in his major tragedies. We may, for want of a better word, describe the phenomenon as Bottulism.

By a curious irony this man of evil repute rose to civic dignity in Stratford. Although Bott had no record of previous service to the corporation, this body in 1564 made him an alderman. During the plague that ravaged Stratford the same summer, Bott contributed 4*s*. for the relief of victims: more than anybody, including the bailiff, and four times what John Shakespeare gave. The following spring, in May 1565, the corporation expelled Bott for speaking opprobriously of its members. In his place they elected John Shakespeare. The two men knew one another.

Bott had earlier secured a marriage between his daughter Isabella and John Harper. 'Being himself a plain and simple-minded man', and still a minor, Harper was over his head in debt. To avoid the forfeiture of his inherited lands, he followed his father-in-law's counsel and entered into a conveyance. That was in April 1563. Bott's machinations, worthy of an Edmund, involved substituted deeds and names, and a seal surreptitiously obtained for Bott by his daughter. In effect, the Botts by such 'policy' assured themselves of Harper's lands should Isabella die without issue.

The stage was now set for the murder which Roland Wheler describes in a volume of depositions, 'together with numerous letters, briefs, informations, &c., on both sides' of Lodowick Greville and William Porter, defendants, *versus* Francis Alford, plaintiff; '*this confused and intricate suit*', as the calendar for June 1571 describes it. By occupation a shoemaker, Wheler had now and then performed services for Bott in return for some odd shillings and a cow. He gives an account of the crime none the less harrowing for the dry legal phraseology in which it is couched:

> the said Bott having in this wise forged the said dedes and so conveyed the said landes / the said Bottes daugter wief of the said John Harper did dye sodenly and was poysoned with rattes bane and therewith swelled to death / And this deponent knoweth the same to be true for that he did see the wief of the said Bott in the presence of the same Bott delyver to the said Harpers wief in a spone myxt with drynke the said Poysonn of Rattes bayne to drynke which poysonn she did drynke in this Deponentes presence the same William Bott by and at that tyme leanyng to the beddes fete / And this Deponent saieth that the said William Bott did see this when it was don And this deponent saieth that after the wief of the said William Bott had so geven the said drynke to the said Harpers wief the said Harper and this deponent did see hir lay a thinge under a grene Carpett.

This 'thinge' Harper offered to taste, thinking it brimstone, 'but by the perswacion of this deponent who suspected it to be Rattesbayne he did forbeare'. Mrs. Bott, her husband's willing accomplice, was not Isabella's mother but a second wife. As Wheler deposes, 'He knewe william Bott to have two wives alyve at one tyme'. The first wife Wheler had taken for Bott to Thorne near Lichfield.

It is strange, if the testimony is a true report, that Bott never stood trial for murder, although various individuals—William Underhill, William Sheldon, and others—knew of the crime; but Wheler deposes that it was hushed up because, were Bott hanged, 'Mr Clopton and the saied John Harper shoulde both lose all their lands which the said Bott had beguyled them of'. The Stratford register lists the burial, on 7 May 1563, of 'Isabella, uxor Johannis Harper de Henley-arden'. (Incidentally Wheler, whose testimony on the point might have been clearer, seems to think the victim was Lettice, Isabella's sister. By 1571 Lettice too was dead, as was the second Mrs. Bott. The bereaved husband had taken a third wife. Given the lapse of years, and the complicated family relationships among the Botts, a degree of confusion on the deponent's part need not surprise us.)

By the time Shakespeare acquired New Place it had long since passed from Bott into the possession of the Underhill family. William Underhill bought the house in 1567. Pictured by an unfriendly witness as 'a subtle, covetous, and crafty man', this Underhill sold New Place to the dramatist in May 1597, and two months later died mysteriously at Fillongley, near Coventry, after orally bequeathing 'all his lands' to his first-born, Fulke. In 1599 the heir, still a minor, was hanged at Warwick for poisoning his father. Thus twice associated with the fortunes of New Place, either in fact or allegation, is murder of kin—a father of his daughter, and a son of his father—by poison for the estate.

Shakespeare's own father was buried in the churchyard of Holy Trinity on 8 September 1601. Precisely when the dramatist wrote *Hamlet* is not known, but he turned to the subject around this time. Bott had long since expired of natural causes with felony in his heart; he was laid to rest at Snitterfield on 1 November 1582, the same month in which Shakespeare applied for a licence to marry Anne Hathaway. Bott's unedifying career, as that of Fulke Underhill, is far removed from the larger spheres of the Court and national politics which usually attract investigators seeking topical contexts for Shakespeare; but even the most exalted achievements of the literary imagination may take on an unexpected dimension from the circumstances of such obscure provincials. One wonders, then: during one of those periodic flights from the capital to Stratford, as he tended the gardens of New Place, and *Hamlet* was percolating subliminally in his brain, did Shakespeare ever pause to consider his house and its heritage?

However that may be—and we can merely speculate—he did prudently safeguard his claim to New Place from any flaw in the title springing from the foul play associated with the previous owner's decease. Under such conditions family estates might become forfeit to the Crown. Therefore, when Fulke's younger brother Hercules (born 6 June 1581) came of age, he at once confirmed conveyance of the Great House to '*Willelmum Shakespeare, generosum*' by means of a Final Concord (*finalis concordia*). Very likely Hercules went through these motions at Shakespeare's request. For the confirmation of his title Shakespeare paid a prescribed fee equal to one quarter of the yearly value of the property. This second Concord superseded the *finalis concordia* of 1597, the finality of which had become potentially doubtful. In most respects the new document follows the old word for word, but in describing the vendee as '*generosus*', or 'gentleman', it is the first to recognise the new status conferred on the Shakespeares by the 1596 Grant of Arms.

The fine, moreover, characterises New Place as a messuage with two barns (or granaries), two gardens, and two orchards, with appurtenances ('*uno mesuagio duobus horreis duobus gardinis & duobus pomariis cum pertinenciis*'). Orchards had not been specified in the earlier concord. They probably do not represent an addition to the property, only a previously overlooked feature. A garden at New Place had first received mention in 1563, when an indenture (now in the Folger Shakespeare Library) cites 'all that his [Clopton's] Capitall mesuage & garden therunto belonginge' in Chapel Street.[1] Two years later, when Bott brought an action for trespass against Richard Sponer, a painter two doors down from New Place, he charged his neighbour with appropriating twelve pieces of timber, worth 40*s*., from his 'barne yarde nighe le New Place gardyn'.

No doubt apples grew in Shakespeare's orchards, and roses in his gardens. In the plays and poems he mentions half a dozen different apples—crab, pippin, bitter-sweeting, pome-water, applejohn, and leather-coat—and refers more than a hundred times to roses, specifying no fewer than eight varieties.[2] Tradition holds that Shakespeare planted a mulberry tree in his garden. Malone, in 1790, reports that a Hugh Taylor, then eighty-five,

> lived when a boy at the next house to New-Place; that his family had inhabited the house for almost three hundred years; that it was transmitted from father to son during the last and the present century, that this tree (of the fruit of which he had often eaten in his younger days, some of its branches hanging over his father's garden,) was planted by Shakspeare; and that till this was planted, there was no mulberry-tree in that neighbourhood. Mr. Taylor adds, that he was frequently, when a boy, at New-Place, and that this tradition was preserved in the Clopton family, as well as in his own.[3]

Maybe, Malone speculates, Shakespeare planted his mulberry in the spring of 1609, when by King James's command, many hundred thousand of the young trees were imported from France for the encouragement of silk manufacture.

Vines too, most likely grape-vines, grew at New Place, and in time achieved local celebrity. In January or February of 1631, the first baronet of Stowe, Sir Thomas Temple, wrote from his seat at Wolverton in Buckinghamshire to instruct his steward Harry Rose

> to ride to Stratforde upon Avon at your next opportunity & to desire Mr Hall Phiscon from me to desire him to suffer Harry Rose, or any better in skill, to gather some few budes that is 2 or 3 of the fairest of those budes on some few shutes of the last yeares vines. His house is neare to the house of my brother Peter Temples wife, to whom I would have yow putt her in minde to request the same Mr Hall (which she promised to

1 Folger Shakespeare Library MS. Z.c.36 (100). ME, 90, alludes to the 1563 document.

2 See the chapter, 'Shakespeare and His Garden', in Fripp, *Shakespeare: Man and Artist* (1938), ii. 465–7.

3 William Shakespeare, *Plays and Poems*, ed. Edmond Malone (1790), vol. i, pt. 1, p. 118, n.6.

22 ROLAND WHELER'S DEPOSITION, JUNE 1571 (extract). *Public Record Office, State Papers Domestic, SP 12/79. I found the Wheler deposition, in transcript, among the papers of the late E. Tangye Lean, which at the invitation of his widow, Mrs. Doreen Lean, I examined in London in 1976. These voluminous papers consist mainly of transcripts, photocopies, and the like, of documents that Lean was assembling*

when it was don did this deponent saieth that after the

weif of the said William Holt had [illegible] the said drinke

to the said Harpers weif the said Harper and this deponent

did see hir lay a thinge under a greene Carpett and she beinge

gon furth of the Chamber the said Harper mistrusted what

she had hidden there went to the same Carpett and this deponent

[illegible] wth hym to see and there they espyed rattesbayne where

wherwith the said Harpers weif had before drunke, but they

not knowing it to be rattesbayne the said Harper saied it

was brymstone and offered to have tasted of the same, but

by the perswasion of this deponent who suspected it to be

rattesbayne he did forbeare And this deponent saieth that

dyvers persons dare well knowe and understande of the

aforesaid matter and of the deth of the said Harpers

weif who dyed of the poysonyng as is aforesaid.

The deponent and her husband found the ratts bane [illegible]

The deponent suspected it to be rattsbane

76

151

for a book on Shakespeare in his Warwickshire context. Mrs. Lean has since donated these materials to the Shakespeare Birthplace Trust, which has made them available to students at the Records Office in Stratford-upon-Avon. The deposition is here reduced by about one fifth.

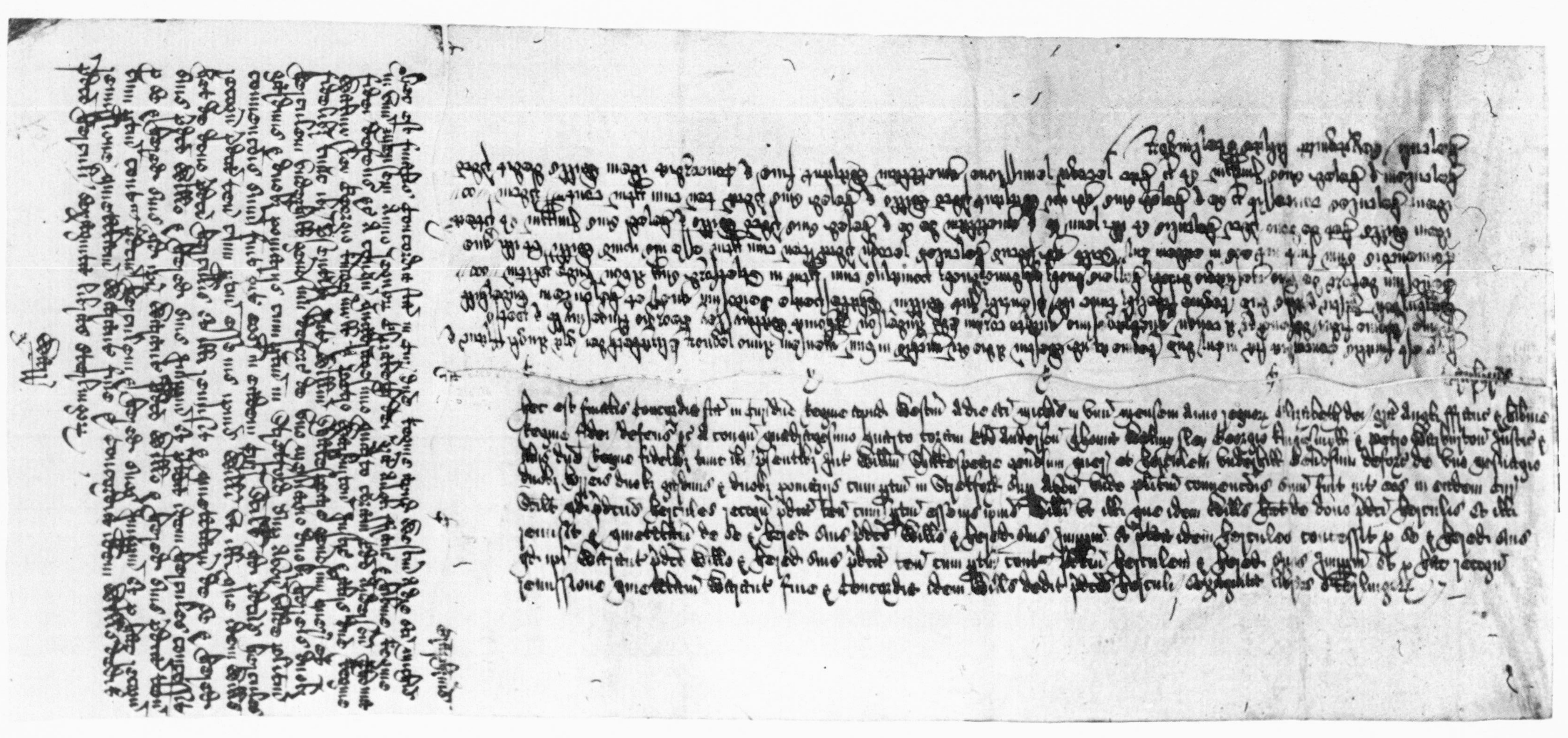

23 HERCULES UNDERHILL RECONFIRMS THE NEW PLACE CONVEYANCE TO SHAKESPEARE, 1602. *Folger Shakespeare Library MSS. Z.c.36 (110) and Z.c.36 (111); Public Record Office, Court of Common Pleas, Feet of Fines, C.P. 25 (2)/237, Michaelmas 44 & 45 Eliz. I, no. 15. Transcript: TB, 42 (extract); EKC, ii. 96 (extract); BRL, ii. 355–6 (text and translation). The seller's copy appears at the top, with the purchaser's alongside. The third copy was kept by the court. The chirographer, or court officer appointed to engross fines (or chirographs), inscribed the tripartite Concord on a single piece of parchment, which he then divided along wavy lines into copies for the court files, the vendor, and the purchaser. These copies fit together exactly. Those originally held by the vendor and purchaser were preserved by Sir John Clopton (d. 1719), and subsequently by the Ingrams of Wolford and their heirs the Severnes of Shropshire (ME, 158, n. 8). Richard Sims of the British Museum, examining the manuscript collections of J. E. Severne, came upon these copies, and announced his discovery in* The Athenaeum *for 13 February 1886, p. 241. Acquired by H-P, the two documents eventually passed into the collection of Henry Clay Folger, and thence to the Folger Shakespeare Library. In* A Calendar of the Shakespearean Rarities . . . preserved at Hollingbury Copse *(1887), where they are listed as item 140, H-P describes them as 'Quite perfect, and in the same condition in which they must have been when in the poet's own hands' (p. 51). They remain in that condition. The documents are here reduced by approximately one half.*

me), to gratifie me with some such sutes of his vine, which my sister commended much to me, which I now chuse this time, the same being seasonable, though not the best seasonable.

These 'vine settes' he asked Rose to plant 'without faile' in Dassett Court orchard—'neare the Bees, adding some sand in the morter pitt to the rootes with beastes bloud, if it may be gotten'—and also to 'sett som 2 or 3 of those shutes to be planted heare at wolverton'. Peter Temple's wife Katherine, referred to in the letter, was (before 1640) living across the road from New Place, at the house on the corner of Chapel Street and Scholars' Lane which now receives visitors as the Falcon Hotel. Two other Temple letters mention the same vines.[1]

For some years Shakespeare's descendants—his daughter Susanna and her husband John Hall, and their daughter Elizabeth, married first to Thomas Nash and then to John Bernard—lived at New Place, which formed part of the poet's entailed estate. In April 1653 Elizabeth Bernard, by then twice widowed, executed a deed conveying the property after her decease to trustees, who were directed to sell it and apply the proceeds as she would 'declare and nominate'. In 1675 Sir Edward Walker, once Secretary of War to Charles I, bought New Place, apparently as an investment, for he never resided there. When Walker died two years later, he devised the house to his daughter Barbara, who had married Sir John Clopton. Thus did New Place return to the family of the original builder.

Some earlier historians inferred that the Cloptons razed the house early in the next century, but it seems rather to have been re-edified on neo-classic principles and 'improved' with a Georgian façade. That was in 1702. It is a question whether New Place was rebuilt by Sir John or by his second son Hugh, to whom the father had conveyed it, subject to a life interest, on 20 January 1700. There appears to be more to this affair than the several deeds, preserved in the Shakespeare Birthplace Trust Records Office, relate; but most likely Sir John had the work done, although probably with borrowed money which Hugh undertook to repay.

In 1753 the Revd. Francis Gastrell, retired vicar of Frodsham, acquired New Place, which had already, some years before Garrick's Jubilee, begun to attract the attention of the curious wending their pilgrim steps to the seat of Shakespeare's birth. Six years later Gastrell hired a carpenter to cut down and chop into firewood Shakespeare's mulberry tree, thus sparing himself 'the trouble of shewing it to those whose admiration of our great poet led them to visit the poetick ground on which it stood'. As further insurance against such tiresome intrusions, and in protest against paying full rates for a house he occupied only part of the year, Gastrell demolished New Place and, amid curses and execrations, departed Stratford forever.

The now vacant site passed through various hands before Halliwell-Phillipps in October 1861 bought it with money raised by public subscription. By this means the site came to the Stratford Corporation, and subsequently to the Birthplace Trust. No owner after Gastrell has ever ventured to rebuild New Place, but another spreading mulberry, grown from a scion of the tree Shakespeare reputedly planted, still flourishes in the Great Garden.

II. The Addenbrooke Suit, 1608–9

Twice Shakespeare prosecuted debtors, thus conferring upon them their own inglorious niches in literary biography. One of these unfortunates was Philip Rogers, an apothecary who sold drugs and tobacco, and also ale (plenty of Stratfordians sold ale), in his High Street shop. Rogers held the lease of five cottages which he sublet to poor tenants but, with five mouths to feed, he often got into financial scrapes. Two clergymen sued him to collect debts, as did his surgeon George Agar, who had treated him for an ulcer; Rogers, in turn, went to law to recover a book, Gale's *Certain Works of Chirurgerie*, which (he charged) Valentine Palmes had unlawfully detained.[2] As regards the Shakespeares, Rogers had run up a bill for twenty bushels of malt at different times between March and May of 1604. Usually the womenfolk in Jacobean households attended to the brewing, so Rogers may have dealt with Anne. He borrowed an additional 2*s*. on 25 June, but paid back only 6*s*. of the total of £2.1*s*.10*d*. owed. At some time (when is not clear, as the

1 'A Document Concerning Shakespeare's Garden', *The Huntington Library Bulletin*, i (1931), 199.
2 Fripp, ii. 792–3; ME, 92.

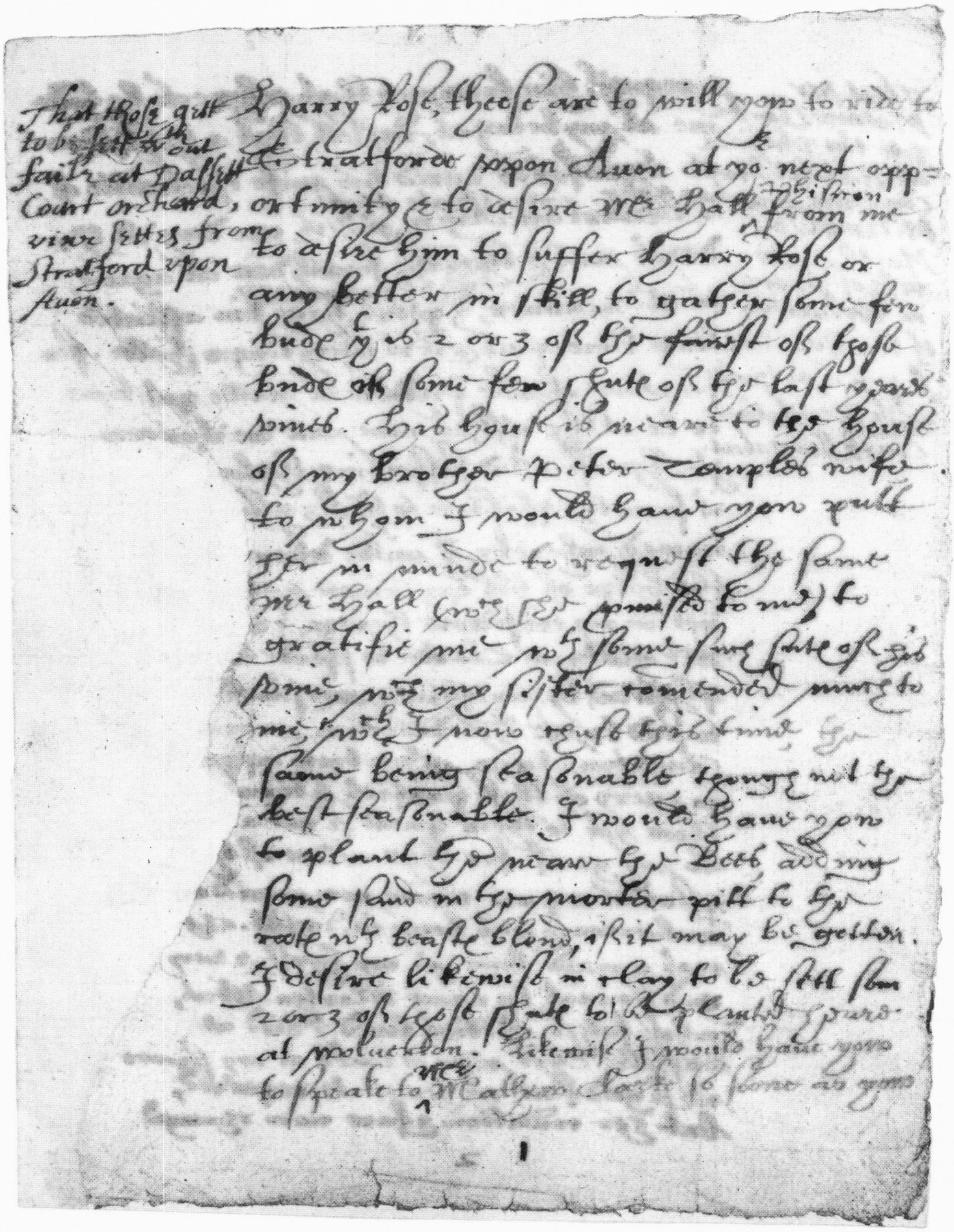

note of hearing is undated) Shakespeare brought suit. The documents do not disclose the upshot of the action.[1] The dramatist's other debtor, John Addenbrooke, owed him £6 in 1608. Who he was remains uncertain, although apparently he did not reside in the borough. A John Addenbrooke in 1584 bought the advowson—the right to nominate one's choice for a vacant benefice or living—of Tanworth, and parted with it the following year; he recovered a debt of 40*s.* at Stratford in 1594. Nothing further is known of him. The Hatfield Manuscripts (xiv. 150) around 1600 record 'one Addenbrooke' as selling licences to make starch in Warwick. He or some other may have been the John Addenbrooke that Shakespeare sued. Whoever he was, the documents in his case, unlike those for Rogers, tell the complete story of the progress and resolution of the litigation.

1 The only extant record in the case (Shakespeare Birthplace Trust Records Office, MS. EK 27/5) is reproduced in *DL*, item 143, p. 182.

24 THE VINES OF NEW PLACE: SIR THOMAS TEMPLE'S LETTER, 1631. *Huntington Library MS. STT 2145. Transcript:* The Huntington Library Bulletin, *i (1931), 200–1; BRL, ii. 586* (*extract*); *ME, 91* (*extract*). *Temple's continuation of the letter on the verso deals with medical matters.*

Such civil causes were heard by the Stratford Court of Record, which (under the charter of 1553) had jurisdiction over cases of debt, up to a maximum of £30, arising within the borough, as well as trespass, stolen goods, and the like.[1] The court met fortnightly, if required, with the bailiff presiding and (as his executive officers) serjeants at the mace. Court-appointed common

1 On the Stratford Court of Record, EKC, ii. 117, is concisely informative; for the relevant provision in the charter, see *MA*, i. 11.

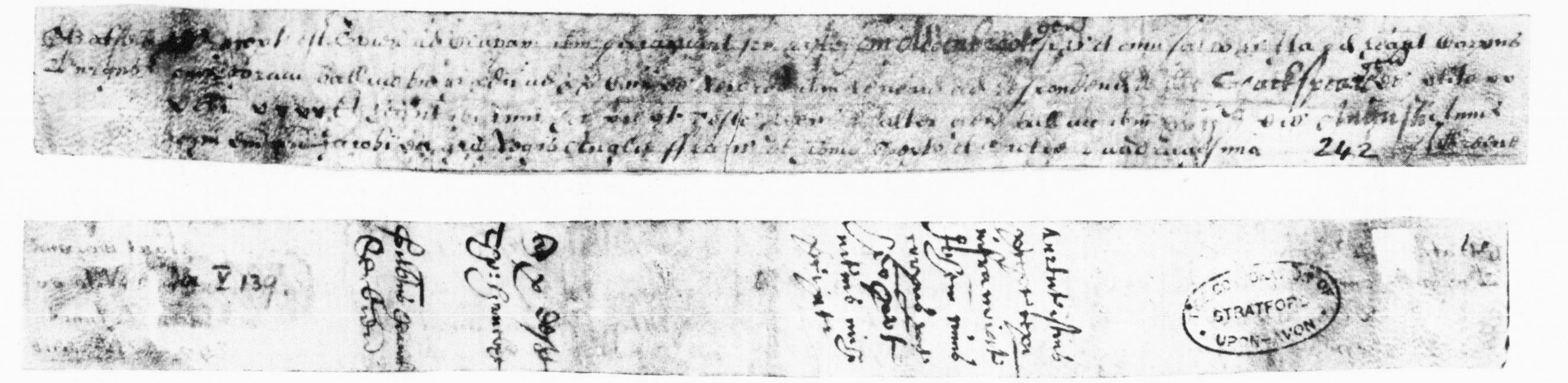

25 JOHN ADDENBROOKE ARRESTED, 17 AUGUST 1608. *Shakespeare Birthplace Trust Records Office, Misc. Doc. V, 139. Transcript: H-P,* Outlines, *ii. 78; BRL, ii. 393–4 (text and translation). R. B. Wheler discovered the action and published this item, as well as item 31 below, in his* History and Antiquities of Stratford-upon-Avon *(Stratford-upon-Avon, [1806]), pp. 144–5.*

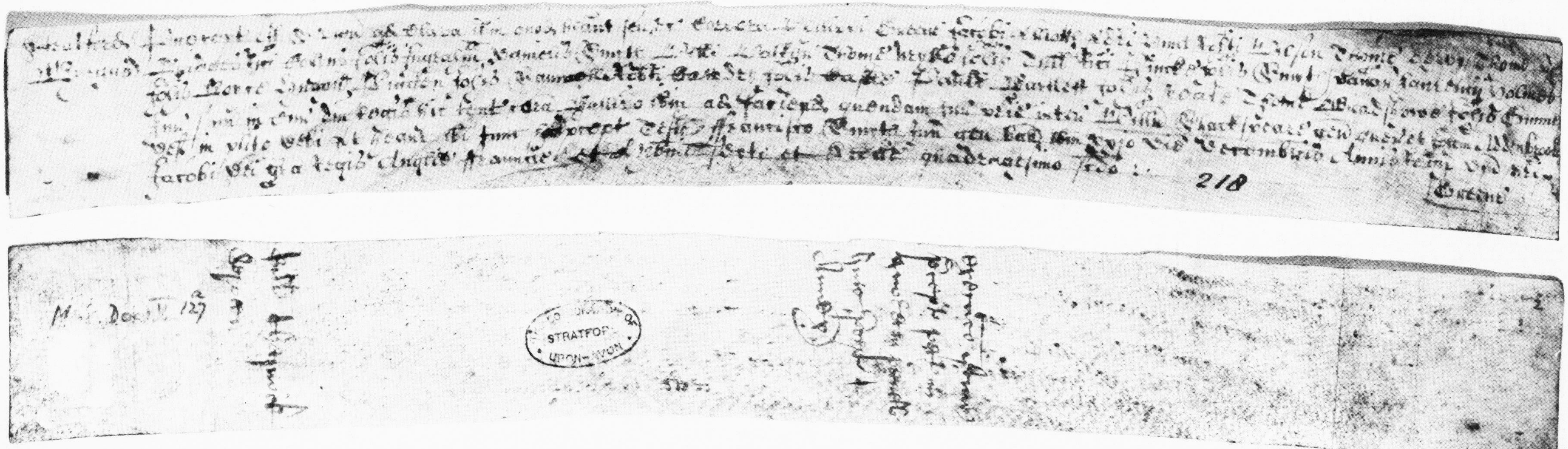

26 THE ORDER TO EMPANNEL A JURY, 21 DECEMBER 1608. *Shakespeare Birthplace Trust Records Office, Misc. Doc. V, 127a. Transcript: H-P,* Outlines, *ii. 78; BRL, ii. 394–5 (text and translation).*

attorneys received 4*d.* a session for representing the litigants. All save one of the documents in Shakespeare *versus* Addenbrooke bear the signature 'Greene' and the endorsement of either Gilbert Charnock or Francis Boyce, the serjeants. This Greene was Shakespeare's cousin Thomas, then a house guest at New Place.[1] It has been suggested that he acted as Shakespeare's solicitor in the case (William Tetherton had handled the Rogers suit for him); but Greene seems never to have acted for him in this capacity, nor did he draw up his cousin's will. As steward of the borough, however, Greene functioned as clerk of the Court of Record. The bailiff he served (at the outset of the case) was Henry Walker, a well-to-do mercer and popular townsman who had been elected in 1607 and would hold the office twice again, in 1624–5 and 1636–7. He was Shakespeare's friend. When Walker's son William was baptised on Sunday, 16 October 1608, the poet after whom he was named acted as godfather—perhaps, given his professional obligations, by proxy, although in the same month, on the 29th, the King's Men were playing in nearby Coventry. In his will Shakespeare remembered his godson with 20*s.* in gold.

At a time when many schoolmasters earned no more than £10 a year, a debt of £6 was not inconsiderable. Appropriately, therefore, justice took its magisterial course in Shakespeare *versus* Addenbrooke, as chronicled by the seven extant documents.[2] On 17 August 1608 the bailiff issued his *praecipe*, or precept (item 6), directing the serjeants to produce the body of 'Johannem Addenbrooke, generosum' to answer William Shackspeare in an action for debt ('*ad respondendum Willelmo Shackspeare generoso de placito debiti*'). An endorsement, signed by Charnock, 'serviens', noted that Addenbrooke freed himself by producing Thomas Hornebye as his surety. A blacksmith, and a blacksmith's son, Hornby ran his smithy below the Mere in Henley Street, a stone's throw from the Birthplace. He kept an alehouse as well, and frequently stood bail for debtors. Nothing further happened for some months—perhaps Shakespeare hoped Addenbrooke would settle out of court—but on 21 December Charnock summoned twenty-four citizens for the purpose of empanelling a jury (item 7). An undated court record (item 8) rehearses the names of the 'juratores', some from families well enough known from other Stratford records, others less familiar:

> Nomina juratorum inter Willelmum Shakespere generosum versus Johannem Addenbroke de placito debiti. Philippus Greene; Jacobus Elliott; Edwardus Hunte; Robertus Wilson; Thomas Kerbye; Thomas Bridges; Ricardus Collins; Johannes Ingraham; Daniell Smyth; Willelmus Walker; Thomas Mills; Johannes Tubb; Ricardus Pincke; Johannes Smyth, draper; Laurencius Holmes; Johannes Boyce; Hugo Piggon; Johannes Samwell; Robertus Cawdey; Johannes Castle; Paulus Bartlett; Johannes Yeate; Thomas Bradshowe; Johannes Gunne. Quilibet jurator predictus per se separatim manucaptus est per plegios Johannem Doo et Ricardum Roo.

The last sentence, stating that each of the aforesaid jurors has been made a bondsman by pledge of John Doe and Richard Roe ritualises by legal fiction the procedure of old whereby bondsmen for jurors were actually required. Of the jurors listed, Robert Cawdry belonged to the prominent Stratford recusant family; he had in 1600 sued Shakespeare's brother-in-law, the hatter William Hart, for debt. The experience was hardly novel for Hart: two others proceeded against him the same year, including Richard Collins, on the same jury list. Hugh Piggon was likely the son of the Hugh Pigeon, one of the poor folk in Greenhill Street, who was admitted as almsman in 1573.

There followed (item 9) a *distringas juratores* precept calling for attendance of the jurors at the next session of the Court of Record ('*ad proximam curiam de recordo*'). The fifth document (item 10) listed the jurors once again, but recorded Greene and Elliott as ill, and marked twelve names 'juratus'. These comprised the panel finally selected. Having retired, they found for the plaintiff, and assessed costs of 6*s.*8*d.* for their own labours, 4*d.* in costs (*misae*) for the plaintiff, plus 2*d.* damages (*dampna*). The last figure is inconsistent with that of the order (item 11) to arrest and produce Addenbrooke at the next sitting to satisfy William Shackspere, gentleman, for both the £6 of debt and the 24*s.* for damages and injuries he sustained by reason of the withholding of the aforesaid debt: '. . . ad satisfaciendum Willelmo Shackspere generoso tam de sex libris debiti

1 See below, pp. 72–3.

2 On this suit see EKC, ii. 114–18; he summarises the first six documents in the case and transcribes the seventh. BRL, ii. 393–400, mostly follows the analysis of EKC, but is helpful on some of the legal terms.

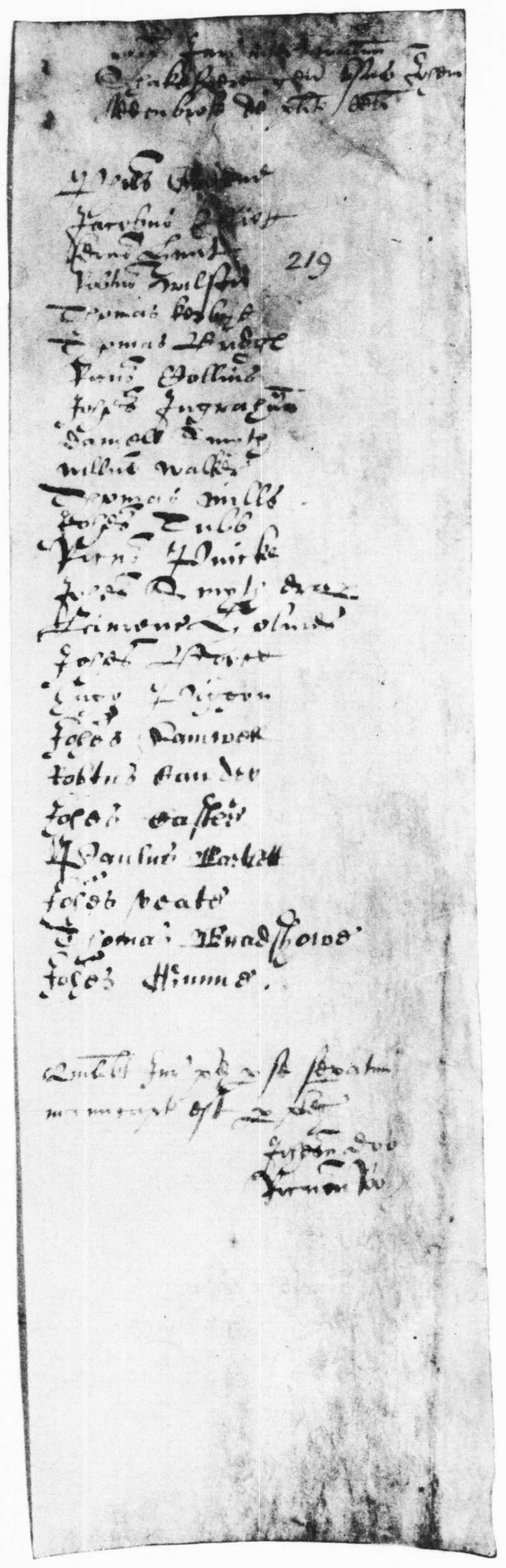

27 THE PANEL OF JURORS, C. DECEMBER 1608. *Shakespeare Birthplace Trust Records Office, Misc. Doc. 127b. Transcript: H-P,* Outlines, *ii. 78; BRL, ii. 395 (text and translation).*

28 THE JURY BOUND, 15 FEBRUARY 1609. *Shakespeare Birthplace Trust Records Office, Misc. Doc. V, 115. Transcript: H-P,* Outlines, *ii. 78–9; BRL, ii. 395–6 (text and translation).*

29 THE JURY FINDS FOR SHAKESPEARE, MARCH 1609. *Shakespeare Birthplace Trust Records Office, Misc. Doc. V, 116. Transcript: H-P,* Outlines, *ii, 79; BRL, ii. 397 (text and translation). Reproduced is the recto, with the jurors named, and the verso, with their verdict and assessment of costs and damages.*

quas predictus Willelmus in eadem curia versus eum recuperavit quam de viginti et quatuor solidis qui ei adjudicati fuerunt pro dampnis et custagiis suis quos sustinuit occacione detencionis debiti predicti'. But, as Francis Boyce's endorsement indicates, Addenbrooke had flown the coop, and was not to be found within the liberties of the borough. Accordingly, in the last precept (item 12), the court ordered Thomas Horneby, 'plegius et manucaptor' (pledge and mainpernor, i.e. bondsman), to show cause why he should not be held liable for the £6 plus 24*s.* costs owed by his delinquent client. Such were the hazards, which Hornby more than once encountered, of the bondsman's vocation.

The Shakespeare records invite biographical fantasy. If the story of his marriage is a subject for sentimental romance, his efforts to recoup debts by litigation lend themselves to melodrama: the poet of humanity becomes a tight-fisted capitalist demanding his metaphorical pound of flesh. Thus, as Sir Sidney Lee, in the age of the robber barons, sees him,

> Shakespeare inherited his father's love of litigation, and stood rigorously by his rights in all his business relations. . . . It is beyond question . . . that at Stratford Shakespeare, like many of his fellow-townsmen, was a frequent suitor in the local court of record. While he was not averse from advancing money to impecunious neighbours, he was punctual and pertinacious in demands for repayment. . . . On February 15, 1609, the dramatist, who seems to have been legally represented on this occasion by his kinsman, Thomas Greene, obtained judgment from a jury against Addenbroke for the payment of 6*l.*, with 1*l.* 5*s.* costs, but Addenbroke left the town, and the triumph proved barren. Shakespeare avenged himself by proceeding against Thomas Horneby, who had acted as the absconding debtor's bail. Horneby had succeeded his father Richard Horneby on his death in 1606 as a master blacksmith in Henley Street, and was one of the smaller sharers in the tithes. The family forge lay near Shakespeare's Birthplace. Plaintiff and defendant in this last prosecution had been playmates in childhood and they had some common interests in adult life. But litigation among the residents of Stratford showed scant regard for social ties, and in his handling of practical affairs Shakespeare caught the prevailing spirit of rigour.[1]

Never mind that Lee mistakenly makes Greene Shakespeare's attorney, or that he errs slightly with respect to the assessment of costs. More serious is his misinformation that Shakespeare frequently resorted to the law in his pursuit of the wretches who owed him money. So far as is known, he petitioned the Court of Record for relief only twice in his lifetime: less than others of his status. Litigation in Shakespeare's Stratford, indeed in Elizabethan England generally, was an everyday pastime, indulged in largely because the legal system furnished no other convenient machinery, such as credit accounts or collection agencies, for the recovery of personal or business debts. Whether Shakespeare and Hornby played together as children the documents fail to reveal, but we may feel reasonably assured that the social fabric of his everyday life did not unravel because on two occasions he preferred not to find himself out of pocket.

III. Thomas Greene and the Welcombe Enclosure

Early in *Bingo*, Edward Bond's play about Shakespeare, a representative of the powerful neighbourhood landholders, William Combe, visits the dramatist in his retirement at New Place. Combe confirms the gossip about enclosure. He explains the issues, not so much (one suspects) for Shakespeare's benefit as for that of a modern audience only dimly aware, if at all, of the agrarian revolution taking place in his England.

> We're going to enclose—stake out new fields the size of all our old pieces put together and shut them up behind hedges and ditches. Then we can farm in our own way. Tenants with long leases will be reallocated new land. Squatters and small tenants on short leases will have to go: we shan't renew. That leaves you, and some others, who own rents on the land.[2]

'The rents', Shakespeare recalls. 'I bought my share years ago out of money I made by writing.' Enclosure meant conversion from tillage to grassland, corn to sheep. The prospect of fatter returns beckoned the entrepreneur; as Combe points out: 'Sheep prices are lower than corn prices but they still give the best return. Low on labour costs! No ploughing, sowing, harvesting, threshing, carting—just a few old shepherds who can turn their hand to butchery. Sheep are pure profit.' By engendering scarcity of grain, enclosure pushed up the price of bread; it swelled the poor rolls with dispossessed small renters. The Stratford town council, already burdened with seven hundred almsfolk—roughly a third of the population—opposed the Welcombe enclosure. In the play Combe has come to enlist not Shakespeare's partisanship but his neutrality. 'Don't support the town or the tenants', he urges. 'When the council write, ignore them. Be noncom-

1 Sidney Lee, *A Life of William Shakespeare* (4th ed. of revised version, 1925), pp. 321–3.

2 Quotations are from Edward Bond, *Bingo: Scenes of Money and Death* (1974).

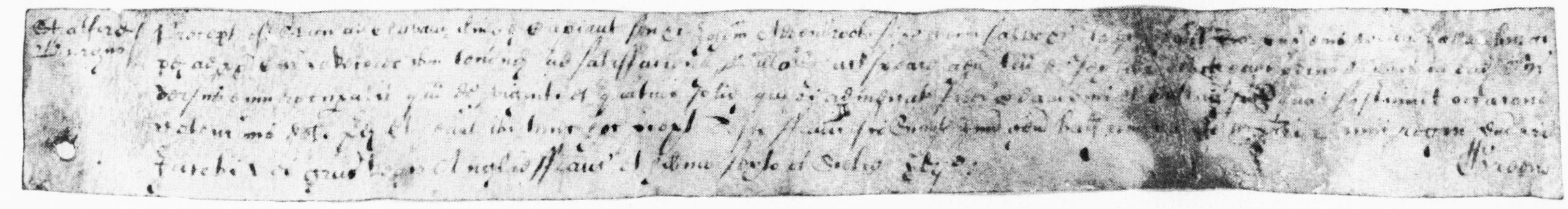

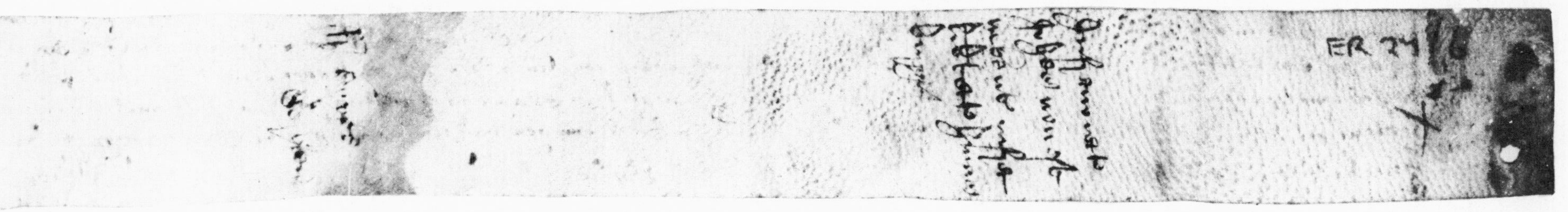

30 ADDENBROOKE ORDERED TO SATISFY THE VERDICT, 15 MARCH 1609. *Shakespeare Birthplace Trust Records Office, MS. ER 27/6. Transcript: H-P,* Outlines, *ii. 79; BRL, ii. 397–8 (text and translation).*

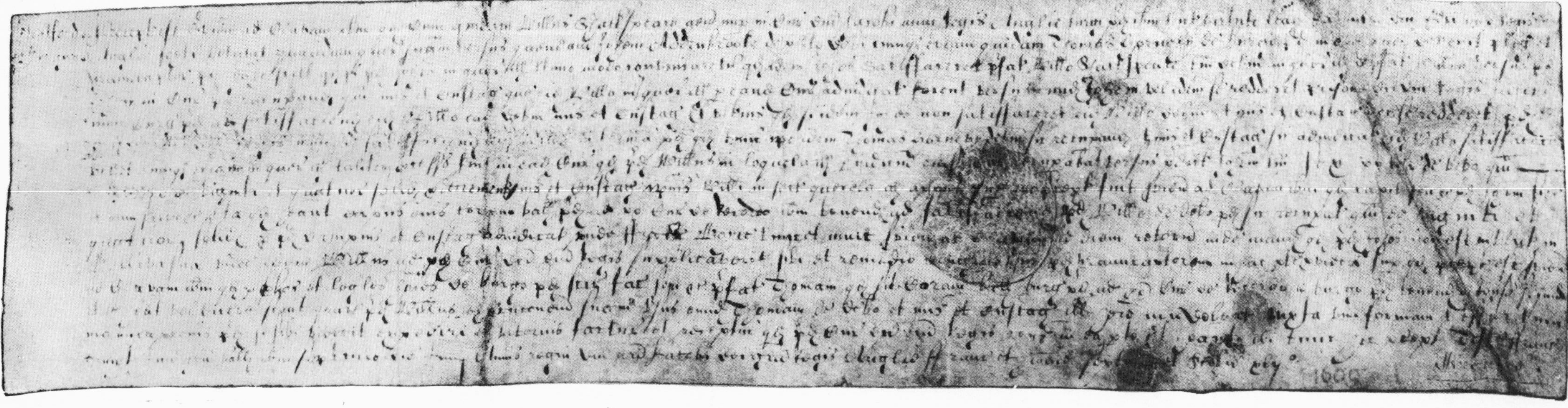

31 THE ORDER AGAINST THOMAS HORNBY, 7 JUNE 1609. *Shakespeare Birthplace Trust Records Office, MS. ER 27/7. Transcript: H-P,* Outlines, *ii. 79–80; EKC, ii. 115–16; BRL, ii. 398–400 (text and translation).*

32 THE WEST VIEW OF WELCOMBE HILLS. *From the title-page of John Jordan*, Welcombe Hills, near Stratford upon Avon, a Poem, Historical and Descriptive (*1777*).

mittal or say you think nothing will come of it. Stay in your garden.' So he offers an agreement guaranteeing Shakespeare his present rents after enclosure. Shakespeare does not sign, not yet—he wants independent assessors to validate the figures. But in the next scene, six months later, Combe returns with a document and an ink pot, and Shakespeare signs. Subsequently we see the poor suffer. Shakespeare takes poison. He reviews his life. 'Was anything done?' he repeatedly asks before he dies.

Thus, in these *Scenes of Money and Death*, does Bond dramatise Shakespeare's last days. As a plausible reconstruction *Bingo* need not detain anybody; Bond is merely using Shakespeare as a vehicle for his own preoccupations respecting the artist in society. But of the many plays that have been written about Shakespeare's life, no other that I know focuses on the Welcombe enclosure. Bond feels the biographers have neglected the subject too; that most, apart from Chambers, barely notice it. He exaggerates, but he has a point; the affair, having no bearing on poetry or the theatre, usually receives perfunctory treatment—Robert Speaight dismisses in a paragraph 'this rather tedious controversy'.[1] That controversy, however, enables us to see Shakespeare, who was of an age as well as for all time, in his local context of a small Midlands town in the second decade of the seventeenth century where he commanded respect as a leading citizen for his material rather than artistic achievements. Moreover, the controversy itself holds intrinsic interest, involving as it did intrigue, cajolery, and bullying tactics. Ditches were dug and surreptitiously filled; harsh words were spoken, and violence flared while Combe laughed on horseback. Finally, at the Lent Assizes of 1616, Sir Edward Coke, Chief Justice of the King's Bench, told Combe to 'set his mind at rest': there would be no enclosure of the Welcombe fields. Shake-

1 Robert Speaight, *Shakespeare: The Man and His Achievement* (New York, 1977), p. 369n.

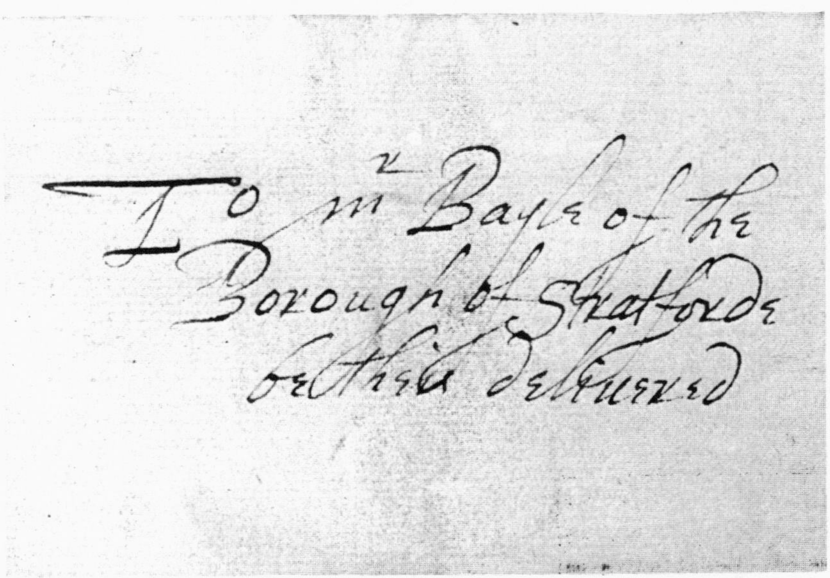

To m^r Bayle of the
Borough of Stratforde
be these delivered

33–5 COMBE DENIED. *Correspondence preserved in the Stratford Records Office illustrates the subsequent course of the controversy. In a letter of 23 December 1616 addressed to Henry Smith, then bailiff, Combe adopted a conciliatory tone, assuring Smith that he had especially ordered his workmen not to dig any part of the common, 'because I would not give you nor the rest of the freeholders enie just exceptions and if they have exceeded there commission what you like not of shall be altered'. Combe had not, however, abandoned hope of enclosure, as the substance, which follows, makes clear:*

but if they have diged upon mine owne lande, which I thinke they may lawfullie doe, both by the law of god and man, . . . I hope you will not out of your christian profession, (if yt weare in your power) goe about to hinder yt: I pray you therfore, let my workmen with your love continue at ther labour, beinge to soe good ende: And doubt not but if you be of a contentious speritt, you shall somtime duringe life have better occation to except against.

The bailiff's reply, dispatched for speedy delivery on Christmas Eve, wasted no time on ceremonial courtesies. 'Sir', Smith wrote,

You might yf yo^w pleased take notice that whether the place bee yor owne or noe, you may not by digginge of ditches diminishe or hinder other mens Commons . . . yf yor unlawfull Caryage in such diggynge move not yor Conscience blinded as yt seemeth with a desire to make yor self Riche by other mens losse, nor the Contynuall most grave and godlie Charge of the Judges at the Assises nor the mynysters Threatnyngs against Inclosures, nor the many suites have beene in all respectfull and loveinge manner made unto you not to worke harme to soe poore a Corporacion and wronge to soe many men as have Common may not move you to desist. I pray you give leave that such Course and suites bee used against you and yor Diggers as may Cause you see yor present and former errors prayinge you not to accounte yt Contencion for men by lawfull meanes to defend theire auncient rightes but by lookeinge homeward to Confesse that the authors of strife are the begynners of newe thinges.

On 12 March 1618 the Archbishop of Canterbury, the Lord Chamberlain, Sir Edward Coke, and others signed a letter to Combe affirming the decree of the Justices of the Assizes, and ordering that any enclosures made contrary to that order 'bee forthwith layd open as formerly ther were: As alsoe that the launde converted into pasture bee againe made arable for Corne and grayne, accordinge to the course of husbaundry there. And lastly that the Meeres, and Banckes bee restored, and made perfect'. Combe had no choice now but to acknowledge defeat, which he ungracefully did.

No. 26 Wheler Collection
p. 43

C No 213

88

71

Mr Bayly: I did especiallie charge my workemen that they should not digge anie parte of the common because I would not give you nor the rest of the freeholders anie iust exceptions and if they haue exceeded there commission what you like not of shall be altered. but if they haue digged upon mine owne lande which I thinke they may lawfullie doe both by the law of God and man for the preservation of corne and avoidinge of unnecessarie suites which may growe for want of a mounde betweene the riuer and the more: I hope you will not out of your christian profession (if yt weare in your power) goe about to hinder yt. I pray you therfore let my workemen with your loue continue at their labour beinge to soe good ende: And doubt not but if you be of a contentious spirit you shall somtime duringe life haue better occasion to except against. And soe desiringe to remaine your frende, if you giue me noe other cause doe rest

xxiii Dec. 1616

Your neybour

Wm Combe

33 WILLIAM COMBE'S LETTER TO HENRY SMITH, BAILIFF OF STRATFORD-UPON-AVON, 23 DECEMBER 1616. *Shakespeare Birthplace Trust Records Office; shelfmark: ER 1/1/72. Transcript: Ingleby,* Shakespeare and the Enclosure of Common Fields at Welcombe, *Appendix, Item V, p. 18.*

No. 26 Wheler Collection 90
p 43 Stratford Inclosure
C No 211 69

Sr you might yf yow pleased take notice that whether the place
bee yor owne or noe, you may not by diggings of ditches x x
diminish or hinder other mens Commons, you are not ignorant
of the late Lord Cheif Justices Order by yor Consent made for
preventinge of tumult, whereof there was an unhappie x x
beginninge, yf yor unlawfull Carriage in this digginge ~~were~~ were
not yor Conscience blinded as yt seemeth with a desire to make yor
selfe rich by other mens losse, ~~were~~ nor the Contynuall most
grave and godlie Charge of the Judges at the Assises nor
the manyfold Threatnings against Inclosures, nor the e-
arnest suite have beene in all respectfull and loveinge manner
made unto you not to worke harme to the peace & Corporation
and wronge to soe many men as have Common may not move
you to desist. I pray you give leave that such Course and x x
suites bee psecuted against you and yor diggers as may cause you
see yor ~~error~~ offence and former prayinge you not to terme
yt Contempt for men by lawfull meanes to defend theire x x
auncient rights. but by lookinge homeward to confesse that
the Authors of strife are the begynners of newe thinges. Thus
prayinge you lett us of Stratford and my selfe in especiall
to have yor love. I rest

one ever desirous of yor love and
of peace:

Henry Smith Bayliffe://

24 Dec. 1616

To the worll my much honored
friende: William Combe
Esquire theis bee dd wth speed

34 THE BAILIFF'S REPLY TO COMBE, 24 DECEMBER 1616. *Shakespeare Birthplace Trust Records Office; shelfmark: ER 1/1/73. Transcript: Ingleby,* Shakespeare and the Enclosure of Common Fields at Welcombe, *Appendix, Item VI, p. 18.*

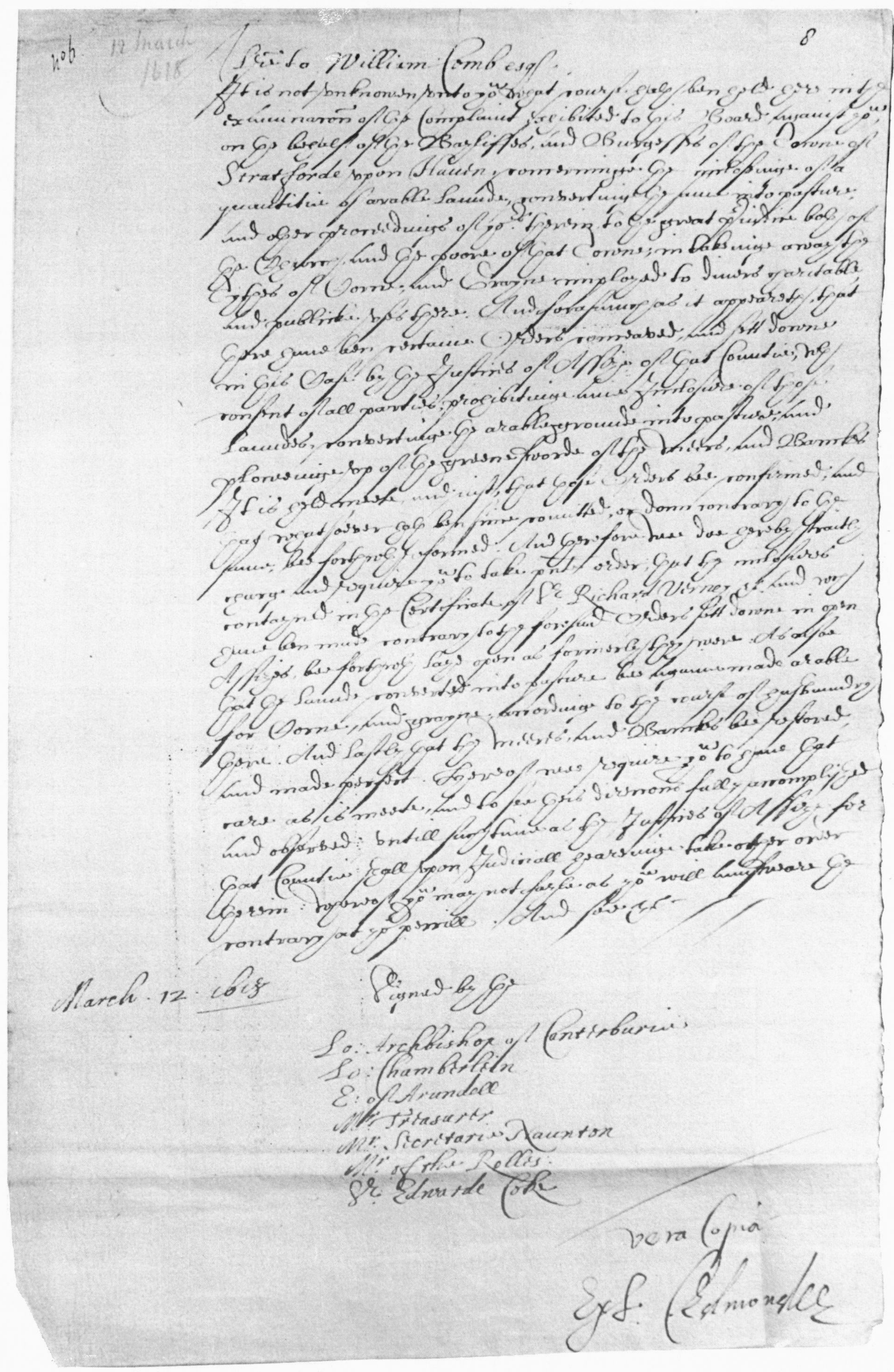
8

12 March 1618

To William Combe esq.

March 12. 1618

Signed by the

Lo: Archbishop of Canterburie
Lo: Chamberlein
E: of Arundell
Mr Treasurer
Mr Secretarie Naunton
Mr of the Rolles
Sr Edwarde Coke

vera Copia

35 THE JUSTICE'S ORDER CONFIRMED, 12 MARCH 1618. *Shakespeare Birthplace Trust Records Office; shelfmark: BRU 15/7/6. Transcript: Ingleby,* Shakespeare and the Enclosure of Common Fields at Welcombe, *Appendix, Item VII, p. 19. This document, here reduced, is a contemporary copy of the original.*

speare by then was dead. Enclosure eventually did take place, but that was in another century.[1]

At stake for Shakespeare were the returns from his half interest in a lease of tithes of 'corne, grayne, blade, and heye' from three neighbouring hamlets of Stratford: Old Stratford, Welcombe, and Bishopton. This interest he acquired, for the goodly sum of £440, from Ralph Hubaud in 1605 (the indenture is reproduced in *DL*, item 155, pp. 193–4). On 28 October 1614 William Replingham, an attorney serving the enclosure activists, agreed to compensate Shakespeare or his assigns for any loss of tithes resulting from 'anie inclosure or decaye of tyllage'. This document (*DL*, item 189, p. 232) provides the basis for Combe's solicitation in *Bingo*. It is also true that Shakespeare (as Combe requests in the play) when consulted said nothing would come of the enclosure drive. But Bond gives the facts an unwarranted significance when he suggests that Shakespeare's neutrality in effect amounted to endorsement. Combe needed all the declared support he could muster if he hoped to overcome the almost unanimous resistance of the Stratford corporation. Shakespeare's failure to intervene—for whatever reason—conferred no advantage, as the event shows; for Replingham, Combe, and their party failed.

Much of our information concerning these events derives from Thomas Greene.[2] Prominent for many years in Stratford affairs, he left his tracks in the municipal records, while his numerous memoranda and other personal papers—he was by habit of mind as well as by vocation a note-taker—are fortunately preserved in the Birthplace Trust Records Office. We know Greene better than we do most of Shakespeare's fellow townsmen. The son of a Warwick mercer, he entered the Middle Temple in 1595, with the Marstons, father and son, as sureties; the son, John, would later achieve eminence as a satirist and playwright. Greene was admitted to the bar in 1600, and the next year began representing the Stratford corporation as solicitor. In this capacity he negotiated in London a new charter, which James at length granted in 1610. Meanwhile he had in 1603 become (by patent) Steward of the borough, and from 1603 until 1617 he served as Town Clerk. As Clerk he kept the minutes for council sessions in the Guild Hall. The corporation in 1611 voted to make John Greene (Thomas's brother, also an attorney) or Abraham Sturley his deputy, and to reward the two officers with half the proceeds of the Court of Record. In Stratford Greene reared six children. Three died young and were buried in Holy Trinity churchyard.

Like Shakespeare, Greene had a reversionary interest in the Welcombe tithes, for which he is reported to have paid £300 in 1609. The next year the corporation sprang to his defence when made aware that Greene 'standeth secretlie scandalized and unjustly sklaundred bie unknowen aucthores, That he hath hearteofore deceaved and dealt evillie with us in buyinge of one Humfrie Coles esquier an intereste in tithes the inheritance wheareof is in us'; to the contrary, the corporation goes on record, Greene 'for his fidelitie and endevors in our behalfes allwaies used us verie well'. With Shakespeare and seventy others, Greene in 1611 contributed to the cost of prosecuting in Parliament a bill 'for the better Repayre of the high waies and amendinge divers defectes in the Statutes alredy made'. The name of 'm^r^ Thomas Greene esquire', set down for a donation of 2*s*.6*d*., appears second, after the chief alderman. In the end he felt the town had let him down; when Thomas in 1617 decided to pack up and leave Stratford, selling his house and tithes for a lower than anticipated price, he lamented not receiving 'recompense to a greater value for my golden dayes and spirites spent in Stratfordes Service'. With these golden days past, the Greenes settled in Bristol, although Thomas pursued a successful career as barrister in London. There he kept his ties with the Middle Temple, where he was appointed successively Reader, Master of the Bench, and (in 1629) Treasurer. In his will, dictated on 5 November 1640 and proved the next July by his widow Lettice, Greene remembered, in addition to his children and grandchildren, the cathedral church of Bristol.

This busy professional man now and then spared some time for literary dabblings. He may or

1 These events I have recounted in some detail in my *DL*, pp. 230–4. They are also dealt with by Fripp, *Shakespeare*, ii. 805–12, and by ME, 136–8. Bond cites as his own source—an authoritative one—EKC, ii. 141–52. Joan Thirsk, *Tudor Enclosures* (1959), may be recommended as a concisely authoritative brief review of the varieties of enclosure, motives, legislation, and other aspects of the question, with special attention given to the Midlands.

2 On Thomas Greene I have found most useful ME, 127–32, 136–9 *passim*. Also valuable are EKC, ii. 149–52; Fripp, *Shakespeare*, i, ii *passim;* Rupert Taylor, 'Shakespeare's Cousin, Thomas Greene, and His Kin: Possible Light on the Shakespeare Family Background', *PMLA*, lx (1945), 81–94.

may not be the Thomas Greene who saluted his new monarch in 1603 with the poem *A Poet's Vision and a Prince's Glory*, at the end of which he threatens to try again 'if this prosper but successefullie'; but he probably contributed the sonnet honouring the Warwickshire poet Michael Drayton in the 1603 edition of *The Barons' Wars*. Greene could not, however, have been responsible—as sometimes alleged—for the 1602 modernisation of *The Seven Wise Masters*, which purged that witty narration of its 'rude and barbarous' phrase and penning; for a recently recovered unique copy of a 1576 edition, now in the British Library (shelfmark C.142.c.15), is similarly equipped with the address of 'Thomas Greene Gentleman to the learned Reader'. In Stratford, Greene left behind among his papers Latin verses, as well as such philosophical ruminations as 'Love is not to be so suppresed with Wisdom. . . . Cause a Lover Loveth his Torment'.[1]

The enclosure crisis led Greene to seek out Shakespeare's counsel, but ties of kinship as well as interest drew the two together. In his diary Greene more than once refers to Shakespeare as his cousin, and, although the Elizabethans employed this term loosely, some blood relationship or matrimonial connection probably existed.[2] For a while, perhaps more than a year, Greene enjoyed the hospitality of New Place. That was in 1609, when he and his family were waiting to take possession of a house occupied by George Badger. Greene had bought from the Crown St. Mary's House, adjoining the Churchyard in Old Town—'A pretty neate gentleman like house', he described it afterwards, 'with a pretty garden and a lyttle yonge Orchard standinge very Sweete and quiett'. But Badger put off moving. 'I was content to permytt yt [the delay] without contradiccion', Greene noted on 9 September, '& the rather because I perceyved I mighte stay another yere at newe place.'[3] In December 1611 the Greenes, Thomas and Lettice, joined Judith Shakespeare in witnessing a deed of sale for Elizabeth Quiney and her son Adrian. Despite these dealings Shakespeare does not name his cousin in his will.

Greene, however, mentions Shakespeare a number of times in his memoranda. On 5 September 1614 the Town Clerk drew up a list of 'Auncientt ffreeholders in the ffieldes of Oldstratford and Welcombe'. The name of 'M[r] Shakspeare' heads the rest, with his holdings described thus: '4. yard Land, noe common nor ground beyond gospell bushe, noe grownd in Sandfield, nor none in slowe hill field beyond Bishopton nor none in the enclosure beyond Bishopton'.[4] From 15 November 1614 to 19 February 1617, when debate over enclosure raged, Greene kept a diary. An entry for 17 November 1614 records a visit to 'Cosen Shakspeare', just returned to town; 'he & M[r] Hall say they think there will be nothyng done at all'. On 10 December, Greene was looking in vain for Replingham at the Bear and New Place. Two weeks later, on the 23rd, he wrote to Shakespeare about the corporation's opposition—'I alsoe wrytte of myself to my Cosen Shakespeare the Coppyes of all our oathes m[a]de then alsoe a not of the Inconvenyences wold gr[ow] by the Inclosure'. An entry for 9 January 1615 reveals that Thomas Lucas, Shakespeare's Gray's Inn solicitor, suggested that Greene's name be included when the articles between Replingham and Shakespeare were being drawn up ('one Thomas Greene, gent.' duly appears in the agreement). Two nights later, over dinner, Replingham gave Greene reassurances, mentioning 'his agreement for me with my cosen Shakpeare'. A cryptic memorandum for September (day unspecified) has caused puzzlement: 'W Shakspeares tellyng J Greene that I was not able to beare the encloseinge of Welcombe'. One may wonder why Shakespeare should have found it necessary to tell Greene's brother what he must have already known, and why John should have thought this communication interesting enough to repeat to Thomas. And why did the latter record it? Perhaps a slip is involved—*beare* for *barre* or *I* for *he*—but at this distance in time we cannot say. It is, however, abundantly clear from the various memoranda that the prospect of enclosure stirred anxiety in Greene; he had promised the corporation in writing, 'as the Steward & Counsellour of the sayd Borough to assist them agaynst the sayd inclosure', and he was as good as his word. There is not the slightest evidence that Shakespeare shared his cousin's disquiet. On this occasion, as on others, he seems to have preserved his negative capability.

1 ME, 128.

2 Taylor speculates on the possibilities in 'Shakespeare's Cousin', pp. 81–94.

3 Shakespeare Birthplace Trust Records Office, Misc. Doc., XII, 103; EKC, ii. 96; ME, 131–2.

4 Shakespeare Birthplace Trust Records Office, Corp. Rec., Misc. Doc., I, 94; *DL*, item 188, p. 231. Transcript: EKC, ii. 141; BRL, ii. 457.

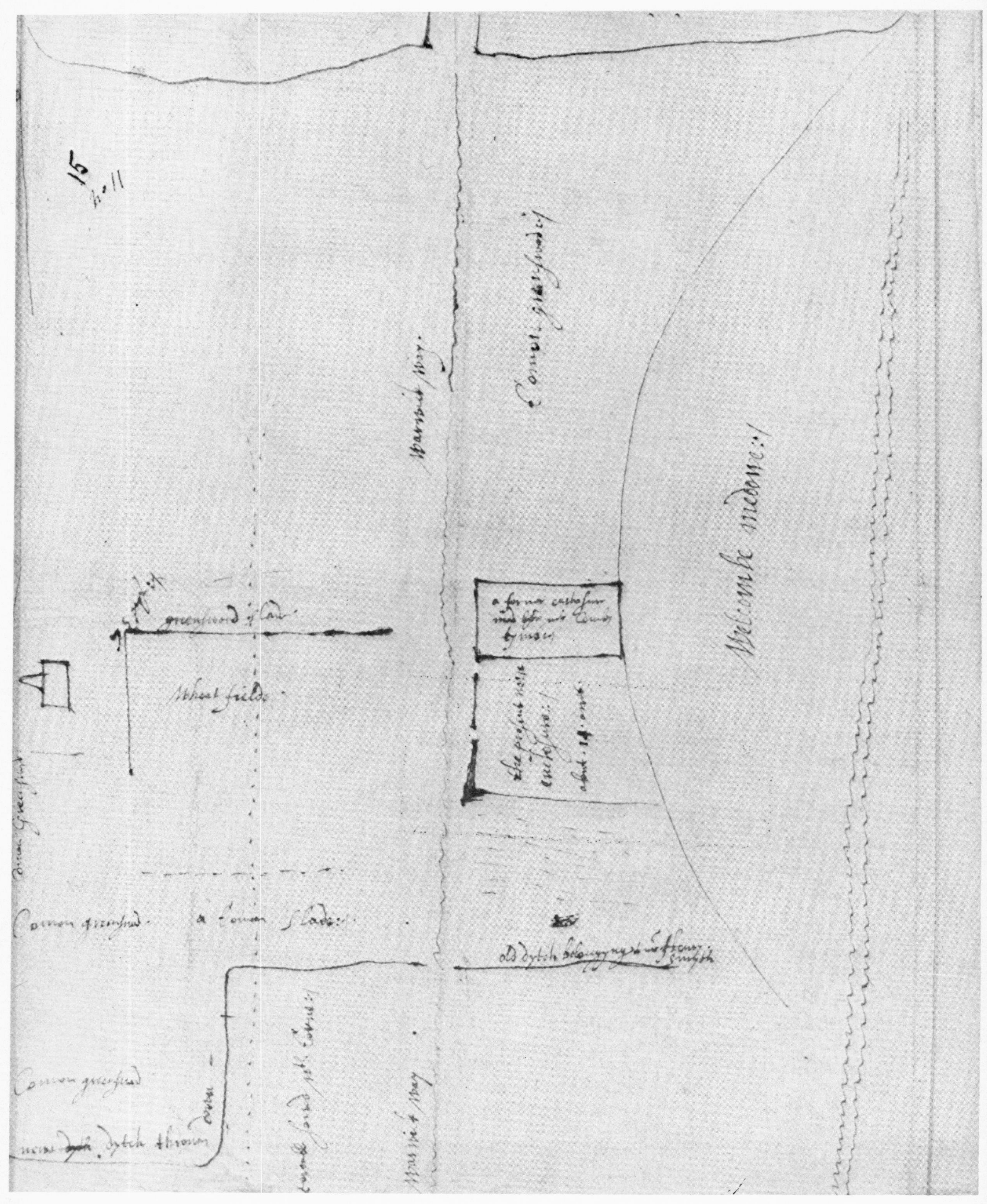

36 THE WELCOMBE COMMONS. *Shakespeare Birthplace Trust Records Office, MS. Misc. Doc., Vol. 7, no. 11. C. M. Ingleby publishes a line facsimile of this sketch, which he describes as 'among the Stratford Muniments'* (Shakespeare and the Enclosure of Common Fields at Welcombe . . . (*Birmingham, 1885*), *p. xii*).

37 THOMAS GREENE'S *DIARY*, 15 NOVEMBER 1614 – 19 FEBRUARY 1617. *Shakespeare Birthplace Trust Records Office, Corp. Rec., Misc. Doc., XIII, 26a, 27–9.*

The Greene memoranda surfaced in the last century. In 1885 C. M. Ingleby published Shakespeare and the Enclosure of Common Fields at Welcombe, being a fragment of the Private Diary of Thomas Greene, Town Clerk of Stratford-upon-Avon. *This slender folio, printed in Birmingham for private subscription in an edition of fifty numbered copies, reproduces in autotype the four leaves, comprising eight pages, of Greene's diary, accompanied by a letterpress transcript furnished by Edward Scott, an Assistant Keeper of Manuscripts at the British Museum. Greene's rapid, crabbed hand has presented difficulties even for experienced palaeographers; difficulties which are compounded by the faded ink and mottled paper. The first leaf was discovered by the Stratford antiquary Robert Bell Wheler, who published several extracts in his* Guide to Stratford-upon-Avon (*Stratford-upon-Avon, 1814*). *Wheler leaves blanks where the manuscript defeated him. H-P came upon the remaining three leaves in a volume of miscellaneous documents in the Muniment Room of the corporation, and noted their existence in his* Descriptive Calendar of the Ancient Manuscripts and Records in the possession of the corporation of Stratford-upon-Avon (*1863*), *p. 396, items 27–9. Ingleby first provided facsimiles and a full transcript. No attempt to supersede his work has since been made, although EKC published selected extracts* (*ii. 142–3*), *as has BRL, ii. 458–63. Nor has Ingleby's book, scarce from the outset, ever been reprinted. It perhaps says something about the attentiveness of even specialist readers that thirty years went by before one, Mrs. Charlotte Carmichael Stopes, discovered that Ingleby had inadvertently transposed pages six and seven of the diary* (Shakespeare's Environment (*1914*), *pp. 86–7*). *The reversal makes hash of the sequence of events, and leads Ingleby to the improbable conclusion that one entry referring to the dramatist 'records, five months after the death of Shakespeare, the statement of Shakespeare himself'. The statement noted by Greene was in fact* (*as Mrs. Stopes points out*) *made by Shakespeare seven months before he died.*

For the present volume we have photographed afresh the eight pages of Greene's diary. Modern technology makes it possible to improve upon the legibility of Ingleby's autotypes. The reader will, I fear, still not find the going easy. A printed transcript of Greene's jottings, with their marginalia, interlineations, deletions, and occasional double columns, presents problems of another kind. To furnish some guidance I have thought it well to reproduce Scott's transcript alongside the facsimiles. He places square brackets around expansions of abbreviations and inverted commas around scored through words, but is otherwise faithful to Greene's format. It goes without saying that I have restored the correct order of both facsimiles and transcripts.

1614

[illegible]

Jovis 17 No: my Cosen Shakspeare comyng yesterday to towne I went to see him howe he did he told me that they assured him they ment to inclose noe further then to gospell bushe & so upp straight (leavyng out part of the dyngles to the ffield) to the gate in Clopton hedge & take in Salisburyes peece: and that they meane in Aprill to servey the Land & then to gyve satisfaccion & not before & he & Mr Hall say they think there will be nothyng done at all.

[illegible]

r[emember] Martis 15 No: [uembris] 1614 "Mr." I asking Mr. Manneryng how they did meane to deale w[i]th me about my p[ar]t interest of tythes where they ment to enclose he told me I should haue no wrong & that I should rather gett a peny th[en] a half penny & then agayne I should rather gett ij[d.] then loose a penny & sayd he was desirous to b[uy] my whole interest of my Tythes I asked him whether he hadd ever thought w[i]th himself what they were w[orth] & he being in haste to goe vpp "ito" into the Court of Chancery sayd he must be gone he would speak w[i]th me soone or send [Mr.] Replyngham Nath[anael] was w[i]th me.

Agaynst Whitehall Wall I mett w[i]th Mr. Replingham whoe promised to come to me at aftir noone saying "he" I should be satisfyed & "as for the towne" I askynge him howe the Towne should be satisfyed he sayd he ca[red] not for their consents.

Rec[eiued] (16 No: [uembris] 1614 at 4 clock aftirnoone a L[ette]re from Mr. Bayly & Mr. Alderman dated 12 *No: [uembris]* 1614 touching the Inclosure busynes: & sent Nath[anael] to see yf Mr. W[illiam] Combe were in Towne & he returned to me & [in] Mr. Wyatts presence sayd he was not in Towne.

Jovis 17 No: [uembris] "as" my Cosen Shakspeare "has" commyng yesterday to towne I went to see him howe he did he told me that they assured him they ment to inclose noe further then to gospell bushe & so vpp straight (leavyng out part of the dyngles to the ffield) to the gate in Clopton hedge & take in Salisburyes peece: and that they meane in Aprill to servey the Land & then to gyve satisfaccion & not before & he & Mr. Hall say they think there will be nothyng done at all.

This mornyng I did send to "speake with" see yf Mr. Tho: [mas] Combe were in Towne & Nath[anael] returned me answere that he went forth of the Towne yesterday.

Mr. Wyatt aftirnoone told me that Mr. Wryght hadd told Mr. Combe that the enclosure would not be & that yt was "end" at an end I sayd I was "susp" the more suspicious for those might be words used to make vs careles I willed him to learne what I (*sic*) could and I told him soe would I.

At night I drew the peticion and gave yt Edmund to wryte fair that J Greene & Mr. Wyatt might see yt before yt were "pre" wrytten to be presented to the Lords.

18. No: [uembris] "I" in the mornyng I gave yt Edmund to shew yt to J Greene that he might "mak" consider of yt & "acq" come amongst vs to acquaynt Mr. Wyatt w[i]th yt, J Greene being shewed yt, aftir noone sent mee word he lyked not of yt but would talke w[i]th me of yt.

About 3 of the clock aftir noone I sent Edmund to R Wyrlye he told (as "I s"* Edmund sayes from him) Mr. Replingham that seying myself to plan for myne owne interest I would be ruled by S[i]r H. Raynsford & Mr. Barnes & he answered none better & that I should have a peny for a peny. And sayd "they" howe Mr. Replingham assured him they ment to inclose but to "gost" gospell bushe & noe further.

The same day Nath[anael] was answered that S[i]r R. Verny was come to the Towne but was not to be spoken w[i]th vntill the morow mornyng.

19 in the mornyng I went to him & desired him if he cold not procure Sir ffrancis Smyth to exchange &c. then "he" that he would be pleased to confyrme him in his promise that he would not part w[i]th yt to any. & he sayd he would & that he would be in the Country & would be contented yf he were named w[i]th S[i]r H. Raynsford & the rest he would do the towne the best good he could.

The same mornyng I tooke w[i]th "the" mee the peticion to Westm[inster] to shewe yt my Cosen graves & (*sic*) but could not fynd him:

21. in the mornyng J Greene sayd that at night he would come & present the peticion with me the same day at afternoone: he drew me asyd in my chamber & told me that J Rednall this day in the mornyng willed him to tell me that some body from Mr. Manneryng hadd bene w[i]th S[i]r ffr[ancys] Smyth & that S[i]r ffr[ancys] Smyth hadd answered him as he hadd answered viz that he would keepe his Land himselfe.

22 Mr. Henry Smyth told me that Mr. Wright told him that my Lo[rd] Carew would "oppose" not agree to furder any Inclosure at Stratford but would rather hynder yt if he could.

The same day Edmund told me "at" that R Wyrley within halfe an houre told him that I was much excepted vnto for makeing such mighty opposicion agaynst the Inclosure & that Mr. Manneryng & Mr. Replingham would be w[i]th him to the aftir noone.

I also asked my brother Nevile after my Cosen Graves xptian name that wee might ("yf" as I thought we should) imploy him in a busynes at the Counsell table.

---

* That is "I s[aye]" erased.

24 aftir noone Mr. Wyatt told me that Mr. Wryght w[i]thin theis 2 houres told him that they were in framyng an answere to the L[ett]res wrytten from Mr. Baylyff and the Company this L[ett]re. And that my lo[rd] Carewe did intend to oppose the inclosure there to be made all he might, alsoe Mr. Wyatt told me that about ffryday "laf" laste he spake

Mr. Manneryng

w[i]th Mr. Manneryng whoe told him that yf he might not doe yt well &c. he cared not for inclosyng and "cared" cared not howe little he did meddle therein.

28. No[uembris] at night Mr. Replinghams speche w[i]th me & my opposynge yt. I sayd I did it accordyng to the trust in me reposed by the Baylyff &c. & howe I was tyed to them &c. and as for myne owne particuler interest I would not vary from what I hadd sayd before & soe wee parted.

3. Dec[embris] Mr. "Baylye" W Barnes Jun[ior] at night told me that Mr. Combe was gone to London: & then I told "th" him that I would have the Lands seene that I might knowe howe to make reasonable demands of Mr. Manneryng.

5 Dec[embris] at a Hall the Company agreed that .6. should goe to Mr. Combe in the name of all the rest to present their Loves & to desire he would be pleased to forbeare to inclose & to desire his love as they wilbe reddy to deserve yt.

Arthur Caudry rather desirit the inclosure might rather stay then goe on, W Euet did "not" wish yt might not take effect. E Hunt would not consent w[i]thout S[i]r ffr[ancys] Smyth but desirit for his owne part yt might not goe on:

Goeing to Mr. Combe.

10 Dec. that the survey there was past, & I "went" came from Wilson to look Mr. Replingham at the beare & at new place but missed him & on the narowe sid but he was not to be spoken with:

9 Dec. aftir Mr. Bayley & wee hadd spent some 4 or 5 houres with the overseers of the poore he Mr. Alderman & I Mr. Baker Mr. Shawe & Mr. Chandler went accordyngly to Mr. Combe whose answere was he should be gladd of our loves & that the inclosures would not be hurtfull to the Towne that he hadd not to doe w[i]th yt but to haue some proffytt by yt & that he thought Mr. Manneryng was soe farre ingaged therein as that he would not be intreated & therefore he would not bestowe his labour to entreate him in any sorte saying if the froste broke the dychynge would goe presently forward.

11 Dec. "I" being Sunday I acquaynted Mr. Bayly that I hadd a byll reddy drawen & prayed "th" him to appoynt a Hall & he puttyng yt of till ffryday I sayd yt desired haste & wished yt might be on the morowe & soe yt was sumoned.

They wold have had my interest in the part to be inclosed.

12 Dec. at the Hall the byll was reade. & stayeth till Mr. Bayly Mr. Alderman "Mr. Ba" myself & Mr. Baker haue bene at Stoneley & aftir some dispute of my consentynge I at their instance did write that I declare my prouins to be by all lawefull & reasonable meanes to assist them as their Steward and Counseller to w[i]thstand the inclosure & howe I hadd given my word for it & then Mr. Walford challengyng I ought to Mr. W[illiam] C[ombe] well I know where one told me he would help me to a Lease for .20. yeres yet to come of the same tythes & a bond of 100[li] to perform yt: ——* & that Thomas Rutter sayd that Mr.

Curres:

T[homas] C[ombe] sayed they were all Curres & sayd of "&" the[m] spitting that one of the dogges such a one as Walford was the cause of sendyng Hitchcocks to prison: And that n[ow]? Mr. W. Barnes sayed that Mris. Reynolds denyed yt for when the enclosure was, Mr. Replyngham sayd yt was not yet for Mr. Combe, but hadd bene surveyed & when Mr. "Replyn" Manneryng knewe the valor thereof yt might be Mr. Combe might have yt before any other.

* Here follow two or three words, apparently a legal phrase in French or Latin. It has been suggested by Mr. E. Maunde Thompson, that they may be "Eust licen[ce] de con[corder]." There certainly was a kind of bond called "Licentia Concordandi."

14 Dec my goeing to Mr. Wrights with E Rawlyns but he was gone to Worcester. & thence to Mr. Nashe about the Chauncell & he told me of the arbitrations. & the 100[li] & the churchyard.

The same day my "as" tryeing my Cosen Baker what he would say about their buyeing the interest of the tythes.

15 Dec being Thursday I told Mr. Ashe & my Cosen Baker what I thought a Commoner might doe as touching throweing downe of dy[tches] being same day he & Mr. Bayly for him told me that Sir Tho[mas] Leyghe stayed in London all xpmas &c. & soe Mr. Manneryng [was] not lyke to come downe & I vrgyng that some Course might be taken for "say" stayeing the inclosure, my Cosen Baker yt were not fytt any thing were done vntill they did see that he did sett a diggyng.

Survey of the Landes:

Mr. Bayly alsoe then told me at his house that James Elliotts & Arthur Cawdry hadd taken a vewe of all the errable Lands: but being busy yt being markett day he cold not stay about yt to shewe yt me. 506 Lands.

20. at the College before Sir Henry Raynsford (at such tyme as Mr. Byshope was there about Mr. Lane) Mr. Combe in gret earnestnes sayd nowe I can not hynder the inclosure now I sight* Mr. Manneryng: And after at my "door" pale door before John Watkyns & W. Martyn I told Mr. Combe that the words between vs were but speeches "in the ton" of pleasure & not to preiudice me with Mr. Manneryng & he sayd noe yt made noe mater & noe Advantage to be taken of them.

21 Our goeing to Clarden.† Mr. Spencer sayd Ld Chancery‡ was their friend in Chancery. Councell table Sir ff. Grevill sent to me? he wold have vs peticion to the Kyngs Chancery case of annoying Sir Tho[mas] Lucy.

Heu vivunt homines tanquam mors nulla sequetur
Et velut informis fabula vana fide
Mors certa est incerta dies hora agnita nulli
Extremam quare "tu" quamlibet esse "diem" puta
Fleres si scires "vnam" vnum tibi tempora mensem
Rides cum non sit forsitan vna dies
Qui modo sanus erat nunc lecto egrotus adheret
Estque cinis subito qui modo ciuis erat.

[Alas! men live as though no death will follow,
And as if it were an insubstantial tale, devoid of credit.
Death is certain, uncertain the day—the hour known to none;
Wherefore think any day to be thy last.
Thou wouldst weep if thou knewest thy time to be but a single month:
Thou smilest (incredulous) to be told that perhaps it may be but a day.
He who yesterday was hearty now keeps his sick bed,
And our fellow-townsman of an hour ago is all at once become dust and ashes.—Ed.]

23. Dec. A Hall. L[ett]res wrytten one to Mr. Manneryng another to Mr. Shakspeare with "the" almost all the com[panyes] hands to eyther: I alsoe wrytte of myself to my Cosen Shakspeare the Coppyes of all our oathes mde [made?] then alsoe a not of the Inconvenyences wold g[row] by the Inclosure.

Edmund Rawlyns well remembreth that? in my best Chamber told me I should have? for my tythes viz that evenyng he sent for me to th? and to speake about Mr. Lanes busynes:

* Probably written by mistake for "side with."
† Claverdon.
‡ A slip of the pen for "Chancellor."

27

28

29

30

1614

Tho[mas] Combes callyng the Companye doggs & Curres (testis Tho[mas] Rutter:

26 the agree[men]t was made between Mr. Walford & Mr. Chandler at Clarden.

27. there was a meeting at the Hall & the same day the book & a l[ett]re drawen.

28 they were sent to Mr. Gylb[e]rd whoe, the same day went to Clarden. but shewed noe l[ett]res.

29 he brought me the "boo" draught of the book agayne & that night I added Covenants as I thought most agreeable to T[homas] C[ombe] his mynd.

30 A Hall called: where those Covenants were shewed & agreed to be annexed to the book & to be sent to Mr. Gybbe[r]d & a L[ett]re from them which there I wrote & del[ivered] all to Mr. Chandler being party to the book to be caryd & spedd w[hi]ch he undertook presently to goe about.

1 Ja[nuarij] aftir evenyng prayer in my study at home Mr. Chandler shewed the book drawen & Mr. Gybb[e]rds answere on yt before Mr. Bayly Mr. Alderman Mr. Barker Mr. Gybbes Mr. Wilson & others.

Munday 2 Ja[nuarij] at Mr. Baylyes & my rydyng to Balsall that mornyng "th" Tho[mas] Parkers Lease ingrossed was deli[vered] to Mr. Chandler by Edmund Rawlyns.

3 Ja. 1614 at Warwick Mr. Spencer told me that Mr. W. Combe sayd to him that I should be very fully satisfyed.

"Wensday 4" Thursday 5 Ja[nuarij] they were sealed at Stratford by Mr. Parker "&" but not by his wife. (as I was told by the lessees answere to the Wilsons) that day the the surrender of E. H. was drawen & sealed & then I heard of "but" first but sawe not Mr. Manneryng his L[ett]res.

Saturday 7 Ja. at night Mr. Bayly Mr. Barker Mr. Walford & Mr. H Smyth came from Mr. Woods w[i]th his answers to demands drawen by my Cosen Baker in wrytyng:

Threatnyng such as throw down the ditch.

The same day at night (as Mr. Chandler told me 9 Ja. in the mornyng) Mr. W. Combe told Baylys he heard that some of the better sort would goe to throwe downe the dytche & sayd I O wold they durst* in a threatnyng maner w[i]th very great passion & "ag" anger.

Threatnyng to do the town all the mischeif "they" he cann.

The same .9. day in the mornyng Mr. Chandler came as he sayd from Mr. William Combe whoe sayed they were a Company of factious knaves & hee "bad him" asked him what do you meane all & whoe doe you meane to which he made noe answere at all: but sayd he will doe them all the mischeif he cann.

Sayd they were purtan knaves and underlings in their colour.

Spades privatly sent.

9 Ja: & he now told me that Mr. Walford & he had privately sent their spades before & that by & by they would goe throwe downe some of the dytch, I aduised that they wold goe in such pryvat maner as that "the none" none might see them goe least others might perhapps followe in Companyes & soe make a riott or a mutyny:

Sly rode to his Mayster.

r[emember] Sly upon the first dayes offryng to fyll the dytch by h [? by & by] Mr. H Smyth made a cesser vntil he hadd rydden to Mr. W Combe & at his returne went to worke agayne. q[uere] what day that first day was.

his Covenantyng w[i]th Mrs. Reynolds.

his Covenantyng at first w[i]th Arthur "Cawdrye" Cawdrey.

Mr. Replyngham 28 Oct[o]bris articled w[i]th Mr. Shakspeare & then I was "recommended" putt in by T Lucas.

9 Ja: about .3. of the clock aftirnoone came to me willed me to propound a peace promised me x$^{li.}$ to buy a geldyng to doe yt. lyked not amysse of a friendly suit to end yt willed me to moue S[i]r Henry Raynsford therof I sayd my mocion wold be taken to be to favourable I knowyng their fixed resolucions I sayd he wold acquaint them that I moved "th" him to that end and then as good moue yt of myself. threatned that w[i]thi[n] this .12. moneth "he" all the ffields should be layd downe greensward if they did not agree: I told him yt was knowen that "I" he was here & that I thought I did nothing but both sydes heard of yt & therefore I caryed myself as free from all offence as I could; I told "them" him I would "bef" do yt before Wednesday night to some of the principall of them. but prayed him yf any thing were done to London or otherwise in the meane tyme touching that busynes "he wold" (as I was bound to them in all fidelity for I must do for them such lawfull things as they desired) that he would not account yt an vnfashionable dealyng in me to do in the meane tyme any thing I cann. he confessed that there was nowe about 600 Lands to be layd downe from arrable to pasture & that S[i]r Tho[mas] Lucy promised he would helpe him to a Lease of the tythes of ground adioynyng for the foldynge of his Lambes in yeanyng tymes. All which I told him was not vnthought of: aftir some speches that he should think himself beholdyng vnto me yf I could bring an end to passe he aftir many promises & protestacions that I should be well dealt w[i]thall he departed & I brought him to the doore Michaell only & Herne attendyng his comyng in my Hall: & Edmund Rawlyns w[i]th them: Amongst other speeches he told me that "my Lo: C" Mr. Manneryng once purposed to procure my Lo[rd] Chauncellour to wryte to the Company. I sayd yt wold have bene respectfully receyved & "wi" very duetyfully answered. & I told him the substance of all Mr. Manneryngs & Mr. Replynghams speeches & myne at the towne & of my seekyng Mr. Replyngham at his last being here.

I did yt the same night at their commyng downe to me anon aftir viz. Mr. Bayly Mr. Baker Mr. Walford Mr. Chandler.

---

* That is, "Aye, O would they durst!"

10 Januarij 1614 [illegible]

[illegible]

11 Januarij 1614

[illegible]

1. [illegible] 25 [illegible]

2. [illegible]

3. [illegible]

4. [illegible] 25 [illegible]

[illegible]

Thursday 12 Ja. [illegible]

[illegible]

12 Ja. 12 Ja. [illegible]

[illegible]

10. Januarij. 1614. at the quarter sessions: Mr. Archer was spoken to as a Justice of peace & a Commoner to help at the Sessions for preventyng breach of the peace.

At Mr. Baylyes instance we viz. he, myself Mr. Baker Mr. Walford & Mr. Chandler alighted at the Byalyes (*sic*) for that part was so fytt to goe privately to Mr. Wards & thence to Mr. Hales, we went & there agreed as there we hadd together resolved none shall be spoken of but the dyggers & noe mencion at all of Mr. M Mr. R or Mr. Combe. agree the peticion shall not be putt vpp. went to Mr. Halls & shewed him as to Mr. Ward our feares of tumult & howe on Monday people came to looke on when Mr. Walford & Mr. Chandler were there. desired his advice as also that he wold persuade Mr. Combe there might be stay made & to enforme my Lo[rd] Compton thereof. & to putt him in mynd of his promise to the Countrey at the last "dig" dyggynge, & being sett in Court Mr. Stapelton asked what I hadd to say that he might despatch me & I sayd I was not reddy but sent for Mr. Ward who happely mett Mr. Replyngham in the Court about the Hall & proposed stay of enformyng the Court which "J" Mr. Bayly being nere Mr. Ward yelded to. Aftir dyner at Mr. Wards house agree[men]ts were made in these words. "10 Januarij 1614."

Respect to Mr. Combe.

My Lo[rd] Comptons promise at last dyggyng.

10 Januarij 1614.

Yt is agreed for preventyng of Tumults and avoydyng of meetyng of the people of Stratford & "Bi" Byshopton for the present.

1: That any further dytchyng stay vntill the .25. of March next.

2. That there be noe ploughing on the Common or any part thereof vntill then.

3. And yt ys ment there shalbe a cartway left vnder Rowley. and other vsuall ways to lye open.

Not done but stopped since.

4. Yt ys ment that there shalbe noe throweing downe of the dytches alreddy sett vpp but aftir such wayes as aforesayd, vntill aftir the sayd 25 day of Marche.

Subscribed W Walford W Chandler Thomas Greene. "W" Thomas Ayng his marke W Ayng his marke.

While this was doeing as yt stands, the dytches by women & "Chid" Children of Byshopton & Stratford were fylled vp agayne.

Before dyner tyme I never sawe Tho[mas] Greene Tho[mas] or W Aynge. and I hearteIy thanke almighty god I never gave the lest allowance in any tumultuous courses but protested agaynst yt & as yet never "was" gave any Counsell to any Bishopton mann in these busynes.

On Wednesday being the xj[th] day. anon aftir the Court Mr. Parsons told Mr. Bayly & me in the Hall that Mr. Lucas sayd that the other syde being X Mr. Walford & Mr. Chandler might have gone .9. & noe ryott & shewed him many cases as he sayed yester night in that poynt but I dissented & lyked not that Course "by" but confessed yt was true in case of a mylston or a great peece of tymber that soe many might goe as were sufficiently able to cary yt away or lade yt.

Q[uere] this opinion of riotts.

At night Mr. Replingham supped w[i]th me & Mr. W Barnes was to beare him Company where he assured me before Mr. Barnes that I should be well dealt w[i]thall "as n" confessyng former promisses "& th" by himself Mr. Manneryng & his agreement for me w[i]th my Cosen Shakspeare:

Thursday .12. Ja. in the mornying the Company did meet & there Mr.Barker Mr. Walford Mr. Chandler Mr. Henry Smyth Mrs. Quyney Lewes Hiccox & Laurence Wheeler e[x]pressly to Mr. Replinghams face disagreed to the intended inclosure & these Mr. Bayly "from Mr." & Mr. Baker from Mr. John Lanes mouth declared that he would never agree while he lived & sayd he would enter for a forfyture vpon his tenants for a former forfyture yf ever they did agree therevnto: and all desired that Mr. Manneryng wold stay all proceedyngs "and at party" to inclose: & at partyng Mr. Replyngham sayd he wold gyve names to Mr. Baylyf for doing Justice vpon the women dyggers: & yt was answered that then Justice should "be" be done:

Disagreers 12 Ja. 12 Ja. Re:

On ffryday .13. Ja: being an hall day and the accompt day about .2. of the clock in the aftirnoone he came to the Hall & shewed a note of names, of whom he sayd he would gyve some names to Mr. Baylyff (but not of all) that he would bynd them to their good behaviours & then w[i]thout at the Court table he wrote a L[ett]re to S[i]r Henry Raynsford: I told Mr. Replingham they would cry o[u]t of me as if I did "cas" cause to be bound for my Clarks proffits but I cared not the Law should by myne advise be executed upon them:

16. Mr. W Combe rod as was sayd toward London.

14. I went to Clyfford to speake w[i]th S[i]r Henry Raynsford but he was at Brodeway.

9: ffebruary [illegible]

[illegible]

Speeches of buying the royalty of the fishing — Ingram

[illegible]

[illegible]

value of the Inclosures — 12 February [illegible] 250 [illegible]

23 marcij [illegible]

1614 — [illegible]

[illegible] 25 marcij [illegible]

[illegible] 27 marcij [illegible]

[illegible] 28 marcij [illegible]

1615 — 27 marcij [illegible] 30 marcij [illegible]

29 marcij [illegible]

[illegible]

1 Apr. 1615 [illegible]

[illegible] 10 march 1615

2 Apr. [illegible]

[illegible] at the Inclosure [illegible]

3. Apr. [illegible]

7. Apr. [illegible]

8. Apr. [illegible]

12 Apr. [illegible]

10 Apr. [illegible]

19. Apr. [illegible]

20. Apr. [illegible]

9: ffebruarij. myself Mr. Chandler J Greene & Edmund Rawlyns being w[i]th Mr. Manneryng he sayd all dyggyng & ploweing should stay till Easter:

Speeches of buyeing the royalty of S[i]r Arthur Ingram

Then he & Mr. Ryplingham sayd they were "to buy" about to buy the Royalty of S[i]r Arthur Ingreham and that w[i]thin an houre before they hadd hadd some speeche together to that effect.

Mr. Ryplingham alsoe denyed that he gave yt forth as by Mr. Bayly & Mr. Aldermans L[ett]re was purported touchyng a dyggyng in of a lesse Inclosure.

Value of the intended Inclosure

Sunday . 12. Februarij Mr. R Moore shewed "me the" me the particuler, as offred to be sold by Mr. Combe; ratyng the intended Inclosure at 250[li] per annum.

1615
Mr. Chaundler sayd Mr. Combe vpon his carryeing him the peticioun called him knave a many tymes & told him he lyed.

22 Marcij at a Hall a peticion was agreed vpon to be exhibited to my Lo[rd] Chief Justice at Coventrey where I was w[i]th yt & yt was set down 25 Mercij at the assises syttyng in Court but his Lo[rdship] would be putt in mynd of yt agayne at Warwick & there Mr. Combe 27 Mercij at night by my Lo[rds] appoyntement mett vs before my Lo[rd] & hadd the peticion w[i]th him to Answere the poyntes therof & answered "th" by trauerse of the poyntes. my Lo[rd] ordered "prout" 28 Marcij at the delyuery of the nisi prius prout patet per ordinem.

1615

28 Mercij at night at my Commyng home my wif told me yt was sayd while we were "as" at the Assises that "there" yt should not be enclosed but there should be .4. shepheards kept to keepe shepe there & all should be layd doune to greensward: & this from Mris. Reynolds & 30 Marcij Mr. Collyns sayd he lykewise heard soe much:

29 Marcij aftir noone Mr. W Combe "rode" by himself & Mr. Tho[mas] Combe or one of them in the ffields dealt w[i]th Laurence Wheeler & Lewes Hiccox to "se" make choice of Land for Mris. Reynolds: but they sayd they would not meddle without their "Landlady" Landlady (meanyng Mris. Reynolds) & this Mris. Reynolds acquaynted my wif w[i]thall in "Mris." Mr. Collyns presence at my house:

1 Apr[ilis] 1615. "Mr. B" being Saterday Mr. Baker told me at his shopp howe that the day before he was in S[i]r W Somervilles & Mr. Combes Company a huntyng in Awson ffields & there Mr. W Combe told him he might thanke me for the peticion, & that he would sell all & offred to sell him the l[li] [£50] per annum lyeing in Bridgtowne amongst my lo[rd] Carewes Land there. & that he for his part "never" ment not to enclose &c.

r. Febr & March 1615

2 Apr. Mr. Parsons being Alderman told me that Mr. Combe questyoned with him why he was soe agaynst the inclosure & he sayd as Mr. Baker hadd sayd to him they were all sworne men for the good of the Boroughe and to preserve their Inherytaunces & therefore they would not have yt sayd in future tyme that they were the men which gave way to the vndoeing of the towne. tellyng Mr. Combe that all the .3. fires were not soe great a losse to the towne as the Inclosure wolde be.

3. fires not so great a loss as the Inclosure wold be

3. Apr. ex relacione Mris. Reynolds to my wif. Thomas Combe yesterday being Palmsunday payd to Mris. Mary Nashe xxx[li] part of the l[li] which she was to have for her good will to depart w[i]th her estate:

"5" 7. Apr. being goodfryday Mr. Barker commyng to the Colledge to Mr. T C[ombe] about a debt he stood surety for Mris. Quyney "he" W C[ombe] willed his brother to shewe Mr. Barker noe favour & threatned "that" him that he should be served vpp to London within a ffortnight. (and so yt fell out:

8. Apr. being Saterday T C[ombe] payeing me the half yeres rent for the tythes in my garden told me there would be noe inclosure that went not "on." on.

12 Apr Mr. P recityng to T Rogers his being beaten at his house.

10 Apr Mr. B his mencionyng of T C[ombe] his kickyng & beatyng his sheppard at Meons demandyng his wages.

19 Apr. W C[ombe] rayled at Laur[ence] Wheeler & Lewes Hiccox for plougheing w[i]thin the intended inclosure vt ait Mr. Barker Mris. Reynolds.

20. Apr. they & Mr. "an" Nashe & many other t[enan]tes as is sayd ploughed there vpon their owne Land, with w[h]ich W C[ombe] was very angry.

[illegible]

26 Julii [illegible]

26 [illegible]

[illegible]

14 Aug 1615 Mr Barker dyed. [illegible] Sept. Mr Shakspeare tellyng J Greene that I was not able to beare the encloseinge of Welcombe.

5 Sept. his sendyng James for th'executours of Mr Barker to agree as ys sayd with them for Mr Barkers interest.

10 Sept. [illegible]

12 Sept. [illegible]

16 Sept. 1615. [illegible]

[illegible]

21 Sept. [illegible]

22 Sept. 1615 [illegible]

[illegible]

25 Sept. [illegible]

[illegible]

Vpon the moweing of Welcombe Medowe Mr. W C[ombe] "opp" his eatyng vpp the grasse thereof which hadd wont to be preserved vntill M[ichaelmas] to help their wheat soweing.

25 Julij. Commyng from Glouc[ester] [?] P Rosewell nere Marston told me that W C[ombe] hadd sent S[i]r E Greville a fatt wether & ment to vse S[i]r "Ar" E Grevilles favour to S[i]r Arthur Ingram to buy the Royalty of old Stratford for Mr. Combe for better furthryng his enclosure & to end the difference between P Roswell & him.

26 W C[ombe] & Th[omas] C[ombe] rod to Mylcott to S[i]r Arthur Ingram to Mylcott:

Easter terme his payeing for 2 bylles one agaynst Hiccox [?] Replingham the other agaynst Mr. Barker [?] Browne. } W Combe payd for the wrytyng of the bylles & for draweing them & soe Mr. Dastons man told Edmund Rawlyngs.

8 Augusti Sir Henry Smyth & others their puttyng vpp the peticion for eatyng vpp "Welcomb" Welcombe medowe w[i]th sheepe.

1615 14 Aug Mr. Barker dyed. { Sept W Shakspeares tellyng J Greene that I was not able to "he" beare the encloseinge of Welcombe.

5. Sept. his sendyng James for the executours of Mr. Barker "concerning" to agree as ys sayd w[i]th them for Mr. Barkers "inf" interest.

10 Sept Mr. W Barnes told his vncle in my hearyng at Clyfford that Mr. Combe hadd bought their interest & gave them x[s] in earnest & was to pay xl[li] more:

12 Sept. ffr. Ben? & J Samwell at my house told me of Mr. W Combe syttyng at his. being appoynted to "look of" be taken of him by holder 6[d] & of John Yate iiii[d] for their pyggs before they could have them forth of the pownde & howe that ffr Aynge was dryven to sue a Replevyn:

16. Sept. 1615 S[i]r Henry Raynsford repeated to me howe that he hadd told Mr. J Nashe "howe" that Mr. W Combes best way was to agree w[i]th me & that Mr. W Combe therevppon "se" went to S[i]r Henry & thanked him for his kyndnes therein & told S[i]r Henry that he would gyve me satisfaccion so as I would procure the townes consent & that Mr. Combe told him that H Smyth would lett him have "the" his Land lying w[i]thin the enclosure the Towne being compounded "w[i]tha" w[i]thall & that Arthur Cawdrey answered him that he would never consent w[i]thout the Towne & that he hadd a house & other things more profitable to him them "th" his Land was: & that he hadd rather loose his Land then loose their goodwilles & S[i]r Henry also nowe told me that P Rosewell hadd spoken with him "& then" within this few dayes & told him that thoughe Mr. Combe have bene at Mylcott yet he shalbe sure never to have any royalty there & that he would sue Mr. W Combe in accions of trespas vpon trouer for carryeing away his Corne and will alsoe sue Tho[mas] Combe vpon a bond of "xl[li]" 400[li] for that he enjoyeth not the doales there but hadd his Corne soe carrydd away & will sue W Combe in the Starre Chamber for ryotts & alsoe seek relief in equity against Mris. Hyatt: "& fyn" & told Sir Henry Raynsford that Sir E G would stick to him: & that S[i]r Arthur Ingram "would goe" was gone into the North with Riche merchants & would perhapps sell there & buy all the Royalties at Stratford: & my answer touchyng my self was that seeing my advantage touching Mr. Manwayryng I would be gladd to see what composicion in reddy money he would offer me for otherwise I would not deale with him. Sir Henry alsoe told me howe Mr. Combe sayd he should "dymys" dymynyshe my tythes 30[s] per annum there. by the [?] harrowing of his ground at Ingon:

Arthur Cawdrys speeche.

W Combe his Ryotts about P Rosewell his Corne:

dimynish my tythes 30[s] per annum:

21. Sept. Mr. Collyns told Mr. R G that W C[ombe] would have a Commission of Concealments & then gett a yere of the corne & "sayd" questyons whether the yeres tythes did passe the rents payd in lieue of Tythes.

22. Sept. 1615. Sir Henry Raynsford told me that Mr. Combe hadd spoken with him & sayd he would not agree with me vnles he agreed with all the rest & that he sayed he would "ly down" lay downe all his Land to pasture nowe & at 2 yeres end yt would yeld him as much proffyt as otherwise & that he would plough at Ryon & by that meanes he might lay down his land in the Common ffyelds.

ploweing at Ryon Clyfford.

28 Sept. Mr. Nashe & Thomas Greene offryng the tax for the poore to Mr. Combe he wold not signe yt vnles I might be asmuch as himself as x[s] on a mark or thereabouts: & then R G told me of his quarrellyng with Tho[mas] Greenes man about diggyng clay in the wastes.

Wastes.

.6. Octobris. T L[ucas] his being at the Hall about his money.

14 December 1615 [illegible]
[illegible]
[illegible]
[illegible] October [illegible]
[illegible]

19 Dec. 1615 [illegible]
[illegible] 4 [illegible] 5 days [illegible]

26 Dec. 1615 [illegible] Court [illegible]
[illegible]
[illegible]

[illegible]

24 Feb. 1615 [illegible] Sheriff [illegible]
[illegible]
[illegible]
[illegible]
[illegible]

27 Feb. [illegible] Sheriff [illegible]
[illegible]
1 marcii [illegible]
[illegible] Thomas [illegible]
[illegible] 27 [illegible]
[illegible] Thomas [illegible]
[illegible] Sheriff [illegible]
[illegible]

[illegible] 27 [illegible]
[illegible]
[illegible]
[illegible]
[illegible]

2 marcii 1615 [illegible] Richard [illegible]
[illegible] Thomas [illegible] William [illegible]
[illegible]
[illegible]
[illegible]

5 marcii 1615 [illegible]
[illegible]

14 Decembris .1615. Mr. ffr[ancys] Smyth sen[ior] at the Hall told me that Mr. Tho[mas] C[ombe] within a fewe dayes before told him that his brother would plowe this yere for his good but next yere would lay yt downe to spyte me.

The same day there Mr. Baker told me that they questyoned my Lo[rd] Cheif Justices authority to make any such order as was made there being nothyng dependyng before him.

19. Dec. 1615. poore blynd Hiccox dryven to gett a replevyn of Mr. Collyns for replevyeing "cattle" his milch cattle taken by the Heyward in other mens corne. the highe Sheryff denyeing yt him for 4 or 5 dayes.

26. Dec. 1615 T L his raylynge vpon & beatynge J Courte:

to sett downe the procedyngs about shewyng the dyggers the Coppy of my Lo[rds] order & their Answere about Mr Tho[mas] Combe & the highe Sheryff.

21 febr. 1615. agreed and entred in the book at a hall that the enclosure should be made a Towne cause & "be" the charges be defrayed out of the towne revenewes.

24 febr. 1615. the Highe Sheryff & Mr. Tho[mas] Combe at the bridge end toward the woodyard "told" being told by Mr. Baker that he marveyled he would contrary to my Lo[rds] order enclose and digg in the Common. they answered they hoped my Lord could not hynder "them for wi" men for doeing with their owne as they pleased. & that the dytch was mad but to save "their" Mr. Sheryff his Corne, sayeing they had gyven [money] to my Lo[rd's] gentlemen to work my Lord & that was no good ymployment of their towne revenewes.

27. ffebr. Mr. Sheryff sayd that which was done "was" was done agaynst his will &
1 Marcij
yet on ffryday .1. Marcij Mr. Baylyff Mr. Alderm[an] myself Mr. Walford Mr. "Henry" Chandler Mr. Henry Smyth ffr[ancys] Boice? & Richard Hasler went to see the Inclosure (ffranc[ys] Bois & Richard Haseler being gone to the lower end) one John Terry Thomas Hiccox William Whitehead & Michaell Pigeon were in fynyshyng the enclosure consystyng of 27 ridges acres length a peece & 3 headlands those fellowes sayd that yt was true that Mr. Thomas Combe & Boughton did (in Mr. Sheryffs absence at London) warrant them & they would defend them & that Mr. Highe Sheryff did nowe sett "hi" them on worke & badd them take noe discharge at any mans hands whoesoever & he would see they should take noe harm.

W Morrell al[ia]s Webbe

28 febr. coram m[agist]ro Gybbard "W" Webbe Morrell "sayd" told me in my study that Mr. Sheryff before Val[entine] Tant sayd to him yf he were not out of authority he would send him to the Gaole & havyng dyvers tymes ympounded his shepe. badd him tell my Lord Cooke that he would for euery seuerall tr[espa]s have a seuerall accion agaynst him. & for every vj^{d} dammage wold recover agaynst him vj^{li}.

.2. Marcij. 1615. Mr. Chandlers man Richard Ward went to the place where they were dyggyng & Stephen Sly John Terry Thomas Hiccox William Whitehead & Michaell Pigeon assalted him soe as he could not proceede with throweing downe the dytches & Sly sayd yf the best in Stratford "came" were there to throwe yt downe he wold bury his
q[uere] plus
head in the bottom of the dytche:

.3. Marcij. 1615. Sir Henry Raynsford at Clyfford told me of Mr. W Combes tellyng him that he was to pay my Lo[rd] lx^{li} per annum for xxj yeres for the Land he sold my
barne
Lord & hadd "the" my lords barne into the bargayne.

[illegible]

[illegible]

[illegible] 1616 [illegible]

[illegible] 1616 [illegible]

[illegible] 1616 [illegible]

[illegible] Welcombe [illegible]

Welcombe meadowe [illegible]

19 February 1616 [illegible]

[illegible] Mr Chaundler [illegible]

[illegible]

At Warwick Assises in Lent 1615 & 1616 my Lo[rd] Chief Justice willed him to sett his heart at rest he should neyther enclose nor lay downe any earrable nor plowe any "greenswar" auncient greensward.

Wednesday in Easter weeke the Company aftir some speeches at the Colledge with Mr. Sheryff caused their answere to be entred in the booke viz. they desired his goodwill but would euer withstand any enclosure.

J Greene — 10 Apr. 1616 at Welcombe "he" Mr. Highe Sheryff told my brother he was out of hope ever to enclose & sayd Mr. Reynolds should have his Articles agayne as soone as he could fynd vpp the same.

r the times of his proposiciones in wrytyng at the Hall & "his." their Answere thereto.

4 Sept. 1616. Mr. Henry Smyth told me That Mr. Sheryff said he wold distreyne their Cattle & they should not have them replevyned vnles they sued a replevyn from London & by reason therof there did forbeare to putt in their Cattle.

5 Sept. 1616. Mr. Hall told me of G Bennes sayeing what he w[ou]ld do to Lucas & that Mr. Sheryff sayd L[ucas] could not be an honest man for he hadd noe religion in him.

About 8 Sept. T Combe & V Tant upon fightyeng at Bishopton?

The sheryffs lyeing in the dytches a fyeld to keep other men's sheep forth of Welcombe Meadowe.

19 februarij. 1616 his "meetyng" commyng downe to Mr. Bayly & vs & sayeing yt is true it is a wronge to dygg vpon the greensward but a Judge of Assise would gyve but small damages & that yf yt should not be layed downe all this styrre would not bee. Mr. Chandler & alij We come for our Comon & that is "this" [? arrainged] by dyggyng on the "g" greensward, Combe to the dyggers Maysters goe on with your busynes I will beare you out thoughe yt cost me 500li:

Mr. Baker — He sayeth one accion & noe more for dyggynge, & on yeres punyshment for layeinge downe & noe more for ever.

EXPLANATORY NOTE.

The presence of ? shews that a word has been omitted, as being undecipherable or illegible. A reading in [ ], with ? also included, is tentative only; while one that is probably right, but still somewhat doubtful, is preceded by [?]. A comparison of such with the autotypes will enable the reader to appreciate the force of these indications of doubt.

The letters supplied, where a word is abbreviated in the manuscript, are enclosed in [ ].

3
Shakespeare's Handwriting

'To be briefe', Martin Billingsley urges in *The Pen's Excellency, or The Secretary's Delight*, 'the Art of *Writing* is so excellent, and of such necessary use, that none ought to be without some knowledge therein, since the excellency of no Art without it can be made knowne or manifest.'[1] In Shakespeare's day Englishmen wrote mainly in the native secretary hand. Most women did not write at all. Other hands were available for special purposes. Billingsley enumerates half a dozen, including bastard secretary, 'gotten of the Secretary', and for 'divers purposes exceeding graceful; as for Engrossements, Epitaphs for Tombes, Titles of Bookes'; also Roman, much used in the universities; Court, the hand of the King's Bench and Common Pleas, employed too for a variety of legal records; and Chancery, the hand of the High Court of Chancery, for charters and certain official documents.

Secretary, however, was the workaday script used by businessmen and officials in the conduct of their mundane affairs, and by poets and playwrights in their endeavours of art. This is not the place to survey in detail the characteristics of this ruggedly inelegant cursive hand, to which able guides are available; but a few of the salient features are the use of two minuscule *f*'s for the majuscule, the numerous distinct forms for lower-case *r*, and the indistinguishability of minuscule *u* and *n* (hence the confusion as to whether Shakespeare in 1605 bought his moiety of a lease of tithes from Ralph Hubaud, or Huband, of Ipsley).[2]

In this period another hand, of alien origin, was making inroads in England: the reformed calligraphy generated in the early fifteenth century by the artistic and humanistic impulses of the Italian Renaissance. When Shakespeare was receiving his schooling in the 1570s, the new script had already for some time been taught to the children of the upper classes—Edward VI and Lady Jane Grey, for example, had mastered fine Italian hands. But the old ways – and penmanship – persisted, at least for a time, in provincial communities like Stratford; there the children in the local grammar school learnt secretary. By the mid seventeenth century, however, the Italian hand dominated, and by 1700 secretary had for all practical purposes vanished. In printing an analogous revolution had by then long since been effected, with roman type replacing black letter.

The chapter 'Handwriting' by Sir Edward Maunde Thompson in *Shakespeare's England* (Oxford, 1916), i. 284–310, remains, after over half a century, a useful introduction. Giles E. Dawson and Laetitia Kennedy-Skipton (now Yeandle), *Elizabethan Handwriting 1500–1650* (New York, 1966), is a valuable modern guide, containing an informative introduction and numerous specimens in facsimile, with accompanying transcriptions.

I. The Authenticated Signatures

His old friends from the King's Men marvelled at Shakespeare's fluency with the pen.[3] 'His mind and hand went together', Heminges and Condell wrote in a famous passage of their preface to the First Folio: 'And what he thought, he uttered with that easinesse, that wee have scarse received

1 Martin Billingsley, *The Pens Excellencie, or The Secretaries Delight* [1618], sig. C2.

2 ME, 105, establishes the spelling on the basis of variants such as 'Hubalt', 'Hubatt', 'Hybote', etc., in the Stratford records.

3 In a profile of Mel Brooks in *The New Yorker* (30 October 1978), Kenneth Tynan cites Brooks's opinion that Shakespeare was 'a terrible writer'—'He had the worst penmanship I ever saw.' The Baconians, in their more earnest fashion, have anticipated Brooks: Sir Granville G. Greenwood dismisses several authenticated signatures as 'terrible scrawls' in *Is There a Shakespeare Problem?* (1916), and others have echoed the same opinion. In fact, however, Shakespeare was a perfectly capable penman in the rugged native hand.

from him a blot in his papers.' Modern study of the printed texts suggests they exaggerated—Shakespeare did revise. Posterity would exchange much for a few holograph specimens of those lines, blotted or unblotted; but we are not so fortunate. The only authenticated examples of Shakespeare's handwriting are six signatures to legal documents, plus two brief additional monosyllables, and even these have not gone wholly unchallenged. They comprise eighty-five characters, of which seventy-six are still legible. Meagre as the sampling is, it furnishes specimens of eleven lower-case letters (*a*, *e*, *h*, *i*, *k*, *l*, *m*, *p*, *r*, *s*, *y*) and three capitals (*B*, *S*, *W*). The six signatures all date from the last four years of Shakespeare's life, between May 1612 and March 1616, when his playwriting career had for all practical purposes ceased. All appear on legal documents. Only one may be described as an ordinary, everyday signature. The signatures are, in chronological sequence:

(a) 'Willm̄ Shakp' (Shakespeare's deposition in the Belott–Mountjoy action, 11 May 1612. Public Record Office, Court of Requests, Documents of Shakespearian Interest, Req. 4/1).

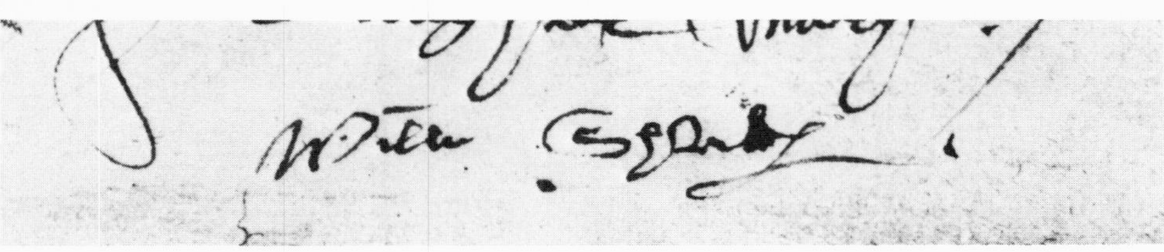

38 BELOTT–MOUNTJOY DEPOSITION: SHAKESPEARE'S SIGNATURE, 11 MAY 1612.

(b) 'William Shakspēr' (The Blackfriars Gate-House Conveyance, 10 March 1613. Guildhall Library). As the ink of the *r*, which extends over the edge of the tag on to the parchment of the deed, is slightly fainter than the rest, one may reasonably gather that the signator added the final character after momentary hesitation—an inference supported by the fact that the abbreviation mark appears above the *e*, its normal position if that were the last letter.

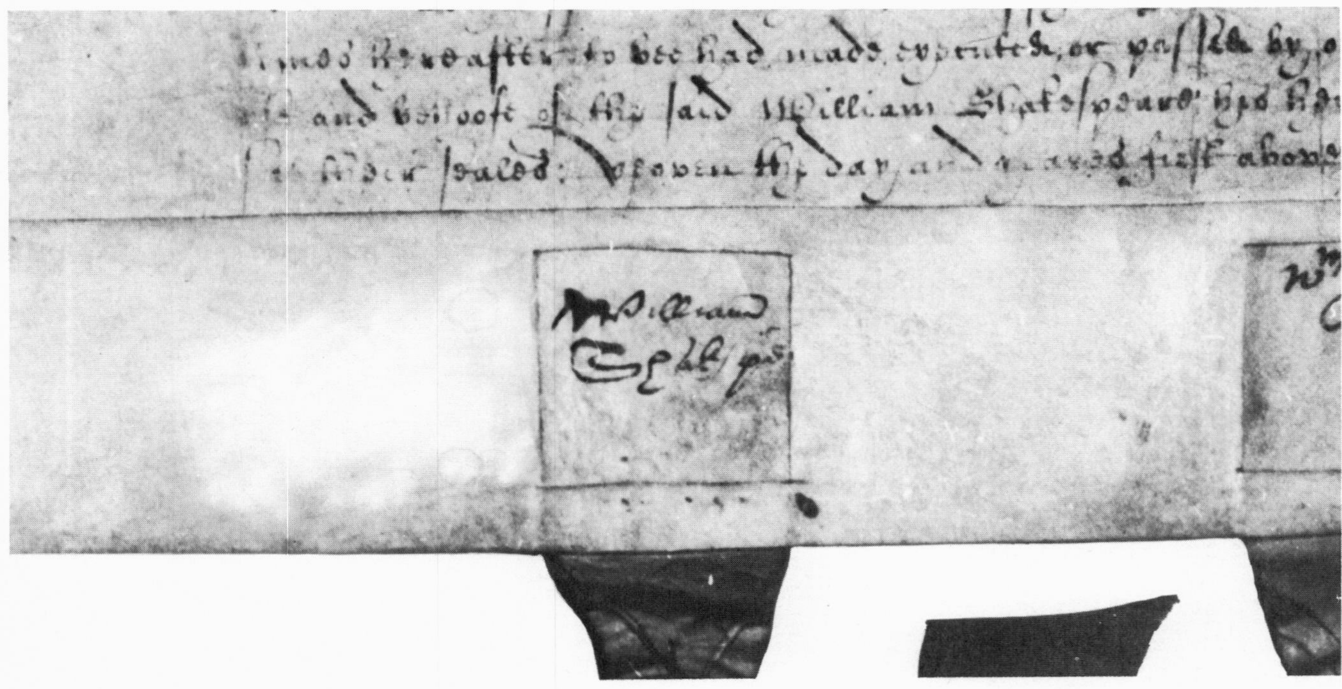

39 BLACKFRIARS GATE-HOUSE CONVEYANCE: SHAKESPEARE'S SIGNATURE, 10 MARCH 1613.

(c) 'Wm Shakspē' (The Blackfriars Gate-House Mortgage Deed, 11 March 1613. British Library, MS. Egerton 1787).

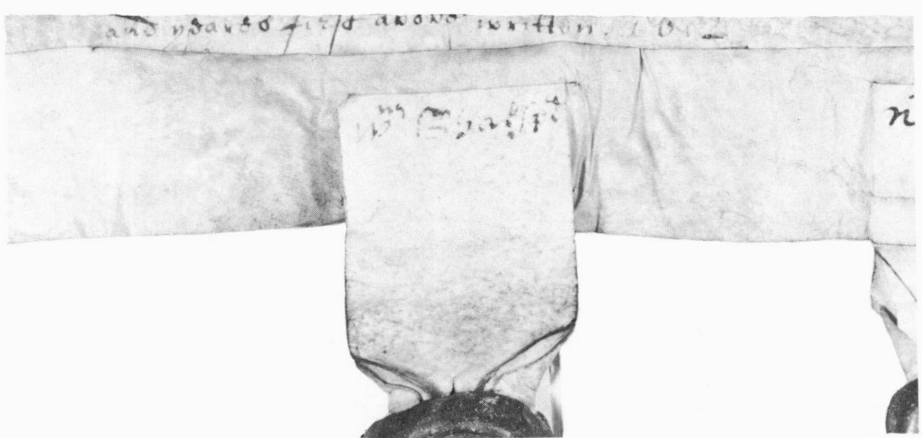

40 BLACKFRIARS GATE-HOUSE MORTGAGE DEED: SHAKESPEARE'S SIGNATURE, 11 MARCH 1613.

(d) 'William Shakspere' (Shakespeare's Last Will and Testament, sheet 1. Public Record Office, Principal Probate Registry, Selected Wills, Prob. 1/4). Time, that universal mouse, has nibbled away the bottom of the sheet, obliterating most of the surname; what remains is faded. When Maunde Thompson published a photographic facsimile in 1916, the condition of the signature was poor, but (as items 41 and 42 reveal) further deterioration has since taken place. This signature was probably already the worse for wear when George Steevens provided the first imperfect facsimiles of the three signatures to the will in the Johnson–Steevens edition of *The Plays of William Shakspeare* (1778), vol. i, facing p. 200; but the early plate gives us the spelling.

41 LAST WILL AND TESTAMENT, SHEET ONE: SHAKESPEARE'S SIGNATURE, 25 MARCH 1616. *As reproduced in Edward Maunde Thompson,* Shakespeare's Handwriting *(Oxford, 1916), illustration No. 4. The will was then still in Somerset House.*

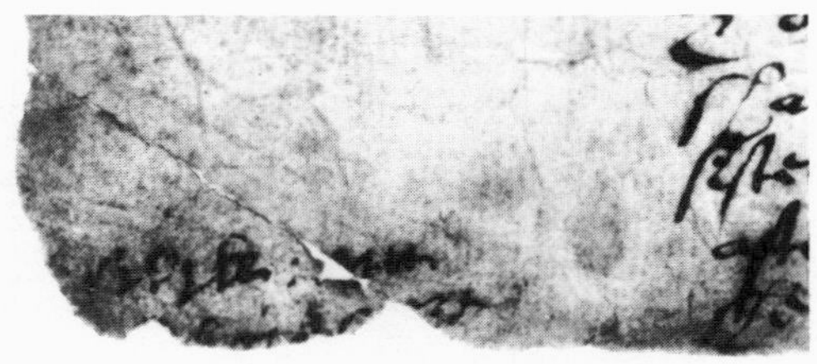

42 LAST WILL AND TESTAMENT, SHEET ONE: SHAKESPEARE'S SIGNATURE, 25 MARCH 1616. *The signature today.*

43 LAST WILL AND TESTAMENT: SHAKESPEARE'S SIGNATURES, 25 MARCH 1616. *Shakespeare's signatures to the three sheets in the Steevens facsimile,* The Plays of William Shakespeare, *ed. Steevens and Johnson (1778), vol. i, facing p. 200.*

(e) 'Willm̄ Shakspere' (Shakespeare's Last Will and Testament, sheet 2).

44 LAST WILL AND TESTAMENT, SHEET TWO: SHAKESPEARE'S SIGNATURE, 25 MARCH 1616.

(f) 'By me William Shakspeare' (Shakespeare's Last Will and Testament, sheet 3). Some earlier authorities (e.g. Malone and Madden) give the surname as *Shakspere*, the *a* of the unsteady second syllable being interpreted as an ink-blot rather than a letter. That the *a* is, however, a character is demonstrated by the connecting stroke linking it with the *r* that follows; as Thompson observes, 'He would not have linked a smudge.'[1] The medial *s* is possibly a brevigraph for *es*. I include facsimiles of the signature actual size, and also enlarged.

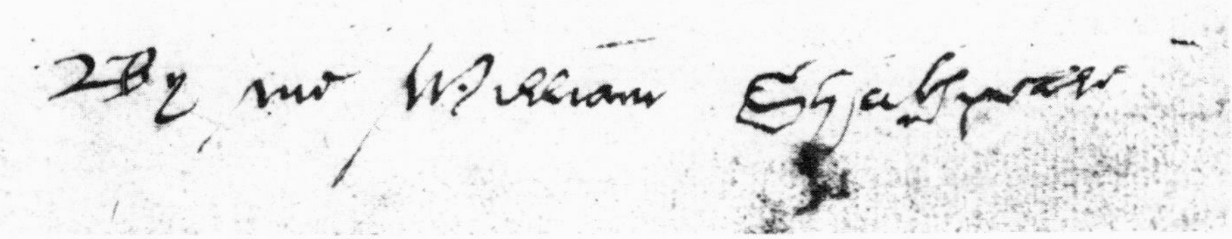

45 LAST WILL AND TESTAMENT, SHEET THREE: SHAKESPEARE'S SIGNATURE, 25 MARCH 1616.

46 LAST WILL AND TESTAMENT, SHEET THREE: SHAKESPEARE'S SIGNATURE, 25 MARCH 1616. *The signature enlarged twice.*

It will be observed that, even in this limited sampling, considerable variation exists respecting spelling and abbreviation. During the Elizabethan period it was not uncommon for someone to vary the form of his own name, although such fluctuation on two successive pages of the same document is not so usual. Variations of handwriting will appear less self-evident to modern students for whom secretary is an alien calligraphy—to the novice one minuscule *k* may look much like another, while to the trained eye these forms differ considerably. As Dr. Samuel A. Tannenbaum puts it, with the exquisite tact for which he was celebrated, 'To one unfamiliar with the old English script . . . the mistaken identity of one specimen of writing with another specimen written in that calligraphic system is as easy and as natural as it is for a white man who does not have frequent contacts with negroes to mistake one for another, *i.e.*, to fail to see the distinguishing

1 Edward Maunde Thompson, 'Handwriting', *Shakespeare's England* (Oxford, 1916), i. 306n.

individual features.'[1] The spectrum of variation among the six authenticated signatures is in fact sufficiently wide to prompt one recent student, Michael L. Hays, to question the authentication. Apropos of the will, he reminds us of an observation, made over half a century ago by the distinguished palaeographer Hilary Jenkinson, 'that in the Elizabethan period (and later) a clerk taking down or copying a deposition might himself sign it with the name of the deponent', and repeats Tannenbaum's corollary, 'that a testator's name may represent the signature of another in his stead'.[2] Jenkinson writes authoritatively on the Court hand, but he gives no supporting documentation for his assertion, and even the pronouncements of experts require the corroboration of evidence. If such evidence exists, I am unaware of it; and even then, Tannenbaum's corollary does not necessarily follow: a will is not a deposition. What is clear is that the hand that signed Shakespeare's testament is not the same as the one that set it down, although, Shakespeare studies being what they are, a few have argued, rather perversely, that Shakespeare both penned and signed his will. The last sentence of the document begins, 'In witness whereof I have hereunto put my Seale . . . '. Collins or his scribe has scored through the word 'Seale' and written 'hand' above. Such an alteration suggests that the will, as originally devised, called for Shakespeare's seal *in place of* his signature, but that (as it turned out) the testator could muster the strength to sign himself. A seal was required (as Henry Swinburne, our authority of last resort on Elizabethan wills, observes) when the will was 'neither written by the testator, nor by him subscribed'; the absence of the seal implies the presence of the testator's signature.[3]

Anyway, such latitude as exists among the Shakespeare signatures can be accounted for by two circumstances. Firstly, abnormal conditions affect five of the six signatures. Two were constrained by the narrow dimensions of the parchment tags inserted through slots at the foot of legal documents for the attachment of seals; three were set down by a man shortly to die. Secondly, while signatures sometimes remain constant, it is not unusual for them to vary; in this period George Chapman, for example, sometimes signed in English script, sometimes in Italian, while Edmund Spenser's signature fluctuated markedly.[4] One may reasonably conclude that all six signatures were set down by the same man, William Shakespeare.

The peculiarities of Shakespeare's eleven minuscules and three majuscules have been analysed in minute detail by Sir Edward Maunde Thompson. He notes the bold *h–a* linkage in the Belott–Mountjoy deposition, 'the pendent bow of the *h* being carried up above the line in an arched curve and merging with the *a*, which by this action is left open at the top like a *u*.'[5] Except in his fifth signature, Shakespeare uses the Italian form of long *s* in the medial position—the only concession he made to the new fashion in handwriting.[6] He seems to have written lower-case *e* with the loop reversed. Noteworthy too is the crossbar of the *p* (which some have taken for an Italian long *s*) in the deposition signature: a long horizontal stroke to indicate abbreviation of the second syllable of the surname, *per* (or *sper* or *spere*). In three of the signatures Shakespeare places an ornamental dot within the final loop of the *W*, a feature paralleled by capital letters (not only *W* but also *C*, *O*, and others) in sundry lay as well as scribal hands. But the most discussed feature of Shakespeare's handwriting is the open *a* with horizontal spur at the back which appears in the deposition signature and 'which is so marked that it may be regarded as a personal peculiarity'. It also turns up more than once in the 'Sir Thomas More' fragment. Thompson, who kept watch for occurrences of the spurred *a* in this period, reported in 1923 that he could find none except those in Shakespeare's signature and the 'More' fragment, although he and a

1 Samuel A. Tannenbaum, *Problems in Shakspere's Penmanship* (New York, 1927), p. 71.

2 Hilary Jenkinson, 'Elizabethan Handwritings: A preliminary Sketch', *The Library*, 4th Ser., iii (1922–3), 31; referred to by Michael L. Hays, 'Shakespeare's Hand in *Sir Thomas More*: Some Aspects of the Paleographic Argument', *Shakespeare Studies*, viii (1975), 248.

3 Henry Swinburne, *A Briefe Treatise of Testaments and Last Willes* (1590), ff. 191v–2.

4 R. C. Bald cites these examples in '*The Booke of Sir Thomas More* and its Problems', *Shakespeare Survey 2* (Cambridge, 1949), p. 54.

5 Thompson, 'Handwriting', p. 308.

6 In three of the signatures, however, the *h* resembles the Italian form; but this letter may be in the 'set hand' which preceded secretary, and whose *h* was very similar to the Italian. See R. A. Huber, 'On Looking Over Shakespeare's "Secretarie"', *Stratford Papers on Shakespeare*, ed. B. A. W. Jackson (Toronto, 1961), pp. 61, 70n.

colleague had examined 'numerous documents' and 'many collections of MSS'.[1] Other instances have been noted since, however, although perhaps not minutely identical, and the form is clearly less extraordinary than Thompson thought.

Palaeography easily slips across the indistinct border separating it from graphology; thus experts have intensively scrutinised the three signatures to Shakespeare's will for clues to the health of the testator. Dates have significance in this context. When Francis Collins, Shakespeare's solicitor, recopied the first sheet of his client's will he wrote 'Januarij' at the top, then crossed out the word and put 'martij' above. The alteration suggests that Collins prepared a draft in January, probably (although not certainly) of 1616, and returned for late revisions on 25 March 1616. A month later Shakespeare died. Presumably he was dying before he was dead, but we have no concurrent medical testimony. According to the Revd. John Ward, 'Shakespear Drayton and Ben Jhonson had a merry meeting and it seems drank too hard for Shakespear died of a feavour there contracted.'[2] The report of the vicar of Stratford may be true, but coming as it does a half-century after the event, it must be taken *cum grano*; in any event, perfect memory, for self-evident practical reasons, counted for more than perfect health—as Swinburne puts it, 'the integritie of the minde, and not of the bodie, is required in the testator'.[3] Nevertheless, the declaration in the exordium is the only contemporary evidence we have as to Shakespeare's condition during the last weeks of his life.

This testimony later pathologists, trusting to will and Ward, have supplemented. One may choose from (among others) diagnoses of *angina pectoris*, typhoid fever, typhus, Bright's disease, apoplexy, epilepsy, shaking palsy, chronic arteriosclerosis, pulmonary congestion, locomotor ataxia, mental fatigue (a real killer), chronic nicotinism, gluttony, or debauchery; or whatever combination seems most agreeable.[4] Despite these differences, the authorities agree that Shakespeare was pretty sick. Thompson, who resists such excesses of the clinical spirit, does offer some observations on the poet's condition. Comparing the testamentary signatures with the others, especially that of the deposition, he remarks on 'the painful contrast between the handwriting of sickness and the handwriting of health'. The 'weakness and malformation of the surname' on the third sheet of the will testify strikingly to mortal illness. 'Although Shakespeare lived for nearly a month longer, till the 23rd April, there can be no question that at the date of the execution of the will he was sorely stricken: of this the imperfections in the handwriting of the signatures afford ample evidence.'[5] Elsewhere, in a letter to *The Times Literary Supplement* (12 June 1919), Thompson cautions readers to 'remember that, at the time of the execution of his will, Shakespeare was a dying man, and, moreover, was apparently suffering from some nervous affection (writer's cramp, perhaps) which prevented his writing legibly and, in fact, on this occasion caused his signature to break down deplorably'. Maybe; the indifferent eye may indeed remark the wavering of an unsteady hand in the surname. But the terms chosen by Thompson are perhaps excessively dramatic, or unwarrantedly diagnostic, and one may wonder whether he would have reached precisely the same conclusion if he did not know that Shakespeare had only a month to live.

II. Doubtful and Spurious Signatures

Every once in a while a sixteenth- or seventeenth-century book comes to light with a fly-leaf or title-page signature purporting to be Shakespeare's. These almost invariably arouse deep distrust. 'It is a rule with me never to bother my head about autographs of Shakespeare IN BOOKS, not believing in any of them', wrote the greatest of Victorian Shakespeare scholars and collectors, near the end of his life, to the bookseller William Grose.

1 Thompson, 'The Handwriting of the Three Pages Attributed to Shakespeare Compared with his Signatures', *Shakespeare's Hand in the Play of Sir Thomas More* (Cambridge, 1923), p. 72n.

2 *DL*, item 201, p. 242.

3 Swinburne, *Briefe Treatise*, f. 61v.

4 Tannenbaum, himself a physician, lists a number of these armchair diagnoses in his *Problems*, pp. 74–7.

5 Thompson, *Shakespeare's Handwriting* (Oxford, 1916), p. 11.

If you find me one *on a deed* you will then most likely be able to open the purse-strings of
Yrs faithfully
J. O. Halliwell-Phillipps[1]

The cynicism is understandable; there had been too many false alarms over books, which after all represent cheap shots for the forger. Old books are fairly easy to come by, easier than deeds; and in such a game it scarcely matters if the copy is defective. All one has to do is dip pen in some antique-seeming concoction, and copy, with plausible variations, one of the existing Shakespeare signatures readily available in facsimile. It helps if the book selected is one Shakespeare is known to have used for a source, such as Plutarch's *Lives* or Holinshed's *Chronicles*; but a work with no recognised Shakespearian connection may serve the laudable end of spurring scholarship to establish one. A half-century ago Tannenbaum claimed that he had traced 109 books with purported Shakespeare signatures, seventy-nine of them the product of William-Henry Ireland's industry, in public and private repositories in England, Scotland, France, and the United States.[2] There must be many others. Ireland once took the pains to draw up a catalogue of Shakespeare's library (offered as 'by the Bard himself'); it boasts such items as Marlowe's *Doctorre Faustus*, Hackulyte's *Voyages*, and, among later acquisitions, Heywood's *Silver Age* and *Brazen Age*, both dating from 1613.[3] Still, the possibility always exists that a genuine survival from Shakespeare's library has over the centuries been gathering dust somewhere. Three from the past deserve more than passing notice. These are, in ascending order of plausibility, a copy of Ovid's *Metamorphoses* in the Bodleian Library, Florio's translation of Montaigne in the British Library, and Lambarde's *Archaionomia* in the Folger Shakespeare Library. All have at one time or another won support in responsible quarters. Thus they also illustrate the pitfalls of belief.

In January 1864 the Bodleian Library acquired, as part of the stock of a London bookseller, W. H. Elkins, a dog-eared copy of the Aldine edition of the *Metamorphoses*, printed in octavo at Venice in 1502. The book contains numerous Latin annotations, as well as schoolboy pen-and-ink sketches of gibbets, hanging bodies, faces, and the like. On the title-page appears a shaky abbreviated signature, 'W^{m} Sh^{e}', or 'Sh^{r}' or 'Sh^{re}' (it is no longer readily decipherable, if it ever was). Opposite, on the inside front cover—the fly-leaf has long since gone—a previous owner has placed this inscription in an archaic, or pseudo-archaic, hand:

This little Book of Ovid was given to me by W. Hall who sayd it was once Will. Shaksperes
T. N.
1682

Not until the tercentenary of Shakespeare's birth, a vintage year for the emergence of Bardic mementoes and relics, was the public made aware of the existence of this curiosity. In 1916, another tercentenary, the book, designated MS. Autogr. f. 1, found a place in the *Catalogue of the Shakespeare Exhibition held in the Bodleian Library*.

Believers must justify their faith. 'The theory is', according to Bodley's distinguished Librarian, Falconer Madan,

that the book was knocking about in some country town such as Stratford-on-Avon, was embellished as described by a grammar school boy, and was picked up by Shakespeare after his retirement to his native town, between 1611 and 1616, and inscribed with his name. His presumably increasing ill-health would tell on his handwriting, and after his death the little Ovid would remain in the family till his grand-daughter (a Hall) died in 1670, and might pass through a relative of her to T. N. in 1682.[4]

The W. Hall referred to in the note cannot be the William Hall of Lichfield, later prebendary of St. Paul's, who in 1694 dispatched a letter about the Stratford charnel house and Shakespeare's epitaph to Edward Thwaites, the Anglo-Saxon scholar.[5] This William Hall was too young, for

1 Letter of J. O. Halliwell-Phillipps, dated 28 July 1886, MS. Y.c.1225 in the Folger Shakespeare Library.

2 Tannenbaum, *Problems*, p. 160.

3 MS Ogden 54 in the Library of University College, London.

4 Falconer Madan, 'Two Lost Causes and What May Be Said in Defence of Them', *The Library*, 3rd Ser., ix (1918), 98.

5 *DL*, 250–1; EKC, ii. 260–1.

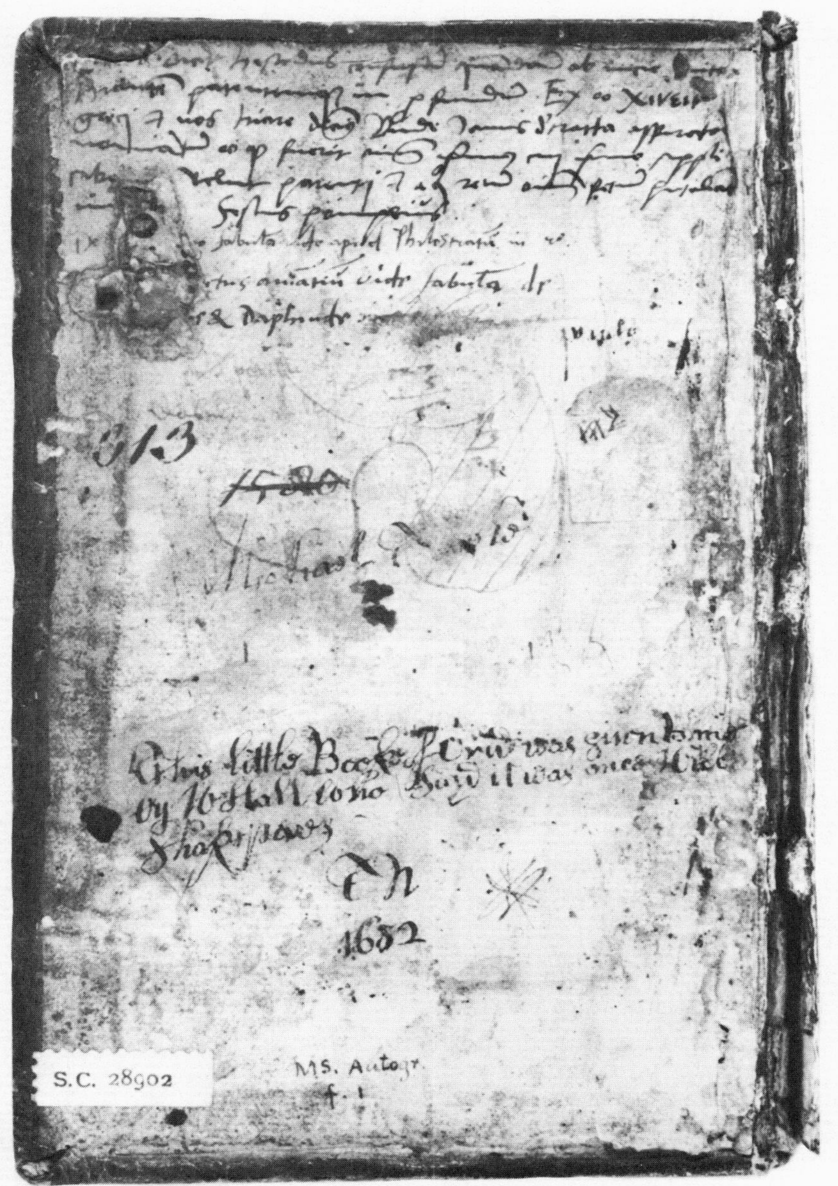

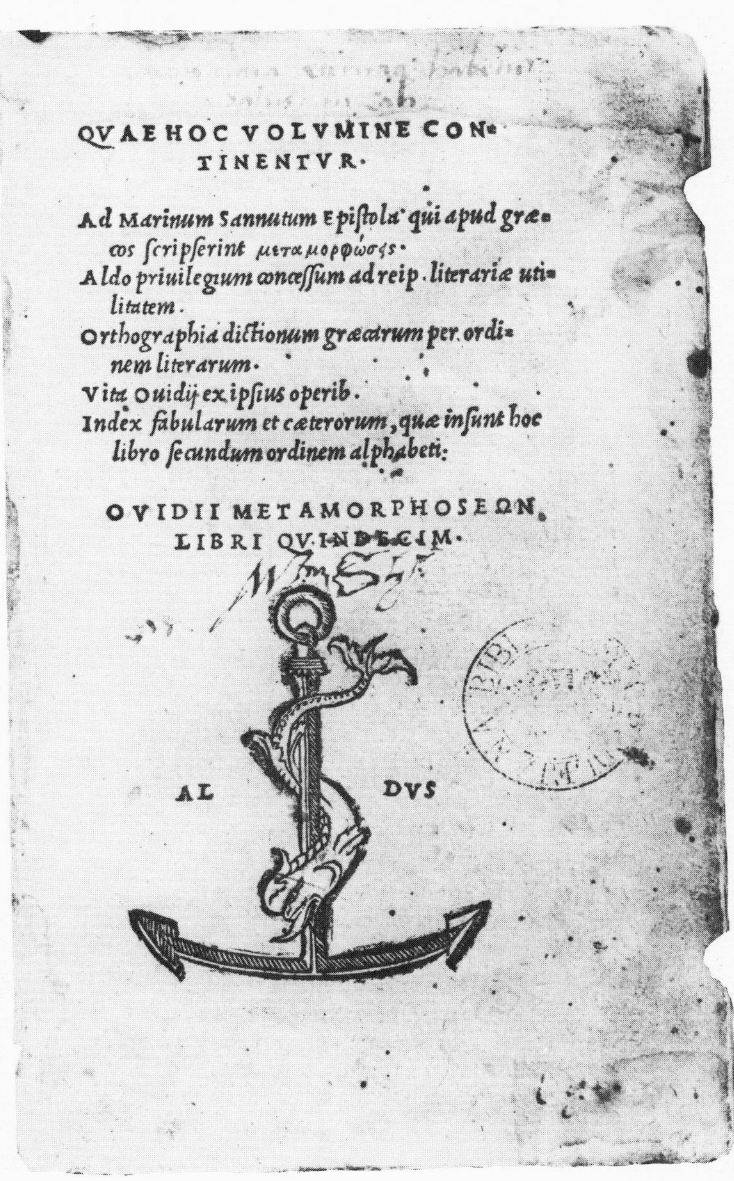
QVAE HOC VOLVMINE CONTINENTVR.

Ad Marinum Sannutum Epistola qui apud græcos scripserint μεταμορφώσεις.
Aldo priuilegium concessum ad reip. literariæ utilitatem.
Orthographia dictionum græcarum per ordinem literarum.
Vita Ouidij ex ipsius operib.
Index fabularum et cæterorum, quæ insunt hoc libro secundum ordinem alphabeti.

OVIDII METAMORPHOSEΩN LIBRI QVINDECIM.

AL DVS

47 THE OXFORD OVID (1502): TITLE-PAGE AND INSIDE FRONT COVER.

he took his B.A. from Queen's College, Oxford, in 1694. Another William Hall, however, was residing in Stratford from 1660 until at least 1684.

These reconstructions cut little ice with the age's most respected authority on Shakespeare's handwriting. When Sir Edward Maunde Thompson pronounced the Ovid autograph a forgery, Madan challenged him to publish his proofs. This Thompson obligingly did, with devastating effect, in *The Library* for July 1917. He demonstrated that the signature was a palpable forgery modelled on the subscription to the second sheet of Shakespeare's will. From this specimen the fabricator took his two majuscules. The testator's *W* furnished 'the fine introductory looped up stroke' absent from the other genuine signatures. True, the forger's *S* differs, in the concavity of the base curve, from the one in the will, but he seems to have consulted not the original document but Steevens's 1778 facsimile, which converted Shakespeare's secretary form into the Italian. The lower-case *h* also derives from the same signature, but the Blackfriars gate-house conveyance supplied the *m* of the Christian name, followed so literally as to include the apparently inadvertent pendent tag. As regards T. N.'s accompanying note, Thompson argued that this embellishment, also a fake, was originally dated 1602 rather than 1682, but that the forger, justifiably insecure about his command of Elizabethan script, altered the *o* to *8* to make it more safely modern. In the end Sir Edward dismisses with relief this 'clumsy fabrication'.[1]

1 Thompson, 'Two Pretended Autographs of Shakespeare', *The Library*, 3rd Ser., viii (1917), 212.

Stung, Madan replied the next year in *The Library*. As regards the note, he endeavoured to vindicate the year 1682, the *8* (he claimed) being 'the ordinary flat-topped 8', and cited other manuscript material where the hand offers a similar general appearance. Madan has a point about the date; but the heart of the case resides in the autograph itself, and here his defence is feeble. The very title of Madan's essay, 'Two Lost Causes and What May be Said in Defence of Them' (the other lost cause being the 1468 Oxford Jerome), acknowledges the force of Thompson's arguments.

The British Library Montaigne belongs in another class. In faded brown ink, this autograph, spelt 'Willm Shakspere', appears on the bottom half of the lining paper—originally the fly-leaf—facing the title-page of a copy of the 1603 folio first edition of John Florio's English translation of the *Essays*. The book was generally unknown until 1837, when Sir Frederic Madden, Keeper of Manuscripts in the British Museum, provided a sketchy provenance in a letter addressed to the Society of Antiquaries. Madden reports that the copy had been owned by the Revd. Edward Patteson, vicar of Smethwick in Staffordshire, some three miles from Birmingham, and thus near the Shakespeare country. How or when it came into Patteson's hands Madden cannot say, although he reports as 'very certain' that 'previous to the year 1780, Mr. Patteson used to exhibit the volume to his friends as a curiosity, *on account of the autograph*'.[1] The book passed to the minister's son, the Revd. Edward Patteson of East Sheen in Surrey; in 1836, through the good offices of a Mr. Barnwell, it was brought to the Museum for Madden's inspection. In June 1838 that institution purchased the relic from the bookseller Pickering, who had himself acquired it, only a month earlier, for £100 by auction at Evans's of Pall Mall. The Museum forthwith placed the volume on public display.

An experienced palaeographer, conscious of how contemptible were the Chatterton and Ireland forgeries, Madden did not doubt that in the 1603 Montaigne he had found the real thing. 'The present autograph *challenges and defies suspicion*', he declared in his letter to the Antiquaries, 'and has already passed the ordeal of numerous competent examiners, all of whom have, *without a single doubt*, expressed their conviction of its genuineness'.[2] But he supplies no further details, nor does he enter upon any palaeographical analysis. It fell to Madden's former underling at the Museum, Thompson, to furnish such an analysis some eighty years later. By it he undermined the confident conclusions of his former chief. Sir Edward sets about his task with, as he says, 'a natural pang of regret'; but he also generously reminds readers that, when Madden examined the autograph, photography was not yet available, nor had the Belott–Mountjoy deposition been discovered.

In his detailed analysis of the signature Thompson notes the disproportion of the letters, especially the gigantic scale of the *W*, unparalleled in the true Shakespeare autographs. Except for the two *ll*'s and the *pe*, which are linked, the letters are not written continuously, as was Shakespeare's practice. The long Italian *s* does resemble Shakespeare's; but the *W* is 'ignorantly conceived', and the *p*, wanting the characteristic loop, 'offends so flagrantly against all the characteristics of the English *p*, that it must be denounced as a spurious imitation'. Even without the weight of other evidence, the *p*, Thompson felt, sufficiently condemned the signature as a forgery, albeit a superior one.[3]

As with the Ovid, his judgement prevailed. He was of course in a position to help make it prevail; in 1872, when Thompson was Director, the Museum withdrew the Montaigne from exhibition. Now and then someone has attempted to reopen the case. Tannenbaum has made the most elaborate argument for the authenticity of the signature, to which he devotes an entire chapter of his *Problems in Shakspere's Penmanship*. He comes on strong, in a barrage of nouns:

> The pictorial impression made by 'Montaigne' is one of unquestionable genuineness; there is about it that naturalness, boldness, abandon, freedom, directness, straightforwardness, which one associates with genuineness. The writing strokes have the smoothness, directness, uniformity and continuity of genuineness. There is

1 Frederic Madden, *Observations on an Autograph of Shakspere* (1838), p. 5. Italics Madden's.

2 Ibid., p. 6. Italics (again) Madden's.

3 Thompson, 'Two Pretended Autographs', p. 206.

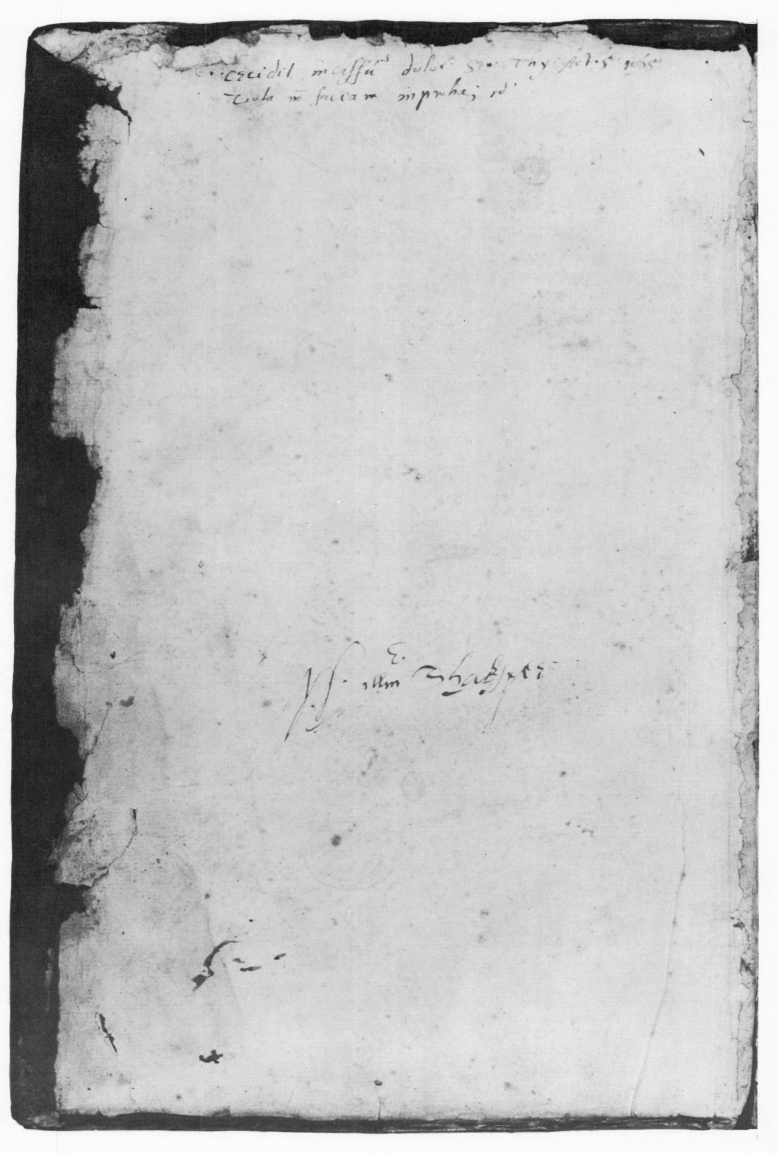

48 THE BRITISH LIBRARY MONTAIGNE (1603), LINING PAPER, FRONT COVER: THE PURPORTED SHAKESPEARE SIGNATURE. *British Library, C.21.e.17.*

no sign of the hesitation, deliberation, doubt, patching, mending, or drawing which we associate with forgery and which are so strikingly and unequivocally apparent in the abbreviated 'signature' in the Bodleian Library's copy of the 1502 edition of Ovid's *Metamorphoses*.... [1]

Thus does Tannenbaum apply his science of bibliotics. He rather undermines his palaeographical polemics by reproducing a photograph of the Florio signature alongside another signature, labelled as spurious, from a copy of Rastell's *Statutes*. Both look very much like the work of the same cunning hand.[2]

In 1929 George C. Taylor, in an interesting brief article, observed that Edward Capell was the first to draw attention to Shakespeare's indebtedness to Montaigne, in a note to *The Tempest* which appeared in part 4 of volume ii of Capell's *Notes and Various Readings to Shakespeare* in 1780, a publication that students have often misdated. If the Revd. Patteson exhibited the Montaigne volume (as Madden says) *previous to the year 1780*, that took place before Shakespeare's awareness of Montaigne had become public knowledge. What, therefore, Taylor asks, would the motive for forgery have been?[3] These arguments, like Tannenbaum's, prove ineffective. Madden's casual reference to a date is mere uncorroborated hearsay; and spurious Shakespeare signatures appear at random in all sorts of old books, the Rastell *Statutes*, for example. That a forger inserted one in a copy of Montaigne's *Essays* without knowledge of a Shakespeare connection does not strain credulity. Thompson's arguments here, as with the Aldine Ovid, remain unassailable.

The Lambarde signature raises more complex issues. William Lambarde is today best known for his *Perambulation of Kent* and for an exchange with his sovereign in her Privy Chamber at East Greenwich in August 1601 (the last month of his life), when he was Keeper of the Records in the Tower of London. The latter conversation took place half a year after the Essex rebellion, for which the conspirators had commissioned the Lord Chamberlain's Men to mount a special performance of Shakespeare's *Richard II* at the Globe. The Queen, Lambarde reports, fell upon that monarch's reign, saying 'I am Richard II. know ye not that?' To which he replied, 'Such a wicked imagination was determined and attempted by a most unkind Gent. the most adorned creature that ever your Majestie made'. She had the last word: 'He that will forget God, will also forget his benefactors; this tragedy [*Richard II*] was played 40tie times in open streets and houses.'[4] In his own time Lambarde was chiefly esteemed for his *Eirenarcha: or of the Office of the Justices of the Peace*, which went through eight editions between 1582 and 1610. In 1568 Lambarde brought out *Archaionomia, sive de priscis anglorum legibus libri . . .*, a quarto compilation, in some three hundred pages (140 numbered leaves), of old English ecclesiastical laws. On the left-hand page Lambarde gives the Anglo-Saxon text—this was one of the earliest books to use Anglo-Saxon type—and, on the right, a Latin translation or paraphrase. *Archaionomia* gained wide respect in the legal profession as a source for precedents, although it never entered a second impression.

On 27 November 1938 a copy with scattered underlinings and annotations was one of two unspecified titles offered for sale by Sotheby's (catalogue item 505) as part of a lot of four that included Heylin's *Microcosmos*. For the sake of the Heylin the Folger Shakespeare Library bought the four books for £1. The Library had no particular use for the Lambarde—it already owned five copies—and besides, this one, stiffly bound in vellum, had suffered water damage which left the title-page badly crumpled. But when the binder routinely smoothed it out, one could see an inscription above the ornamental border—'This to be kept for ye impression is [out?] nor like to be renew'd'—and underneath, on the border itself, what appeared to be a signature. Several members of the Folger staff—Giles E. Dawson, James G. McManaway, and Edwin E. Willoughby—studied the signature in every available way. Owing to bleeding of the ink, they found that the best way to inspect it was from the underside, with the help of a magnifying glass. They photographed the signature; they made use of the ultra-violet and infra-red lamps. In the laboratory

1 Tannenbaum, *Problems*, pp. 162–3.

2 W. H. Kelliher of the Department of Manuscripts of the British Library makes the point; see Robert Ellrodt, 'Self-Consciousness in Montaigne and Shakespeare', *Shakespeare Survey 28* (Cambridge, 1975), p. 38, n. 2.

3 George C. Taylor, 'The Date of Edward Capell's *Notes and Various Readings to Shakespeare, Volume II*', *Review of English Studies*, v (1929), 319.

4 EKC, ii. 326–7.

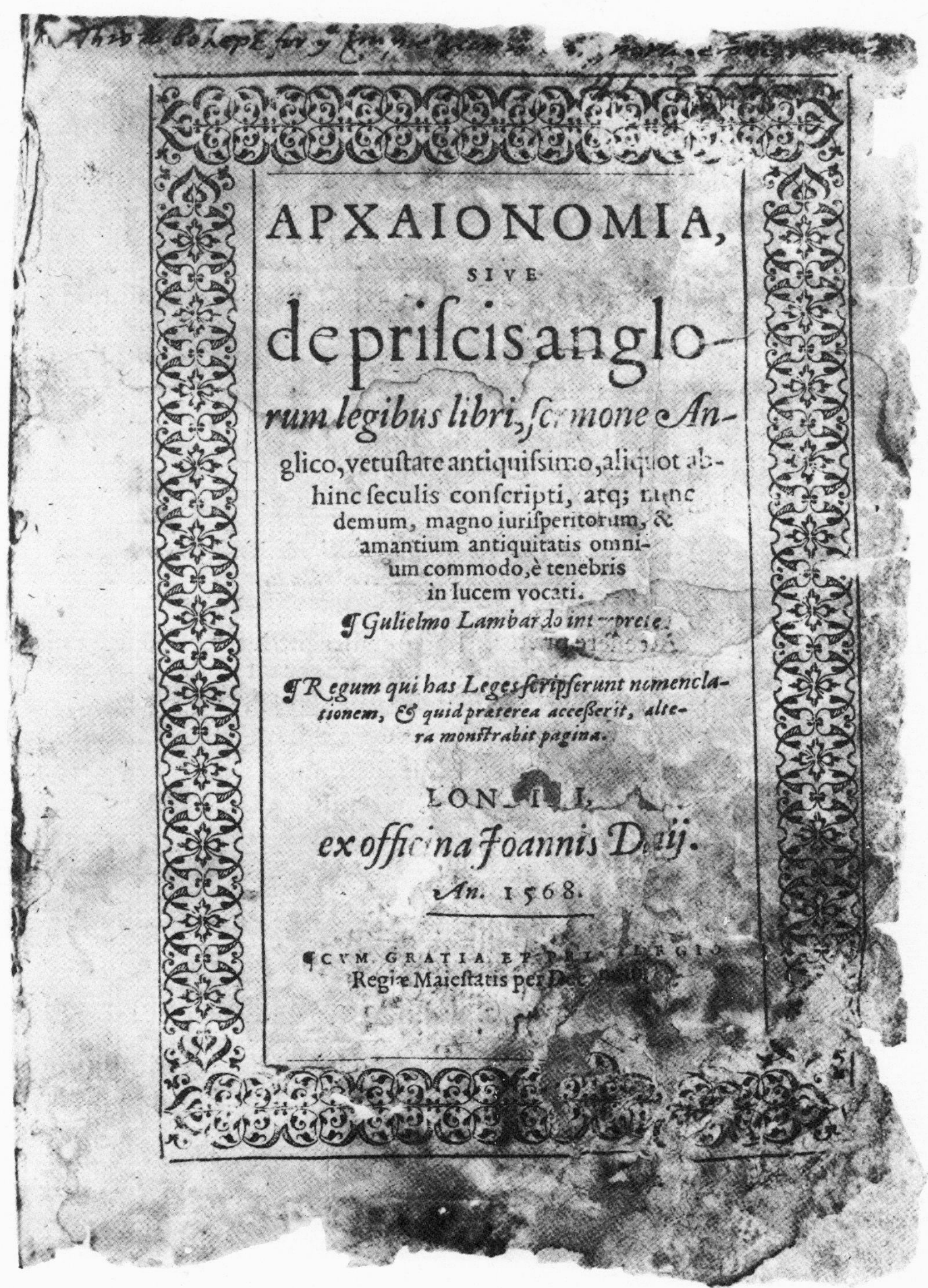
APXAIONOMIA,

SIVE

de priſcis anglo-
rum legibus libri, ſermone Anglico, vetuſtate antiquiſsimo, aliquot ab-
hinc ſeculis conſcripti, atq; nunc
demum, magno iuriſperitorum, &
amantium antiquitatis omnium commodo, è tenebris
in lucem vocati.

¶ Gulielmo Lambardo interprete.

¶ Regum qui has Leges ſcripſerunt nomencla-
tionem, & quid praeterea acceſſerit, alte-
ra monſtrabit pagina.

LONDINI,

ex officina Joannis Daij.

An. 1568.

¶ CVM GRATIA ET PRIVILEGIO
Regiae Maieſtatis per Decennium.

49 WILLIAM LAMBARDE, *ARCHAIONOMIA* (1568), TITLE-PAGE. *Folger Shakespeare Library, MS. V.a.230.*

of the United States Archives, experts subjected the signature to microscopic, photographic, and other tests, as well as comparison with Shakespeare's known handwriting. When all was said and done (Dawson reported in 1942) 'it persisted in looking like "W Shakspere" '. The *Shaks* was reasonably clear, the *p* following somewhat less so, and the rest—*ere* or *ear* or *er*—not confidently decipherable.

But is the signature genuine? A relevant consideration is the presence, inside the front cover, of these words in an eighteenth-century hand: 'Mr. Wm Shakspeare Lived at No 1 Little Crown St Westminster NB near Dorset Steps St James's Park.' No other reference to such an address for Shakespeare has come down. Whoever put it in the book must have been prompted to do so

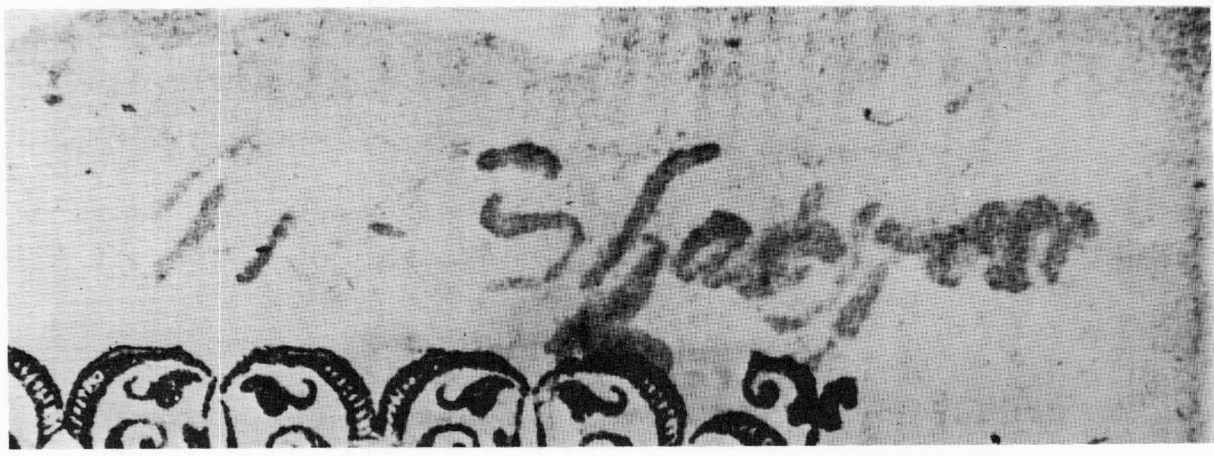

50 WILLIAM LAMBARDE, *ARCHAIONOMIA* (1568): THE FOLGER SIGNATURE. *The signature, as here reproduced, has been photographed from the back with mirror reversal of the image; enlarged four times.*

because of the signature, which no doubt was at one time more legible. The systematic numbering of London houses goes back only to 1765, when Parliament enacted legislation requiring it. Little Crown Street seems by then to have disappeared, for it is not included in Pine and Rocque's exhaustively detailed *Plan of the Cities of London and Westminster* (1746), which however lists a Crown Court not far from Derby Court. Maybe, McManaway wondered in *Notes and Queries* in 1939—the first allusion, albeit indirect, to the Folger volume—Crown Court once served as an alternative name for Little Crown Street?[1] However that may be, we can at least trace the signature back as far as the late eighteenth century.

In the Folger Library's decennial report for 1931–41, Adams discussed the Lambarde volume briefly. Dawson in 1942 drew it to the attention of a wider scholarly audience in a paper read before an English Institute meeting at Columbia University, and published the next year in the *English Institute Annual*. Dawson enumerated four possible ways of accounting for the presence of the signature in the book:

> (1) It is a forgery; (2) It was written by some unknown person practicing penmanship or writing the name down with no intent to defraud; (3) It is the signature of some unknown person named W. Shakespeare; (4) It is the autograph signature of William Shakespeare the dramatist.[2]

One by one Dawson discounts the first three. The signature looks more like an authentic Shakespeare autograph than does any known forgery, or even any of the possibly genuine signatures; in the eighteenth century the art of literary fabrication had not yet far advanced—witness William-Henry Ireland's brief but astonishing success with the Norfolk Street papers. In the end Dawson has left only the fourth and last option, which he embraces with a scholar's caution: '. . . that William Shakespeare wrote his signature on this title page, perhaps because he owned the book—a strange volume indeed for his library'.[3]

The next year Adams allowed enthusiasm freer rein. Doubtless Shakespeare and Lambarde, moving in the same small Elizabethan world of letters, knew one another, and it is 'highly likely' that Shakespeare took an interest in Anglo-Saxon. While not claiming certainty, 'so far as modern science can tell', Adams concluded, 'there seems to be no reason to question the antiquity of the signature, and a palaeographical study points to its being the autograph of the poet'.[4] He cites the findings of the United States Archives authority:

1 'Little Crown Street, Westminster', query signed 'J. G. M.', *Notes and Queries*, clxxvii (1939), 478. McManaway does not cite the inscription, or book, that prompted his query.

2 Giles E. Dawson, 'Authenticity and Attribution of Written Matter', *English Institute Annual, 1942* (New York, 1943), p. 97.

3 Ibid., p. 100.

4 Joseph Quincy Adams, 'A New Signature of Shakespeare', *Bulletin of the John Rylands Library*, xxvii (1942–3), 259.

At the end of several months of investigation, Dr. Tate reported that, after applying all the tests known to him, he could discover no evidence that the signature was not contemporary with the poet, and hence what it purported to be, namely a genuine signature of some person named 'William Shakespeare'; and that after comparing its individual letters with those of the dramatist's acknowledged signatures, he believed it to be in all likelihood from the same hand.[1]

Adams mentions chemical analysis as one of the tests performed. But the report of Vernon D. Tate, Chief of the Division of Photographic Archives and Research, dated 15 December 1939 and preserved in the Folger Library, tells a somewhat different story. 'No chemical tests of ink or paper have been made,' he states, 'and it is considered impossible to determine the age of ink by any known test.'[2] Tate's conclusions are more restrained than Adams reports: '. . . it is apparent that the evidence is inconclusive. . . . It is exceedingly difficult to make a statement proving or disproving the authenticity of this signature on the basis of the materials at hand.'[3] I doubt that Adams, a scholar of unimpeachable reputation, set out deliberately to mislead; the exhilaration of having obtained—was it possible?—a genuine Shakespeare signature for his beloved library, the only such signature in the United States, swept aside ingrained scruples, and (I expect) led him unconsciously to distort the laboratory findings of his impartial expert.

Surveying Shakespeare's small Latin and less Greek, T. W. Baldwin in 1944 described the claim of the Lambarde signature as 'respectable'. There the matter rested, a temporary casualty of the Second World War, until, in 1950, an experienced palaeographer, Charles J. Sisson, remarked sceptically—if somewhat obscurely—on the signature:

A number of marked variations from any known signature or from normal Secretary hand causes doubts, after examination of the original, fortified by expert opinion of the reproduction, not least in respect of the *h* and of the style in general. It might perhaps even suggest a *memoriter* imitation of the Mortgage signature. The claim is, however, supported by the recency of the revelation of the signature in the process of ironing, as also by the reference to Shakespeare (written in later) as resident in Westminster.[4]

The *Archaionomia* signature, however, has characteristics of several of the known signatures, including the Belott–Mountjoy deposition, not discovered until this century; so the suggestion of *memoriter* imitation hardly bears scrutiny. In 1958 Hereward T. Price accepted Lambarde as genuine, although on the basis of the tests commissioned by Adams rather than on independent inspection; his advocacy smacks of special pleading.[5] Three years later, Sisson's hesitance received support from an unexpected quarter. R. A. Huber, whose expertise derives from criminal investigations rather than palaeographical studies, found the new signature 'too "all new"', especially as regards proportions, spacing, and the like.[6] These strictures do not add up to much; the Lambarde signature (if it is genuine) was written under different conditions from the others, and presumably some years earlier, so such differences are not too startling.

The Folger signature was therefore not exactly an unknown quantity when a young American academic, W. Nicholas Knight, created a stir over it in 1971. He re-examined the writing with the aid of ultra-violet light, and detected a dot in the last arc of the *W*, and following this letter a lower-case *m*, unraised, but with a horizontal bar, signifying abbreviation, above. These findings Knight announced in an article forthrightly entitled 'The Seventh Shakespeare Signature', in *The Shakespeare Newsletter* for May 1971, and in discussions with newspaper reporters. He reports that these palaeographical features—not noted by Dawson—were confirmed by the Folger Library's Curator of Manuscripts, Mrs. Laetitia Yeandle. In a note following the article, Louis Marder, editor of *The Shakespeare Newsletter*, cautiously describes Knight's work as 'a very interesting piece of research'. The newspapers, giving the story prominent coverage, reacted less cautiously.

1 Ibid.

2 Vernon D. Tate, 'Preliminary Report on the Examination of a Signature Appearing on the Title-Page of "Apxaionomia, sive de priscis anglorum legibus libri, sermone anglico", London, 1568', correspondence files (1931–47) in the Folger Shakespeare Library, pp. 11–12. Tate's covering letter is dated 15 December 1939.

3 Ibid., p. 11.

4 Charles J. Sisson, 'Studies in the Life and Environment of Shakespeare since 1900', *Shakespeare Survey 3* (Cambridge 1950), p. 4.

5 Hereward T. Price, 'Shakespeare's Classical Scholarship', *Review of English Studies*, N.S., ix (1958), 54–5.

6 Huber, 'On Looking Over Shakespeare's "Secretarie"', p. 69.

'A Wesleyan University English professor, combining electronic detective work with deduction based on his literary and legal knowledge of Elizabethan England, believes he has authenticated the only signature of William Shakespeare known to exist outside England and shed new light on the poet's expertise in law.' So Henry Raymont reported in *The New York Times* on 19 August. Raymont further observed that 'dealers estimate a Shakespeare autograph to be worth about $1-million'. A *Christian Science Monitor* headline (30 July 1971) thereupon trumpeted the '"million-dollar dot"'. Newspaper articles following Dawson's announcement in 1942 had reckoned the value of a Shakespeare autograph at $50,000; but inflation and hyperbole will have their way.

Inflation of another kind marks the substantial book (325 pages) Knight spins out of the signature, *Shakespeare's Hidden Life: Shakespeare at the Law, 1585–1595* (1973), an exercise in what might have been but probably never was. He revives, none too persuasively, the old and generally discredited theory that Shakespeare during the Lost Years occupied himself as a lawyer's scrivener. Knight exaggerates Shakespeare's knowledge of the law, while his own knowledge of the Inns of Court is insecure.[1] He tends to lose sight of the fact that the Chancery litigants in the nineties were John and Mary Shakespeare, not their son William. 'What follows . . . ', Knight says in his first chapter, 'is a re-creation, and not a fantasy'.[2] But it is a fantasy, not a re-creation; Shakespeare's hidden life remains stubbornly private. But what counts, after all, is the signature. Of this autograph, 'only the seventh known', Knight claims, 'although this extraordinary bit of faded writing has been known to scholars for some time, some strange reticence of scholastic perversity has prevented giving it consideration in print'.[3] Strange reticence? Where are the Dawsons and Adamses of yesteryear? In his book Knight elaborates on his previous palaeographical arguments, but adds nothing substantive that is new.

His well-publicised researches, which served to rekindle interest in the signature, seem not to have reached Lambarde's most recent biographer, Retha M. Warnicke, who includes no index reference to Knight or (for that matter) Shakespeare in her *William Lambarde, Elizabethan Antiquary, 1536–1601* (1973); but then, the historians and the literary people sometimes have different fish to fry. Knight did, however, succeed in smoking out Roderick Eagle, the anti-Stratfordian, who declared in a letter to *The Daily Telegraph* (24 August 1971) that the Folger copy of Lambarde's *Archaionomia* had once belonged to him: he had bought it in 1915, for half a crown, from a junk shop at Forest Hill, a London suburb, and had subsequently lent it to William T. Smedley, well known in Baconian circles. One does well not to lend books; Smedley failed to return his copy, and after his death it turned up in the Sotheby's sale. Eagle concluded that the signature was an Ireland forgery, and retained his equanimity. 'I feel quite satisfied', he assured the public, 'that by losing the book I am not the poorer by £400,000!'[4]

On 4 August 1977, Mrs. Laetitia Yeandle being present, I once again inspected the title-page, which is in exceedingly fragile condition, with the aid of a magnifying glass and ultra-violet light. Examination revealed, following the *W*, possible vestiges of an *m*, consisting of what may be two minims. Over these apparent minims there was possibly a horizontal bar, although this might also be a flick in the last stroke of the *W*. A dot was also evident in the final loop of the *W*, but, to the unaided eye, this feature could equally represent a swelling in the printed decorative border. The dot—or was it a speck?—was, however, visible from the back under ultra-violet light; still it could have been, as Mrs. Yeandle had noted years earlier, a bleed-through of the design, which was broken at that point. A few days later, on 8 August, we were joined by Mr. Robert MacClaren of the United States Archives, who came armed with a microscope. Magnification of approximately one hundred times revealed fairly decisively that the dot of the *W* was what it appeared to be, a dot, physically placed with pen and ink on the poor-quality, bibulous paper. MacClaren recommended ion-beam analysis as a logical next step.

Where, then, do we now stand with respect to the purported Shakespeare autograph in the Folger copy of Lambarde's *Archaionomia*? Ireland, who so conscientiously assembled a library for

1 See R. J. Schoeck's notice in *Shakespeare Quarterly*, xxvi (1975), 305–7.

2 W. Nicholas Knight, *Shakespeare's Hidden Life: Shakespeare at the Law 1585–1595* (New York, 1973), p. 25.

3 Ibid., p. 124.

4 Roderick L. Eagle, 'Travels of a "Shakspere" Signature', *The Daily Telegraph*, 24 August 1971, p. 12.

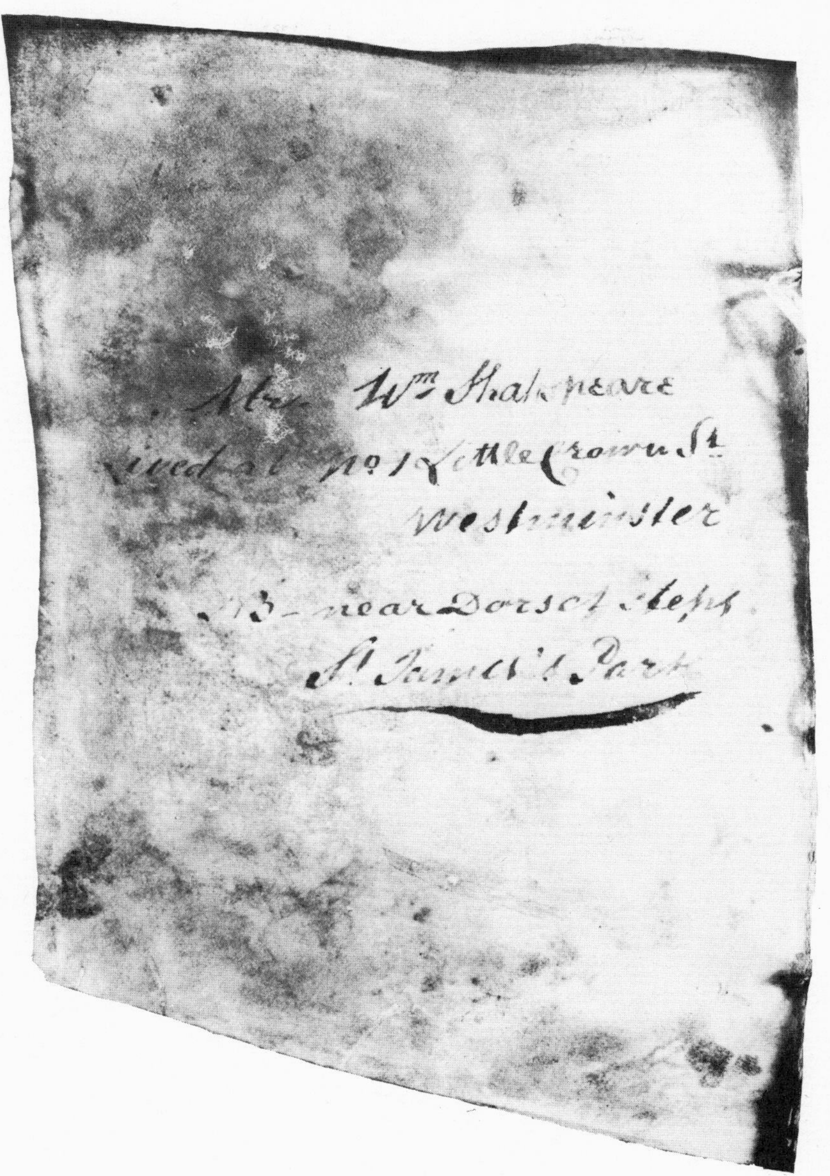

51 WILLIAM LAMBARDE, *ARCHAIONOMIA* (1568): THE LITTLE CROWN ST. NOTE. *Inside front cover, Folger Shakespeare Library MS. V.a.230.*

Shakespeare, seems not to have forged this signature. It is, however, oddly positioned for either a faked or genuine signature, and the volume in which it appears still seems an odd choice for Shakespeare's library. The absence of any provenance, however sketchy, is discouraging. More than thirty years after the dust was stirred, allowed to settle, then once again resifted, Dawson, who did the first stirring, thinks there is a better chance that the signature is genuine than that it is not. That strikes me as a fair statement of the position. Handwriting analysis alone cannot resolve the question, and it seems unlikely, so long after the event, that evidence of another sort will be forthcoming. The Lambarde signature makes a better claim to authenticity than any other pretended Shakespeare autograph but it is premature, to say the least, to classify it as the poet's seventh signature.

To broaden the spectrum of this survey of Shakespeare's handwriting, I include a few specimens of unquestionably forged signatures. For other forgeries, on a grander scale, see pp. 117–154.

III. The 'More' Fragment

The same volume of *The Library* that contained Maunde Thompson's exposure of two pretended Shakespeare autographs also carried an article by Percy Simpson supporting the Shakespearian ascription of a portion of a manuscript play in the British Museum; you win some and you lose some. The manuscript fragment, evidently holograph, is Addition IIc of Harley MS. 7368, 'The Booke of Sir Thomas Moore'. The addition, the 'Ill May-Day' scene, comprises three pages with 147 lines, plus a single speech-prefix, 'all'. Alexander Dyce first edited the play in 1844 for the Shakespeare Society. Some years later, in 1871, Richard Simpson suggested, on literary grounds, that a part of the manuscript was by Shakespeare. The next year a more considerable scholar, James Spedding, the respected biographer and editor of Bacon, supported the attribution on palaeographical grounds, pointing out resemblances between the Addition and the five signatures then known. In 1911 the Malone Society published W. W. Greg's classic edition of the play. Five years later Thompson launched a controversy that has reverberated to this day when, in *Shakespeare's Handwriting*, he set forth detailed arguments for the autograph character of the fragment. He reiterated his case in 1923, when he was in his eighties, in an important collection of papers, *Shakespeare's Hand in the Play of Sir Thomas More*, to which Greg contributed a chapter on the several hands in the manuscript. Much follow-up discussion ensued in the correspondence columns of *The Times Literary Supplement*, and elsewhere, all through the decade. The literature of this debate is too extensive for summary and analysis here, but fortunately one can refer interested readers to a pair of excellent retrospective articles: R. C. Bald, '*The Booke of Sir Thomas More* [*sic*] and its Problems', *Shakespeare Survey 2* (Cambridge, 1949), pp. 44–65, and Harold Jenkins, 'A Supplement to Sir Walter Greg's Edition of *Sir Thomas More*', included in the lithographic reprint (1961) of Greg's edition, and also in Malone Society *Collections*, vol. vi, 1961 (1962), 179–92.

First-hand study of 'Sir Thomas More' has been handicapped as a result of a misguided early attempt to protect the manuscript. Around the middle of the nineteenth century, after the appearance of the Dyce edition, some unknown person pasted thick, semi-opaque tracing paper on both sides of six of the crumbling leaves, and also patched holes with gummed paper. It is a case of the cure being worse than the disease. With the passage of time the tracing paper darkened, and the paste thickened, leaving much of the writing illegible. The mutilation affected two of the three pages of Addition IIc. It was possible, in a more enlightened day, to remove the tracing paper from f. 8^{v}, which however remains badly impaired; f. 8 is hopeless, while f. 9 escaped desecration. For a while the Museum authorities felt constrained to remove the manuscript from circulation because of the brittle condition of the paper (Jenkins did not have access to it); but it now is available once again, with individual leaves encased in blocks of glass. The best preserved page, f. 9, is kept on permanent display in a case in the Manuscript Saloon.

I have discussed the authorship in my *Internal Evidence and Elizabethan Dramatic Authorship: An Essay in Literary History and Method* (1966), pp. 104–7 et passim, and considered it within the context of a narrative biography in my *William Shakespeare: A Documentary Life* (1975), pp. 157–60. Here I shall limit my remarks to palaeographical considerations, and especially to contributions made since the surveys of Bald and Jenkins.

First a word about the chief peculiarities of the hand, most of which Thompson pointed out more than half a century ago. There is the anomalous *k* (with a heavy comma added to finish the small loop) of the second will subscription, and paralleled by 'knees' at l. 110, which lacks the cross-bar. Greg disputes the occurrence of this form in hand D. The latter, however, manifests three forms of the letter *k* used by Shakespeare. As noted above, he employed the Italian form of the long *s* in four of his signatures; only two Italian forms, an *s* and an *r*, occur in the Addition, in a single word, the speech-prefix 'Seriant' at l. 17. Although Thompson is inclined to attach evidential value to the *s*, others are understandably sceptical, as it is a capital in 'More'. The unusual formation of Shakespeare's *p* (in the Blackfriars gate-house mortgate deed), involving a descender followed by a cross-stroke, and then a third stroke to finish off the top of the loop, may be observed in the three instances of 'peace' at l. 50. Shakespeare's use of a downstroke preliminary to an upstroke (noticeable in the *m* of 'me' and the *W* of 'William', forming in the latter what has been described as an 'elongated needle eye') finds parallels in the Addition (ll. 75, 95, 130, 144). But the most discussed form is the spurred *a* of the deposition autograph, which also appears in 'that' of l. 105, and elsewhere, although less closely approximated. As previously indicated, the spurred *a* is less extraordinary than Thompson and others have thought, although Sisson reports that he never encountered another. There are also discrepancies between hand D and that of the six signatures: the *h*'s differ; Shakespeare neglects to dot his *i*'s, while D generally does. Whatever is the date of 'Sir Thomas More', and the date is debatable, a number of years must have intervened between the composition of Addition IIc and the penning of the signatures. Differences are therefore to be expected, quite apart from normal everyday variations in a hand. What counts is the cumulative impression.

In an interesting brief article in *The Times Literary Supplement* (22 April 1977), 'Theobald, *table/babbled*, and *Sir Thomas More*', Giles E. Dawson employs palaeographical (as well as orthographical) evidence from the Addition to reconstruct how the Folio compositor of *Henry V* may well have misread *babld* (II.iii.17) as *table*. On the basis of negative checks Dawson concludes that 'The probability of finding any other hand than hand D in which they [these characteristics] all abound is one in many thousand.' The argument is plausibly ingenious, if slightly marred by a slip: for the Folio reading is not *table* but *Table*. The mistake exemplifies the ubiquity of error; what happened to Dawson, an experienced hand with hands, could happen to anybody. In any event, we do well not to ignore the voices of caution, which have of late become increasingly numerous.

Although R. A. Huber, working of necessity entirely from photocopies, was unable to avail himself of the facilities of the Crime Detection Laboratory at the Ottawa headquarters of the Royal Canadian Mounted Police, he provides a most judicious evaluation of the evidence concerning the handwriting of the Addition. His conclusions bear quotation:

> Hand D, indisputably, shows similarity to the Shakespeare signatures in some letter forms in general, and in a few even more specific respects. There is admittedly a similarity in writing size, expansion, and quality—as represented particularly in Shakespeare's writing by the conveyance signature—and in the relative heights of certain letters. It is difficult, nevertheless, to reconcile certain salient differences [e.g. the *h*'s, *y*'s, and dotted *i*'s]. Physical infirmity alone cannot account for divergences in fundamental structures. . . .
>
> The similarities that are present clearly put Shakespeare within the relatively small group of writers of the time who could have written Hand D. In the light of the differences noted, however, the evidence is *not* sufficiently strong to justify a positive identification of the poet.[1]

Fifteen years afterwards, Huber found a supporter in Paul Ramsey, whose essay, coyly entitled 'Shakespeare and *Sir Thomas More* Revisited: or, a Mounty on the Trail', adds little of substance to the article. Mainly Ramsey accentuates the negative, emphasising 'the principle that what does not fit is more important than what does fit'.[2] Such a principle, valid as far as it goes, will seem less novel to students of authorship attribution than it does to Ramsey.

A more considerable exercise in scepticism is Michael L. Hays's paper, 'Shakespeare's Hand in *Sir Thomas More:* Some Aspects of the Paleographic Argument'. He effectively scores palaeographical pretensions to scientism by noting the frequency of reliance on 'general' or 'personal' impressions. The history of authorship investigations is, indeed, littered with the bones of failed exercises in pseudo-objectivity. Hays remarks on the quantitative meagreness of the control data, i.e. the six signatures; he draws attention to inconsistencies in Thompson's arguments over the years—inconsistencies that Hays is inclined to ascribe not to changes of opinion but, less charitably, to tactical requirements of the moment. Sometimes Hays presses his case unconvincingly, as when (as we have seen) he casts doubt on the integrity of the Shakespeare autographs. Moreover, his own comments are uninformed by any direct experience of the primary materials. Still, he does undermine faith in the validity of an attribution based on palaeographical grounds alone.

That is, if such faith prevailed in the first instance. Fifteen years earlier, Sisson, who accepts the identification of hand D as that of Shakespeare, had said (respecting Huber's caveats) that 'they bear out on the whole the general view of recent scholar–paleographers that a convincing case for identification cannot rest upon handwriting alone, but depends upon the cumulative effect of other evidence converging upon a positive conclusion supported by a reasonable probability derived from handwriting'.[3] Of course, as E. G. Fogel has remarked in a different but analogous context, zeroes, however plentiful, still add up to zero. The crucial consideration, as regards the

1 Huber, 'On Looking Over Shakespeare's "Secretarie"', pp. 65–6.

2 Paul Ramsey, 'Shakespeare and *Sir Thomas More* Revisited: or, a Mounty on the Trail', *Papers of the Bibliographical Society of America*, lxx (1976), 333–46.

3 'Postscript' to Huber, p. 76.

'Ill May-Day' scene, is that the varieties of evidence—palaeographical, literary (imagery, ideas, and the like), and textual (e.g. the spelling *scilens*)—are rather more than ciphers; nor is the configuration of data, which are encouragingly varied, merely the sum of the individual items. The arguments for Shakespeare's authorship have power. G. Blakemore Evans, recognising that power, has seen fit to find space for the three pages (plus another speech of twenty-one lines not claimed to be holograph) in *The Riverside Shakespeare*, of which he is textual editor. He is not the first to include the scene in a collected edition, and we may expect others to follow suit. At the same time, the ascription to Shakespeare remains a theory, not a fact, and in the absence of external evidence is destined to continue so.

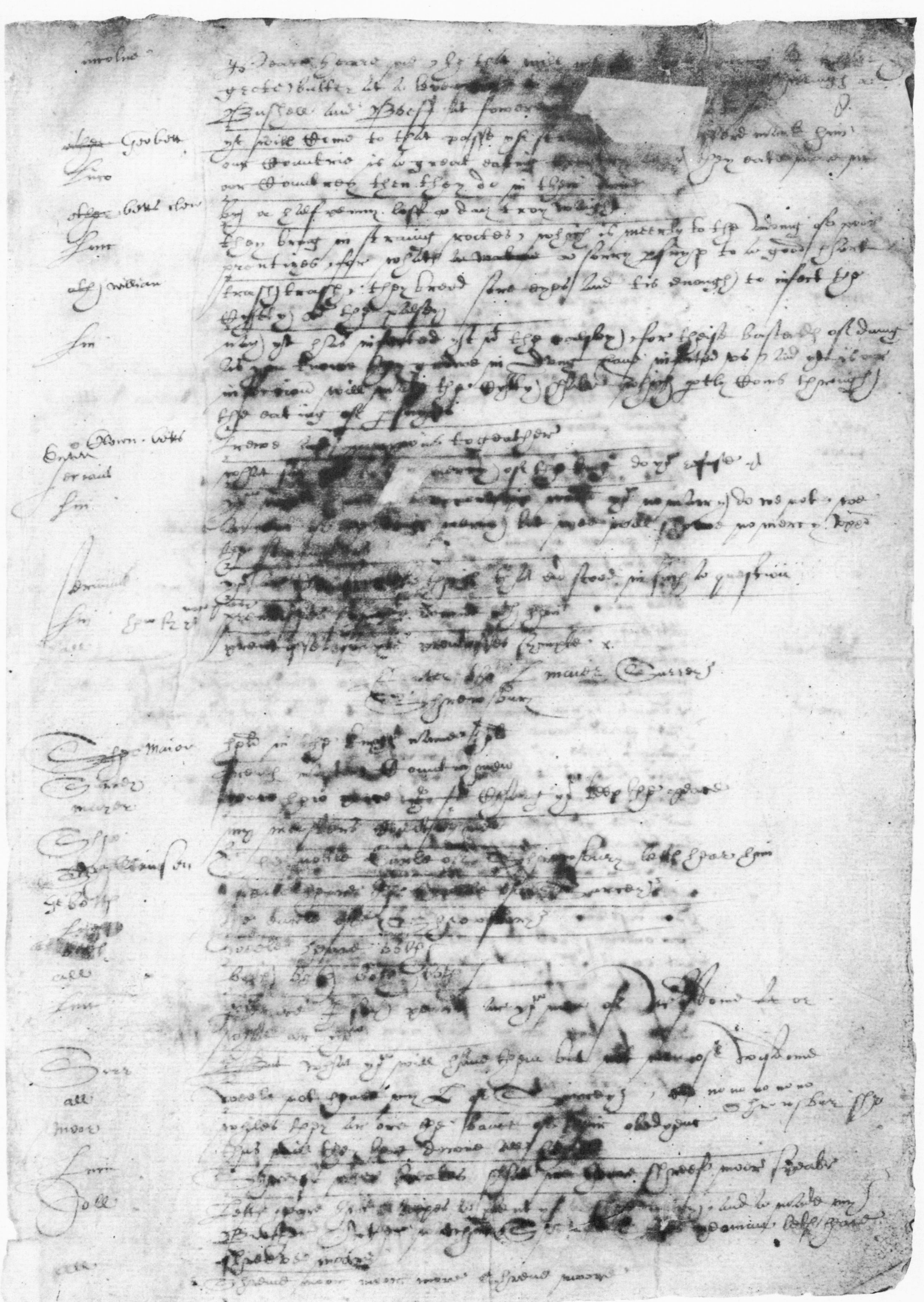

52 'SIR THOMAS MORE', ADDITION IIc, f. 8. *British Library MS. Harley 7368.*

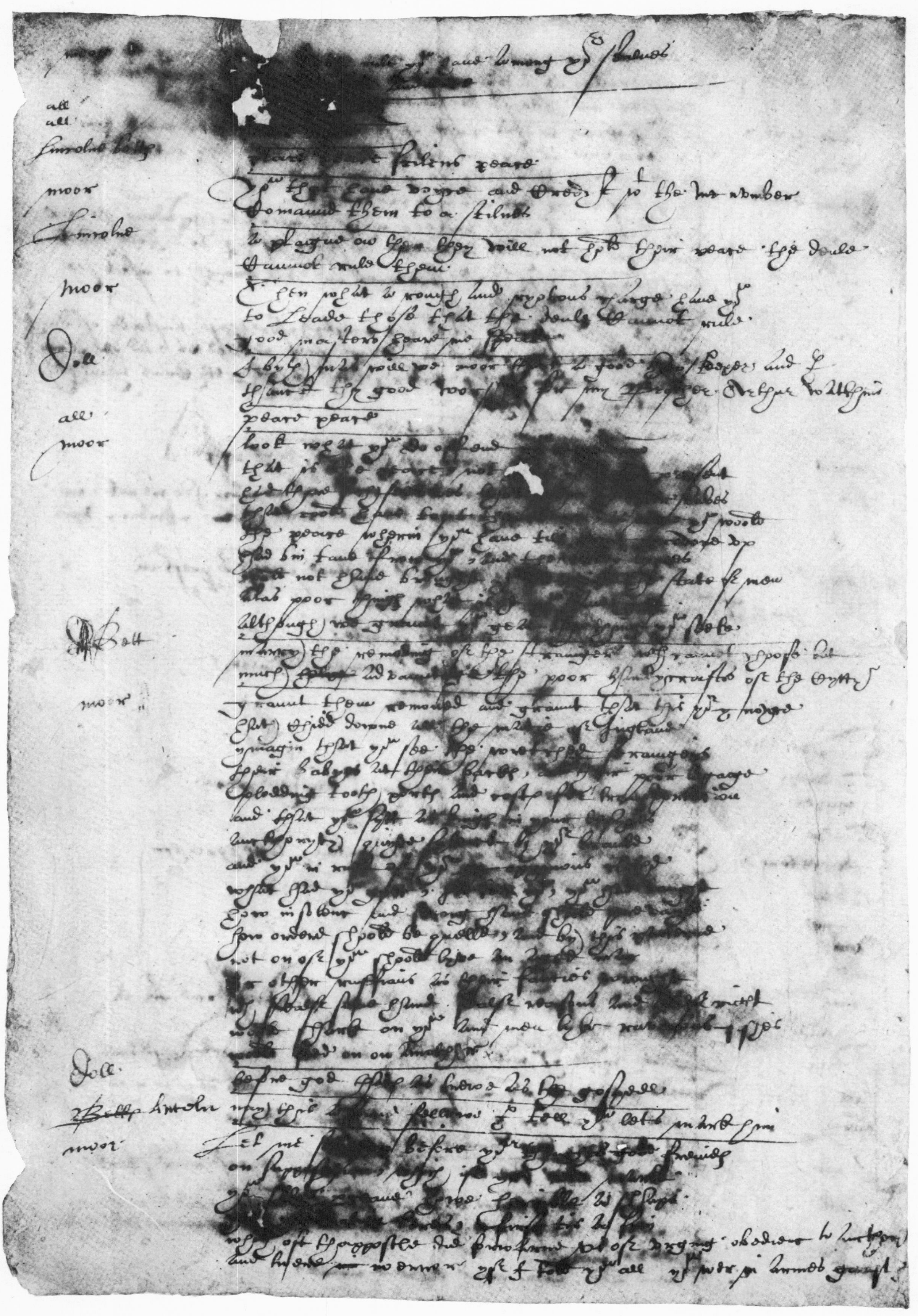

53 'SIR THOMAS MORE', ADDITION IIc, f. 8v. *British Library MS. Harley 7368.*

Opposite:
54 'SIR THOMAS MORE', ADDITION IIc, f. 9. *British Library MS. Harley 7368. Reproduced beneath the page is the speech-prefix 'all' on the verso.*

9

all marry god forbid that

moo nay certainly you are
for to the king god hath his offyc lent
of dread of Iustyce, power and Comaund
hath bid him rule, and willd you to obay
and to add ampler maiestie to this
he ~~god~~ hath not ~~le~~ only lent the king his figure
his throne and sword, but gyven him his owne name
calls him a god on earth, what do you then
rysing gainst him that god himsealf enstalls
but ryse gainst god, what do you to your sowles
in doing this o desperat as you are.
wash your foule mynds with teares and those same hands
that you lyke rebells lyft against the peace
lift vp for peace, and your vnreuerent knees
~~that~~ make them your feet to kneele to be forgyven
~~is safer warrs then euer you can make~~
~~whose discipline is ryot; why euen your hurly~~
~~cannot proceed but by obedienc~~ ~~tell me but this~~ what rebell captaine
as mutynes ar incident, by his name
can still the rout who will obay a traytor
or howe can well that proclamation sounde
when ther is no adicion but a rebell
to quallyfy a rebell, youle put downe straingers
kill them cutt their throts possesse their howses
and leade the maiestie of lawe in liom
to slipp him lyke a hound; ~~sayeng~~ say nowe the king
as he is clement, yf thoffendor moorne
shoold so much com to short of your great trespas
as but to banysh you, whether woold you go.
what country by the nature of your error
shoold gyve you harber go you to ffraunc or flanders
to any Iarman province, ~~to~~ spane or portigall
nay any where ~~why you~~ that not adheres to Ingland
why you must needs be straingers, woold you be pleasd
to find a nation of such barbarous temper
that breaking out in hiddious violence
woold not afoord you, an abode on earth
whett their detested knyves against your throtes
spurne you lyke doggs, and lyke as yf that god
owed not nor made not you, nor that the elaments
wer not all appropriat to your Comforts.
but Charterd vnto them, what woold you thinck
to be thus vsd, this is the straingers case
and this your mountanish inhumanyty

all fayth a saies trewe letts ~~vs~~ do as we may be doon by

~~all~~ Linco weele be ruld by you master moor yf youle stand our
freind to procure our pardon

moor Submyt you to theis noble gentlemen
entreate their mediation to the kinge
geve vp yor sealf to forme obay the maiestrate
and thers no doubt, but mercy may be found yf you so seek

all

4
Shakespeare Forgeries: Ireland and Collier

When a great man leaves behind no letters, diaries, or personal memorabilia of any kind, perhaps inevitably a credulous public will, with the passage of time, be mocked with those spurious inventions alone capable of gratifying curiosity and rendering the god human. Thus it happened with Shakespeare. Apart from a single *jeu d'esprit* (the fabricated Peele letter of 1763), the history of Shakespearian forgery begins in the closing years of the eighteenth century, after the enthronement of Shakespeare as National Poet and culture hero. The coronation ceremonies, presided over by the premier actor of the age, David Garrick, had taken place in Stratford in 1769. Now the stage was set for William-Henry Ireland. His puerile forgeries contrast instructively with those of John Payne Collier a half-century later, illustrating how in mischievous, as in more praiseworthy human pursuits, progress may be registered. Since I have already related the story in some detail in my *Shakespeare's Lives*, I shall here deal more compendiously with the principal events, incorporating however a few titbits of new information that have come my way since 1970, and allowing myself (here and there) to express second thoughts on the significance of familiar events.

I. William-Henry Ireland

William-Henry, whose meteoric two years of celebrity failed to escape the usual fate of meteors, was the only son of Samuel Ireland, an illustrator and antiquarian collector with magpie tendencies. He discreetly supplied (for profit) the needs of other collectors, and enjoyed some success with a series of books that combined a leisurely narrative of touristic perambulations with decorative engravings—insipid but technically better than adequate—of prospects and public buildings. In 1790 Ireland published *A Picturesque Tour through Holland, Brabant, and Part of France*, which set the pattern for subsequent volumes dealing with the English scene. He would pick a river—the Medway, the Thames, the Wye—and follow its meandering course. His *Picturesque Views on the Upper, or Warwickshire Avon, from its Source at Naseby, to its Junction with the Severn at Tewkesbury* (1795) includes a section on Stratford and our earliest depiction of Anne Hathaway's Cottage, which has since served for so many picturesque views. Ireland made notes and sketches for this volume during a visit to the Shakespeare country in the summer of 1794. His son accompanied him.

The pair tagged along while John Jordan, a failed wheelwright and autodidact who had found his niche as unofficial Stratford *cicerone*, pointed out the Shakespeare shrines. Samuel sketched the Birthplace interior, the Guild Chapel, Holy Trinity, with the Janssen monument, the poet's courting chair in Anne Hathaway's Cottage, and Shakespeare's crabtree, then still standing by the side of the road leading to Bidford. At Clopton House the gentleman-farmer occupant, a Mr. Williams, regaled Ireland with a tale about a roaring bonfire he had made, not a fortnight since, of bundles of papers bearing Shakespeare's name, in order to provide space in a small chamber for some young partridges. Samuel cursed bitterly, lamenting to heaven that he had not arrived sooner, while his son absorbed the scene in silence. After the day's excursions, over dinner at the inn, William-Henry listened to his father's transports upon 'the immortal and divine Shakspeare'.

When they returned to London and their house in the Strand looked after by Mrs. Freeman, *née* Anna Maria de Burgh Coppinger, Samuel's housekeeper and mistress (William-Henry's mother), the father's Shakespearian ecstasy gave no sign of abatement; instead 'his encomiums',

William-Henry reports in his *Confessions*, 'were unceasing; and he would frequently assert, that such was his veneration for the bard that he would willingly give half his library to become possessed even of his signature alone'.[1] William-Henry in due course supplied rather more than that. With furious energy he produced a whole library of Shakespeare signatures and documents. His demons urged him on to prove to the world his own genius and to win the approval of an aloof parent: once, while they were on the Thames, Samuel pointed out Pope's villa and, patting his son on the head, sighed, 'I fear you will never shine such a star in the hemisphere of literary fame'. The world, so far as it took note of William-Henry at all, deemed him a blockhead. This his father had concluded, with supporting documentation from the boy's Ealing schoolmaster, who informed 'Mr. Samuel Ireland', William-Henry later recalled, 'that I was so stupid as to be a disgrace to his school, and that, as he found it impossible to give me the least instruction, he would much rather I should not return after the holidays, as he (Mr. Shury) conceived it was no better than robbing Mr. Ireland of his money'.[2] This disgrace he gleefully reports in a section labelled 'Stupidity when a Child'. The Shakespeare forgeries would change all that. Of course a minor inconvenience was that William-Henry could not shine in the hemisphere of literary fame without also unmasking himself as an impostor.

The course of the imposture, from inception to exposure and its grotesque aftermath, is amply documented; in fact there exists almost a surfeit of primary materials in the form of published polemics and apologias, as well as manuscript diaries, letters, scrapbooks and marginalia, much of which Ireland's biographers have ignored. But the central documents are the compulsive confessions of William-Henry's mature years. They alone record how he set about his task, the impressions made by his forgeries when he first showed them to his father and visitors, and (not least) his own emotions. His printed *Confessions* of 1805 boasts the title-page motto, 'The whole truth, and nothing but the truth', to which he added in his own hand (in a Folger copy), 'So help me God'. But William-Henry's nemesis, Edmond Malone, was unimpressed by such solemn avowals of veracity. In his copy, now in the British Library, he wrote: 'There is as much *falsehood* in this Rogue's *Account* of his impudent forgery, as there was in the forgery itself; for scarcely a single circumstance is represented truly in all its parts.'[3]

He *was* a rogue, and even his *mea culpa* posturings harbour palpable lies. These begin (chronologically) with his birth-date. William-Henry claims that he embarked upon his fabrications 'at the age of seventeen years and three quarters'. In a marginal note alongside this statement Malone wrote, 'another *falsehood*', and he is right: the Ireland family Bible, now in the possession of Stuart B. Schimmel of New York, records William-Henry's birth on 2 August 1775. Thus he was nineteen when, on 16 December 1794, he presented his father with the first Shakespeare paper, a lease entered into by William Shakespeare and John Hemynge 'of thone Pte', and Michael Fraser and his wife Elizabeth 'of the othere Pte'. William-Henry's trifling deviation from truth in this instance served two functions: it demonstrated the precocity that is one manifestation of genius, and extenuated the guilt of a youthful offender. Still, despite the false leads strewn through the confessions, one can piece together the story of how the hoax was successfully perpetrated—provided one treads warily, acknowledging uncertainties, and wherever possible corroborating William-Henry's testimony from other sources.

The aforementioned lease was inscribed on a piece of old parchment torn from a rent-roll at Bingley's Chambers in the New Inn, where William-Henry day-dreamed away his afternoons as a conveyancer's clerk; he always had the wit to use genuine old paper or parchment. For ink he employed a concoction supplied by the bookbinder Laurie, consisting of three different fluids used to marble the covers of calf bindings. Because the ink appeared very faint when dry, the forger would hold his document for a few seconds over a fire, which darkened the colour but also—a regrettable side-effect—produced scorching. Still, few noticed. For the seals appended in former times to legal instruments, William-Henry plundered old deeds, scooped out cavities in the wax, inserted the pendent parchment tags, then refilled the cavities with melted fresh wax (old wax

1 *The Confessions of William-Henry Ireland* (1805), p. 45.

2 Ibid., p. 3.

3 Shelfmark C.182.aa.7, flyleaf.

crumbled), and finally rubbed soot and coal-ashes over the new seals to make the shade uniform. Handwriting models for Shakespeare were furnished by the signatures to the Blackfriars gate-house mortgage and the poet's will. These William-Henry claimed, falsely, to have taken from the facsimiles to the Johnson–Steevens *Shakespeare*. In fact he used Malone's 1790 edition; the latter would get credit for nothing. Discovery presented a constant threat, so the forger worked with pell-mell haste. Once Montague Talbot, a fellow clerk with theatrical aspirations, surprised him in the act. He was welcomed into the conspiracy.

For his second experiment William-Henry struck out more boldly and attempted Shake-spearian phraseology and handwriting, but prudently he did not stray from legal formulae, in this case a promissory note undertaking to repay his 'good and Worthye Freynd John Hemynge' £5.10*s*. 'for hys greate trouble [the Ireland forgeries abound in references to troubles taken] in settling and doinge much for me at the Globe Theatre'. Never mind that promissory notes did not yet exist, or that the document is dated 'September the Nynth 1589', a full decade before the construction of the Globe. Nobody yet knew when the theatre was built. In this forgery, as in almost all the others, William-Henry disdains any punctuation whatever. The 'Note of Hand' is in the familiar palsied scrawl of the Ireland papers. Needless to say, it shows no command of the Elizabethan secretary hand, but is evidently a travesty of the wavering signatures to Shakespeare's will. That the uncouth scripts of the Ireland forgeries deceived anyone may today seem incredible; one can only surmise that early English handwriting had become (except for a handful of scholars) an unknown calligraphy. Anyway, most of the deceived had no pretensions to such expertise. Suitably impressed with the antique paper and ink, they turned to the transcriptions supplied by William-Henry.

Prosaic legal instruments hardly stretched the imagination of a genius; soon he was embarking upon Shakespearian flights. The Profession of Faith, designed to undermine the assumption (fostered by the purgatorial Ghost in *Hamlet*) that the playwright had embraced Catholicism, contains not a single reference to the Blessed Virgin and the Saints amongst its pieties, in the most affecting of which Shakespeare implores his creator to 'cherishe usse like the sweete Chickenne thatte under the coverte offe herre spreadynge Wings Receyves herre lyttle Broode ande hoverynge oerre themme keepes themme harmlesse ande in safetye'. (The orthography, with its promiscuous terminal *e*'s and doubling of consonants, furnishes one of the more delicious pleasures of the forgeries.) Here, as was his wont, Shakespeare improves upon Scripture. 'O Jerusalem, Jerusalem, killing the prophets and stoning those who are sent to you!', Jesus laments in the Temple, in Matthew's Gospel: 'How often would I have gathered your children together as a hen gathers her brood under her wings, and you would not!'

An epistle from Queen Elizabeth thanking 'goode Masterre William' for his 'prettye Verses' proved that Shakespeare had admirers in the best circles. Master William's letter to Anna Hatherrewaye demonstrated the tenderness of his conjugal affection. Accompanying the letter was a lock of bardic hair—short, straight, and wiry, as (to William-Henry's astigmatic eye) Droeshout had represented it—tied with thick woven silk fetched from an ancient patent where it had served to affix the Great Seal; also a quintet of verses addressed to the same object of adoration. The second stanza affords a fair specimen:

Though fyckle fortune prove unkynde
Stille dothe she leave herre wealthe behynde
She neere the hearte canne forme anew
Norre make thye Willys love unnetrue[1]

Other treasures included a letter to Southampton, whose bounty nourished the hand of gratitude, 'which Bllossommes Bllooms butte never dyes itte cherishes sweete Nature ande lulls the calme Breaste toe softe softe repose'; also Southampton's reply, noting that his favourite had accepted only half the proffered bounty.

1 For the Ireland forgeries I quote from the texts given by William-Henry himself in *Miscellaneous Papers and Legal Instruments under the Hand and Seal of William Shakspeare* (1796), unpaged. Not surprisingly, Ireland's transcriptions sometimes differ, as regards accidentals, from the invented papers reproduced in facsimile in the same volume, and (more markedly) from later copies made by the author for collectors.

Profeſſion of Faith.

I BEYNGE nowe offe ſounde Mynde doe l
thatte thys mye wyſhe wille atte mye deathe
acceeded toe as I nowe lyve in Londonne and
mye ſoule maye perchance ſoone quitte thys p
Bodye it is mye deſire thatte inne ſuche caſe I n
bee carryed to mye native place ande thatte
Bodye bee there quietlye interred wythe as
pompe as canne bee ande I doe nowe inne th
mye ſeyriouſe Moments make thys mye profeſſ
of fayth and whiche I doe moſte ſolemnlye bel
I doe fyrſte looke toe oune lovynge and greate
ande toe hys gloriouſe ſonne Jeſus I doe alſoe
leyve thatte thys mye weake ande frayle Bo
wille retturne toe duſte butte forre mye ſoule
God judge thatte as toe hymſſelfe ſhalle ſe
meete O omnipotente ande greate God I am
offe Synne I doe notte thynke myſelfe worthye
thye grace ande yette wille I hope forre evene
poore pryſonerre whenne bounde with gallyng I
evenne hee wille hope for Pittye ande whenne
teares offe ſweete repentance bathe hys wretc
pillowe he then looks ande hopes forre pardo
thenne rouze mye Soule ande lette hope th
ſweete cheriſher offe alle afforde thee comf
alſoe O Manne whatte arte thou whye conſide
thou thyſelfe thus greatelye where are thye g
thye boaſted attrybutes buryed loſte forre ev
inne colde Deathe. O Manne whye attemp

55 THE PROFESSION OF FAITH. *From Folger Shakespeare Library MS. W.b.497. This compilation consists of Ireland forgeries mounted with the corresponding printed transcripts; also portraits of Shakespeare, extracts from Rowe's Life, and specimens of Mrs. Freeman's handwriting. Ireland fed, literally as well as figuratively, off his notoriety by turning out souvenir scrapbooks for well-heeled collectors of curiosa. Thus the Profession of Faith as here reproduced is an imitation of a forgery. For it Ireland consulted the reader's convenience by following the lineation of the quarto edition of* Miscellaneous Papers and Legal Instruments, *published in the same year as the folio.* *The Profession continues on the next page.*

Profession of Faith.

toe searche the greatenesse offe the Almyghtye
doste butte loose thye labourre more thou
pteste more arte thou loste tille thye poore
e thoughtes arre elevated toe theyre summite
thence as snowe fromme the leffee Tree droppe
disstylle themselves tille theye are noe more
d Manne as I am frayle bye Nature fulle offe
yette greate God receyve me toe thye
nme where alle is sweete contente ande
ynesse alle is blysse where discontente isse
re hearde butte where oune Bonde offe freynd-
e unytes alle Menne Forgive O Lorde alle
synnes ande withe thye grete Goodnesse take
lle to thye Breaste O cherishe usse like the
Chickenne thatte under the coverte offe herre
ynge Wings Receyves herre lyttle Broode
hoveringe oerre themme keepes themme
esse ande in safetye

Wm Shakspeare

That Shakespeare had a patron the world already knew from the dedications of his two narrative poems; his Deed of Gift to Ireland breaks new ground. An Elizabethan William Ireland, haberdasher, had existed, and was recorded as being in 1604 a tenant of the Blackfriars gate-house that Shakespeare acquired nine years later. It was not, however, previously realised that this William Ireland had the additional Christian name Henry, or that he had participated in the exploit gratefully remembered by the poet in the Deed of Gift sealed and delivered on 25 October 1604:

Whereas onne or abowte the thyrde daye of the last monethe beyng the monethe of Auguste havynge withe mye goode freynde Masterre William Henrye Irelande ande otherres taene boate neare untowe myne house afowresayde wee dydd purpose goynge upp Thames butt those thatte were soe toe connducte us beynge muche toe merrye throughe Lyquorre they didd upsette oure fowresayde bayrge alle butte myeselfe savedd themselves bye swimmyng for though the Waterre was deepe yette owre beynge close nygh toe shore made itte lyttel dyffyculte for themm knowinge the fowresayde Arte Masterre William henrye Irelande notte seeynge mee dydd aske for mee butte oune of the Companye dydd answerre thatte I was drownynge onn the whyche he pulledd off hys Jerrekynne and Jumpedd inn afterre mee withe muche paynes he draggedd mee forthe I beynge then nearelye deade and soe he dydd save mye life and for the whyche Service I doe herebye give hym as folowithe!!!

Dearesste Anna

As thou haste alwaye founde mee toe mye Worde moste
trewe soe thou shalt see I have stryctlye kepte
mye promyse I praye you perfume thys mye poore Locke
withe thy balmye Kysses forre thenne indeede shalle Kynges
themmeselves bowe ande paye homage toe itte I doe assure
thee no rude hande hathe knottedde itte thye Willys alone
hathe done the worke Neytherre the gyldedde bawble thatte
envyronnes the heade of Majestye noe norre honourres moste
weyghtye wulde give mee halfe the joye as didde
thysse mye lyttle worke forre thee The feelinge
thatte dydde neareste approache untoe itte was thatte
whiche commethe nygheste untoe God meeke ande
gentle Charytye forre thatte Virrtue O Anna doe I
love doe I cheryshe thee inne mye hearte forre thou
arte ass a talle Cedarre stretchynge forthe its branches
ande succourynge the smallere Plants fromme nyppynge
Winneterre orr the boysterouse Wyndes Farewelle toe
Morrowe bye tymes I wille see thee tille thenne
Adewe sweete Love

Thyne everre

Wm Shakspeare

56 SHAKESPEARE'S LETTER TO HIS DEAREST ANNA. *From* Shakspeare's Manuscripts, *vol. i,* Kynge Lear &c, *f. 111, in the collection of Mrs. Donald F. Hyde at Four Oaks Farm, New Jersey. The transcription appears in Ireland's* Confessions, *f. 123, in the Hyde collection.*

Opposite:
57 THE SHAKESPEARE LOCK. *From Ireland's* Confessions, *f. 124, in the collection of Mrs. Donald F. Hyde at Four Oaks Farm, New Jersey.*

The

Remaining part of the
Lock of Hair.

On the ensuing Page will be
found a full Account of the
Epistle from Shakspear to his
Love Ann Hatherway

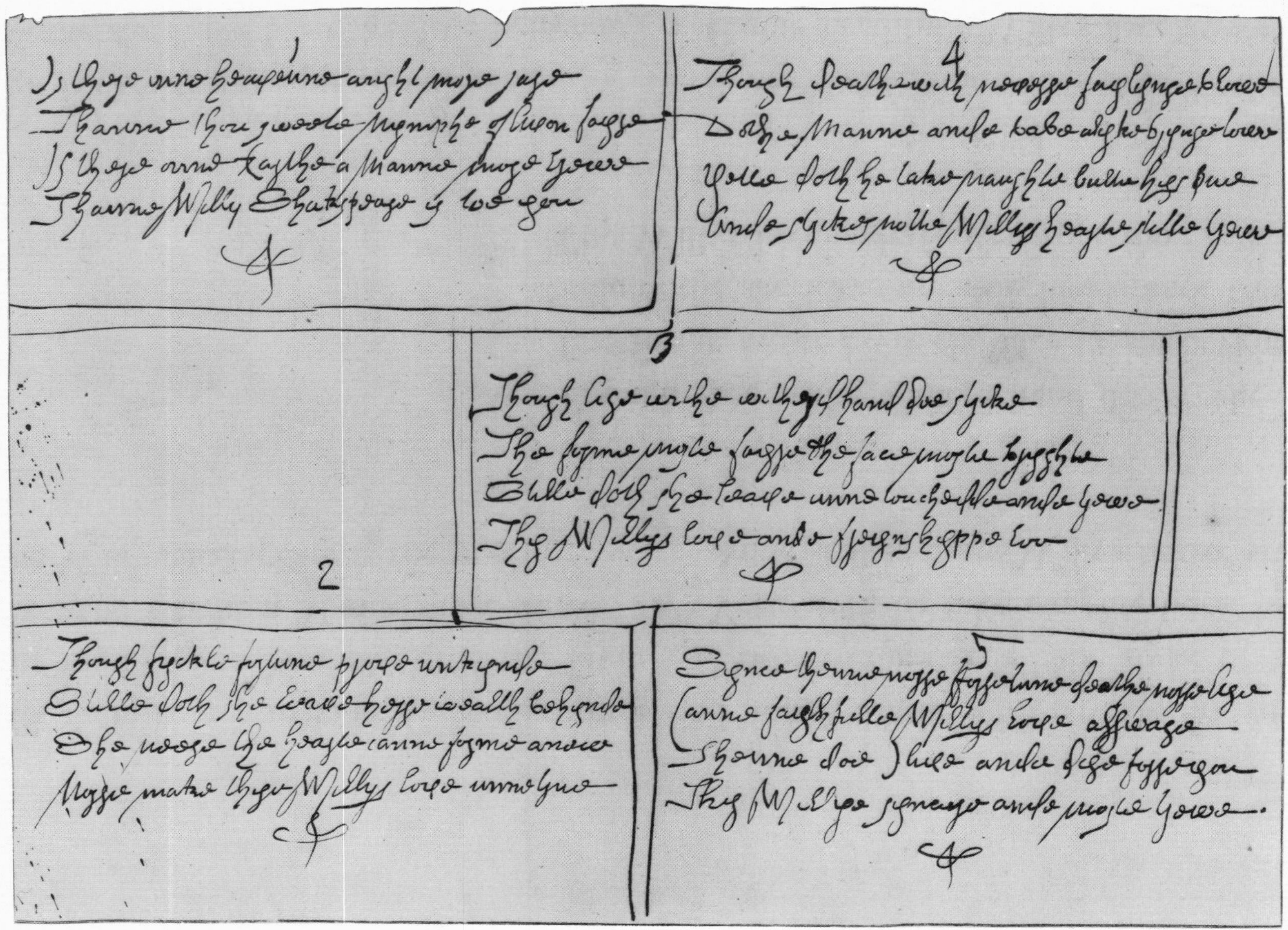

58 SHAKESPEARE'S VERSES TO ANNA HATHERREWAYE. *From* Miscellaneous Papers and Legal Instruments under the Hand and Seal of William Shakespeare, *1796. Underneath an inserted portrait of Samuel Ireland opposite the title-page of Folger Shakespeare Library copy no. 2* (*shelfmark: PR 2950.A22a.Cage*), *used for this facsimile, William-Henry notes that the copy was intended for presentation to the gentleman-owner of the papers: 'I was requested by my Father to enquire of him* [*Mr. H*] *in what manner he would have the Volume bound my answer was blue Morocco . . .'. The bookseller William Scott provided the binding. When the copy proved undeliverable to the intended recipient, the forger exchanged it for some black-letter volumes in Scott's shop.*

The bequest, made to Ireland and his heirs or next of kin 'for everre', includes the manuscripts of *Kyng Leare* (not yet written) and *Kyng henry thyrde of Englande*, one of Shakespeare's less well-known plays. Shakespeare also expressed his devotion poetically in 'Tributary Lines' thanking 'hys freynde hys IRELAND. . . . Modelle of Virretue Charytyes sweeteste Chylde'; in effect Ireland expresses poignant emotion for Ireland.

By inventing William Henrye our William-Henry (whose own antecedents were dubious) provided himself with a genealogy; one, moreover, congenial to adolescent fantasies of romantic heroism. More practically, he established his claim to the Shakespeare Papers in the event that—as a visitor to Norfolk Street suggested might conceivably happen—some descendant of Shakespeare came forward to claim them.

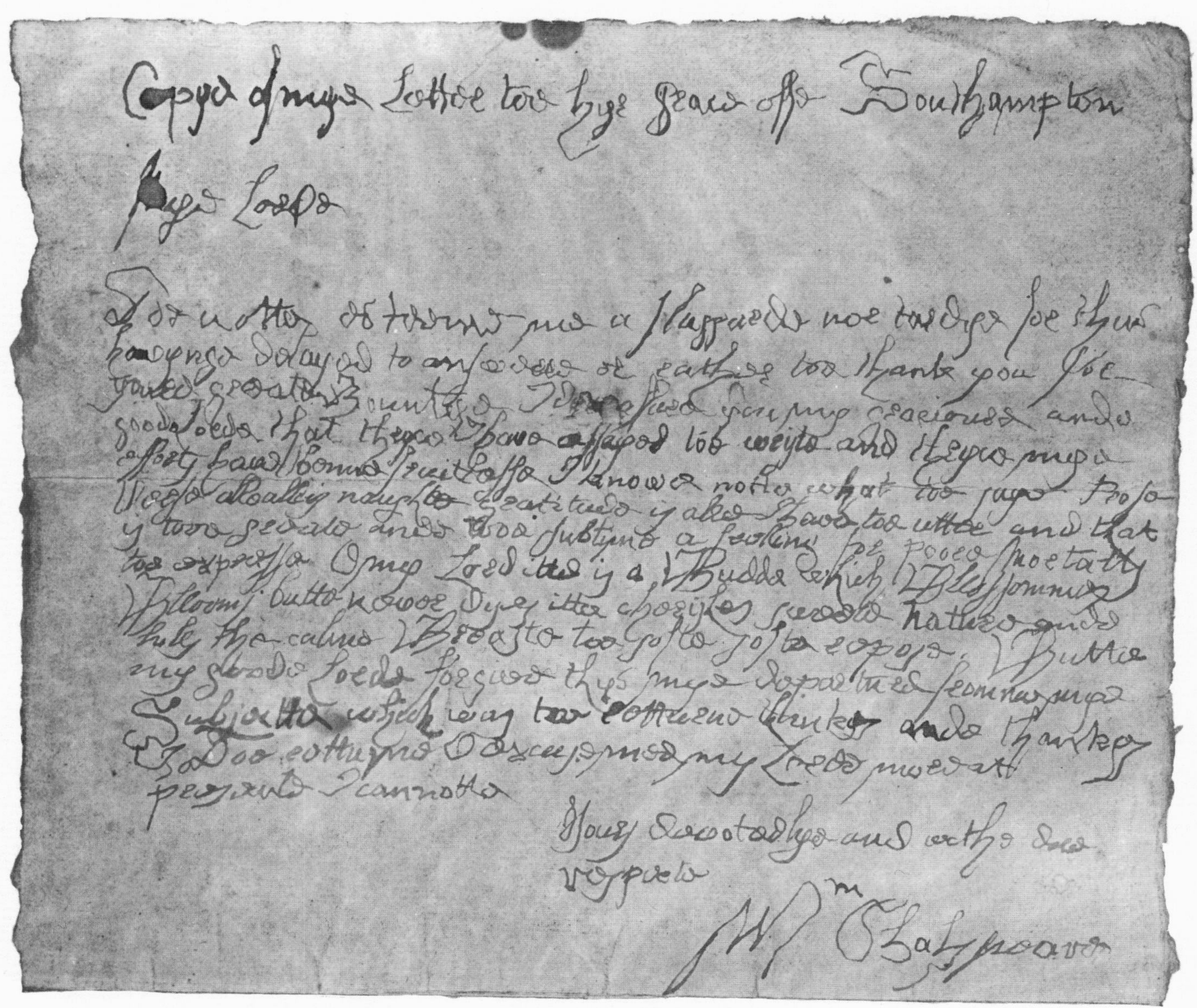

Copye of mye Letter too hys grace offe Southampton

Mye Lorde

59 SHAKESPEARE'S LETTER TO SOUTHAMPTON. *From* Shakspeare's Manuscripts, *vol. i,* Kynge Lear &c, *f. 113, in the collection of Mrs. Donald F. Hyde at Four Oaks Farm, New Jersey. Ireland furnishes a transcription in his* Miscellaneous Papers and Legal Instruments.

Most imposing is a complete manuscript of *Kynge Leare* in the author's hand (and therefore completely innocent of punctuation), which makes numerous improvements upon the received texts. Thus Kent's unfortunately truncated final speech—'I have a journey, sir, shortly to go. / My master calls me; I must not say no'—is at last given entire and uncorrupted:

Thanks Sir butte I goe toe thatte unknowne Land
Thatte Chaynes each Pilgrim faste within its Soyle
Bye livynge menne mouste shunnd mouste dreadedde
Stille mye goode masterre thys same Journey tooke
He calls mee I amme contente ande strayght obeye
Thenne farewelle Worlde the busye Sceane is done

Years later, no less discriminating a judge than William-Henry himself allowed he was 'so arrogant as to believe [these lines] would not injure the reputation of Shakspeare'.[1]

If Ireland's *Leare* purged Shakespeare's tragedy of the ribaldry and other unworthinesses foisted upon the playhouse copies by the vulgar actors, the forgeries in general served a similar virtuous

1 *Confessions*, p. 118.

60 SHAKESPEARE'S PORTRAIT. *From* Shakspeare's Manuscripts, *vol. i, f. 108, in the collection of Mrs. Donald F. Hyde at Four Oaks Farm, New Jersey. When Samuel Ireland, more knowledgeable about pictures than he was about old manuscripts, dismissed the sketch as 'an inexplicable paper and of no consequence', William-Henry retrieved his credit by the next day producing a letter in which Shakespeare teasingly describes the portrait as a 'whymsycalle conceyte'. The significance of the 'witty conundrum', as William-Henry terms it, forthwith became the subject of learned investigation, but to no avail.*

purpose, and reveal their perpetrator as a youth of generous sentiment and fastidious morality. Shakespeare emerges as a sincere adherent of the Established Church, a loving husband, generous friend, and correct playwright. No Dark Lady casts a shadow over these Shakespeare Papers.

In order to pass off his fabrication William-Henry had to establish some sort of pedigree for them, and so he invented Mr. H, a wealthy young gentleman who kept the papers, along with

61 JOHN NIXON, THE OAKEN CHEST, OR THE GOLD MINES OF IRELAND, 1796. *Item D.G. 8884 in the Department of Prints and Drawings of the British Museum. Mary Dorothy George* (Catalogue, *vii. 98) notes that gold was discovered in the Wicklow Mountains in autumn 1795. A merchant in Basinghall Street, London, and talented amateur artist, John Nixon was a caricaturist of some hilarity. He exhibited frequently at the Royal Academy between 1784 and 1815, and was for some years secretary to the Beefsteak Club. His views included seats of the nobility and gentry in England and Ireland. Nixon died in 1818. The print is here reduced by about one half.*

bundles of other old documents, in a large chest in his chambers. Having taken a fancy to William-Henry, he was content to let him use these curiosities as the latter deemed fit, on condition only that Mr. H's identity and abode remained hidden. So Samuel was told. Eventually he entered into correspondence with (in his phrase) 'the gent', who was importuned for more documents—'not only papers but pictures drawings &c'—and, above all, for a personal interview, so as to

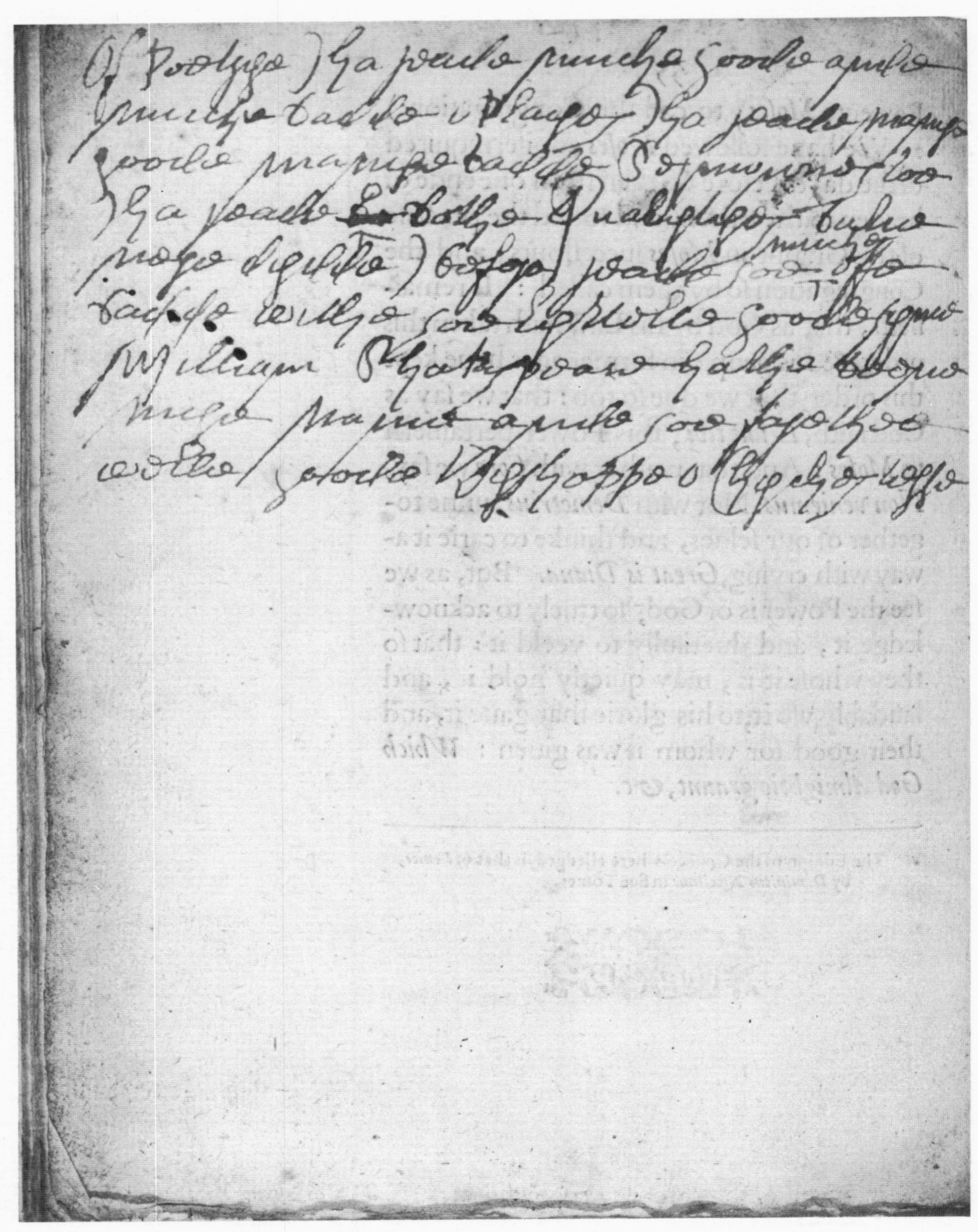

62 SHAKESPEARE PASSES A LITERARY JUDGMENT. *From Lancelot Andrewes,* A Sermon Preached before the Kings Majestie at Hampton Court, Concerning the Right and Power of calling Assemblies . . . *(1606), sig. H2ᵛ; copy in the collection of Stuart B. Schimmel of New York City. The transcription (opposite) is included in the same volume.*

resolve the inevitable questions about provenance which William-Henry's testimony could not on its own answer. Mr. H, however, preferred to dwell on the excellences of William-Henry. 'The more I see of him the more I am amaz'd—', the gent confessed. 'If your *Son* is not a second Shakspeare I am not a *Man.*' True. In this letter, as in others from Mr. H, William-Henry did not bother to disguise his hand. His father never noticed.

Samuel had early on shown some of his treasures to antiquarian acquaintances—the Revd. Dr. Samuel Parr, for example, and Joseph Warton, the editor of Pope—who bestowed appropriate homage. In February 1795 Ireland threw open the doors of his house in Norfolk Street to the public. So great was the press that he was forced to limit admission to ticket-holders (subscribers

Of Poetrye I ha reade
muche goode ande muche
badde Playes I ha reade
manye goode manye badde
Sermonnes toe I ha reade
o bothe Qualytyes butte
nere dydde I before reade
soe muche offe badde withe
soe lyttelle Goode synce
William Shakspeare hathe
beene mye Name ande soe
farethee welle goode Byshoppe
o Chychesterre —

to a forthcoming edition of the Papers) and their guests. The faithful came: Francis Webb, secretary at the College of Heralds, and George Chalmers, who, even after the balloon burst, would produce two large volumes of *Apology for the Believers in the Shakspeare-Papers*; also (a few months before his death) James Boswell. For some time Boswell studied the exhibits set before him, and, having refreshed himself with a warm brandy and water, knelt down before a volume of the papers and said, 'I now kiss the invaluable relics of our bard: and thanks to God that I have lived to see them!' With reverence he kissed them, then left. Thus William-Henry describes the visit, and if one is tempted to doubt this report, as others, it is confirmed by Samuel, whose account is (not unexpectedly) rather less colourful.[1] The great scholar Joseph Ritson, not yet mad, also came to Norfolk Street, and left in silence; he was not amused. The Prince of Wales expectedly kept aloof from the throng, but royal recognition came to Samuel in the form of an audience at Carlton House.

1 See John Mair, *The Fourth Forger: William Ireland and the Shakespeare Papers* (1938), p. 66n.

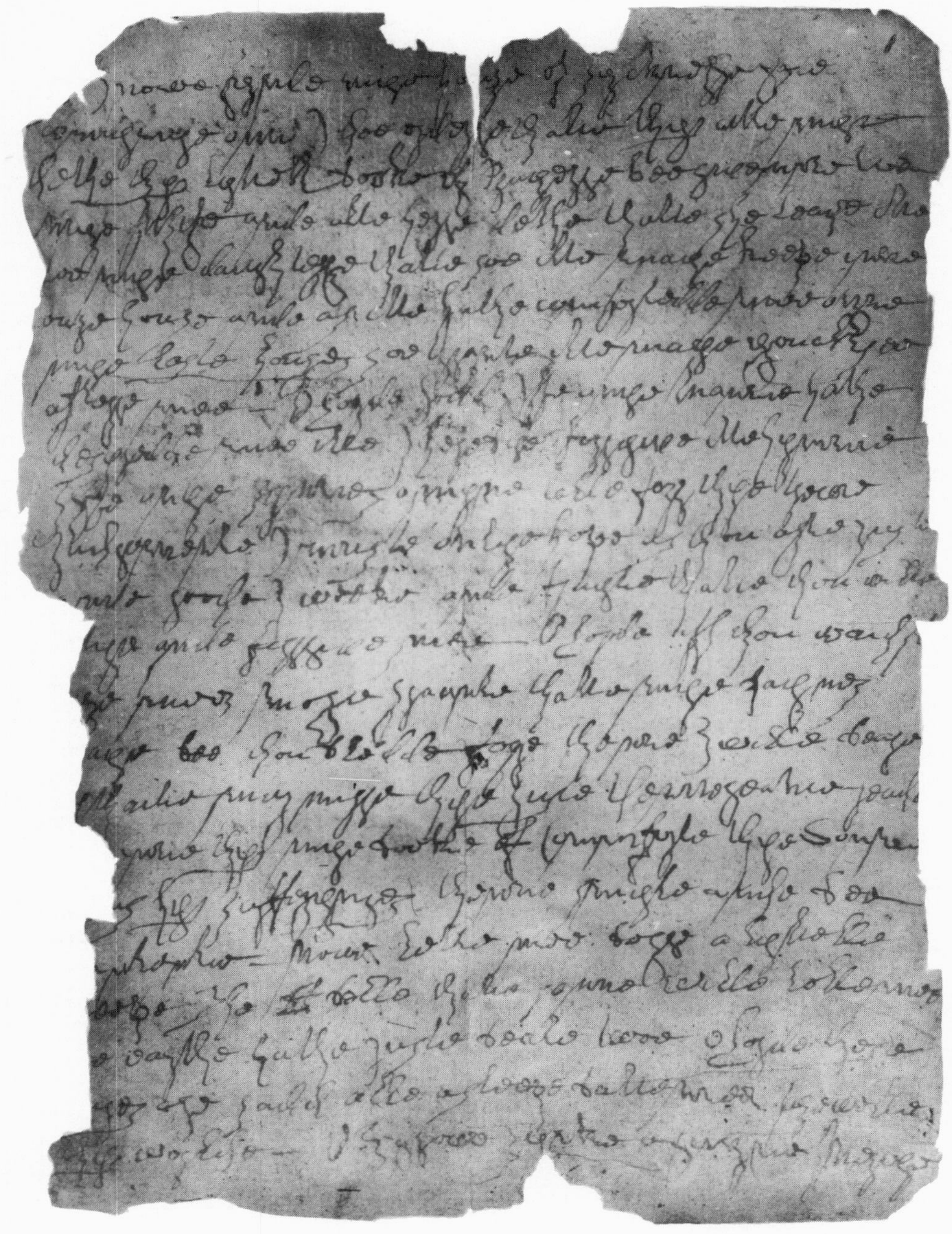

The greatest Shakespearian authority of the age also stayed away. Malone, unwilling to be drawn into making a pronouncement based upon a cursory viewing, tried to borrow the documents for inspection in the privacy of his own study. Using the artist Ozias Humphry as intermediary, he made the approach (at a second remove) through Thomas Caldecott, a minor Shakespeare devotee and editor on the periphery of the Ireland circle. It was an unwise choice: Caldecott loathed Malone, and gleefully returned word to him (*via* Humphry) that Samuel had no intention of showing the Shakespeare Papers 'to any Commentator or Shakspere monger whatever'. Malone had no choice but to bide his time.

His opportunity came when Samuel published his edition of *Miscellaneous Papers and Legal Instruments under the hand and seal of William Shakspeare: Including the tragedy of King Lear and a small fragment of Hamlet, from the original MSS. in the possession of Samuel Ireland, of Norfolk Street.* This ludicrously sumptuous folio comprised—in addition to transcriptions—numerous facsimiles of the Shakespeare Papers, some in colour. The volume, published on Christmas Eve 1795, gave Malone all the ammunition he required. Meanwhile, at Drury Lane Theatre, plans moved ahead for the first performance of *Vortigern*, a new manuscript play by Shakespeare recovered from Mr. H's inexhaustible treasure-chest.

This is one of the worthy Mr. Saml. Ireland junior's impudent & clumsy forgeries.
The paper has been fried by the hot poker till it has cracked to pieces F.D.

63 SHAKESPEARE'S DEATHBED TESTIMONIAL. *Bodleian Library, MS. Douce e. 8. Neither this declaration nor Shakespeare's animadversions on the Bishop of Chichester (item 62) appear in* Miscellaneous Papers and Legal Instruments. *The appended note is by Francis Douce.*

On 31 March 1796 Malone published *An Inquiry into the Authenticity of Certain Miscellaneous Papers and Legal Instruments, published Dec. 24, MDCCXCV. and attributed to Shakspeare, Queen Elizabeth, and Henry, Earl of Southampton: Illustrated by fac-similes of the genuine hand-writing of that nobleman, and of her Majesty; a new fac-simile of the hand-writing of Shakspeare, never before exhibited; and other authentick Documents.* This four-hundred page book, the astonishing product of two months' labour, represents a total assault on the pretensions of the Shakespeare Papers; Malone deploys all his awesome power as a scholar—and prosecuting attorney—against this 'imputed trash' in its every aspect: provenance, handwriting, orthography, diction, and historical circumstances.

Such bombardment the papers could not sustain. *Vortigern*, acted two days after the appearance of Malone's *Inquiry*, was hooted off the stage, a fiasco to which Kemble's subversive performance contributed. In November, William-Henry owned up to his delinquencies in *An Authentic Account of the Shaksperian Manuscripts, &c.*, designed to absolve Samuel and to win forgiveness for what was, after all, 'the act of a boy'; his sole object, he protests, was to give his father pleasure. The latter in the same month published *Mr. Ireland's Vindication of his Conduct, respecting the publication of the supposed Shakspeare MSS.* In this apologia he sought not to authenticate the papers but to defend his character against the aspersions of Malone, who had branded him with the name of impostor. Pathetically Samuel rehearses, from the preface to *Miscellaneous Papers and Legal Instruments*, the circumstances that brought the papers into his hands; he quotes exculpatory letters from his son and Montague Talbot; he solemnly protests his innocence. All to no avail. Miserable, he returned to the pamphlet wars again with *An Investigation of Mr. Malone's Claim to the Character of Scholar, or Critic*, undated but probably 1797. The disputed documents he now describes as presenting a 'doubtful and mysterious question'; Malone, no less than they, has become his obsession. So he cites, from Elizabethan sources, spellings (e.g. *ande*, *archebishop*, *doe*) and usages (*complement*, *excellence*, etc.) which Malone claimed did not then exist. Ireland scores some points, but they hardly mattered; Malone did not deign to reply.

Still Samuel's demons drove him on. The year before his death he published *Vortigern* and *Henry II*, in his preface excoriating Malone, with his 'mass of dulness and self-conceit', mere 'trash', and averring that nothing could 'induce him to believe that great part of the mass of papers in his possession are the fabrication of any individual, or set of men of the present day'.[1] In an inexpressibly sad Advertisement to *Henry II* he confides in the public—why should they care?—that he has seen his son only once in nearly three years, and that he cannot credit William-Henry's confessions, 'as they stand in direct opposition to what had been before solemnly stated as fact'. He is incapable, he reiterates in a final italicised paragraph, of deliberate imposture or of laying before the public as genuine any papers in which he did not himself believe.

His avowals fell on deaf ears. Samuel's reputation, and along with it his business, collapsed. Obloquy was heaped upon him. The columns of one newspaper compared him with Abraham offering up his own son Isaac as a sacrifice; Samuel lacerated himself by clipping it out and pasting it in his scrapbook. But what stung the worst was Gillray's savage engraving which shows him clasping to his bosom 'Ireland's *Shakspeare*': it bears the title, 'Notorious Characters. N° 1.'; and, below, this inscription: 'Mr Bromley in his Catalogue &c. p. 390. has erroneously put this Portrait into his SEVENTH Class.—It ought to have appeared in the TENTH. See the Contents of it. p. 449.' Samuel duly turned to the page, and found that the class referred to was that of 'Convicts and persons otherwise remarkable'. In his desperation and anger he thought of instituting libel proceedings, a course from which his solicitor prudently dissuaded him. Eventually hope deserted Samuel, while illness wasted his body. In July 1800, his spirits and his heart broken—so his physician remembered him—he died.

A few years before Ireland's death, just as the dust had begun to settle, a reasonably balanced view of the *affaire* was set down by Caldecott. He had been among the first to view the Shakespeare Papers, and followed the course of the imposture attentively. It was largely Caldecott who furnished Samuel with the material for his *Investigation.* On 30 November 1797 he wrote to a friend in the country:

> The real secret of this audacious & wholesale Imposture has not yet been divulged: &, tho' the world, naturally enough, will never be brought to believe, that the Son & Father were not knowingly playing into one anothers hands, I have been throughout the whole of this business, & am now, thoroughly satisfied, that Ireland, the Father, was both innocent, & intirely ignorant of the Authors as he was of the management of this Fraud. He was, I am assured, the dupe of a Son, to whom it may have been, that he had given an example & in part accomplished in Arts, w^h were after practised against himself. The Son has published to the World, that he is the author of every thing sent out into it or exhibited in this business. This in the extent stated (i.e. that he was capable of writing the small pieces first produced) no Individual throughout it ever gave the smallest credit to. His Father was strongly persuaded, that by some artifice, Fraud or worse he got possession of some antient Papers & Instruments; & that from some such materials these were by somebody (some of them probably by himself) manufactured. Neither one or the other of them to my certain knowledge are capable of writing a sentence of English correctly, or know even the common parts of Speech.[2]

1 *'Vortigern' . . . and 'Henry the Second'*, ed. Samuel Ireland (1799), p. v.

2 Letter inserted in a bound volume of pamphlets, entitled *Shakespeare Papers*, in the Folger Shakespeare Library; shelfmark: PR 2950.B5. Copy 2. Cage.

The Spirit of Shakspere appearing to his Detracters

Tremble, thou wretch,
That hast within thee Undivulged crimes.
Unwhipp'd of justice.
Shakspeare.

Ah me, Ah me, O dear, O dear,
What Spectre's this, approaching here.

Surely tis Shakspeare's injured shade.
It fills my soul with so much dread
It is, it is, thus on our knees,
Let's strive his anger to appease.
O Father of the British Stage.
Whose wit has charm'd from age to age

Pardon the base unworthy flame.
That Burnt to rob thee of thy fame
But now this Solemn mockry's o'er
Thy gracious mercy wee implore
We'll never more disgrace thy page.
Our Brains were gone a pilgrimage

64 SILVESTER HARDING, THE SPIRIT OF SHAKSPERE APPEARING TO HIS DETRACTORS, 1796. *Item D.G. 8883 in the Department of Prints and Drawings of the British Museum. Like Nixon (item 61), Harding implicates the entire family in the Ireland forgeries: Samuel, his mistress/housekeeper, and their two daughters, besides William-Henry. The brother and partner of the printseller Edward Harding, Silvester (1745–1809) achieved some reputation for his portraits of theatrical personages and his book illustrations, including the 150 plates, mostly derivative, provided for* Shakespeare Illustrated, by an assemblage of Portraits & Views, appropriated to the Whole Suite, of our Authors Historical Dramas, to which are added Portraits, of Actors, Editors, &c. *(1793). The print is here reduced.*

Caldecott, it is clear, has—like Samuel and the rest—underestimated William-Henry's powers of invention; but he has gauged public opinion accurately enough.

For despite the son's several confessions the world held Samuel equally or more guilty. William Mason's verses in 1797, vilifying the 'Four forgers born in one prolific age', make Samuel—not William-Henry—the fourth son of Fraud, after Lauder, Macpherson, and Chatterton. Mason's lines were duly appended to the Gillray engraving. In his obituary for Samuel Ireland in the *Gentleman's Magazine* for September 1800, the anonymous memorialist remarked:

It was averred, both by father and son, that the imposition originated with, and was entirely conducted by, the young man, without the privity or participation of his parent; but this fact many strong circumstances lead us to doubt: the complicity appears obvious, and it even seems that some part of the forgery could not have been conducted by the son alone.[1]

The belief in Samuel's complicity persisted. In 1855 a contributor to *Willis's Current Notes* went so far as to allege that the father devised the whole affair, with his elder daughter inventing the forgeries, while 'the redoubtable William Henry was merely a copier'. In the *Life* long accepted as standard, Sidney Lee seems to implicate Samuel when he speaks of 'the fraud of the Irelands', and William Jaggard, in his *Shakespeare Bibliography*, finds it 'difficult to believe him entirely free of blame'.

Yet the Ireland papers in the British Library attest to Samuel's gullibility; he actually did correspond with Mr. H. A wise father knows his own son; but this one was not wise. A letter to one G. Charles George, dated 26 June 1797, shows how slow reason was in breaking down the fortifications of credulity. 'My opinion is—', Samuel said of the Shakespeare Papers, 'that they have been stolen—& that he [William-Henry] is afraid to declare ye truth for fear of Consequences.'[2] On his deathbed Samuel declared, in his physician's presence, 'that he was totally ignorant of the deceit, and was equally a believer in the authenticity of the manuscripts as those which were even the most credulous'.[3] Ireland's will contains the following bequest: 'I give to my son William Henry Ireland the repeating watch I have generally worn with the seals appendant and as I wish to die in peace and good will with all mankind I hereby freely and sincerely forgive my said son for having made me the innocent agent of mischief and imposition and do give unto him 20 pounds for mourning.'[4] Such testimonials must carry weight, and more recent students, while acknowledging the complexity of Samuel's character, have tended to accept him at his word.

They have not, however, reckoned with a tantalising insight furnished by William-Henry's *Full and Explanatory Account of the Shaksperian Forgery*, an unpublished manuscript in the Hyde Collection at Four Oaks Farm in New Jersey. This manuscript antedates the more cunningly rationalised 1805 *Confessions*. Among the non-literary documents dealing with theatrical and pecuniary matters, and designed mainly to swell the store of papers, was (William-Henry relates) a note recording payment to Shakespeare of £50 for 'oure Trouble' in playing before the Earl of Leicester in his house; another acknowledges the reimbursement. William-Henry dated one of the Leicester receipts 1590, although that nobleman had died two years earlier. This mistake Samuel at once realised when his son presented the document. In his alarm William-Henry offered to burn the note immediately, but his father prevented him—maybe the receipt was dated on some later occasion, or confused with another. Finally they agreed to tear off the date. When William-Henry recast this episode for his published *Confessions*, he excluded his father's participation and made himself the discoverer of the year of Leicester's death. Somehow the uncensored version reached Malone, for in his copy he wrote alongside the passage, 'This whole statement is *false*. The father was privy to the tearing off the date; as this writer [i.e. William-Henry] has acknowledged *under his hand*.'

To how much else was he privy? 'In Justice to my father & to remove the Reproach under

1 *The Gentleman's Magazine*, 2nd Ser., vol. 1, pt. ii(1800), 902.

2 Folger Shakespeare Library MS. S.b.119. The letter is included in a grangerised copy of *Miscellaneous Papers*.

3 John Latham, *Facts and Opinions Concerning Diabetes* (1811), p. 176.

4 Quoted by Bernard Grebanier, *The Great Shakespeare Forgery: A New Look at the Career of William Henry Ireland* (1966), p. 284.

which he has Innocently fallen respecting the papers publish'd by him as the MSS of Shakspeare', William-Henry avouches in a document dated 24 May 1796, among the Ireland papers in the British Library,

> I do hereby solemnly declare that they were given to him by me as the genuine productions of Shakspeare & that he was & is at this Moment unacquainted with the source from whence they came or with any Circumstance concerning them save what he was told by myself and which he has declared in the preface to his Publication.[1]

The certificate, in William-Henry's hand, and witnessed by Albany Wallis—antiquarian enthusiast and solicitor friend of Samuel in Norfolk Street—as well as by Wallis's clerk, was carried as an advertisement by the *True Briton* on 11 June. This unequivocal exoneration of the father should be persuasive. But in a note, also among the Ireland papers, Samuel reveals that the confession was composed not by the penitent, but by Wallis; an aroma of collusion clings to William-Henry's protestations.

That Samuel's moral character was not irreproachable is confirmed by a letter he addressed to Sam—as he usually referred to his offspring—on 16 June 1796. Formerly he had refused to acknowledge that William-Henry had brains enough to perpetrate the fraud; now he advises his son to persist in what had become a vicious hoax:

> In my letter of yesterday I forgot to hint to you, ye dangerous predicament you stand in, if you are as you say the writer &c of these deeds. Your Character if you insist on this will be so blasted, that no person will admit you into their house, nor can you any where be trusted – therfore do not suffer yourself from Vanity or any other motive to adhere to any such Confession.[2]

Here the voice of parental solicitude is not unmixed with cynical expedience. Still, only an inhumanly rigid moralist will fail to sympathise with the pressures behind the beleaguered Samuel's counsel. The sum of the evidence does not lead me to conclude that Samuel was his son's partner in a deliberate hoax. Rather, his urge to believe was so overpowering as to overcome rational scruples. The unconscious, one suspects, called the tune.

So it did, after another fashion, for his son. 'What is most moving', William-Henry's most recent biographer has written of the 1805 *Confessions*, 'is the constant desire to clear Samuel Ireland's name, the profound admiration for his father, and a complete unwillingness to blame him for anything.'[3] In fact his motives were less pure. He protested that he aimed merely to please, but he also resented. The ambivalence of his feelings towards his father surfaces near the end of the *Confessions*, in a chapter entitled 'Mr. Samuel Ireland's Prejudice'. William-Henry writes:

> As a proof of the persecuting spirit which was unceasingly displayed to my detriment, I may mention that the warm emotions of the heart were discarded by Mr. Ireland [he is always Mr., never simply 'my father'], who dreaded any connexion whatsoever with me; fearful lest the world should brand him with countenancing me, and thereby be led to infer that he had been secretly concerned in the fabrication of the manuscripts.[4]

The dual nature of William-Henry's emotions found inspired expression in the Shakespeare Papers. They were in the first instance a bid for love, and in the end an instrument of psychic aggression. Malone had to share his triumph with his victim.

'How then stands the account?', William-Henry asks in the last chapter of his *Confessions*.

> I began the fabrication in the belief that by an innocent delusion I could please one whom I was anxious to gratify, and the persuasion (which I believe will be allowed not unnatural to a youth) that, if the deception were even exposed, the boldness of the attempt would have gained me praise for my ingenuity rather than censure for my deceit.—May it not therefore be concluded that I was not instigated by a desire to *injure any one*?[5]

'Secondly', he continues, '*I really injured no one.*' It is a curious claim in the light of the fate that

1 British Library MS. Add. 30346, f. 239.
2 Ibid., f. 249^v. The manuscript is Ireland's own copy of his letter to his son.
3 Grebanier, *Great Shakespeare Forgery*, p. 292.
4 William-Henry Ireland, *Confessions*, pp. 270–1.
5 Ibid., p. 303.

overtook Samuel Ireland. Malone, unmoved by pity for either father or son, is prompted by loftier public considerations to remark in a marginal note: 'So cheating 350 persons of four guineas each, is doing no injury to anyone: to say nothing of the general injury to literature by such a forger.' Fair enough; but if the subscribers to the *Miscellaneous Papers and Legal Instruments* found themselves cheated of expectation, they did receive a unique—if bizarre—volume for their four guineas, and literature has survived whatever injuries the Irelands inflicted. After almost two centuries the affair of the Norfolk Street Shakespeare Papers still amply rewards the curiosity of those inclined to explore the by-ways of eighteenth-century letters.

II. J. Payne Collier

The mitigating factor of extreme youth, which William-Henry with some overprotestation pleaded, was unavailable to J. Payne Collier. Already experienced in the law (he had been called to the Bar) and journalism (he had been a reporter with *The Times* and then, for legal and parliamentary affairs, with the *Morning Chronicle*), Collier was in his forties when he embarked upon his first fabrications. In any event, he saw himself as requiring no extenuation. He perpetrated his forgeries with cool deliberation; publicly he confessed nothing, and even in his voluminous correspondence, diaries, notations, and autobiographies, the few references to guilt and remorse are couched in generalities that fall short of a direct admission of culpability. Collier's lifetime spanned almost a century. In 1883, shortly before his death at the age of ninety-four, when he was in disgrace with fortune and men's eyes, he set down a sort of epigraph to the manuscript autobiography that to this day remains unpublished. 'My life', the quavering hand reads, 'from first to last, has been a hard-working one, I do not on that account look back upon it with any displeasure—rather the contrary.'[1]

Much of the satisfying hard work went into his Shakespeare forgeries. They first surfaced in 1831, in his three-volume *History of English Dramatic Poetry to the Time of Shakespeare; and Annals of the Stage to the Restoration*, which with shrewd diplomacy he dedicated to the Lord Chamberlain, an office then occupied by the Duke of Devonshire. The *History* established the characteristic Collier pattern of mingling genuine with spurious contributions.

Thus the magician pulled from his hat the Manningham *Diary* resting unnoted among the manuscript riches of the British Museum. On 15 March 1602 Manningham (then studying law at the Middle Temple) set down the anecdote which shows Shakespeare pre-empting Burbage for the favours of a stage-struck citizeness, and triumphantly informing the disappointed lover that William the Conqueror preceded Richard the Third—the latter being one of Burbage's celebrated rôles. Collier prints the item; also the entry—less entertaining but of greater historical importance—describing a performance of *Twelfth Night* at the Middle Temple the previous month.

Along with his account of the *Diary*, Collier gives the text of a seven-stanza 'Ballade in praise of London Prentices, and what they did at the Cock-pitt Playhouse in Drury Lane'. The ballad begins:

> The Prentices of London long
> Have famous beene in story,
> But now they are exceeding all
> Their Chronicles of glory:
> Looke back, some say, to other day,
> But I say looke before ye,
> And see the deed they have now done,
> Tom Brent and Johnny Cory.

Further along occurs a reference to

> False Cressid's hood, that was so good
> When loving Troylus kept her.

1 J. Payne Collier, *Autobiography*, Folger Shakespeare Library MS. M.a.230. The half-sheet on which this passage appears is unpaged.

Collier suspects here an allusion to Shakespeare's *Troilus and Cressida* as surreptitiously acted at the Cockpit; although, yielding to the imperatives of caution, he allows the possibility that another play on the same theme may have existed. The ballad, presented as copied 'from a contemporary MS.', is judiciously praised for possessing 'a good deal of spirit', which clearly it has.[1] The manuscript has never turned up, and the Ballade of the Cock-pitt may be reckoned a Collier invention.

So too the 'remarkable paper' dealing with the proposed Blackfriars Theatre renovation that alarmed residents of the district in 1596. They had petitioned the Privy Council to block the repairs; now the Chamberlain's Men—with the name of William Shakespeare appearing fifth out of eight—counter-petitioned to allow the work to proceed. This curiosity, for which Collier claims no more than the status of a copy, antedates (he points out) by seven years any other authentic document naming Shakespeare. (Presumably he means theatrical notices; discovery of the Exchequer account of 15 March 1595 citing Shakespeare as a payee of the Chamberlain's company lay some decades off.) The counter-petition achieved its end: performance did not temporarily cease at the Blackfriars. So Collier concludes. In fact Shakespeare's troupe first began playing at the enclosed, artificially illuminated playhouse more than a decade later. The whole episode is a scholar's fanciful theory rationalised with manufactured evidence.

Despite these aberrations, and organisational and other deficiencies, the *History* marks an important stage in the Romantic revaluation of the Elizabethan drama. Still the three volumes sold meagrely, and eventually the publishers, John Murray, wholesaled them. Never mind; the dedication had worked wonders. The Duke of Devonshire presented Collier with a hundred pounds, sponsored his membership of the Garrick Club, and arranged his entrée to Holland House. Further—and more practically—the Duke made Collier his librarian and literary advisor, with an annual pension of £100 for these agreeable part-time occupations. One thing leads to another. Thus favoured, Collier made the acquaintance of Lord Francis Egerton (soon to become Earl of Ellesmere), who opened to him the doors of Bridgewater House.

There, randomly heaped up in large bundles, lay the papers of Egerton's ancestor, Sir Thomas Egerton, Baron Ellesmere: Keeper of the Great Seal to Queen Elizabeth, and Lord Chancellor in the next reign. His documents and correspondence the Revd. H. J. Todd had already in part classed, but many items dating from 1581 to 1617, Sir Thomas's years of office, had remained unexplored, indeed unopened, from the time they were first tied together, perhaps by the Lord Keeper himself. His descendant, who in 1833 would come into his title and a patrimony estimated at £90,000 per annum, generously gave Collier 'instant and unrestrained access' to the Ellesmere papers, 'with permission to make use of any literary or historical information' he could glean from them. As, alone and unsupervised, he immersed himself in the Bridgewater House papers, the temptation to augment research with fabrication proved irresistible.

Many years later Collier recalled the occasion of his 'discoveries': how he rapidly examined the papers and, hastening to his patron, read them aloud to him. At his Lordship's request, Collier transcribed the documents, and left with him both the originals and copies. Events now moved quickly. Let Collier tell the story in his own words:

> Going again to Bridgewater House (I think it must have been on the very next day, for I was all eagerness to pursue my search) I overtook his Lordship about to enter the door, having just alighted from his horse. He told me that he had seen Mr. Murray, the publisher, who offered to give me £50 or £100 (I believe the smaller to have been the sum) if I would put the documents into shape and write an introduction to them. I declined the proposal at once, saying that I could not consent to make money out of his Lordship's property. Lord Ellesmere appeared a little surprised at my hyper-squeamishness, and replied, with his habitual generosity, that the documents were as much mine as his, for though I had found them in his house, but for me, they might never have been discovered till doomsday.[2]

Indeed they might not have been.

From Bridgewater House, Collier took all the newly discovered documents, along with his

1 Collier, *The History of English Dramatic Poetry to the Time of Shakespeare; and Annals of the Stage to the Restoration* (1831), i. 401–4.

2 *Mr. J. Payne Collier's Reply to Mr. N. E. S. A. Hamilton's 'Inquiry' into the Imputed Shakespeare Forgeries* (1860), p. 35.

7040
11750 1608

1.

ffor avoiding of the playhouse in the Blacke ffriers

Impr. Richard Burbidge owith the ffee and is alsoe a sharer therein his interest he rateth at the grosse summe of 1000li for the ffee and for his foure shares the summe of 933li 6s 8d	1933li. 6s 8d
Item Laz ffletcher owith 3 shares wch he rateth at 700li that is at 7 yeares purchase for eche share or 33li. 6. 8d one yeare wth an other	700li
Item W. Shakspeare asketh for the wardrobe and properties of the same playhouse 500li and for his 4 shares the same as his fellowes Burbidge and ffletcher 933li. 6s 8d	1433li. 6s. 8d
Item Heminges and Condell eche 2 shares	933li. 6s. 8d
Item Joseph Taylor one share and an halfe	350li.
Item Lowing one share and an halfe	350li.
Item foure more playeres wth one halfe share unto eche of them	466li. 13s. 4d
Suma totalis	6166. 13. 4
Moreover the hired men of the companie demaund some recompense for their greate losse and the widowes and orphanes of playeres who are paide by the sharers at divers rates & proportions soe as in the whole it will coste the L. Mayor and Citizens at the least	7000li

65 THE SHARE OF SHAKESPEARE AND OTHERS IN THE BLACKFRIARS THEATRE. *Huntington Library, MS. EL 11750. Transcript and commentary: Collier,* New Facts, *pp. 21–6; C. M. Ingleby,* A Complete View of the Shakspere Controversy *(1861), pp. 246–7. The page is here reduced by approximately one quarter.*

transcripts, to his friend Thomas Rodd, the antiquarian bookseller in Great Newport Street. Rodd in 1835 printed them with Collier's analysis, in *New Facts Regarding the Life of Shakespeare*. This little volume of some fifty pages takes the form of a letter to Thomas Amyot, treasurer of the Society of Antiquaries: a wonderfully apt strategy, for the Amyot connection reinforced Collier's scholarly credentials, while the epistolary mode permitted an informal excursiveness that softened the documentary austerity of the content. There were no facsimiles. Published in an edition limited to fifty copies, the book was mostly given away rather than sold, although a few copies passed over the counter to Rodd's customers. In his Advertisement Collier disingenuously justified the small printing on grounds that few would be interested in additions to biographical knowledge of Shakespeare. But he could afterwards claim, no doubt with truth, that he made not a farthing on this or his other scholarly publications of the time. He sought—and received—other rewards.

Five of the documents announced in the *New Facts* name or allude to Shakespeare.

The first reveals that as early as 1589—three years before the dying Greene pilloried 'the onely Shake-scene in a countrey'—the dramatist was a sharer, with fifteen others, in the Blackfriars Theatre. Collier's paper assures the Lord Keeper that 'her Majesties poore Playeres', with the Burbages, father and son, heading the roster and 'William Shakespeare' appearing eighth, 'have never given cause of displeasure' by bringing unfit interludes on to the stage of their 'blacke Fryers playehouse'.

The second record, 'For Avoiding of the Playhouse in the Precinct of the Blacke Friers', itemises the pecuniary value of the several sharers' holdings. Shakespeare's interest comes to £1433. 6*s*. 8*d*. for his four shares and for the wardrobe and properties (valued at £500). The worth of the whole enterprise is put as at least £7000: an outlandish figure.

There follows perhaps the most intriguing paper, a letter subscribed with the initials 'H. S.' and recommending to Lord Ellesmere (now Lord Chancellor) the bearers, two of the chief members of the King's company. One is Richard Burbidge, described in vaguely familiar terms as 'a man famous as our English Roscius, one who fitteth the action to the word and the word to the action most admirably'; while the other ('till of late an actor of good account in the cumpanie') has composed some of the best English plays. 'This other', he goes on,

> hath to name William Shakespeare, and they are both of one countie, and indeede almost of one towne: both are right famous in their qualityes though it longeth not to your Lordships gravitie and wisedome to resort unto the places where they are wont to delight the publique eare. Their trust and sute nowe is not to bee molested in their waye of life whereby they maintaine them selves and their wives and families (being both maried and of good reputation) as well as the widowes and orphanes of some of their dead fellows.[1]

The letter, regrettably not the original but merely a '*copia vera*', is set down on a half sheet of paper. Collier surmises that 'H. S.' stands for Henry Wriothesley, third Earl of Southampton. Perhaps not surprisingly, the discoverer of this curious paper sufficiently savours its other revelations: that the Burbages hailed from Warwickshire (as some had previously suspected), that Shakespeare's histrionic gifts were reckoned of a lower order than Richard Burbage's, and that the playwright quitted acting somewhat later than generally supposed. Collier does not neglect to point out good-naturedly a minor error on Southampton's part: Shakespeare's patron, no scholar, has exaggerated the antiquity of the Blackfriars Theatre. It is a nice touch.

The next document, which 'purports' (Collier's word) to be a draft warrant for a patent or Privy Seal, appoints Robert Daiborne, William Shakespeare, and others to instruct the Children of the Queen's Revels playing in the Blackfriars and elsewhere. Collier infers that around the time—the warrant is dated 4 January 1609—the Blackfriars Theatre was threatened with demolition, and that Shakespeare contemplated shifting his interest to another theatrical operation. The Daiborne warrant has a gilt edge, but not until some time later was it noticed that the paper on which it was written had apparently been cut from a book (in the Bridgewater collection?) with a pen knife.

The last document is an original letter, undated but assigned to 1603, in which Samuel Daniel

1 Collier, *New Facts regarding the Life of Shakespeare* ... (1835), p. 33.

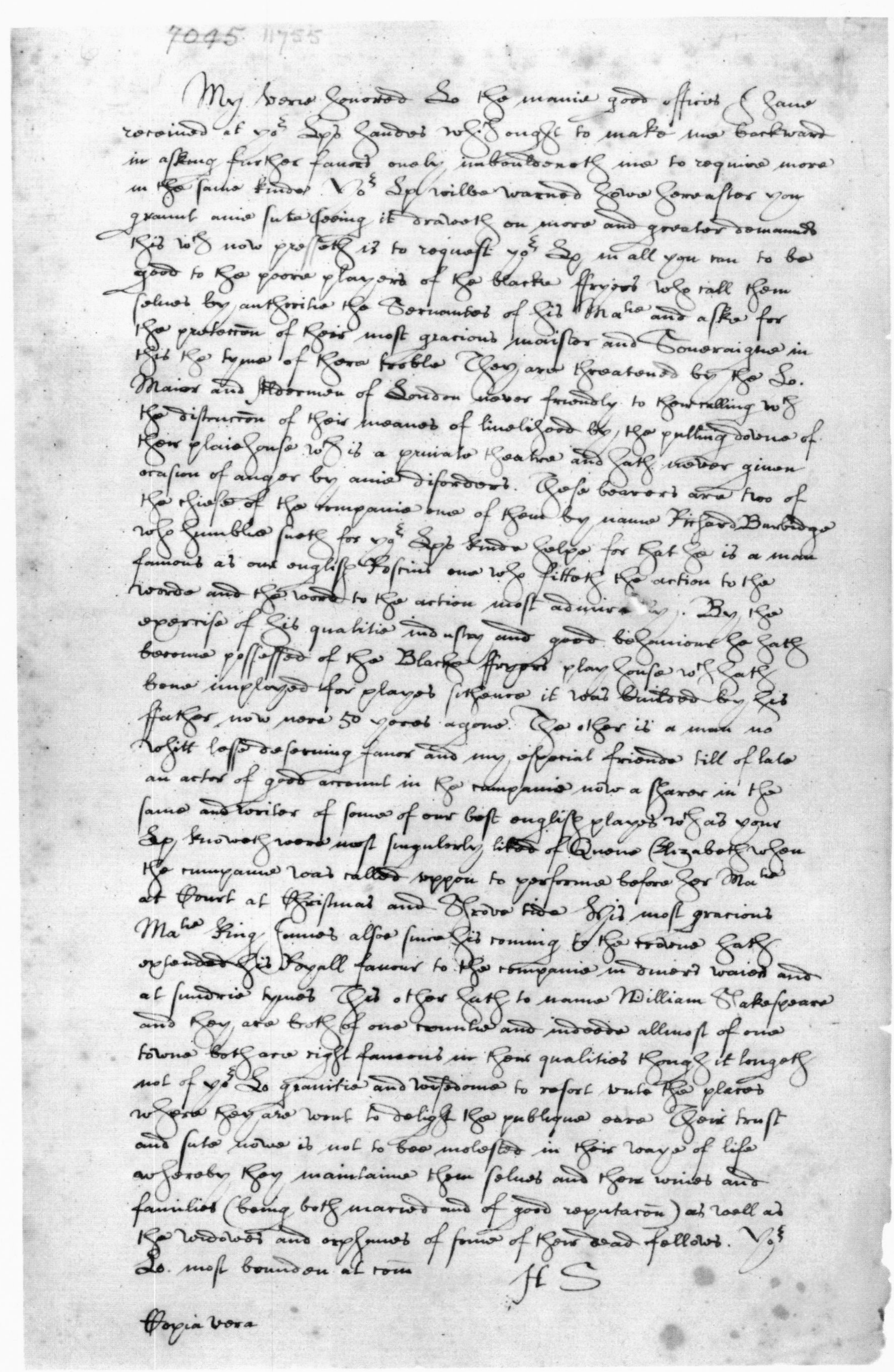

My verie honored Lo. the manie good offices I have
received at yor Lps handes wch ought to make me backward
in asking further favors onely imbouldeneth me to require more
in the same kinde. Yor Lp wilbe warned howe hereafter you
graunt anie sute seeing it draweth on more and greater demaunds
this wch now presseth is to request yor Lp in all you can to be
good to the poore players of the blacke ffryers who call them
selves by authoritie the Servaunts of his Matie and aske for
the protection of their most gracious maister and Soveraigne in
this the tyme of there troble. They are threatened by the Lo.
Maior and Aldermen of London never friendly to their calling wth
the distruction of their meanes of livelihood by the pulling downe of
their plaiehouse wch is a private theatre and hath never given
occasion of anger by anie disorders. These bearers are two of
the chiefe of the companie one of them by name Richard Burbidge
who humblie sueth for yor Lps kinde helpe for that he is a man
famous as our english Roscius one who fitteth the action to the
worde and the worde to the action most admirably. By the
exercise of his qualitie industry and good behaviour he hath
become possessed of the Blacke ffryers playhouse wch hath
bene imployed for playes sithence it was builded by his
ffather now nere 50 yeres agone. The other is a man no
whitt lesse deserving favor and my especiall friende till of late
an actor of good account in the companie now a sharer in the
same and writer of some of our best english playes wch as your
Lp knoweth were most singularly liked of Quene Elizabeth when
the companie was called uppon to performe before her Matie
at Court at Christmas and Shrovetide. His most gracious
Matie King James alsoe sins his coming to the crowne hath
extended his royall favour to the companie in divers waies and
at sundrie tymes. This other hath to name William Shakespeare
and they are both of one countie and indeede allmost of one
towne both are right famous in their qualities though it longeth
not of yor Lo. gravitie and wisedome to resort unto the places
where they are wont to delight the publique eare. Their trust
and sute nowe is not to bee molested in their waye of life
whereby they maintaine them selves and their wives and
families (being both maried and of good reputacion) as well as
the widowes and orphanes of some of their dead fellows. Yor
Lo. most bounden at com.

H S

Copia vera

66 THE 'H.S.' LETTER. *Huntington Library, MS. EL 11755. Transcript and commentary: Collier,* New Facts, *pp. 31–8; Ingleby,* Complete View, *pp. 256–61. The page is here reduced by approximately three tenths.*

Right trustie and welbeloued &c James &c To all Mayors Sheriffes Justices of the peace &c Whereas the Queene our dearest wife hath for her pleasure and recreation appointed her servauntes Robert Daborne &c to provide and bring upp a convenient nomber of children who shalbe called the children of her Ma[tie] revelles Knowe yee that We haue appointed and authorized and by these presentes doe appoint and authorize the saide Robert Daborne Willm Shakespeare Nathaniel ffield & Edward Kirkham from time to time to provide and bring upp a convenient nomber of children and them to instruct and exercise in the qualitie of playing Tragedies Comedies &c by the name of the children of the revelles to the Queene within the blacke ffryers in our Cittie of London & els where within our realme of England. Wherefore we will and commaund you and everie of you to permitte her said servauntes to keepe a convenient nomber of children by the name of the children of the revelles to the Queene and them to exercise in the qualitie of playing according to our Royall pleasure Provided allwayes that noe playes &c shalbe by them presented but such playes &c as haue receiued the aprobation and allowance of our Maister of the Revelles for the tyme being And these our lres shalbe yor sufficient warraunt in this behalfe In Witnesse whereof &c 4° die Janu 1609

Bl ffr and globe
Wh ffr and parishe garden
Curten and fortune
Hope and Swanne
} All in & neere London

Rendo ponortie
Widdowes mite
Antonio kinsmen
Triumph of truth
Touchstone
Mirror of life
Grissell
Engl tragedie
ffalse ffriendes
Hate and Love
Taming of S
K. Edw 2

Stayed

67 THE DAIBORNE WARRANT. *Huntington Library, MS. EL 11754. Transcript and commentary: Collier,* New Facts, *pp. 41–7; Ingleby,* Complete View, *pp. 252–6. The warrant is here reduced by approximately one quarter.*

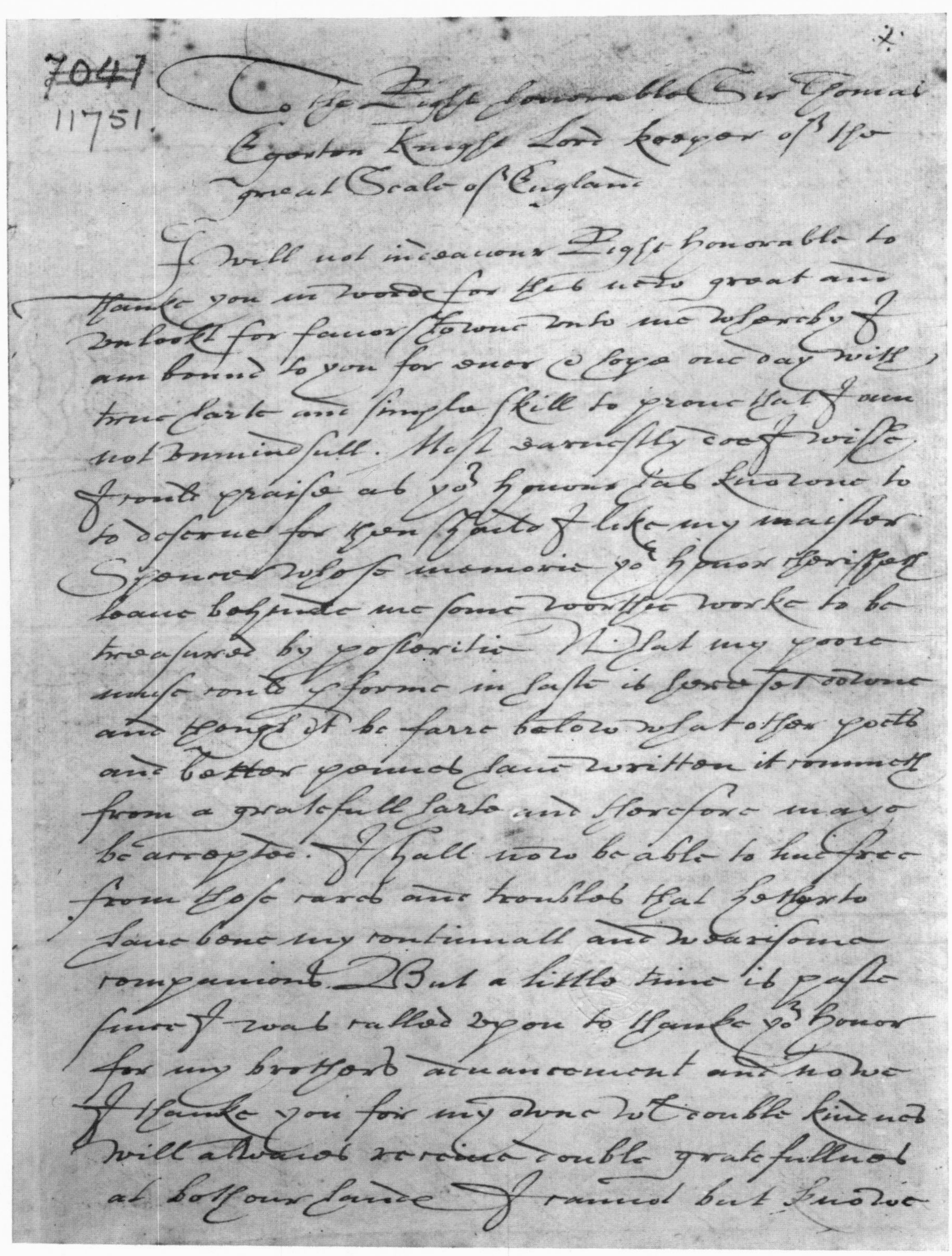
7041
11751

To the Right honorable Sir Thomas
Egerton Knight Lord keeper of the
great Seale of England

I will not indeavour Right honorable to
thanke you in words for this new great and
unlookt for favor showne unto me whereby I
am bound to you for ever & hope one day with
true harte and simple skill to prove that I am
not unmindfull. Most earnestly could I wishe
I coulde praise as yor honour is knowne to
to deserve for then should I like my maister
Spencer whose memorie yor honor cherisheth
leave behinde me some worthie worke to be
treasured by posteritie. What my poore
muse could performe in haste is here sett downe
and though it be farre belowe what other poets
and better pennes have written it commeth
from a gratefull harte and therefore maye
be accepted. I shall now be able to live free
from those cares and troubles that hetherto
have bene my continuall and wearisome
companions. But a little time is paste
since I was called upon to thanke yor honor
for my brothers advancement and nowe
I thanke you for my owne wch double kindnes
will alwaies receive double gratefulnes
at bothe our handes. I cannot but knowe

68 THE SAMUEL DANIEL LETTER. *Huntington Library, MS. EL 11751. Transcript and commentary: Collier,* New Facts, *pp. 47–51; Ingleby,* Complete View, *pp. 247–9.* *The letter here continues on pp. 143–4.*

thanks his protector Sir Thomas Egerton for helping to advance him to the post of Master of the Queen's Revels. 'I cannot but knowe', Daniel confesses,

> that I am lesse deserving then some that sued by other of the nobility unto her Majestie for this roome: if M. Draiton, my good friend, had bene chosen, I should not have murmured, for sure I ame he wold have filled it most excellentlie: but it seemeth to myne humble judgement that one who is the authour of playes now daylie presented on the public stages of London, and the possessor of no small gaines, and moreover him selfe an Actor in the Kings Companie of Comedians, could not with reason pretend to be Mr of the Queenes Majesties Revells, for as much as he wold sometimes be asked to approve and allow of his owne writings.

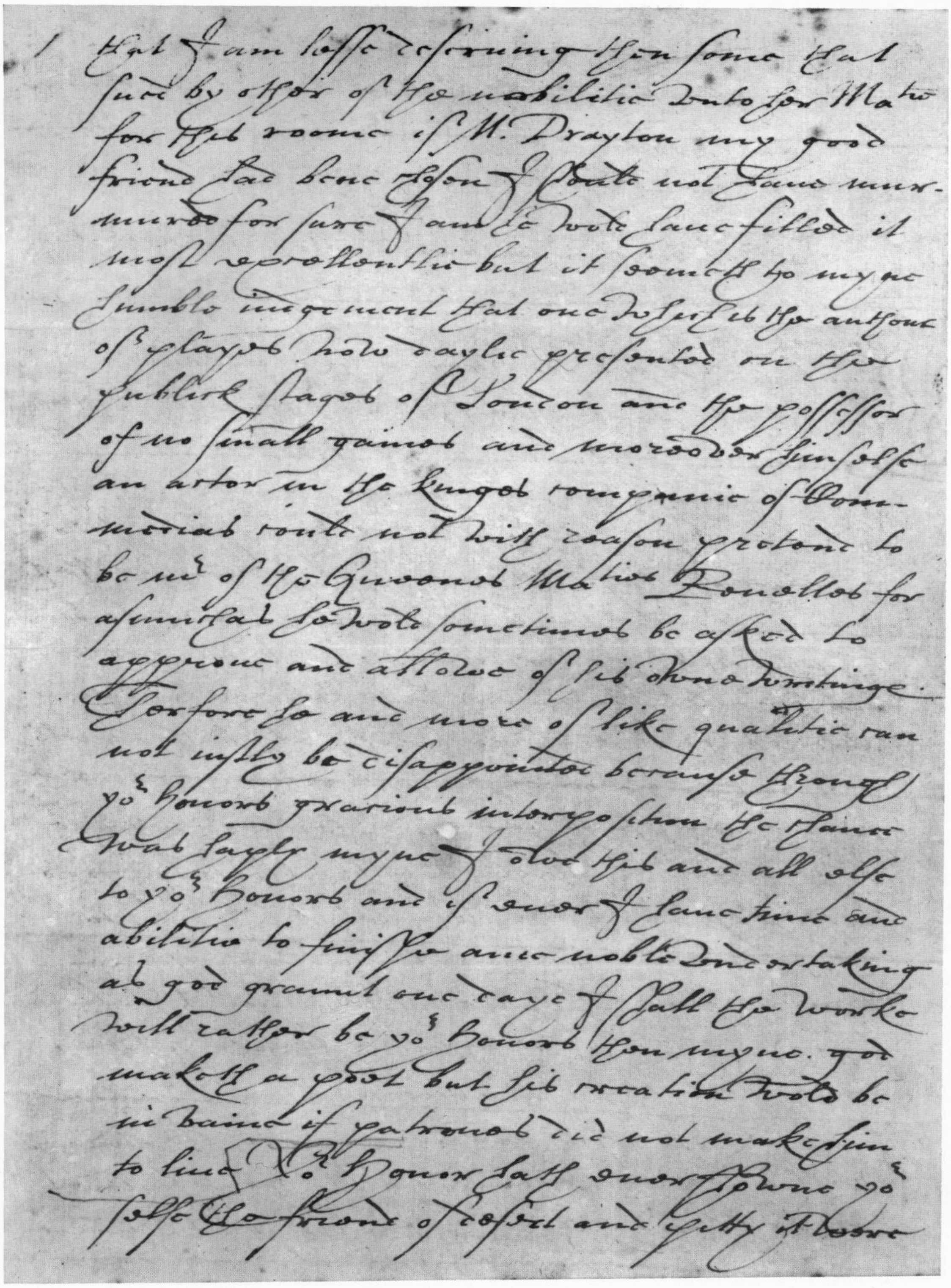

Therefore, he, and more of like quality, cannot justlie be disappointed because through your Honors gracious interposition the chance was haply myne.[1]

Needless to say, the unpreferred playwright without cause for complaint must be Shakespeare.

That these 'new facts' are the spurious inventions of their discoverer no doubt detracts somewhat from their value, without entirely depriving them of interest. A couple of lesser contributions round out the offering: a second Daniel letter, a Privy Council order of 23 December 1579 protecting Leicester's men. But Collier, as was his wont, did good as well as mischief. So he makes available for the first time the text of the 1602 foot of fine reaffirming the conveyance of New Place from Hercules Underhill to William Shakespeare: a document of which Malone (as his

1 Ibid., pp. 48–9.

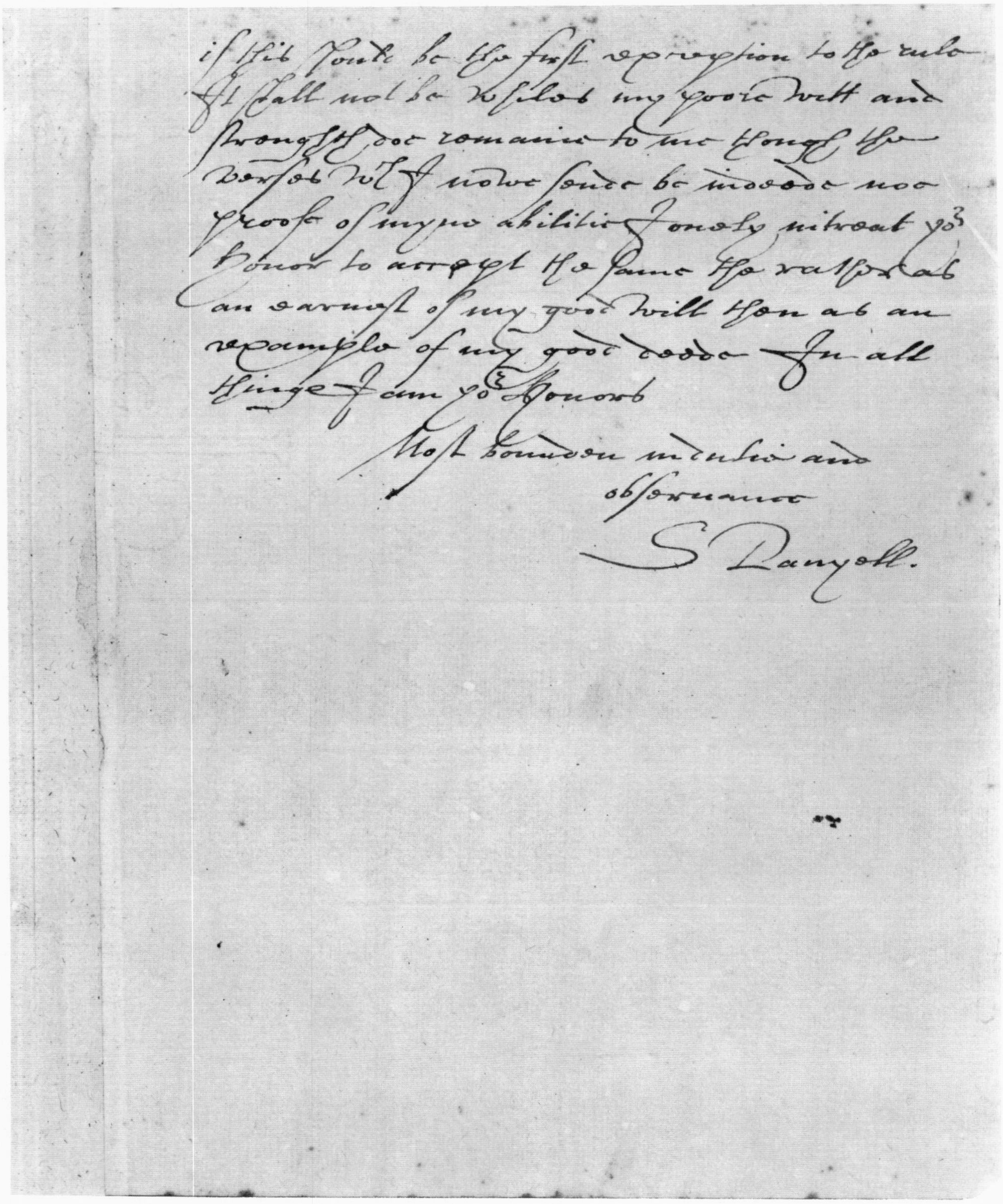
if this shoulde be the first exception to the rule
it shall not be whilst my poore witt and
strength doe remaine to me though the
verses wch I nowe sende be indeede noe
proofe of myne abilitie I onely intreat yor
honor to accept the same the rather as
an earnest of my good will then as an
example of my good deede In all
things I am yor Honors
Most bounden in dutie and
observance
S Danyell.

private correspondence reveals) knew the existence, but which he never got round to publishing. Such bread-and-butter recoveries apparently produced little elation; the foot of fine rates only a footnote from Collier.

'When I took up the copy of Lord Southampton's letter and glanced over it hastily', he recalls in *New Facts*, 'I could scarcely believe my eyes, to see such names as Shakespeare and Burbage in connection in a manuscript of the time. There was a remarkable coincidence also in the discovery, for it happened on the anniversary of Shakespeare's birth and death.'[1] When Sir Frederic Madden, Keeper of Manuscripts at the British Museum, encountered this passage in the copy

1 Ibid., p. 38.

presented to him by the author, he underscored Collier's reference to the anniversary, and expressed his incredulity with three exclamation marks in the right-hand margin. In the left he wrote, 'I can believe *my eyes*—and I know this letter is a *forgery*, and more, I believe that Mr. C. could name the forger.'[1] That was, as one of Sir Frederic's pencilled notes signifies, twenty-five years after the publication of *New Facts*. By then the house of deceit which Collier had so painstakingly erected had come crashing down round him. But for a long period expressions of scepticism were few, and mostly muted. Charles Knight and Joseph Hunter voiced doubts, but when Collier produced the 'H.S.' letter—the most sharply suspected document—before the council of the Shakespeare Society (of which he was the director) he won the support of Thomas Wright, a founding member, and other respected judges.

The tergiversations of Halliwell (not yet Halliwell-Phillipps) chart the evolution of expert opinion. He was only twenty-seven when his *Life of Shakespeare* appeared in 1848. It contains numerous illustrations, but the author reserves pride of place for a full-page facsimile, facing the first page of his text, of a portion of the Southampton letter. 'The fac-simile', Halliwell remarks, '. . . will suffice to convince any one acquainted with such matters that it is a genuine manuscript of the period. No forgery of so long a document could present so perfect a continuity of design. . . .'[2] In December 1847 Halliwell wrote respectfully to Collier, assuring him that he had (on the latter's advice) secured the Earl of Ellesmere's permission to include a facsimile of the Southampton letter, and expressing conviction that 'nothing will tend so much to vindicate its authenticity'.[3] That Halliwell should offer himself as an attorney for the defence of course implies the threat of prosecution. Five years later he had changed sides. In *Observations on the Shakspearian Forgeries at Bridgewater House; Illustrative of a facsimile of the spurious letter of H.S.*, in 1853, Halliwell once again reproduced the letter in facsimile, this time in its entirety; but now he announced, on the basis of his own examination conducted at Bridgewater House, that all the Shakespearian manuscripts preserved there were 'modern forgeries'. (Actually he had not inspected all of them, for he was able to find there only a recent transcript of the Daniel letter.) In facsimile the 'H.S.' letter looked genuine enough, but the original produced a different impression, 'the paper and ink not appearing to belong to so early a date'.[4] Publicly the eight-page leaflet created few ripples. Halliwell had, after all, printed it for private circulation, and not even by innuendo had he impugned the *bona fides* of the super-respectable director of the Shakespeare Society. If the revelations caused consternation in the inner councils of this body, its dissolution later that year came about less from intimations of scandal than from declining membership and pernicious fiscal anaemia; but there can be little doubt that the scandal administered the finishing stroke.

Meanwhile, as a cheerful exponent of the Victorian work ethic, Collier had continued to augment knowledge after his own fashion. The *New Facts* led in 1836 to *New Particulars regarding the Works of Shakespeare*, which was three years later followed by *Farther Particulars regarding Shakespeare and his Works*. Both, like their predecessor, were printed by Rodd in severely limited editions, and both took the form of letters. Now Collier chose highly esteemed clergyman-scholars as recipients, Alexander Dyce for *New Particulars* and Joseph Hunter for *Farther Particulars*. These 'tracts'—Collier's term for them—inimitably blend genuine and spurious discoveries. Thus *New Particulars* offers the first notice of Ashmolean MS. 208, Simon Forman's 'Book of Plays'. While researching his *History of English Dramatic Poetry* at the Bodleian Library, Collier had heard that a manuscript existed there containing eyewitness notes of performances of Shakespeare at the Globe. He tried to track the items down, but was accidentally put off the scent until, some six or seven years later, a cataloguer there chanced upon the *Book of Plays* and immediately transmitted a copy to Collier.[5] He was lucky that way. More than luck lies behind the notice of a performance of *Othello* recorded in Sir Thomas Egerton's accounts for Elizabeth's entertainment at Harefield during three nights, from 31 July to 2 August, in 1602:

6 Aug. 1602. Rewardes to the Vaulters Players
and Dauncers. Of this £10 to Burbidge's
players for Othello . . . 64 18 10

1 *New Facts*, Folger Shakespeare Library; shelfmark: PR 2951.C64.As. Col.

2 James Orchard Halliwell, *The Life of William Shakespeare* (1848), pp. 224–5.

3 Letter, dated 18 December 1847, in Folger Shakespeare Library (MS. Y.c.1207 (1–2)).

4 Halliwell, *Observations* . . . (1853), p. 8.

5 See above, pp. 16–17.

According to Collier these accounts, at Bridgewater House, were in the hand of Sir Thomas's steward, Sir Arthur Mainwaring. Collier notes that the entry proves that Malone's date for *Othello*, 1604, is too late.[1] Collier may well be right—Malone's date *is* rather late—but he has used forged evidence to make his point. Later, when the heat was on him, he maintained that he had been led to his quarry by the former librarian at Bridgewater House: Todd, by then old and deaf, had told him 'he knew that such a circumstance [the *Othello* performance] was mentioned in some MS'.[2] Regrettably Todd was unable to verify Collier's report. He was dead.

In *Farther Particulars* Collier returned to the Manningham entry for *Twelfth Night*. After turning over collections of Italian Renaissance plays for many years, he announces, he has managed to find a 1582 edition of Nicolò Secchi's *Gl'Inganni*—apparently the source for Shakespeare's comedy that Manningham had in mind. Collier also prints 'The Inchanted Island', a long ballad by 'R.G.', the narrative of which recalls *The Tempest*. He corrects the text, sorting out transposed words—'The transcriber was not a very accurate penman'—and reports that 'Mr. Douce called it "one of the most beautiful ballads he had ever read", and shook his venerable head (as was his wont) with admiring energy and antiquarian enthusiasm at different passages in it'. Collier himself was 'by no means prepared to give it so high a character', even if, to be sure, it was 'vastly better' than, say, Thomas Jordan's ballads.[3] Collier's audacity is here breathtaking. The venerable Douce, like the deaf Todd, was lately dead, and 'The Inchanted Island' is the inspired outpouring of Collier's own muse.

The Dulwich College muniments did not escape his indefatigable searches. While collecting materials for his *History of English Dramatic Poetry*, Collier inspected the Henslowe papers in the college library. Malone had been there earlier, and (in his 1790 *Shakespeare*) was the first to publish extracts from the *Diary*, that unique storehouse of information about Elizabethan stage conditions. Between Malone's death in 1812 and Collier's initiative a generation later, nobody seems to have consulted the Dulwich papers, although they were in 1819 lent to the then Archbishop of Canterbury. Under the auspices of the Shakespeare Society, Collier in 1841 published his *Memoirs of Edward Alleyn*, which he followed four years later with a verbatim transcript of the *Diary*. Thus were these invaluable records first made available *in extenso*. To be sure, as it was Collier's melancholy duty to report, Shakespeare's name nowhere appears in Henslowe's *Diary*. Still, Collier improved the manuscript with a number of forged insertions, at least one of which has a suggestive Shakespearian bearing. In an entry for 14 January 1603, where Henslowe had left a space for a title of a play by Chettle and Heywood, Collier supplied the blank with *Like Quits Like*, and in a note sagely observed that just possibly 'this may have been a play on the same story as Measure for Measure', in which (near the end) occurs the line '*Like doth quit like*, and Measure still for Measure'.[4] Elsewhere Collier inserted other omitted titles, and he was not above making deletions where these suited his purposes: preferring (for example) to regard the *Jeronimo* played on 7 January 1597 as a revival rather than new, he erased Henslowe's 'ne'. His *modus operandi* was always to make the evidence fit the thesis. Ever more receptive to fact than to speculation, the world applauded.

The Henslowe papers afforded greater scope than the *Diary* for Collier's special gifts. By producing a 'breif noat taken out of the poores booke', comprising the names of all the inhabitants of Southwark assessed for the weekly payments towards poor relief, he establishes that Shakespeare was residing there in 1609. Collier invents fifty-seven names, including a Mrs. Sparrowhauke and Ferdynando Moses; 'Mr Shakespeare', rated at 6*d*., heads one of the three subdivisions of the list. (Later, when this document provoked denunciation as a clumsy forgery, Collier insisted that Malone had seen it when he—Collier—was a child of seven, and had referred to it in his *Inquiry*;

1 Collier, *New Particulars regarding the Works of Shakespeare* . . . (1836), pp. 57–8.

2 Collier, *Reply*, p. 35n.

3 Collier, *Farther Particulars regarding Shakespeare and his Works* (1839), pp. 54–63.

4 Philip Henslowe, *Diary, from 1591 to 1609*, ed. Collier (Publications of the Shakespeare Society, no. 28; 1845), p. 230.

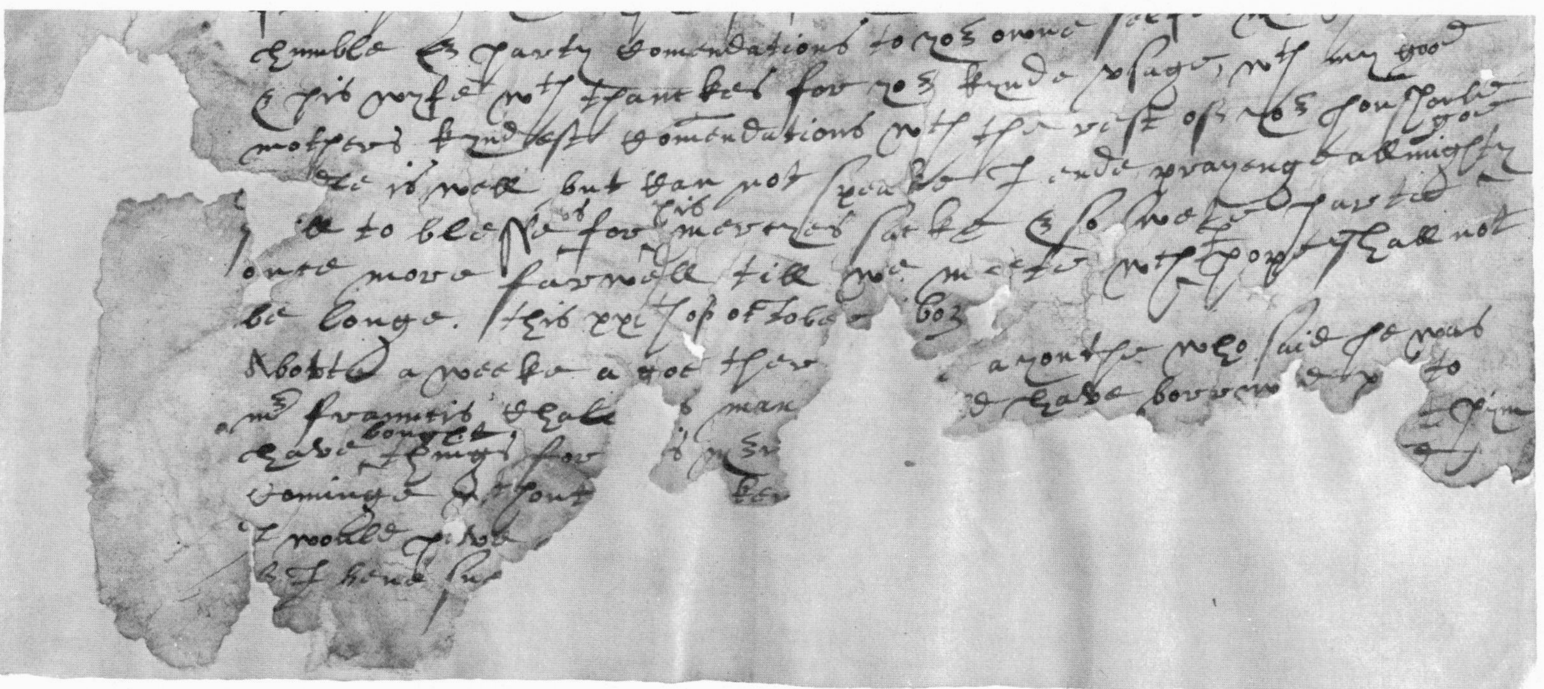

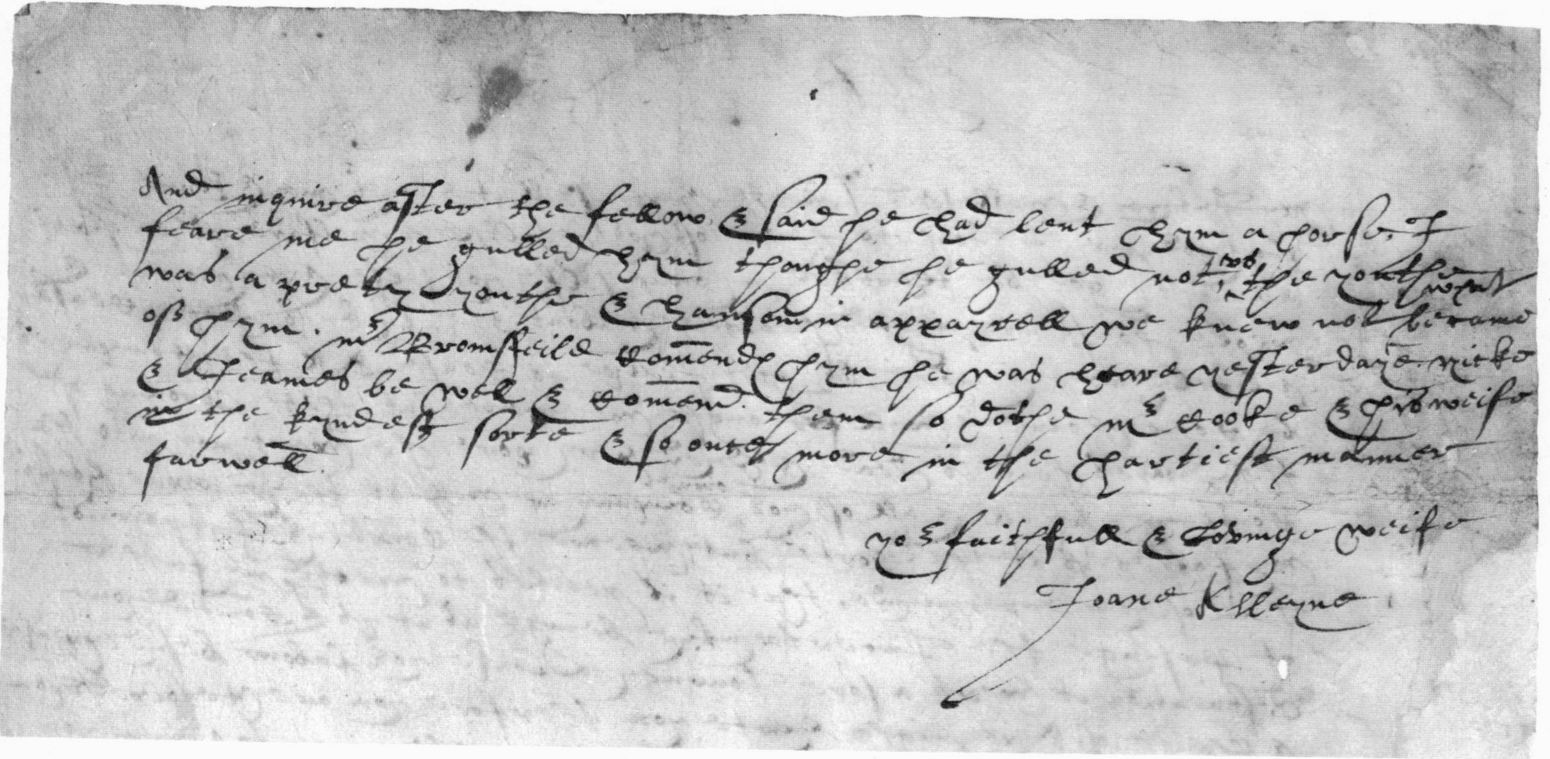

69 THE JOAN ALLEYN LETTER, 21 OCTOBER 1603. *MSS. i, art. 52, among the Henslowe Papers at Dulwich College. Ingleby transcribes the postscript and discusses it in his* Complete View, *pp. 279–88. Both Collier and Ingleby misdate the letter 20 October 1603.*

but Malone mentions no such paper.)[1] More daring was Collier's treatment of the letter addressed by Joan Alleyn on 20 October 1603 to her actor-husband, her 'intyre and welbeloved sweete harte'. This letter, which is genuine and touchingly evocative of life in the capital in time of pestilence, Collier transcribes with (by the standards of the day) reasonable scrupulousness. But

1 A copy of the list does appear on the back of a letter addressed to Malone and inserted at p. 210 of a specimen of the *Inquiry* at the British Library (C.45.e.23). EKC reports that the copy is not in Malone's hand (ii. 389); he here follows D. T. B. Wood, 'The Revels Books: The Writer of the "Malone Scrap"', *R.E.S.*, i (1925), 73. The volume in the British Library belonged formerly to Collier.

the postscript at the bottom, being defective, tempted him dangerously. According to Collier, the paper was in 'a most decayed state', breaking away 'in dust and fragments at the slightest touch'. Where it was 'most rotten', with several hopeless deficiencies, occurred the notice of Shakespeare. He gives the postscript thus:

Aboute a weeke a goe there came a youthe who said he was Mr Frauncis Chaloner who would have borrowed x^li^ to have bought things for * * * and said he was known unto you, and Mr Shakespeare of the globe, who came * * * said he knewe hym not, onely he herde of hym that he was a roge * * * so he was glade we did not lend him the monney * * * Richard Johnes [went] to seeke and inquire after the fellow, and said he had lent hym a horse: I feare me he gulled hym, thoughe he gulled not us. The youthe was a prety youthe, and hansom in appayrell: we knowe not what became of hym. Mr Benfield commendes hym: he was heare yesterdaye. Nicke and Jeames be well, and comend them: so doth Mr Cooke and his wiefe in the kyndest sorte, and so once more in the hartiest manner farwell.[1]

Years afterward, when the postscript had returned to haunt him, Collier insisted that Shakespeare's name had been earlier present in this part of the letter, a fact which his dear friend Amyot would affirm, were not that gentleman unfortunately deceased; his informed witnesses had a way of being dead when their services were required. These protestations availed Collier little, for it was noted that no entire line was wanting from the Joan Alleyn postscript, and that the surviving words—still legible—were incompatible with Collier's transcript, which omits nine words from the last four lines of the original. The phrase 'Mr Shakespeare of the globe' could never have appeared in the text.

Why did Collier in this way convict himself? For convict himself he did, on evidence which, not being dependent upon the special expertise of the palaeographer or chemist, any layman could understand. Any visitor to Dulwich who inspected the paper could see for himself that Joan Alleyn's letter was not, as Collier lied, crumbling into dust. He would see too that the postscript was irreconcilable with the published text. Did Collier in his megalomania assume that the world would accept his editions as definitive and that the documents he had transcribed would thereafter be spared inspection? Or did his secret guilt crave the humiliation of exposure? More probable, perhaps, that (like other, more mundane, rogues) he experienced a special *frisson* from balancing himself on the edge of the abyss.

He plunged over when he yielded to that last infirmity of an ignoble Shakespeare scholar, an edition of the complete works. For years he had contemplated such a venture, which, unlike his Shakespeare Society publications and limited-edition tracts, offered the promise of handsome pecuniary rewards. In 1841 Collier published a shilling pamphlet, *Reasons for a New Edition of Shakespeare's Works, containing notices of the defects of former impressions, and pointing out the lately acquired means of illustrating the plays, poems, and biography of the Poet.* A new edition, both he and his publisher (Whittaker and Co.) felt, needed justification, and in the Bridgewater First Folio, Collier produced it. This handsome copy, with exceptionally wide margins, contained—so he announced—manuscript corrections of textual minutiae in a seventeenth-century hand possibly dating from the reign of Charles I. Two decades after the pamphlet appeared, an adversary, looking back, saw it as signalling a new epoch in Shakespeare criticism. 'It was here', observed C. M. Ingleby, 'that Mr. Collier first appealed to *manuscript authority* for the regulation and emendation of the text of Shakspere.'[2] These annotations, some thirty in number, appeared only in a few of the early plays of the volume, and their quality made it 'a matter of deep regret that the corrector of the text carried his labours no farther'. So Collier remarked of his own forged notes. The Bridgewater Folio corrections (those he found acceptable) were incorporated by Collier in his 1842–4 *Works of William Shakespeare*, which was trumpeted as being based upon 'an entirely new collation of the old editions', and dedicated to His Grace the Duke of Devonshire. Collier would never be guilty of ingratitude.

He carried his labours farther with the Perkins Folio. This 'find' Collier announced in *The Athenaeum* for 31 January 1852. He tells of happening to be in Rodd's shop, years since, when a parcel of books arrived from the country. The consignment, bought at auction (maybe in

1 Collier, *Memoirs of Edward Alleyn* . . . (Publications of the Shakespeare Society, no. 1; 1841), p. 63.

2 C. M. Ingleby, *A Complete View of the Shakspere Controversy* . . . (1861), p. 22.

Bedfordshire; his memory was hazy), included a battered copy of the Second Folio, sans title-page and other leaves, with blotted and dirty pages and a greasy calf binding. On the outside front cover the original owner had written, 'Tho. Perkins, his Booke'. Rodd let the copy go for thirty shillings. Only much later did Collier discover that almost every page bore emendations, some apparently 'highly valuable', in a handwriting of the Commonwealth period. These altered punctuation, spelling, words, phrases, lines, sometimes even pairs of lines. Had the Old Corrector (Collier wondered in *The Athenaeum* for 7 February 1852) consulted manuscripts unavailable to the original editors, or did he draw upon his memory of stage recitations; or were the revisions mere conjecture? Maybe the corrector resorted to all three methods. In a third letter, on 27 March, Collier drew attention to what would become a celebrated emendation, 'bisson (= purblind) multitude' for 'bosom multiplied' in *Coriolanus* ('How shall this bosom multiplied digest / The Senate's courtesy?', III.i.131–2). Even the uncompromising Dyce adopted this correction, which makes sense graphically; but most modern editors retain the Folio reading.

Collier displayed his Folio before the council of the Shakespeare Society (not yet demoralised) and at a meeting of the Society of Antiquaries. Such was the curiosity aroused that he exhibited it again, for the Fellows, in the Library at Somerset House. That summer members of the Shakespeare Society received advance copies of Collier's *Notes and Emendations to the Text of Shakespeare's Plays, from early manuscript corrections in a copy of the folio, 1632, in the possession of J. Payne Collier, Esq. F.S.A.*, a supplemental volume to his edition. Official publication took place early the next year, when the book appeared in a trade edition by Whittaker, who shrewdly judged that it would promote sales of the *Shakespeare*. A German translation followed in 1854, and influenced the great Delius at Bonn. The *Notes and Emendations* made available only a selection from the many thousands of manuscript corrections in the Perkins Folio. A second edition offered more, and in 1856 Collier published a list that purported to be complete, but which in fact comprised fewer than half the annotations. He was always careless.

In the *Notes and Emendations* Collier describes his Folio in greater detail, and notes for the first time that 'many stains of wine, beer, and other liquids are observable: here and there, holes have been burned in the paper, either by the falling of the lighted snuff of a candle, or by the ashes of tobacco'.[1] Thus, more cunningly than Ireland, did the forger cover his tracks. In the same introduction Collier considers the possibility that Perkins was possibly the actor who played Barabas in a 1633 revival of Marlowe's *Jew of Malta*; he knew his stage history. This Perkins was then the foremost actor with Queen Henrietta's men. His Christian name, however, was Richard. Collier knew this too. Might not, then, Thomas have been Richard's descendant? But the player is not recorded as having a son Thomas, although the Richard Perkins buried at St. James, Clerkenwell, may have been his offspring. No help.

Collier also pinpoints the time of his purchase as the spring of 1849. Regrettably Rodd was unable to verify Collier's circumstantial account of the transaction, for, like Amyot, Douce, and other previously cited worthies, he was dead. F. C. Parry, however, was alive and residing in St. John's Wood. This obscure gentleman was in a position to offer 'clear and positive' proof that the Perkins Folio existed, in its annotated state, a half-century previous. He came to Collier's notice in this way: a John Carrick Moore happened to show the *Notes and Emendations* to Parry, who remembered having once owned such a Second Folio, and, from Collier's description and a facsimile page, declared that this was the book, which could (he believed) be traced back to the Perkins family of Ufton Court, Berkshire, one of whom had married the delicious Arabella Fermor of *The Rape of the Lock*. Collier naturally grasped at a provenance thrown in his lap. Twice he visited the elderly Parry, disabled from a fall, and extricated from him a confirmation of the pedigree, which was duly reported in *The Athenaeum* for 4 June 1853. It did not go entirely unnoticed that on neither of his visits to Parry did Collier have the disputed book in hand.

For him 1853 was a year of crisis. The Perkins Folio created a furore that his other improvisations had for over a decade miraculously escaped. First there were the letters in *The Athenaeum*, then correspondence spilled over into *Notes and Queries*. An industrious Shakespeare editor and antiquary, Samuel Weller Singer, vindicated Shakespeare's text *from* [so the title went] *the*

1 Collier, *Notes and Emendations to the Text of Shakespeare* . . . (1853), Introd., p. vi.

As for my Country, I have ſhed my blood,
Not fearing outward force: So ſhall my Lungs
Coine words till their decay, againſt thoſe Meazels,
Which we diſdaine ſhould Tetter us, yet ſought
The very way to catch them.
Bru. You ſpeake a'th'people, as if you were a god,
To puniſh; Not a man of their Infirmity.
Sicin. 'Twere well we let the people know't.
Men. What, what? his Choller?
Cor. Choller? Were I as patient as the midnight ſleep,
By Iove, 'twould be my minde.
Sicin. It is a minde that ſhall remaine a poiſon
Where it is: not poyſon any further.
Corio. Shall remaine?
Heare you this Triton of the *Minnowes*? Marke you
His abſolute Shall?
Com. 'Twas from the Cannon.
Corio. Shall? O God! but moſt unwiſe Patricians: why
You grave, but wreakleſſe Senators, have you thus
Given Hidra heere to chooſe an Officer,
That with his peremptory Shall, being but
The horne, and noiſe o'th' Monſters, wants not ſpirit
To ſay, hee'l turne your Current in a ditch,
And make your Channell his? If he have power,
Then vale your Ignorance: if none, awake
Your dangerous Lenity: If you are Learn'd,
Be not as common Fooles; if you are not,
Let them have Cuſhions by you. You are Plebeians,
If they be Senators: and they are no leſſe,
When both your voyces blended, the great'ſt taſte
Moſt pallates theirs. They chooſe their Magiſtrate,
And ſuch a one as he, who puts his Shall,
His popular Shall, againſt a graver Bench
Then ever frown'd in Greece. By Iove himſelfe,
It makes the Conſuls baſe; and my ſoule akes
To know, when two Authorities are up,
Neither Supreame; how ſoone confuſion
May enter 'twixt the gap of Both, and take
The one by th'other.
Com. Well, on to'th' Market place.
Corio. Who ever gave that Counſell, to give forth
The Corne a'th'Store-houſe gratis, as 'twas us'd
Sometime in Greece.
Men. Well, well, no more of that.
Cor. Though there the people had more abſolute powre,
I ſay they noriſht diſobedience: fed the ruin of the State.
Bru. Why ſhall the people give
One that ſpeakes thus, their voyce?
Corio. Ile give my Reaſons,
More worthier then their Voyces. They know the Corne
Was not our recompence, reſting well aſſur'd
They ne're did ſervice for't; being preſt to'th' Warre,
Even when the Navell of the State was touch'd,
They would not thred the Gates: This kind of Service
Did not deſerve Corne gratis. Being i'th' Warre,
Their Mutinies and Revolts, wherein they ſhew'd
Moſt Valour, ſpoke not for them. Th' Accuſation
Which they have often made againſt the Senate,
All cauſe unborne, could never be the Native
Of our ſo franke Donation. Well, what then?
How ſhall this Boſome-multiplied, digeſt
The Senates Courteſie? Let deeds expreſſe
What's like to be their words. We did requeſt it,
We are the greater pole, and in true feare
They gave us our demands. Thus we debaſe
The Nature of our Seats, and make the Rabble
Call our Cares, Feares; which will in time
Breake ope the Lockes a'th' Senate, and bring in
The Crowes to pecke the Eagles.
Men. Come enough.
Bru. Enough, with over meaſure.
Corio. No, take more.
What may be ſworne by, both Divine and Humane,
Seale what I end withall. This double worſhip,
Whereon part do's diſdaine with cauſe, the other
Inſult without all reaſon: where Gentry, Title, wiſedome
Cannot conclude, but by the yea and no
Of generall Ignorance, it muſt omit
Reall Neceſſities, and give way the while
To unſtable Slightneſſe. Purpoſe ſo barr'd, it followes,
Nothing is done to purpoſe. Therefore beſeech you,
You that will be leſſe fearefull, then diſcreet,
That love the Fundamentall part of State
More then you doubt the change on't: That preferre
A Noble life, before a Long, and Wiſh,
To jumpe a Body with a dangerous Phyſicke,
That's ſure of death without it: at once plucke out
The Multitudinous Tongue, let them not licke
The ſweet which is their poyſon. Your diſhonor
Mangles true judgement, and bereaves the State
Of that Integrity which ſhould becom't:
Not having the power to doe the good it would,
For th'ill which doth controul't.
Bru. Has ſaid enough.
Sicin. Ha's ſpoken like a Traitor, and ſhall anſwer
As Traitors doe.
Corio. Thou wretch, deſpight ore-whelme thee:
What ſhould the people doe with theſe bald Tribunes?
On whom depending, their obedience failes
To'th' greater Bench, in a Rebellion:
When what's not meet, but what muſt be, was Law,
Then were they choſen: in a better houre,
Let what is meet, be ſaid it muſt be meet,
And throw their power i'th' duſt.
Bru. Manifeſt Treaſon.
Sicin. This a Conſull? No.
Enter an Ædile.
Bru. The Ediles hoe: Let him be apprehended:
Sicin. Goe call the people, in whoſe name my Selfe
Attach thee as a Traitorous Innovator:
A Foe to'th' publike Weale. Obey I charge thee,
And follow to thine anſwer.
Corio. Hence old Goat.
All. Wee'l Surety him.
Com. Ag'd ſir, hands off.
Corio. Hence rotten thing, or I ſhall ſhake thy bones
Out of thy Garments.
Sicin. Helpe ye Citizens.
Enter a rabble of Plebeians with the Ædiles.
Men. On both ſides more reſpect.
Sicin. Heere's hee, that would take from you all your power.
Bru. Seize him Ædiles.
All. Downe with him, downe with him.
2 Sen. Weapons, weapons, weapons:
They all buſtle about Coriolanus.
Tribunes, Patricians, Citizens: what hoe:
Sicinius, Brutus, Coriolanus, Citizens.
All. Peace, peace, peace, ſtay, hold, peace.
Men. What is about to be? I am out of Breath,
Confuſions neere, I cannot ſpeake. You Tribunes
To'th' people: *Coriolanus,* patience: ſpeake good *Sicinius.*
Sicin.

70 THE 'BISSON MULTITUDE'. *From the Perkins Folio in the Huntington Library; shelfmark: 56316. STC 22274e. The page here is slightly reduced.*

interpolations and corruptions advocated by John Payne Collier, Esq., in his notes and emendations. While derisively rejecting as an imposture the Old Corrector's improvements, Singer could not bring himself to believe that Collier was other than the victim of a mischievous hoax.[1] Halliwell, his suspicions aroused, visited Bridgewater House, and in the *Observations* delivered his verdict on the 'new facts' without (as we have seen) implicating Collier himself.

The inevitable next step was taken two years later by A. E. Brae in the seven pages of his anonymously printed shilling pamphlet, *Literary Cookery*, which *The Athenaeum*—always Collier's partisan—had refused. Signing himself 'A Detective', Brae is mostly exercised about Collier's purported short-hand notes of lectures delivered by Coleridge in Fleet Street as far back as 1812; but he has, as another principal motive, the mission 'to rescue the outraged spirit of Shakespeare from the incubus of those "marginal corrections", which, to the shame of the nineteenth century, have been permitted, like the unclean birds of old, to settle down upon his text, tearing and mangling, and befouling where they could not destroy'.[2] The pungency here displayed is matched elsewhere in the broadside by references to plagiarism, vulgarity, and imbecility. The accusing finger points unmistakably at Collier himself—'if the scent now opened be effectively followed up', Detective suggests, 'it may, perhaps, at length extort a second confession, similar to Ireland's, of Shakespearean forgeries'.[3]

Brae had gone too far, and Collier sued the publisher, John Russell Smith, in the Queen's Bench for criminal libel. Presiding was Lord Campbell, later to become Lord Chancellor. A Shakespeare enthusiast, Campbell would (a few years afterwards) frame his *Shakespeare's Legal Acquirements Considered* in the form of a letter to his 'old and valued friend' Collier. They had known one another from their law-reporting days on the *Morning Chronicle*. In the affidavit that formed the basis for his prosecution, Collier ignored Detective's snipings at the Coleridge lectures to dwell on the Perkins Folio. Under oath he repeated his account of how the volume had come his way, and solemnly swore:

> I have not, in either of the said editions [of *Notes and Emendations*], to the best of my knowledge and belief, inserted a single word, stop, sign, note, correction, alteration, or emendation of the said original text of Shakespeare, which is not a faithful copy of the said original manuscript, and which I do not believe to have been written, as aforesaid, not long after the publication of the said folio copy of the year 1632.[4]

That this affidavit is wholly untrue goes without saying: Collier had himself made all the corrections, many of them first in pencil (later half erased) in his own undisguised hand, and subsequently in his laboriously acquired but fluent simulation of a seventeenth-century script. But, to Campbell, Collier's oath sufficiently vindicated the moral character of this 'most honourable' man: the distinguished editor of Shakespeare, vice-president of the Society of Antiquaries, beneficiary of a civil list pension of one hundred pounds 'in consideration of his literary merits'. The publisher returned the unsold sheets of *Literary Cookery* to the author, who had no choice but to order suppression. Only fifteen copies had changed hands. Thus Collier won the day. What if he had compounded the crime of fraud with the crime of perjury?

It was a Pyrrhic victory. Only palaeographical inspection now could silence—or validate—the voices of protest, and such inspection the formerly accommodating Collier effectively discouraged by distancing himself from his book. This he presented, as a free gift, to the Duke of Devonshire. Of course the sceptical or merely curious might, if they wished, apply to view the folio at Devonshire House; but not without Collier's knowledge—he was, after all, the Duke's librarian—or the prospect of his intimidating presence. Few applied. Finally, however, a paralytic seizure carried off the old Duke, and his cousin, the seventh to succeed to the title, opted for co-operation with the scholarly world.

Late in the day on 26 May 1858 the Perkins Folio reached Madden at the British Museum.

1 Samuel Weller Singer, *The Text of Shakespeare Vindicated* (1853). In his interleaved copy, now in the Folger Shakespeare Library (MS. W.a.197.cs1287), he added this epigraph: '"It is plain that in this slippery age we live in, it is very easy to make a book look as old as you would have it." Lord Ch. Justice, in Lady Ivy's case; State Trials Vol. VII p. 572[.] But pens can forge, my friend, that cannot write.'

2 [A. E. Brae], *Literary Cookery* . . . (1855), p. 6.

3 Ibid., p. 7.

4 Ingleby (*Complete View*) gives the text of Collier's affidavit (pp. 38–40).

Three weeks later, while turning over the pages leaf by leaf, Sir Frederic noticed the incompletely obliterated pencil notations in the margins; also pencil below ink emendations. His manuscript diary, preserved in the Bodleian Library, records Madden's consternation upon discovering that the forged entries were by Collier, whose hand he knew well and whose probity he had never questioned. Victorian scientism furnished verification. In the Mineral Department of the Museum, M. H. N. Maskelyne, the Keeper, conducted tests—microscopic, chemical, and mechanical—which demonstrated conclusively that the pencil markings lay beneath, not over, the ink, and that the latter was no true ink but a water-colour paint presumably chosen for its pseudo-antique lustre. Parry, visiting the Museum, finally held the borrowed folio in his hands, and denied ever having owned it. Aided by his young assistant, N. E. S. A. Hamilton, Madden uncompromisingly followed Collier's spoor. They scrutinised the Bridgewater House manuscripts, and pronounced all, save one, spurious (the lone exception was also later repudiated). At Dulwich College, Hamilton established that Mrs. Alleyn's postscript could never have included the Shakespeare reference of Collier's transcription. In July 1859 Lord Ellesmere personally delivered to the Museum the Bridgewater Folio, examination of which quickly revealed the forger's pencil trail.

That month a series of letters to *The Times* made public the findings of the Museum authorities. A more comprehensive arraignment followed in 1860, when Hamilton examined the several controverted items—the Perkins Folio, the Alleyn letter, the Bridgewater Folio and papers—in his coolly devastating *Inquiry into the genuineness of the manuscript corrections in Mr. J. Payne Collier's annotated Shakspere, folio, 1632; and of certain Shaksperian documents likewise published by Mr. Collier*. The *Inquiry* did not single out Collier as the fabricator, but accusation was superfluous: all the evidence pointed unmistakably in a single direction. Cornered, the wounded quarry fended off his assailants as best he could. In a letter to *The Times* (7 July 1859) Collier petulantly vowed to write no more letters, but within less than a fortnight he was addressing *The Times* again. On 19 July 1859 he told of a third visit to Parry, this time with the Perkins Folio in hand, and of encountering him in the road near his home. Then and there Collier showed him the volume. 'That was my book', Parry cried, 'it is the same, but it has been much ill-used since it was in my possession.' As subsequently emerged, however, Parry was then supporting himself on crutches, and incapable of handling a cumbersome folio. Thus did Collier grasp at straws. Although he was prepared, he insisted, to vindicate his integrity before a proper legal tribunal, this time he initiated no libel actions. He did, however, publish a pamphlet *Reply* to Hamilton that proved ineffectual. How could it be otherwise? He was, after all, guilty. Finally, in 1861, another solicitor turned Shakespeare scholar, C. M. Ingleby, administered the *coup de grâce* with his *Complete View of the Shakspere Controversy, concerning the authenticity and genuineness of manuscript matter affecting the works and biography of Shakspere, published by Mr. J. Payne Collier as the fruits of his researches*. In this still highly readable account, which oozes disdain (he truly loathed Collier), Ingleby pins down the malefactor like some helplessly wriggling insect. From Collier only silence. The wider literate public, earlier indifferent to the confined brouhaha over the Bridgewater manuscripts, was at last fully aroused by the scandal of the Perkins Folio. Collier's reputation lay in ruins.

Former friends and benefactors now turned their backs. Dyce, one of the ablest textual editors of the day, had defected earlier, venting his spleen in a two-hundred page polemic directed not at forgeries but at Collier's '*deliberate misrepresentation*' of him in his revised 1858 edition of Shakespeare. Still Collier remained a famous authority with loyal admirers; so he soldiered on. In 1870 he printed as Christmas gifts *A Few Odds and Ends, for Cheerful Friends*, poems he had himself composed between the age of eighteen and eighty-one. Six years later he could declare that he was still keeping 'very busy; and occupation with me is happiness—and such occupation! I delight in it more and more.'[1] This delighted occupation was his continuing minute examination of Shakespeare with his 'intellectual microscope' that revealed beauties he had never before noticed. He was in his nineties when, in his *Autobiography*, he alluded evasively to his own rôle in the Perkins Folio affair:

. . . if the proposed emendations are not genuine, then I claim them as mine; and there I intend to leave

1 Autograph letter to F. W. Cosens, dated 11 December 1876, pasted into *A Few Odds and Ends* . . . in the Folger Shakespeare Library; shelfmark: PR4489.C23F5.

> the question without giving myself further trouble: . . . no edition of Shakespeare, while the world stands, can now be published without them: I brought them into life and light, and I am quite ready to be answerable for them.[1]

As for his foes (he wrote in his *Diary*), 'I defy them and charge all my Relations & Friends never to say one word in my defence: if they do, they will incur my heaviest displeasure. I DESPISE ALL MY ENEMIES & spit at them I cannot forgive ALL.'[2] In other entries defiance gives way to bitter regret. 'I am ashamed of almost every act of my life.'[3] But even in the privacy of the diary confessional, with death imminent, he never quite confessed. He enjoyed a last laugh after his own fashion, for he survived many of the adversaries—Dyce, Madden, and others—who had toppled him.

His own mischief has posthumously haunted his name. Collier tampered with so much that anything he handled is inevitably open to suspicion. Doubts have been expressed regarding not only Forman's 'Book of Plays' and the Shakespeare entries in the Manningham *Diary*, but also the seven Coleridge lectures from shorthand notes, although all of these must surely be genuine. Meanwhile further proofs of delinquency accumulate. In a painstaking essay published as recently as 1971, Giles E. Dawson has demonstrated, from palaeographical evidence, that the Old Corrector's notes and the eighty-three interpolated ballads in a manuscript commonplace book in the Folger Shakespeare Library are products of the same hand. The normal inference is that the hand belongs to Collier, who once owned the item.[4] Thus has a modern tribunal ratified the judgement handed down by the Victorian court of scholarly opinion.

What obscure object of desire tempted Collier down the devious path that led to his undoing? After all, he flourished in the long springtime of Shakespeare studies when true discoveries, like strawberries for the gathering, beckoned an enthusiast (such as Collier) of wide reading and limitless energy and application. Dr. Samuel Tannenbaum, by profession a psychiatrist and an early follower of Freud, offers a medical opinion; Collier, he concludes, suffered from 'dementia praecox of the paranoid type'. If this diagnosis disappoints, it is not merely because dementia praecox has long since been consigned to the rubbish heap of disused psychiatric jargon; paranoia remains a familiar household psychosis. Besides, it is true that, when he was old and becoming senile, Collier saw himself as the victim of conspiracies—the familiar paranoid syndrome—and hurled abuse at his detractors. These, however, were not figments of his imagination, but indeed existed. From all that we can gather, Collier was a well-loved husband and father, and a generous friend. 'I hate disputes of all kinds', he once boasted, 'and, if I can help it, I never will mix myself up with any hostility personal or literary.' To this layman he does not sound much like a paranoiac.

Collier's vanity, however, was inordinate. As a young man he had played billiards with Keats, and (he crowed) won. He had sat at Coleridge's feet. Collier fancied himself a poet, but his early *Poet's Pilgrimage* failed ignominiously; one bookseller to whom he brought it advised him 'to put it into prose, and then he would consider it again'. This rejection rankled Collier to the end of his days. 'The only book I ever wrote, that I care for, is my "Poet's Pilgrimage"', he said at the age of ninety-two. His spurious poems and ballads gave scope to the frustrated poet in Collier, and afforded him an opportunity, in the notes to his 'discovered' texts, judiciously to praise his own compositions if others would not. The Perkins Folio allowed him to improve Shakespeare with impersonal authority. By making fools of the public, even the learned, with his impostures, he could revel in his own superiority. The forgeries also enabled him to rationalise with evidence such *idées fixes* as Shakespeare's early connection with the Blackfriars Theatre, which, being wrong, would otherwise want corroboration. Explanations of other, deeper motives that no doubt were present are best left to the psycho-biographers.

More than a century after their repudiation, Collier's discredited theories still crop up in odd places. On a British Airways flight from Heathrow to Dulles in 1977, the souvenir menu featured, along with the *saumon mayonnaise*, a potted biography of Shakespeare. The young Shakespeare, we

1 Collier, *Autobiography*, p. 147.
2 Collier, *Diary*, xxi. 35 (Folger Shakespeare Library, MS. M.a.37).
3 Ibid., xxvi. 40 (MS. M.a.40).
4 Giles E. Dawson, 'John Payne Collier's Great Forgery', *Studies in Bibliography*, xxiv (1971), 1–26.

were informed, 'was soon to become connected with companies of players and the stage and, in 1589, he was involved with the Blackfriars Theatre'. Collier would have rejoiced.

5
Shakespeare Portraits

Surely the lineaments of no historical personage are more familiar than those of Shakespeare. We see the face everywhere: in paintings, sketches, and engravings; on postage stamps, posters, and medals; in Picasso's famous doodle. He lends weight to bookrests, and sends up smoke from carved pipe bowls. His statue, decked with pigeon droppings, stands in public parks. I have even seen Shakespeare's features reverentially enshrined, for secular worship, in a pane of Victorian stained glass. The catalogue of the Grolier Club's tercentenary exhibition in New York City in 1916 lists almost 450 engraved portraits, and the display was selective. Yet only two images have established claims to authenticity: the Stratford bust set within the monument in Holy Trinity Church, and the Droeshout engraving on the title-page (not, as often stated, the frontispiece) of the First Folio. Over the centuries enthusiasts have championed the claims of countless other icons, all of them either doubtful or derivative or spurious. A handful hold more than passing interest because of the possibility that they represent a true likeness, or because of their influence or special qualities as portraits; or simply because they are curiosities. A full-scale enquiry is beyond both the scope of this volume and the author's competence. In the pages that follow I have, however, discussed the more important Shakespearian and pseudo-Shakespearian portraits, as well as some of their offshoots. Even a highly selective portfolio will, I trust, hold interest for the poet's devotees, and perhaps also for *aficionados* of English portraiture.

The short list of essential studies is quite short. In 1824 the versatile James Boaden first surveyed the various known portraits in *An Inquiry into the Authenticity of Various Pictures and Prints, which, from the Decease of the Poet to our own Times, have been offered to the public as portraits of Shakspeare*. This monograph is, within its specialist limits, pioneering work. Three years later Abraham Wivell, a professional portrait painter, issued privately his *Inquiry into the History, Authenticity, & Characteristics of the Shakspeare Portraits*. As his title-page proclaims, Wivell examines critically the opinions of Malone, Steevens, Boaden, and others. He is especially severe on Boaden; rather ungratefully, as Wivell does not scruple to reprint whole chapters from his predecessor. Wivell's own uncouth prose must be read to be believed. A copy of his *Inquiry* in the Folger Shakespeare Library (shelfmark PR 2929.W5) contains the author's annotations, many of them devoted to the futile endeavour of grammatical and stylistic improvement; but some offer supplementary information. In 1848, shortly before his death, Wivell published another *Inquiry into the History, Authenticity, and Characteristics of the Shakspere Portraits* which, if containing nothing revolutionary, has the merit of being much shorter than his first book. J. Parker Norris, *The Portraits of Shakespeare* (Philadelphia, 1885), is a convenient, if pedestrian, summary of information. In his *Life of William Shakespeare* (4th ed. of rev. version, 1925), Sir Sidney Lee includes a compendious chapter on 'Autographs, Portraits and Memorials', pp. 518–43, that one may still consult with profit. *O Sweet Mr. Shakespeare, I'll have his picture: The changing image of Shakespeare's person, 1600–1800* (1964) is a long title for David Piper's little pamphlet, but it is written with a special authority that commands respect. Piper's researches provide the basis for the valuable, if all too brief, section on Shakespeare in Roy Strong's *Tudor & Jacobean Portraits* (1969), i. 279–86.

Most valuable are the scattered contributions of M. H. Spielmann. His survey, 'The Portraits of Shakespeare', for the *Stratford Town Shakespeare* (1904–7), volume x, was also printed separately for private circulation in an edition of twenty-five copies. Spielmann's most important essay, 'Shakespeare's Portraiture', was included in *Studies in the First Folio written for the Shakespeare Association* (1924), pp. 1–52, and also published the same year as a pamphlet, *The Title-page of the First Folio of Shakespeare's Plays*. Other detailed—sometimes, one ungratefully feels, too exhaustively detailed—articles by Spielmann on individual portraits appeared in the first decade of this century in *The Connoisseur*, and were never collected. I have seen a letter from the same period to Lee in which Spielmann mentions his unfinished monograph on the subject. He was still engaged on it in 1932, for in a letter dated 15 September to Mrs. H. C. Folger he refers to his 'large and exhaustive book on the Portraits of Shakespeare'. When Spielmann died in 1948 at the age of ninety he had still not published his crowning work. I have as yet been unable to trace it. A comprehensive study of the Shakespeare inconography, reflecting current knowledge and deploying the scientific techniques unavailable to Spielmann, remains a desideratum.

I. The Stratford Monument

Some time after Shakespeare's death—just when is not known—those he left behind in Stratford, no doubt the immediate family, erected a monument in his honour in Holy Trinity Church. It was in its place before 1623, when Leonard Digges, employing a familiar *topos*, alludes to the monument in his poem 'To the Memorie of the deceased Authour Maister W. Shakespeare', gracing the eighth preliminary leaf to the First Folio:

> *Shake-speare*, at length thy pious fellowes give
> The world thy Workes: thy Workes, by which, out-live
> Thy Tombe, thy name must: when that stone is rent,
> And Time dissolves thy *Stratford* Moniment,
> Here we alive shall view thee still. This Booke,
> When Brasse and Marble fade, shall make thee looke
> Fresh to all Ages . . .

Happily the monument, no less than the book, still survives in the north wall of the chancel, some five feet from the floor.

An entry made in his almanac in 1653 by Sir William Dugdale, greatest of Warwickshire antiquaries, identifies the stonemason: 'Shakspeares and John Combes Monuments, at Stratford sup' Avon, made by one Gerard Johnson'. As was the custom, Dugdale here anglicises the name of Janssen. The latter's father, Gheerart the elder, a Dutch 'Tombe Maker' born in Amsterdam, had emigrated to London in 1567. A certificate of foreigners drawn up in 1593 describes this Janssen as a householder in the parish of St. Thomas Apostle's, Southwark, with his wife Mary and six children—five sons and a daughter, all born in England—as well as four journeymen, two apprentices, and '1 Englishman at work'. With two of his sons (Gheerart the younger and Nicholas) Janssen carried on a flourishing trade as monumental stonemason, working with materials from the Southwark stone-yard in his premises not far from the Globe Theatre. In 1591, for the munificent sum of £200, the Janssens designed and executed tombs for the third and fourth Earls of Rutland; two years after the poet's death the sixth Earl—the same Francis Manners who had rewarded Shakespeare and Burbage for an *impresa*—commissioned an ornate monument for his lately deceased elder brother Roger, the fifth Earl. These memorials were conveyed with elaborate care, by boat and ox cart, from Southwark to Leicestershire, where the family buried their dead in Bottesford Church. But the most elaborate monument created by the Janssens (this one by the elder Gheerart, assisted by Nicholas) was the free-standing Southampton tomb at Titchfield, with recumbent effigies of the second Earl—father of Shakespeare's patron—and his parents, the hands of all three joined in prayer. In Stratford, John Combe—old ten-in-the-hundred—made a testamentary provision of £60 for his tomb in Holy Trinity, and directed that it be completed within a year of his death, which took place in 1615. Combe's recumbent effigy lies hard by the Shakespeare monument in the church, and may well have prompted the dramatist's family to commission Gheerart the younger, although the latter was presumably also known to Shakespeare's fellows in the King's men.[1]

1 William Dugdale, *The Life, Diary, and Correspondence . . .*, ed. William Hamper (1827), p. 99; Hamper gives the notice of Dugdale in the 1593 certificate of foreigners (Appendix II, p. 512). For an account of Janssen and the school of Netherlandish refugees, see Margaret Whinney, *Sculpture in Britain 1530 to 1830* (Harmondsworth, 1964), pp. 12–22. Whinney is more impressed with the quantity than with the quality of their sculptures.

71 THE SHAKESPEARE MONUMENT, HOLY TRINITY CHURCH, STRATFORD-UPON-AVON.

Fashioned structurally from white marble, the Shakespeare monument is a very typical example of Jacobean Renaissance style. Corinthian columns of black marble, with gilded freestone capitals and bases, support the cornice with its square displaying the Shakespeare arms, helm, and crest in bas-relief. On either side of the entablature sit nude boys on small mounds, figure and mound being carved from a single block. The cherubic figure on the left holds a spade; that on the right has his left hand on an inverted torch, its flame extinguished, while his right hand rests on a skull. The little boys represent, respectively, Labour and Rest. It is a familiar symbolism, this 'grotesque allegory' (as one art historian terms it); its significance is confirmed by Nicholas Janssen's 'plot', or illustrative plan, for the tomb of the fifth Earl of Rutland, where almost identical figures are carved, one being explained as a 'portraiture of Labor', and 'the other of Rest'.[1] A second skull forms the pyramidal apex of the cornice. Inside the rounded niche of the monument stands the Shakespeare bust, actually a waist-length figure of life size, carved from soft bluish Cotswold limestone fetched (according to the Revd. Joseph Greene, knowledgeable in such matters) from a Wilmecote quarry. Beneath the bust an inlaid panel of black touchstone carries the familiar epitaph:

JUDICIO PYLIUM, GENIO SOCRATEM, ARTE MARONEM:
TERRA TEGIT, POPULUS MÆRET, OLYMPUS HABET.

STAY PASSENGER, WHY GOEST THOU BY SO FAST?
READ IF THOU CANST, WHOM ENVIOUS DEATH HATH PLAST,
WITH IN THIS MONUMENT SHAKSPEARE: WITH WHOME,
QUICK NATURE DIDE: WHOSE NAME DOTH DECK Y[S] TOMBE,
FAR MORE THEN COST: SIEH ALL, Y[T] HE HATH WRITT,
LEAVES LIVING ART, BUT PAGE, TO SERVE HIS WITT.
OBIIT AÑO DOI 1616
ÆTATIS . 53 DIE 23 APR.

The stone-cutter, no scholar, has shortened the first vowel of 'Socratem'; 'SIEH' (for 'SITH') is a slip of a sort not uncommon in monumental inscriptions. More serious is the unknown author's ignorance of where the deceased actually lies buried. We owe to him, however, the information that Shakespeare died on 23 April in his fifty-third year.[2] At the bottom of the monument are three supporting brackets, two alabaster and a third (a replacement) imitation.

Attention focuses on the bust, representing the subject as author orator. Wearing a sleeveless gown over a doublet, Shakespeare is in the midst of composition: his left hand rests on a quire of paper, his right hand grasps a pen, his mouth opens (revealing a single line of teeth without individuation); either he is declaiming his newly minted verses, or he gawps while in the throes of creation. The posture is conventional for such a subject in portraits and funerary sculpture; an analogous instance is Nicholas Janssen's bust of John Stow erected by the chronicler's widow in St. Andrew Undershaft Church in the City almost a decade before Shakespeare's death. If (as our foremost authority has declared) the Stratford monument has beauty of design and forms 'an harmonious and compact whole', the bust itself—surely the chief attraction—is fairly primitive. The bobbed locks, upturned moustaches, and Van Dyck beard are sprucely barbered; but the nose and eyes—mere elliptical slits with irises and pupils daubed in—are too small for the face. A missing anatomical feature is the bony protuberance over the eyes. The space between nose and lips has struck some viewers as disproportionately long. Once, when Sir Walter Scott had remarked upon this peculiarity, a pair of compasses were produced, and demonstrated that Scott's upper lip was a quarter-inch farther from his nose than Shakespeare's. Spielmann proved to his own satisfaction (by applying a burnt cork to his upper lip) that the moustache of the bust produced an illusion of disproportion. However that may be, the sculpture makes no very lifelike impression, and some have indeed concluded that it was modelled on a death-mask. It has also been suggested that maybe a life-mask was used, but these are not recorded in England before the Restoration. Perhaps the rigidity of the genre dictated the stiffness, touches of vivacity

1 Sidney Lee, *A Life of William Shakespeare* (4th ed. of revised version, 1925), p. 498.
2 See EKC, ii. 1.

72 THE SHAKESPEARE BUST, HOLY TRINITY CHURCH, STRATFORD-UPON-AVON.

being deemed inappropriate for the occasion. Maybe they were also beyond the sculptor's skill.

Today Shakespeare holds a replaceable quill. It was not always thus. The fate of the pen that formed part of the original design illustrates the vicissitudes to which monuments in public places are subject. Abraham Wivell in 1827 reported this communication from a gentleman residing in Stratford:

Dr. Davenport, our vicar, who has been connected as such, and curate of our church for fifty years, informs me, that on his first appointment here, the bust had *a stone pen*, which a young gentleman, a friend of his, just emerged from Oxford, came to see him, having taken the pen out of the fingers, and fiddling with it, in the exertion, let it through his own, on the flags, which assuredly broke it in pieces, an ordinary pen has been occasionally put between the fingers, for the last fifty years.[1]

Vulnerable too was the colouring of the bust. Painted sculptures, except for Meissen figurines, may strike moderns as odd, or tasteless, but they were for long popular. Even the decorative friezes of the Parthenon were once brightly coloured. The Flemings, we know, painted their funerary effigies. Painted statuary was a familiar sight to the Elizabethans. 'I'ld have her statue cut, now, in white marble', Dr. Rut remarks in Jonson's *Magnetic Lady* (V.vii); to which Sir Moth Interest replies:

And have it painted in most orient colours.
Rut. That's right! all Citie statues must be painted:
Else, they be worth nought i' their subtile Judgements.[2]

In *The Winter's Tale* Paulina, after discovering Hermione supposedly carved in stone, implores Leontes:

O, patience!
The statue is but newly fix'd, the colour's
Not dry.

The colours of Shakespeare's effigy were not long dry before the damp of Holy Trinity began to take their toll: as early as 1649 the bust had to be 're-beautified'.

When, by 1746, the 'Curious Original Monument and Bust of that incomparable Poet' had 'through length of Years and other accidents become much impair'd and decay'd', the Revd. Joseph Greene, master of the local grammar school, persuaded a troupe of strolling players headed by John Ward (Mrs. Siddons's grandfather) to perform *Othello* in the Stratford Town Hall, with the proceeds going to defray the expense of restoration. The benefit yielded somewhat less that £17, of which £12. 10*s*. was two years later paid to John Hall, a limner of Bristol, for making the monument 'as like as possible to what it was when first Erected'.[3] How much improvement actually took place is not clear, but a forefinger and part of the adjacent thumb needed replacement, as did the shattered alabaster architraves, for which white marble ones were substituted; the gilding was renewed and the colouring revived. So the monument remained until 1793, when Edmond Malone, the most eminent Shakespeare scholar of the age, out of misguided neoclassical zeal persuaded the vicar of Stratford to have the bust painted white. The lead-base paint was in 1861 removed with solvents, and the colours restored—'in too high a key', in Spielmann's opinion—on the basis of recovered vestiges of the original. The bust suffered desecration again in 1973, when vandals dislodged it from its niche by chipping away some of the plinth. At the time the police speculated that these miscreants 'were seeking valuable manuscripts written by the Bard'. They were presumably unforthcoming.

Thus the monument has suffered the depredations of time and unrespecting hands. One would like to have some idea of the original colours of the bust. The earliest description I have been able to come by occurs in a pamphlet privately printed by John Britton in 1816: 'The hands and face

1 Abraham Wivell, *An Historical Account of the Monumental Bust of William Shakespeare* (1827), p. 22.

2 Spielmann, *Title Page*, p. 13, cites this passage, as well as the more familiar one from *The Winter's Tale*.

3 Joseph Greene, *Correspondence*, ed. Levi Fox (1965), pp. 14–15, 168. Fox supplies an appendix of items connected with the 1746 restoration, pp. 164–73. Greene's correspondence makes it clear that Hall hailed from Bristol and not, as sometimes stated, Birmingham.

were of flesh colour, the eyes of a light hazle, and the hair and beard, auburn; the doublet, or coat, was scarlet, and covered with a loose black gown, or tabard, without sleeves; the upper part of the cushion was green, the under half crimson, and the tassels gilt.'[1] This account of the bust as 'originally painted' in every respect conforms with that of Spielmann a half-century ago:

> The painted face of the bust shows a glow of health usually to be seen only in sculptured effigies. The hair and beard are auburn; the doublet scarlet; the gown black; the falling-band white; the cushion green above and crimson below; the cord and tassels gilt. The eyes are hazel gone dark.[2]

The bust today still wears the same colours, not far removed (one suspects) from the original.

What are we to make of the well-fed gentleman with his short neck, plump sensual cheeks, and vast forehead, who stares at us—rather stupidly, it must be granted—from his station? Evidently the likeness satisfied the family, Dr. Hall probably being the chief sponsor; but they did not boggle at the misinformation in the epitaph. Later responses comprise a spectrum; effigies of great men have their Rorschach aspect. Certainly the bust has had an impact; the forehead, especially, has impressed. Washington Irving in 1815 visited Holy Trinity, and afterwards set down an impression characteristic of many: 'The aspect is pleasant and serene, with a finely arched forehead; and I thought I could read in it clear indications of that cheerful, social disposition, by which he was as much characterized among his contemporaries as by the vastness of his genius.'[3] Serene, with finely arched forehead: this is the Shakespeare of Arnold's celebrated sonnet—the poet of 'victorious brow', smiling and still, 'Out-topping knowledge'. Ingleby a few decades later expressed what is probably still a minority view:

> How awkward is the *ensemble* of the face! What a painful stare, with its goggle eyes and gaping mouth! The expression of this face has been credited with *humour*, *bonhommie*, *hilarity* and *jollity*. To me it is decidedly *clownish*; and is suggestive of a man crunching a sour apple, or struck with amazement at some unpleasant spectacle.[4]

Yet Ingleby found force in the muscular face, and felt that simply *because* the features smacked of caricature, they must retain 'an unmistakeable likeness'. A later age than the Renaissance nurtured the romantic idea of the artist who dies prematurely in his garret of thwarted passion, neglect, and tuberculosis; but Shakespeare was not Keats, and the very burgher-like stolidity of his carved image stirred a sympathetic warmth in some bosoms. Halliwell-Phillipps writes:

> There is, in truth, a convincing and a mental likeness in this monument, one that grows upon us by contemplation, and makes us unwilling to accept any other resemblance. If it has fallen beneath a cloud, the reason must be sought for in the circumstance that an image, the composition of which derives no assistance from the ideal, can scarcely be expected to satisfy the imagination in the delineation of features belonging to so great an intellect. But to those who can bring themselves to believe that, notwithstanding his unrivalled genius, Shakespeare was a realization of existence, and in his daily career, much as other men were, the bust at Stratford will convey very nearly all that it is desirable to know of his outward form.[5]

He was, *in his daily career, much as other men were*. Other men gained and spent. Thus did Shakespeare accommodate himself to the utilitarian temper; that temper which could enshrine him as an example of (in Samuel Smiles's best-selling manual) *Self-Help*. It is from this perspective that we may understand Dover Wilson's aversion to the 'self-satisfied pork-butcher' in Holy Trinity as a twentieth-century reaction against Victorian philistinism. Whatever the limitations of the Stratford bust, and whatever values we may project upon it, it remains an authentic likeness.

Not that its credentials have escaped sceptical inquiry. Any responsible account of the bust must take into consideration a single jarring item of evidence. When, some thirty or forty years after installation, Dugdale printed the first engraving of the monument, it bore an aspect very different from the one we know. In Dugdale's illustration the cherubs balance precariously on the

1 J[ohn] Britton, *Remarks on the Monumental Bust of Shakspeare* . . . (Chiswick, 1816), p. 6.

2 M. H. Spielmann, *The Title-Page of the First Folio of Shakespeare's Plays* . . . (1924). EKC (ii. 184) misquotes the passage, making the cord and tassels black rather than gilt.

3 Washington Irving, *Rip Van Winkle and Other Sketches* (New York, 1882), p. 161.

4 C. M. Ingleby, *Shakespeare; The Man and the Book* (1877–81), i. 79.

5 William Shakespeare, *Works*, ed. J. O. Halliwell-Phillipps (1853–65), i. 230.

73 THE SHAKESPEARE MONUMENT IN DUGDALE'S *ANTIQUITIES OF WARWICKSHIRE* (1656), p. 520. *Wing D2479.*

edges of the cornice, while leopards' heads surmount the capitals. Shakespeare himself has strangely altered; the smug pork-butcher has turned into a decrepit elderly tailor.[1] His cheeks have contracted, the moustaches droop, his mouth is clenched shut. As though in abdominal pain, he clutches a pillow to his stomach, his elbows akimbo. All things being possible in Shakespeare studies, even this dispiriting icon has found its rhapsodist. 'In it there *is* something biographical, something suggestive', Mrs. Charlotte Stopes insists; 'it shows us the tired creator of poems, exhausted from lack of sleep, "Nature's sweet restorer", weary of the bustling London life, who had returned, as soon as possible, to seek rest at home among his own people, and met an over-early death in the unhealthy spring-damps of 1616.'[2] For Mrs. Stopes, the first to undertake a detailed comparison of the engraving with the bust, the former carries greater authority; the sculpture, she thinks, underwent fundamental reconstruction in 1748. But £12. 10*s.* would hardly have bought *that* much alteration. If I read Mrs. Stopes correctly, she seems to think that the mantle was thrown over Shakespeare's shoulders as part of the restoration; but since the figure is carved from a single block of stone, such a change of costume would of course be impossible. Anyway, a rough sketch of the monument made by George Vertue in 1737 and preserved in one of his notebooks—a sketch of which Stopes was unaware—shows the bust as it now appears.

It has always been that way. Errors, both small and substantive, litter Dugdale's numerous, large, and densely factual books; given the speed with which he turned them out, it could hardly be otherwise. One would welcome the chance to compare the drawing Dugdale supplied to his

1 EKC (ii. 185) characterises Shakespeare as a tailor.

2 Charlotte Carmichael Stopes, *The True Story of the Stratford Bust: A Contemporary Likeness of Shakespeare* (1904); reprinted from the *Monthly Review*, April 1904.

17

went to see the church of Stratford

several Monuments one in the rails of the communion Table for Old John a Coomb a rich miser whom in Shakespears time he made an Epitaph — see Shakespears workes.

amonument for Sr Hugh Clopton and his Lady of that Town.

another Monument a Man and Woman hand in hand, not quite half figures (erect) not lying this was made in memory of Judith daughter of Wm Coomb ... she dyed 1649. but this Monument was set up after the restoration — or about 40 years ago only upon one part of the Mont. is Tho: Stanton fecit Holb.

& who the Sculptor of the figures was being done masterly. and some merit.

Rev. Mr Kendrick Minister there. now

Mr Harbord Statuary lives there at Stratford and I commissiond him to make me a Cast from the Bust of Shakespears head on his Mont.

no. 1. on Shakespears grave stone near the rails of the commu table.

Good frend for Jesus sake forbeare
to digg the dust enclosed HEare
blest be the Man that spares these stones
and Curst be he y. moves my bones.

he left 2 daughters
Susanna daughter of Shakespeare, married to John Hall. Gent.
another Daughter married to Mr Nash. of ...

no. 2. his wifes grave stone.
anne .... wife of Shakespeare dyd. aug. 6. 1623.

74 GEORGE VERTUE'S SKETCH OF THE SHAKESPEARE MONUMENT, 1737. *British Library, MS. Portland Loan 29/246, p. 17. Vertue made the sketch when, in the company of the Earl of Oxford, he visited Stratford in October 1737; see Frank Simpson, 'New Place: The Only Representation of Shakespeare's House, from an Unpublished Manuscript'*, Shakespeare Survey 5 (*Cambridge, 1952*), *pp. 55–7.*

75 JOHN BOADEN, SHAKESPEARE IN HIS STUDY, *c. 1825. Folger Shakespeare Library, Art File S527, no. 302. This lithograph, dated 1828, is from a drawing by Thomas Fairland.*

Opposite:
76 THE DROESHOUT ENGRAVING: THE FIRST STATE. *From* Mr. William Shakespeare's Comedies, Histories, & Tragedies *(1623), title-page. Copy in the British Library; shelfmark: C.39.k.15. Other examples of the first state are preserved at the Bodleian and the Folger Shakespeare Library (two examples).*

MR. WILLIAM
SHAKESPEARES
COMEDIES, HISTORIES, & TRAGEDIES.

Publiſhed according to the True Originall Copies.

LONDON

Printed by Iſaac Iaggard, and Ed. Blount. 1623.

engraver Hollar or one of Hollar's assistants—Gaywood or King or Dudley or another, most likely Gaywood—with the engraving itself. Spielmann, who was able to make such a comparison, has a teasing note: 'It is the fact that the original drawing for this engraving is extant and in the possession of a lineal descendant of Dugdale, and that the plate departs in details from the sketch. Why? One of them, obviously, must be wrong. In truth, both are libels on the original.'[1] Evidently, the engraver (and the artist also) took liberties that were customary then, before the camera with its objectively verifying lens was available to inhibit such wayward fancies. At least the engraver got the armorial bearings right, which were what Dugdale cared about most.

The Stratford monument, unsurprisingly, had little impact on later artists and engravers striving to formulate an image, romantic or sentimental, compatible with the imperatives of bardolatry. At least one item, however, invites notice. Early in the last century John Boaden executed a full-length portrait in oil of Shakespeare seated in his Stratford study. He wears the Droeshout ruff. Plutarch and other volumes clutter his desk, along with paper, ink pot, and quill; framed paintings of cherished totems—Queen Elizabeth and the Globe playhouse (from the Visscher panorama)—grace the wall; a window commands a view of Holy Trinity Church. Son of the James Boaden who attempted the first monograph on the Shakespeare iconography, John shared his father's enthusiasm for the theatre and the National Poet. His portrait subjects included Kean, Kemble, and Eliza O'Neill in Shakespearian rôles. Evidently the monumental bust in Stratford appealed to him, for he sketched it with meticulous care for a drawing that was more than once engraved. From 1810 until his death in 1839, the same year in which his father died, Boaden exhibited often at the Royal Academy and the Society of British Artists, turning out pictures which (in the judicious summation of his *DNB* memorialist) 'although pleasing, did not rise above mediocrity'.

II. The Droeshout Engraving

As Digges mentions the Stratford monument in his commendatory poem for the First Folio, it must antedate our only other authenticated likeness: the copper engraving of a younger Shakespeare which ornaments the title-page of the same volume. Underneath the lower left-hand corner of the plate appears the engraver's signature: 'Martin Droeshout sculpsit London'. It is his only title to fame.

Martin (or Marten) Droeshout belonged to the third generation of a Flemish family resident in London. The surname is variously spelt in the records. Martin's grandfather John, a painter and joiner, had crossed the Channel from Brussels—then the South Netherlands—around 1570; the same 1593 certificate of foreigners that cites Janssen describes Droeshout as '24 Years in England'.[2] This John had two sons: Martin, a painter, and Michael, the engraver's father. Some details about the latter may be gleaned from the same certificate. He is listed as living in Bread

Opposite:

77 THE DROESHOUT ENGRAVING: THE SECOND STATE. *From* Mr. William Shakespeare's Comedies, Histories, & Tragedies *(1623), title-page. Copy in the Folger Shakespeare Library, Washington, D.C.; shelfmark: STC 22273, Fo. 1, No. 1. The title-page here reproduced is from a copy presented by William Jaggard to the herald Augustine Vincent, whose device—a muzzled bear holding a banner in its left paw, and a squire's helmet in the right—appears stamped on the front cover of the binding. The inscription is in Vincent's hand. Vincent, a friend of Jaggard, quarrelled with the York Herald, Ralph Brooke, who had in 1602 complained about the grant of arms to 'Shakespear yᵉ Player'. Before coming to the Folger collection, the Vincent copy belonged to the Sibthorp family of Sudbrooke Holme, Lincoln. The volume is described and analysed by Sidney Lee,* A Life of William Shakespeare *(4th ed. of revised version, 1925), pp. 566–7. It is item lxxxvii in Lee's* Census of Extant Copies of the First Folio.

1 Spielmann, *Title-Page*, p. 21n.

2 I quote the certificate from Hamper's text in Dugdale, *Diary*, Appendix II, p. 511. Spielmann, *Title-Page*, p. 25, states that Droeshout settled in London in 1566, and I have previously followed his dating (*DL*, 258). Spielmann may be right, but, as he gives no documentation, I have decided here to follow the certificate, which is particular on the matter.

Ex dono Willi Jaggard Typographi a° 1623

MR. WILLIAM

SHAKESPEARES

COMEDIES, HISTORIES, & TRAGEDIES.

Publiſhed according to the True Originall Copies.

LONDON

Printed by Iſaac Iaggard, and Ed. Blount. 1623.

Street ward, 'a chamber Keeper; no wyfe; born in Brussell in Brabant, but dyd remayne sumtyme in Andwarpe, sometyme in Fryzeland, and sometyme in Zeland, and from thence came hyther. A graver in Copper, which he learned in Brussell'. On 17 August 1595 Michael married Susanna van der Ersbek of Ghent. Of their several children, Martin was baptised 26 April 1601. Thus he was only fifteen when Shakespeare died, and twenty-one when he received the commission to supply an engraving for the imposing Folio volume that was to sell for the high price of £1. One can only speculate as to why the inexperienced young engraver was entrusted with this important assignment. Conceivably a connection with the Janssens had something to do with it. The two families belonged to the same small colony and worshipped together in the Dutch Reformed Church at Austin Friars.

Opposite the title-page appears Ben Jonson's short poem endorsing the portrayal:

This Figure, that thou here seest put,
It was for gentle Shakespeare cut;
Wherein the Graver had a strife
with Nature, to out-doo the life:
O, could he but have drawne his wit
As well in brasse, as he hath hit
His face; the Print would then surpasse
All, that was ever writ in brasse.
But, since he cannot, Reader, looke
Not on his Picture, but his Booke.

Jonson is not, as might appear, imprecise in referring to brass, for the terms *brass* and *copper* were then used interchangeably. The poem itself consists of a tissue of commonplaces, one of which (lines 3–4) echoes Shakespeare's *Venus and Adonis*: 'Look when a painter would surpass the life / In limning out a well-proportioned steed, / His art with nature's workmanship at strife. . . .' How seriously should one take Jonson's eulogy? He knew the subject personally, so his judgment carries weight. But the stanza is routine bread-and-butter verse (no doubt only an oversubtle criticism will discern latent irony in the concluding couplet), and since George Steevens in the eighteenth century, some have doubted that Jonson had ever even seen the engraving he commended.[1] Conceivably his opinion was based on the miniature (which would help account for the linear conception of the engraving) or limning ('a portrait consisting of an outline drawing with perhaps delicate flat washes of colour') from which Droeshout worked.

The First Folio engraving survives in three states. These Charlton Hinman has distinguished in precise detail in his monumental *Printing and Proof-Reading of the First Folio of Shakespeare*:

1. State I is most readily identified by its lack of any shading on the ruff under the ear. Only a few impressions of this 'proof state' of the engraving would seem to have been made before the plate was considerably modified, since State I is represented in the Folger collection by only a single copy, Folg. 2.

2. State II shows shading on the ruff; the high-light in each eye is represented by a small but fairly regular rectangle of white; the silhouette of the hair on the right side is sharp and smooth. Evidently a fair number of impressions were taken from the once-altered plate, for State II is found in six Folger copies (Folg. 1, 7, 13, 14, 20, and 72), and this state is also represented in the Lee facsimile.

3. In State III a small wedge of black pierces from the top of the rectangle of white in each of the eyes; and this state also shows, about midway along the silhouette of the hair on the right side, what may be taken to represent a single hair that is slightly out of place. (These peculiarities are so small as easily to escape notice; but there can be no doubt that they reflect changes deliberately made in the plate and hence that they define a genuine third state.) State III is much commoner than State II. It is to be seen in some two dozen Folger copies.[2]

As the century progressed the printers used the same copper plate for subsequent editions of the Folio. The engraving appears in the identical position in the Second Folio of 1632, and the first issue (1663) of the Third Folio, but was the next year displaced to the frontispiece position, over Jonson's verses, to make room for a listing on the title-page of the seven apocryphal plays added

1 Such short poems, expressing undifferentiated praise, 'were manufactured to order, often without the plate being seen by the versifier' (Spielmann, p. 27).

2 Charlton Hinman, *The Printing and Proof-Reading of the First Folio of Shakespeare* (Oxford, 1963), i. 248–9.

78 THE DROESHOUT ENGRAVING IN THE FOURTH FOLIO. *From* Mr. William Shakespear's Comedies, Histories, and Tragedies *(1685), first preliminary leaf. Wing S2915.*

to the second issue. The same format obtains in the Fourth Folio of 1685. Continued use of the plate resulted in its progressive deterioration. With the Fourth Folio coarse cross-hatching covers most of the engraving, except the background. The face, now swarthy, gleams with oily highlights; there is a stubble of beard around mouth and chin. Thus did the attempt to freshen the plate demean the subject.

The engraving was not that much to begin with. An apparently neckless head sits on its platter of a wired-band, rather like the decapitated Baptist being served up to Salome. The mouth has wandered off to the right, the ear lobe defies anatomy, and the hair (straight rather than bobbed as in the monument) fails to balance on the two sides. Proportions are awry: the head is much too big for the torso; the shoulder wings, for the doublet. (Some have speculated that Droeshout visualises his subject in actor's garb, maybe as the elder Knowell in *Every Man in His Humour*—we know Shakespeare acted in the play. That would help account for Jonson's praise; but such reconstructions are romance. In the engraving Shakespeare wears the costume of a well-to-do gentleman of his day.) Light improbably emanates from several sources at once. It comes from above the head and from left of the nose; it falls on the ruff and where the hair joins the forehead. The shadows are unfortunately not consistent with these lighting sources. In all, a lamentable performance.

Still, even Droeshout has found his panegyrists. The biographer of the Dutch engraver Houbraken has studied the portrait and concluded: 'There indeed we find the features which characterize the author of *Romeo* as well as of him who wrote *Julius Caesar*. What nobility in that forehead! with what feeling is rendered the pensive and penetrating expression of the eyes and of the smile, of which the irony is softened by the sweetness of soul!'[1] Allowance perhaps should be made for the fact that the enthusiast is foreign, but the terms of ver Huell's encomium are not very different from those employed earlier by James Boaden. 'To me', he confesses, 'this portrait exhibits an aspect of calm benevolence and tender thought; great comprehension, and a kind of mixt feeling, as when melancholy yields to the suggestions of fancy.'[2] As Boaden had for a time declared himself a believer in the Ireland papers, he could possibly persuade himself of anything, although he is on the whole a sane and temperate early guide to the Shakespeare iconography. Be this as it may, Droeshout has found a modern admirer in A. L. Rowse, normally properly contemptuous of second-raters:

> The whole impression is dominated by that magnificent bald cranium, like another dome of St. Paul's—plenty of room there for the most lively (and living), the most universal brain among the Elizabethans. It is absolutely convincing. Then there are the arched eyebrows, the large fine eyes that we can see would easily be capable of a wide range of expression, full of intelligence. The nose is large and rather sensual, yet with sensibility indicated in the flare of the nostril—and we know that he had an acute sense of smell. The mouth small and well-formed, with a suggestively feminine curve of the lips, almost a Cupid's bow. The well-rounded cheeks suggest the mobile face of an actor, with easy changes of expression; the face rather hairless, with light moustache and little tuft beneath the lower lip, the hair worn long. What a powerful impression it gives: that searching look of the eyes understanding everything, what a forehead, what a brain![3]

Would the Droeshout engraving, one wonders, have inspired comparable raptures had it portrayed Ferdinando Clutterbook, Shakespeare's tax collector, or some other Elizabethan nonentity?

Still, despite Droeshout's painfully modest talents and the unlikelihood (given his age at the time) of his direct acquaintance with his subject, such evidence as we have goes to confirm the genuineness of the representation. There is Jonson's testimony, already discussed. Shakespeare's old friends from the King's Men, Heminges and Condell, deemed the portrait fit to grace the title-page of a volume dedicated to the two noble lords who, 'prosequuted both them [Shakespeare's plays], and their Authour living, with so much favour'. True, engraving and bust present different images, but the latter depicts an older man. In both, the poet has the same extraordinary perpendicular forehead, and the skull proportions of the two are compatible; so they tend mutually to confirm authenticity.

A word about Droeshout's later career. He went on to engrave other portraits and title-pages, although he never achieved any special eminence. His subjects included General Fairfax, John Donne (prefixed to *Death's Duel*, 1632), and John Howson, Bishop of Durham. In 1634 Droeshout did a frontispiece of Dido stabbing herself for Stapylton's octavo *Dido and Aeneas*, a translation of Vergil's Fourth Book. There are in the British Museum Print Room sets of Droeshout's 'The Four Seasons' and 'The Prophecies of the Twelve Sibyls', the latter copied from Crispin van de Passe. He died around 1652, leaving a corpus of only twenty-two positively identified items.[4] Were it not for his Shakespeare, engraved when he was twenty-one, he would long since have been forgotten.

1 A. ver Huell, *Jacobus Houbraken et son Œuvre* (1875), quoted, in translation, by Spielmann, p. 27.

2 James Boaden, *An Inquiry into the Authenticity of Various Pictures and Prints* . . . (1824), p. 17.

3 A. L. Rowse, *The English Spirit: Essays in Literature and History* (rev. ed., 1966.), pp. 5–6.

4 I follow the descriptive catalogue of Arthur M. Hind, *Engraving in England in the Sixteenth & Seventeenth Centuries* (Cambridge, 1952–64), ii. 351–66. Hind counts sets like *The Twelve Sibyls* as single items.

This Shadowe is renowned Shakeſpear's? Soule of th'age
The applauſe? delight? the wonder of the Stage.
Nature her ſelfe, was proud of his deſignes
And joy'd to weare the dreſsing of his lines;
The learned will Confeſs, his works are ſuch,
As neither man, nor Muſe, can prayſe to much.
For ever live thy fame, the world to tell,
Thy like, no age, shall ever paralell.

79 THE WILLIAM MARSHALL ENGRAVING. *From* Poems: written by Wil. Shake-speare, Gent. (*1640*). STC *22344*. *Copy in the Bodleian Library; shelfmark: Arch. G.f.4.*

The Shakespeare engraving began early to spawn copies and adaptations. First to appear was a frontispiece, by William Marshall, to John Benson's pirated 1640 edition of the *Poems*. An oval portrait surmounts a pastiche of verses lifted from Jonson's eulogy, with a concluding couplet that may (anything is possible) be original. In the lower right-hand corner of the plate appears the signature, 'W.M. sculpsit'. From 1617, when the first engraving with his name was published, until 1650, when he passes from view, Marshall was a prolific engraver of portraits, title-pages, and book illustrations (his cataloguers list over 250 items). Of his life nothing is known. His literary subjects include Milton, John Fletcher, and James Shirley, but he is best known for his illustrations for Quarles's *Emblems* in 1635, followed three years later by *The Hieroglyphics of the Life of Man*. Corbett and Norton sum up Marshall's gifts thus: 'There is a negligible attention to form of any kind; classical design, architectural framework, nature are unimportant to him. His talent lay in the depicting of male and female marionettes, often of very small size, singly or in groups, which he manipulated with a rough facility, his sole aim being to tell a story or convey a message in as simple and literal a fashion as possible.'[1]

His Shakespeare is one such marionette. If Droeshout is unmistakably the source, Marshall introduces a few individual touches. He reverses Droeshout, lengthens the figure, puts a sprig of laurel in Shakespeare's left hand ('this sinistrous decoration', as Boaden terms it), straightens the bottom edge of the ruff, and throws a cloak over the right shoulder. The cloak would appeal to later portraitists. Some authorities, following Walpole, allege that Marshall copied an original by the able John Payne (fl. 1600–40), but no such engraving has ever turned up.

1 *Engraving in England*, iii. 102. Hind died before completing work on the third volume, which was compiled from his notes by Margery Corbett and Michael Norton.

The Fates decree, that tis a mighty wrong
To Woemen Kinde, to have more Greife, then Tongue

80 THE WILLIAM FAITHORNE ENGRAVING. *From* The Rape of Lucrece . . . (*1655*), *frontispiece. Wing S2943. Wing mistakenly describes this as the eighth edition; it is the ninth.*

The second offspring of Droeshout is the oval miniature, about one and a half inches long, that embellishes the top of William Faithorne's frontispiece to the 1655 edition of *The Rape of Lucrece*, showing full-length figures of Lucrece stabbing herself while her husband Collatine stands by astonished. Shakespeare's face has lost some of its fullness, and the lips have widened, but his forehead is as impressively perpendicular as ever. Faithorne seems most comfortable with the ruff of the writer described on the title-page as 'The incomparable Master of our English Poetry, Will: Shakespeare Gent.'.

In the apostolic succession of eighteenth-century editions other favourites for a time supplanted Droeshout. Rowe in 1709 included two versions of Chandos (q.v.), as well as the Dugdale travesty of the monument. But Droeshout returned triumphantly on the frontispiece to the first volume of the immensely influential Johnson and Steevens editions of 1778. The unknown copyist, using as his model the portrait in its first state, wielded a meticulous graver. Versions have since been legion.

III. The Flower Portrait

There hangs in the Shakespeare Memorial Gallery in Stratford-upon-Avon a portrait of Shakespeare that uncannily resembles the Droeshout engraving. Measuring 23½ by 17½ inches, the picture is painted in oil on an ancient worm-eaten panel of English oak over a surface thinly coated with gesso (a plaster prepared from paris or gypsum mixed with glue). Although pronounced 'crudely painted and far inferior in quality to Droeshout's work' by one modern authority, its inferiority may not be self-evident to all viewers. The artist has simplified the embroidery, which in the painting shows as gold against the black of the doublet; he has centralised the mouth, corrected the anatomy of the ear, and rationalised the light, which now proceeds from a single source—gone is the illuminated crescent under the right eye. In the upper left-hand corner of the panel appears an inscription in cursive script, all but invisible in reproduction: 'Willm Shakespeare 1609'. Is this a portrait, painted from life, of the poet in his forty-fifth year, that the young Droeshout copied? So several authorities—among them Sir Sidney Colvin, Sir Edward Poynter, and Dr. Lionel Cust—have concluded.

The painting first surfaced in the last century. Around 1840 H. C. Clements, a connoisseur from Peckham Rye, bought the picture from 'an obscure dealer'. On the back of the box housing his treasure, Clements pasted a note:

> The original portrait of Shakespeare, from which the now famous Droeshout engraving was taken and inserted in the first collected edition of his works, published in 1623, being seven years after his death. The picture was painted nine years before his death, and consequently sixteen years before it was published. . . . The picture was publicly exhibited in London seventy years ago, and many thousands went to see it.[1]

Later Clements averred that a descendant of Shakespeare's family, in whose possession the picture had stayed since it was painted, had presented the relic to him. No record has survived of the exhibition to which Clements alludes, despite the 'many thousands' drawn to it when the Jubilee fever raged. However, the portrait was subsequently displayed at the Crystal Palace and at the Alexandra Palace, where the great fire damaged it slightly. In 1892 Edgar Flower of the prominent Stratford brewing family bought the painting from Clements's executrix. Three years later Mrs. Flower presented it to the Memorial Gallery on the Avon which the family had established and generously supported.

It goes without saying that a life-portrait of the National Poet would have inestimable value, so it comes as no surprise that experts have on more than one occasion scientifically studied the Flower picture with all the technology at their disposal. Examination in 1895–6 revealed evidence of megilp and bitumen (the latter in the hair) still fresh enough to yield to the pin. That need not suggest a deliberate deception, only restoration and repair. For some time authorities had known that the portrait covered over an earlier painting, but only recently has X-ray examination, undertaken at the Courtauld Institute, revealed beneath the present surface a painting by a quattrocento artist showing the Madonna and Child, with St. John; the outline of the Virgin's shoulder is still discernible under Shakespeare's stiff white collar. These investigations, however informative, yield no clues to precedence.

Other evidence does. As always with doubtful attributions, provenance presents a challenge, it being easier (as Spielmann has shrewdly observed) to concoct a picture than a pedigree. We are told that the painting remained for so long hidden because of 'the Puritan ascendency and civil wars, and extinction of the family in direct line which caused most of the personal relics to be dispersed'—a feebly vague accounting. But more telling arguments challenge credulity. As Spielmann observes, 1609 is early days for the cursive script in such inscriptions (one of the *a*'s, moreover, looks suspiciously modern). The portrait, in his opinion, lacks the 'little experimental touches' consistent with a portrait from life: 'the accidents of a face' which give expression, likeness, and life—the colour and folds of the skin and the play and forms of the muscles.[2] And, if Droeshout had this painting at his elbow, why did he eliminate from his engraving the inscription with its interesting titbit of information? An engraver's task being to copy his source, it is unlikely that he would deliberately introduce gross errors of anatomy, proportion, and lighting; much more likely that the painter corrected the engraver's faults. But the most telling evidence of Droeshout's priority is the tell-tale shadow on the ruff of the Flower portrait. From the history of the plate we know it was not a feature of the original, but introduced in the second state. So a copy of the First Folio with the engraving in a later state presumably served the anonymous artist.

His identity has naturally inspired speculation. One candidate is the Dutch master Cornelius Janssen, but this attribution is on various grounds untenable. Enough confusion has surrounded the portrait for a responsible critic, the late Robert Speaight, to assert in his last book that it was

1 Quoted by Sidney Lee, *A Life of William Shakespeare* (4th ed. of rev. version, 1925), p. 531.

2 Spielmann, *The Portraits of Shakespeare* (Stratford-upon-Avon, 1907), pp. 14–15.

81 THE FLOWER PORTRAIT. *The Shakespeare Memorial Gallery, Stratford-upon-Avon.*

painted by Martin Droeshout in 1609—when he was eight years old![1] Droeshout is not known to have painted anything. Conceivably Speaight was thinking of the engraver's uncle Martin, but that suggestion is almost equally implausible.

Whoever did the Flower, it holds much interest as our first painting demonstrably of Shakespeare. Provided, of course, that it is the real thing. One cannot altogether suppress the subversive suspicion that the portrait now hanging in Stratford may—just possibly—be a nineteenth-century fake painted on a handily available old panel by a talented rogue who felt no compunctions about sacrificing the Virgin and Child on the altar of Mammon. Disinterested scientific analysis offers the only chance of settling the matter. Meanwhile the Flower portrait serves often enough as the frontispiece to biographies; Sidney Lee used it, as have A. L. Rowse and the present author, not yet assailed by dark misgivings. The frontispiece to Rowse's *William Shakespeare* (1963) is oddly sophisticated, for, without any signal to the reader, somebody has superimposed the Flower head and ruff, retouched, upon a modern rendering of the doublet and background.

IV. The Chandos Portrait

Painted in oil on coarse English canvas, and of approximately the same dimensions ($21\frac{3}{4}$ by $17\frac{1}{4}$ inches) as the Flower, the Chandos portrait was the first picture presented to the National Portrait Gallery—in 1856 by the Earl of Ellesmere—and has hung there to this day. The painting is in the shape of an oval, a form traceable in British portraiture to the first decade of the seventeenth century, and shows the subject facing slightly to the left, whence derives the light. He appraises the viewer pensively with dark greyish eyes. This Shakespeare—if it is he—wears a brown moustache and a pointed beard. The forehead is ample, although not perpendicular; the hair full at the sides. Over the plain black doublet a small white collar stands open, the drawstrings (visible through the beard) hanging down. In the subject's left ear a gold ring gleams.

The swarthy physiognomy, even more than the 'wanton lips', has stirred xenophobic anxieties. 'It is hard to believe', Spielmann declares, 'that this dark face, of distinctly Italian type, represents one of the pure English Shakespeare stock of the Midlands'.[2] Others have remarked on the Italianate look of the face; a greater number, perhaps, have found it 'decidedly Jewish'. The Jewishness has been rationalised by the suggestion that the portrait shows Shakespeare made up for the part of Shylock; in Shakespeare studies all perplexities have their resolutions. Anyway, better a Jew than a pork butcher if one must make a choice—this bohemian with a golden earring might conceivably have the soul of a poet. Nor is the 'somewhat lubricious' mouth unsuited to an English writer who, in Dr. Rowse's handicapping, is the all-time winner in the sexiness sweepstakes. Whatever the reasons, only Chandos of all the Shakespeare portraits, real or spurious, has challenged Droeshout for popularity. Boaden remarked that 'No picture within the last hundred years has been more frequently copied.'[3] That was in 1824. Many have copied or reproduced it since.

That the picture is English, and of the period, no authority questions. But the first half-century of its existence are Lost Years, a void which, in the nature of things, fancy has filled. Who painted it? In the mid eighteenth century the antiquary Oldys, annotating his Langbaine's *English Dramatick Poets*, remarked on the 'picture of Shakespeare which they say was painted by old Cornelius Jansen, others by Richard Burbage the player'. It is clear from the context that Oldys is referring to the Chandos; but if Shakespeare was the sitter, 'old Cornelius' is unlikely to have painted this life-portrait, for he seems not to have been launched on his career until after the playwright's death. The more interesting Burbage possibility also will not bear scrutiny. The great actor had some reputation as a talented amateur of the brush; but if the picture of Burbage preserved at Dulwich College is, as generally supposed, a self-portrait, he could hardly have executed the professionally accomplished Chandos canvas. Another report, also from the eigh-

1 Robert Speaight, *Shakespeare: The Man and His Achievement* (New York, 1977), p. 346.
2 Spielmann, *Portraits*, p. 7.
3 Boaden, *Inquiry*, p. 39.

82 THE CHANDOS PORTRAIT. *The National Portrait Gallery, London.*

teenth century, ascribes the portrait to '*one Taylor*, a Player & painter contemporary with Shakes[peare] & his intimate Friend'.[1] This player is elsewhere identified as John Taylor. No such player is known to have performed on the Elizabethan stage, but a Joseph Taylor (1586–1652) appears among 'the Principall Actors in all these Playes' listed in the First Folio. Taylor, we are elsewhere told, was celebrated for acting Hamlet 'incomparably well'; Downes reports that he received coaching in the rôle from none other than 'the Author *Mr Shaksepeur*'. Such instruction is improbable, however, as Taylor did not join the King's Men until 1619, when he was called upon to fill the awesome vacancy left by Burbage's death. And if Taylor was, like Burbage, a dilettante artist, no contemporary report confirms that fact. It is also said that he bequeathed the portrait to Sir William Davenant, self-proclaimed Shakespearian by-blow and early custodian of the mythos; but no Taylor will is known to exist. The picture remains stubbornly anonymous.

Still, Davenant may well have owned it. After he died, impoverished and intestate, in 1668, the portrait apparently found its way to the most notable actor of the Restoration theatre, Thomas Betterton, who knew Davenant from the Duke's Company days at Lisle's Tennis Court. Either before or after Betterton—more likely after—the canvas was possessed, according to Steevens and others, by Mrs. Barry (d. 1714), the actress whose Desdemona rivalled that of Mrs. Siddons. Mrs. Barry parted with the picture for forty guineas, a sum large enough to prompt Steevens, aware of her propensities, to wonder ungallantly whether 'the possession of somewhat more animated than canvas, might have been included, though not specified, in a bargain with an actress of acknowledged gallantry'.[2] From Mrs. Barry or Betterton, probably the former, the painting passed to Robert Keck of the Temple, for a sum known to have been forty guineas. Keck died in 1719. With him a verifiable pedigree begins. But the earlier history, implausible or contradictory as much of it is, does (as Piper observes) place the Chandos portrait squarely within the Shakespearian stage tradition.

The portrait next passed into the hands of a Mr. Nicholls of Minchenden House, Southgate, who had wed into the Keck family. When his only daughter married the Marquis of Caernarvon, afterwards Duke of Chandos, the picture became the property of that noble family. For this reason it is called the Chandos portrait.

Its fame antedated the designation. Sir Godfrey Kneller, Lübeck expatriate and Court painter to a succession of English monarchs, made the first recorded copy. This he presented to the age's leading poet, John Dryden, who acknowledged the tribute in his own verse offering to Kneller in 1694:

> *Shakespear* thy Gift, I place before my sight;
> With awe, I ask his Blessing e're I write;
> With Reverence look on his Majestick Face;
> Proud to be less; but of his Godlike Race.
> His Soul Inspires me, while thy Praise I write.[3]

The copy that inspired Dryden passed into the collection of the Earl Fitzwilliam at Wentworth Castle, and is owned by the present Earl. (A handsome large eighteenth-century copy of the Kneller hangs in the Folger Shakespeare Library.)

The Chandos likeness adorns the great sequence of eighteenth-century editions from Rowe onwards, until Steevens in 1778 restored Droeshout to pre-eminence. When George Vertue engraved the Stratford monument for Pope's 1725 *Shakespeare*, his antiquarian conscience did not keep him from substituting the Chandos head for Janssen's. More than once Vertue returned to Chandos. Until recently unknown, his delicate watercolour miniature on vellum shows the

1 As Vertue is the first (c. 1719) to set down a pedigree for the portrait, the entire entry perhaps deserves quotation: 'Mr. Betterton told Mr. Keck several times that the Picture of Shakespeare he had, was painted by one John Taylor a Player. who acted for Shakespear & this John Taylor in his will left it to Sr. Willm. Davenant. & at the death of Sr. Will. Davenant. Mr. Betterton bought it, & at his death Mr. Keck bought it [1719] in whose possession it now is' (*Vertue Note Books*, i (Walpole Society; Oxford, 1930), xviii, 56). He found the information sufficiently interesting to enter it twice in his notebooks (cf. *Note Books*, i. 48).

2 William Shakespeare, *Plays*, ed. Samuel Johnson and George Steevens (1793), i, Advertisement, p. iv.

3 John Dryden, 'To Sir Godfrey Kneller', in Dryden, *Works*, ed. H. T. Swedenberg *et al.* (Berkeley and Los Angeles, 1956–76), iv. 463.

83 GEORGE VERTUE, THE STRATFORD MONUMENT, IN WILLIAM SHAKESPEARE, *WORKS*, ED. ALEXANDER POPE (1725), I. *The plate appears opposite p. xxxi.*

familiar face in profile. Edward Capell, who treasured his copy of the Chandos, included it among his donations to the Library of his beloved Trinity College. In 1760 Sir Joshua Reynolds painted a copy for Bishop Newton which Malone eventually acquired. Certain to the last of the authenticity of the Chandos portrait, and left unsatisfied by Reynolds's not very faithful rendering,

84 GEORGE VERTUE, PORTRAIT MINIATURE OF SHAKESPEARE, 1734 (?). *From the collection of Miss Lois Avery Gaeta of New York City. The frame backing covers the verso, which, according to G. Peirson, who received the picture as a gift in 1815, is signed by Vertue and dated 1734. The last two figures, however, are 'doubtful'. See S. Schoenbaum, 'A New Vertue Shakespeare Portrait',* Shakespeare Quarterly, *xxvii (1977), 85–6.*

85 THE FORSYTH MINIATURE. *Mrs. Helen Forsyth of Hampstead bought the cravat pin with this portrait in 1966 from the Grainger-Brown antique shop opposite the Birthplace in Stratford-upon-Avon. The old lady who sold it to her, Mrs. Forsyth reports, said it had belonged to Lord Aylesford; but the provenance is unknown. So too is the date, although the early to mid nineteenth century is a reasonable guess. The blemish next to the ear has resulted from a reflection, the glass not being safely removable for photography. The portrait is here enlarged.*

Malone arranged for Ozias Humphry to make an elegant crayon drawing at Chandos House. Now in the Folger, the drawing serves as frontispiece to the present volume.

These number among the innumerable sons of Chandos. In due course more distant relations augmented the tribe, while the alchemy of Romanticism worked its transmutations. In her collection in Hampstead, Mrs. Helen Forsyth has a gold cravat pin with a tiny miniature portrait of Shakespeare, only two centimetres long, set in an oval of turquoises and pearls. A watercolour with touches of gouache, the picture is painted on ivory. This Shakespeare has shed some of his years, although the receding hair line displays the familiarly copious breadth of forehead. Evolution has disguised the portrait's lineage, but a few details, especially the collar, testify to the Chandos connection, which is confirmed by intermediary icons. Whoever painted the miniature no doubt idealised, even sentimentalised, his subject: but with his youthful intensity and wonderfully soulful eyes, this Shakespeare, unlike many of the others, might credibly have been a poet and player of genius.

Notwithstanding all these testimonials of imitation, can we accept the Chandos as a genuine life-portrait of Shakespeare? Comparison of the features with those of the Stratford bust and the Droeshout plate has resulted in contrary verdicts. The Chandos 'feature-measurements differing wholly in proportion from those of the Droeshout engraving and the Stratford bust, raise an obstacle it is impossible either to surmount or to circumvent, for it is absolutely incredible that all three can represent the same man'. Thus Spielmann.[1] For Dr. Roy Strong, however, this possibility is not so incredible: 'Working on the basis that the bust and engraving are acceptable images of the poet at different periods of his life there is no reason to believe that they do not represent the same man as appears in the Chandos portrait. The main features tally; only the hair, beard and moustache are differently arranged.'[2] For Spielmann only the hair tallied in the three artefacts. As Strong acknowledges, such comparisons have their subjective aspect.

The present condition of the picture should effectively inhibit confident judgments. Successive restorations have taken their toll of the thinly painted surface, much of which may now be repaint. Infra-red photography gives a clue to the original appearance, but the impartial observer will do well to conclude with Strong that 'The identity of this as a portrait of Shakespeare remains non proven and is likely to remain so.'[3] Still, David Bevington reproduces the portrait on the front cover of his revision of Hardin Craig's complete edition of Shakespeare. Other responsible students have used it and no doubt will continue to do, despite cautionary counsels; for, when all is said, it expresses a humanity to which Janssen's chisel and Droeshout's graver could not aspire.

V. The Janssen Portrait

In 1770 there appeared an edition of *King Lear*, with extensive notes based on collations of early and modern editions, which the editor—discreetly anonymous—offered as a trial balloon for an intended complete edition of Shakespeare's plays on the same principles. The dedication page reads:

TO
CHARLES JENNENS, Esq.
AT
GOPSAL, LEICESTERSHIRE,
UNDER WHOSE PATRONAGE,
BY ACCESS TO WHOSE LIBRARY,
AND FROM WHOSE HINTS AND REMARKS,
THE EDITOR HATH BEEN ENABLED TO ATTEMPT
AN EDITION OF SHAKESPEARE,
THE SAME IS INSCRIBED,
WITH THE GREATEST RESPECT AND GRATITUDE,
BY HIS MOST OBLIGED,
AND OBEDIENT HUMBLE SERVANT,
THE EDITOR

The fulsomely grateful editor was Charles Jennens. Although one may fairly class him as an eccentric, he has an enduring title to fame for having compiled the texts for three oratorios, including the *Messiah*, by his friend Handel. As a collector, Jennens took pride in the pictures which he had brought together in his house in Great Ormond Street, off Queen Square in Holborn, and which afterwards he displayed in the gallery of the splendid residence he erected in Gopsal, Leicestershire. One of these pictures he reproduced, from an exquisite mezzotint by Richard Earlom, as the frontispiece to his *Lear*. The caption states: 'WILLIAM SHAKESPEAR. *From an Original Picture by Cornelius Jansen in the Collection of C. Jennens Esq*^{r}'. Above the head a ribbon scroll bears the appropriate motto '*Ut magus*', from Horace's *Epistle to Augustus* (Book 2, Epistle 1). Thus did the public first learn of the existence of the Janssen portrait.

In December of the same year the *Critical Review* sized up the edition in an anonymous notice identifiable, from its special brand of gleeful malice, as the work of George Steevens. The reviewer does not spare the frontispiece:

1 Spielmann, *Portraits*, p. 9.
2 Roy Strong, *Tudor & Jacobean Portraits* (1969), i. 281.
3 Ibid., i. 279.

We should have been glad indeed to [have] had some better proofs concerning the authenticity of the original, than a bare assertion that it was painted by Cornelius Jansen, and is to be found in a private collection, which we are not heartily inclined to treat with much respect, especially as we hear it is filled with performances of one of the most contemptible daubers of the age.

Steevens returned to the attack in the next number, reaffirming his 'former opinion, that the soul of the mezzotinto is not the soul of Shakespeare'. Jennens, stung, in 1772 published an octavo pamphlet vindicating his edition from the abuse of the Critical Reviewers. 'The soul of a picture cannot be the soul of a man', he complained; 'but a picture may be *like* a man's soul, when it is made to express those qualities and dispositions which we discover him by his writings to have been possest of.'[1] Such is no doubt the case, but Jennens offered none of the 'better proofs' demanded, nor did he make his prize available for inspection. Did he hesitate because exhibition would demonstrate that the motto from Horace did not in fact embellish the painting but was added by Earlom?[2]

Jennens must have acquired the picture after 1761, for it is not in the inventory of his art works listed that year in *London and Its Environs Described.* He died in 1773. As to the immediate fate of the portrait reports conflict, but around 1809 it became the property of the Duke of Hamilton. A decade later it devolved upon his son-in-law, the eleventh Duke of Somerset, who had married Lady Charlotte Hamilton. Their son, the twelfth Duke, bequeathed the painting to his daughter, Lady Guendolen Ramsden. She kept it in the staircase hall, under the overhanging gallery, of her house Bulstrode, Gerrard's Cross, until it was disposed of after her death. In 1932, at the recommendation of the Supervisor of Research, Joseph Quincy Adams, the recently established Folger Shakespeare Library purchased the Janssen portrait, for £226. 9*s.*, from Charles Sawyer, an antiquarian bookseller in New Bond Street. It now hangs in the Exhibition Gallery of the Folger. Before the acquisition it had never been publicly displayed; the painting was not photographically reproduced until 1909.

These are facts; earlier pedigrees are romance. One report, first bruited in 1811, maintains that Prince Rupert, who had sat for Janssen, once owned the portrait. This he left to Ruperta, the Prince's natural daughter by Margaret Hughes, whom a wag thus memorialised:

Should I be hang'd I could not chuse
But laugh at wh-r-s that drop from stews,
Seeing that Mistress Margaret ——
So fine is.

Ruperta married Emmanuel Scrope Howe, and Jennens obtained the portrait (so the story goes) from their descendants. Another, more suggestive, genealogy holds as 'highly probable' that Janssen painted Shakespeare's portrait for the poet's patron, the third Earl of Southampton, 'and that it once hung among the illustrious members of his family, in one of his splendid residences, Tichfield, or Beaulieu, a shining proof of his own genius, taste, and liberality'.[3] Maybe it formed part of the extensive collection that the Dukes of Beaulieu and Beaufort divided between them; maybe one of these exalted personages presented it to the master of Gopsal. Southampton's wife is known to have posed for Janssen; so had their daughter Elizabeth, wearing on her bosom a painting in a blue enamelled case. It is a pretty fancy that Janssen painted Shakespeare for Southampton, but the only supporting evidence is the imagination of its author, James Boaden. Anyway, a similar fancy had served some years earlier when an anonymous correspondent (in fact Steevens) conjectured in *The European Magazine* for December 1794 that the Felton portrait (see below, pp. 184–8) had originally 'belonged to the celebrated Earl whom Shakspeare had previously complimented by the dedication of his Venus and Adonis'. Alas, an inventory of the pictures at Titchfield House in 1731 includes not a single Shakespeare portrait.

Spielmann describes the Janssen as 'the most romantic, artistic, elegant, and pleasing of all the

1 [Charles Jennens], *The Tragedy of King Lear, as lately published, Vindicated from the Abuse of the Critical Reveiwers . . .* (1772), p. 37.

2 Spielmann suggests this possibility in his study, the most detailed undertaken: 'The Janssen, or Somerset, Portrait of Shakespeare', *The Connoisseur*, xxiv (1909), 231–7; xxvi (1910), 105–10. A third instalment, dealing with the more important copies, also appeared in *The Connoisseur*, xxviii (1910), 151–8.

3 Boaden, *Inquiry*, p. 74.

WILLIAM SHAKESPEAR.
From an Original Picture by Cornelius Jansen in the Collection of C.Jennens Esq.
R.Earlom fecit

86 RICHARD EARLOM, FRONTISPIECE TO *KING LEAR*, ED. CHARLES JENNENS (1770).

reputed portraits of the poet'.[1] Just so. It is a sensitive face, the features finely modelled: a long, slightly aquiline nose; somewhat compressed ruby lips; small almond-shaped eyes, their expression courteously inquisitive. The extravagant wired collar of *point coupé* betokens wealth and status, as does the figured silk doublet with gold embroidery. This Shakespeare satisfies a special romantic craving. If the Chandos provides an image of the bohemian artist, here we have the poet as aristocrat. But although worthy of Janssen, the portrait is doubtfully his, and even more doubtfully a picture of Shakespeare.

A degree of confusion surrounds the career of Cornelius Janssen van Keulan. Some say that he arrived in England in 1618, in which case he could not, of course, have painted Shakespeare from life. But Janssen was in fact born in London, of Netherlandish parents, in 1593: the registers of the Dutch Church at Austin Friars record his baptism there on 14 October. Possibly he received his training in Holland. In England he practised under the name of Johnson; art historians follow this anglicised form. As a painter he stands in the long shadows cast by Mytens and afterwards Van Dyck. Still, Janssen established himself as a successful portrait painter whose clientele included county families as well as courtly circles. If his work lacks weight and solidity, he excels in sensitive heads and finely painted lace collars. Janssen's first dated portrait goes back to 1617; the next year Milton, a child of ten, sat for the portrait which now hangs in the Pierpont Morgan Library in New York City. Janssen favoured painted ovals rather than rectangles. He recorded many eminences, among them Jonson; it would be pleasant if his *oeuvre* included Shakespeare. A possible Shakespearian connection for Janssen is suggested by his portraits of Sir Dudley Digges and other members of the Digges family. If the inscription on the Folger painting deserves credence, Janssen was sixteen or seventeen at the time. Such precocity, while not unknown in the annals of art, is rare, and in this instance otherwise unsupported. There is indeed no evidence for Janssen's authorship beyond Jennens's bald assertion in 1770.

1 Spielmann, 'Janssen', *Connoisseur*, xxvi (1910), 110.

87 THE JANSSEN PORTRAIT. *The Folger Shakespeare Library, Washington, D.C.*

Nor does the inscription command implicit trust. Spielmann suspected doctoring—the *6* in *46* might be an *o*, he thought, with the tail added. To this admittedly amateur eye the *6* looks unretouched. Then again, the whole inscription may have been added later to mislead the unwary. Apart from the forehead, the facial measurements fail to tally with the Droeshout engraving or the Stratford monument, although Adams, infatuated with the portrait, thought otherwise. Because of these discrepancies, and the doubts respecting provenance, we must, however reluctantly, class this beautiful picture as a 'supply-portrait'—Piper's term for the questionable icons offered to satisfy the developing market in the eighteenth century for new and romantically appealing images of the Immortal Bard.[1] Piper has privately informed me that he believes the Janssen to be 'a genuine painting of the early seventeenth century, modified in the eighteenth to align particularly the dome of the head to tally with Droeshout and the Stratford monument. An unmodified replica was in the Ellenborough collection, and seems very likely to be identical with a portrait of Sir Thomas Overbury recorded there earlier; the features are very close indeed to those of Overbury in the authenticated portrait of him in the Bodleian Library.' Piper reproduces all three pictures in *O Sweet Mr. Shakespeare, I'll have his picture* (Plate 16, items b, c, d). The appeal of the Janssen portrait, one suspects, owes at least as much to the marvellous collar as to the head surmounting it.

VI. The Felton Portrait

This small oil on oak panel (approximately 11 by 9½ inches) forms part of the display of attributed Shakespeare portraits in the west corner of the Exhibition Gallery of the Folger Shakespeare Library. Shakespeare—assuming it is he—has undergone a strange metamorphosis. Affixed to the elongated goose-egg of a head is a nose 'somewhat flattened, and squaring into the form of the lozenge or diamond'; the light moustache grows downward, the chin is beardless. But two features in especial arrest attention: the ruff—'like nothing but a small portable pillory about the neck', Boaden sneered—and the forehead. If the perpendicular expanse is impressive in Droeshout and the Stratford bust, it is here stupendous; those persuaded that a gigantic brain requires a gigantic casing will derive satisfaction from the Felton physiognomy.

Auctioned off in the Baroness Burdett-Coutts's sale at Christies in May 1922, the picture passed, *via* Rosenbach, into the collection of Henry Clay Folger. Before then it had had a chequered history. The portrait first surfaced when exhibited in 1792 at the European Museum in King Street, St. James's Square. An entry in the sale catalogue reads, 'No. 359. A curious portrait of Shakspeare, painted in 1597.' On 31 May, Samuel Felton of Drayton, Shropshire, and Curzon Street in Mayfair, acquired the curiosity for a meagre five guineas. His curiosity piqued, the purchaser applied to the director of the museum, a J. Wilson, for some information about the picture, and in September Wilson obliged: '—The Head of Shakespeare was purchased out of an old house known by the sign of the Boar in Eastcheap, London, where Shakespeare and his friends used to resort,—and report says, was painted by a Player of that time, but whose name I have not been able to learn.'[2] Two years later William Richardson, a print-seller in Leicester Square, told the celebrated Shakespeare editor George Steevens that a customer had shown him 'an ancient head resembling the Portrait of Shakspeare as engraved by Martin Droeshout in 1623'. A viewing was arranged. Steevens noted on the back of the panel the inscription in an old hand, 'Guil. Shakspeare, 1597. R.N.'. He compared the painting with both the Droeshout and the Marshall plates, and concluded that he held in his hand their original.

He sought to trace the provenance. Wilson supplemented his original account by assuring Steevens that 'this portrait was found between four and five years ago at a broker's shop in the Minories, by a man of fashion whose name must be concealed: that it afterwards came (attended

1 David Piper, *O Sweet Mr. Shakespeare, I'll have his picture* (1964), p. 36.

2 Wilson's letter, as well as other details of the picture's early history, derives from the Proposals published, under the title 'Shakspeare', by William Richardson in 1794; see below, p. 186. The Proposals, with the same title, appeared as an anonymous article in *The European Magazine, and London Review*, xxvi (1794), 277–82. A second article, 'The Authenticity of the New Found Portrait of Shakspeare Asserted', appeared later in the same year in *The European Magazine*, 388–90. George Steevens wrote both pieces.

88 THE FELTON PORTRAIT. *The Folger Shakespeare Library, Washington, D.C.*

by the Eastcheap story, &c.) with a part of that gentleman's collection of paintings, to be sold at the European Museum, and was exhibited there for about three months, during which time it was seen by Lord Leicester and Lord Orford [Horace Walpole], who both allowed it to be a genuine picture of Shakspeare.' One may wonder why, if they so allowed, both these wealthy connoisseurs declined to lay out five guineas for such a prize. But (we are told) its damaged condition discouraged purchase. The panel was split on the right, beyond the ear, and a philistine owner had cut off the bottom, beneath the ruff, in order to accommodate the portrait to a spare frame. Still, one would have thought that even a mutilated portrait of Shakespeare would, if authentic, command five guineas.

In other respects the story could seduce only the credulous. The figments of Shakespeare's imagination, not their creator, made merry at the Boar's Head. Anyway the Great Fire of 1666 reduced all of Eastcheap, including the tavern, to smouldering rubble. Steevens was aware that for years the same feeble explanation had accompanied every purported Shakespeare likeness offered for sale. 'It is . . . high time', he warned, 'that picture-dealers should avail themselves of another story, this being completely worn out, and no longer fit for service.' Yet the story was not so worn that he failed to follow it up. He found the former landlord of the Boar's Head, a Mr. Sloman, who could recall but one picture there, a crude daubing of Prince Hal's Gadshill escapade. Next Steevens tracked down the widow of Sloman's predecessor to Crooked Lane, where she had taken up the trade of wire-worker; but Mrs. Binn was ten years dead. Her apprentice, however, remembered her as often talking about the Gadshill painting, but not of any other. Steevens had to conclude that the Felton portrait had for long gathered dust in some garret or lumber-room, and that the Boar's Head legend had become attached after a resemblance to Shakespeare was noticed.

Nevertheless, the picture *probably* ornamented some club-room in Cheapside which *might also have been* Shakespeare's favourite resort, a gathering place for the wits adorned with their portraits. The one in question was no doubt removed before the fire. And what if the pedigree is false? Steevens quotes Lord Mansfield's argument that 'there are instances in which falsehood has been employed in support of a real fact, and that it is no uncommon thing for a man to defend a true cause by fabulous pretences'. The Felton bears its own 'indubitable' marks of genuineness. Thus did the arch-sceptic proclaim himself a true believer.

When Richardson went ahead with plans to publish two line-engravings of the portrait, Steevens wrote the advertisement which the printseller signed; a strategy of subterfuge which seems to have deceived few—Malone some years afterwards, in his Shakespeariana now in the Bodleian Library, left no doubt as to where he himself stood on the claims of Felton when he recorded 'Mr Geo. Steevens's portrait of Shakspeare, under the assumed signature of Wm Richardson, Printseller'. In December 1794, after Thomas Trotter's octavo plates showing the Felton head with the Droeshout costume appeared, Steevens gave his friends copies as Christmas gifts. (Despite such liberties the engraver had the impertinence to offer his wares as 'From the Original Picture'.) Had the cynic who mocked the pretensions of the Chandos at last found faith? Perhaps, but the reputation of a practical joker dies hard. Boswell, the biographer's son, tells a revealing anecdote:

> There are not, indeed, wanting those who suspect that Mr. Steevens was better acquainted with the history of its manufacture, and that there was a deeper meaning in his words, when he tells us, 'he was instrumental in procuring it', than he would have wished to be generally understood; and that the fabricator of the Hardiknutian tablet had been trying his ingenuity upon a more important scale. My venerable friend, the late Mr. Bindley, of the Stamp-office, was reluctantly persuaded, by his importunity, to attest his opinion in favour of this picture, which he did in deference to the judgment of one so well acquainted with Shakspeare; but happening to glance his eye upon Mr. Steevens's face, he instantly perceived, by the triumph depicted in the peculiar expression of his countenance, that he had been deceived.[1]

Perhaps the imp of the perverse, which always lurked below the surface of Steevens's rationality, had once again taken possession.

1 William Shakespeare, *Plays and Poems*, ed. Edmond Malone and James Boswell (1821), i. Advertisement, p. xxvii.

Engrav'd by W. Sherwin from the Original Folio Edition

89 W. SHERWIN'S FRONTISPIECE TO WILLIAM SHAKESPEARE, *DRAMATIC WORKS*, ED. SAMUEL AYSCOUGH (1790), I. *Of this plate J. Parker Norris writes, 'The entire expression is changed, and it is about as poor a copy as can well be imagined'* (The Portraits of Shakespeare (*Philadelphia, 1885*), *p. 60*)*: rather a surprising verdict from one with as much experience as Norris with Shakespeare portraits.*

Malone pronounced the Felton portrait a fabrication. Boaden gleefully mocked it. In the nineties, as editor of *The Oracle*, he had swallowed whole the Ireland forgeries; he would not be duped a second time. After Mr. H, any mention of an unnamed gentleman was calculated to arouse his deepest suspicions—maybe the portrait had issued, along with all the letters, deeds, and plays, from the treasure chest of Ireland. But the recovery of the Felton head antedates the Norfolk Street scandal by several years, and William Henry, in his *Chalcographimania* of 1814, scornfully lampooned the mere '*scrap*' with 'a German's phiz'.

Steevens, however, posthumously found an ally in Abraham Wivell, Boaden's rival as an authority on the Shakespeare iconography. Wivell examined the picture, and, finding the wood in a decayed state, oiled the back with linseed, which had the unforeseen effect of bringing out the inscription more clearly. This he read as 'Gul Shakspear 1597, RB'. Not surprisingly, it occurred to Wivell that the initials might stand for Richard Burbage. Over a century later, Giles E. Dawson, Curator of Rare Books and Manuscripts at the Folger, removed the panel from the frame and examined the back with a magnifying glass and ultraviolet light. He could find no evidence of writing, although the wood was so rough that traces of ink should have shown in the grain. This circumstance reasonably struck him as 'mighty fishy'. Possibly, he speculated, the inscription was on a slip of paper affixed to the back.[1] But it is difficult to see why linseed oil

1 Dawson describes his experience with the portrait in a letter, dated 30 March 1967, in the Felton Portrait folder / Art Provenance File at the Folger Shakespeare Library.

should have been applied to paper, or how it would have had the effect Wivell describes. Be that as it may, the inscription, even if it once existed, inspires little confidence, for the style of the subject's wired band argues against the date. That fashion (allowing for some margin) had not come in before 1610. Shakespeare was by then forty-six, whereas the portrait depicts a younger man.

The aroma of fish is indeed fairly pervasive. Elizabethan fashion called for moustaches to point up, not down. Fuseli considered the picture Flemish work, and Spielmann thinks he may be right, with the doctored picture baked in the 'Westminster ovens' to produce overnight the mellowed surface of an old master. The inspiration for the retouching was possibly W. Sherwin's frontispiece to Samuel Ayscough's 1790 edition of the *Dramatic Works*, with its 'striking likeness of Shakspeare, from the original Folio edition'. Maybe so. The *Literary Gazette* for 7 July 1827 reports, 'we have the most conclusive evidence that the Felton is a forgery; for it was altered and painted by John Crauch [Cranch]. . . . The story about the boar's head, &c. . . . is an auctioneer's trick.' Cranch died, aged seventy, at Bath in 1821. The writer does not produce his 'conclusive evidence'.

The Felton portrait went through several hands, and in 1870 fetched fifty guineas, no princely sum in the heyday of Bardolatry for a Shakespeare portrait with serious claims to acceptance. X-ray examination at the National Gallery in Washington in 1967 revealed that most of the surface had undergone repainting in the nineteenth century; the portrait underneath seemed, from the style, to date from the seventeenth century. The present features are generally compatible with those of the eighteenth-century engraving of the Felton. In 1964 the Cambridge University Press reproduced the portrait on the dust-wrapper of Nevill Coghill's *Shakespeare's Professional Skills*. The picture testifies to professional skills of a different order.

On 25 January 1979, when this book was already in proof, I visited the Baltimore studio of Peter B. Michaels, the conservator appointed by the Folger to clean the Felton and other portraits in advance of a travelling exhibition sponsored by the Library. He had just completed work on the Felton. The subject's ruff now extended to the left side of the original panel, and had moved about an inch higher on the cheek. On the left side of the ruff, three stripes, not previously visible, corresponded to the three on the right. The formerly bare chin now boasted some fine hair beneath the lower lip. We could find no evidence of an inscription on the back of the panel.

VII. The Ashbourne Portrait

If the doubtful portraits so far treated have in common one feature—their incomplete or otherwise unsatisfactory pedigrees—the large Ashbourne canvas (47½ by 37½ inches) belongs in a special class of more advanced dubiety. For it comes equipped with no pedigree whatsoever, nor even with traditional Shakespearian associations. The picture is first mentioned on 8 March 1847, when the Revd. Clement Usill Kingston, a Second Master of the Free Grammar School at Ashbourne, Derbyshire, sought the counsel of the leading authority of the day on the Shakespeare iconography. 'The way in which I happened to come into possession of it was this', Kingston wrote to Abraham Wivell:

> A friend in London sent me word that he had seen a portrait of Shakespeare, that he was positive it was a genuine picture, and that the owner only valued it as being a very fine painting. Being too poor to purchase it for himself, he advised me by all means to have it. I immediately wrote back requesting him to secure me the prize.

That is all, at least as regards background. Kingston noted a resemblance—which has struck others since—to the Janssen countenance, and did not hesitate to declare his faith: 'In fact, and I speak it with the utmost confidence (though I am sure you will consider me too bold), I really believe it to be the best, and certainly the most interesting portrait of the immortal bard in existence.'[1] Wivell hastened from Birmingham to London for a look, and came away convinced

1 I have been unable to trace Kingston's letter, which in the nineteenth century was in the possession of Samuel Timmins. My quotations are from a copy supplied by Timmins to J. Parker Norris, and printed by him in *The Portraits of Shakespeare* (Philadelphia, 1885), pp. 166–8. Norris incorrectly gives Kingston's Christian name as Clements.

90 THE ASHBOURNE PORTRAIT. *The Folger Shakespeare Library, Washington, D.C.*

'that Shakspere sat to the talented artist for the portrait . . . The Circumstances of the picture being a *half length*, and in so *perfect a state*, is one of the most extraordinary discoveries of the age.'[1] Thus encouraged, Kingston the next year published a handsome large mezzotint by G. F. Storm.

Actually the life-size portrait is three-quarter, not half, length. A dignified figure of contemplative mien stands by a table. He has a high forehead, sensitive long nose, auburn hair, and fair skin. Is the skull on the table a *memento mori*? Or an emblem of the subject's profession (physician or philosopher)? Or perhaps an allusion to *Hamlet*? Whatever the symbolism, the skull supports the subject's right arm; his hand with its tapering fingers holds a book, perhaps a missal, tied with red ribbon. On the cover appears, embossed in gilt, a shield and crossed spears. (Kingston discerned in these ornamental details 'the crest of the Shakespeare family, and the tragic mask'. The eye translates what it sees into its own language. I can discern no Shakespeare crest, and if the shield is a mask, it is not conspicuously tragic.) This gentleman of status wears a multifold lace ruff, a black tight-fitting coat, and, around his waist, a sword or rapier belt of black leather with silver filigree. No weapon is visible. A signet ring adorns the elongated thumb of the left hand, from which dangles a crimson and gold gauntlet. In the upper right-hand corner is this inscription:

ÆTATIS SUÆ 47
A°: 1611.

The portrait has been described as romantic, but it has for this viewer an almost Spanish sobriety.

Eventually the painting came into the collection of Mr. R. Levine of Norwich. After his death Eustace Conway of New York City bought it at a Sotheby's auction in 1928. From Conway, pressed for money during the Great Depression, it passed, for $3500, to Henry Clay Folger. The picture now hangs in the Exhibition Gallery of the Folger Library. Around 1939, Charles Wisner Barrell, secretary–treasurer of the Shakespeare Fellowship (an Oxfordian society), received permission to subject the portrait to infra-red and X-ray photography. There followed an article, 'Identifying "Shakespeare"', in the *Scientific American* for January 1940, in which Barrell announced certain remarkable discoveries. Underneath the present paint lies another portrait, of none other than Edward de Vere, seventeenth Earl of Oxford: his device of the wild boar ornaments the signet ring, and just below the inscription a 'phantom shield' shows the armorial bearings of the Countess of Oxford. The X-rays, moreover, revealed under the phantom shield the monogram of the Dutch portrait painter Cornelius Ketel (1548–1616).

Much discussion followed in the world press. The Folger commissioned an independent X-ray examination by Stephen S. Pichetto, Consultant Restorer to the National Gallery in Washington and also to the Metropolitan Museum of Art in New York. Pichetto concluded that the original painting belonged, at the earliest, to the second half of the seventeenth century, and that the overpainting took place not earlier than the eighteenth century. The monogram apparent to Barrell eluded other eyes; efforts to identify the original subject failed. In 1950 Giles Dawson showed an X-ray photograph of the faintly visible coat of arms to a learned herald at the College of Arms. In this expert's considered judgement the armorial bearings could not be those of the Countess of Oxford, nor of any woman; nor could they be those of the seventeenth Earl. News sometimes travels slowly. John Young writes in *The Times* (25 May 1977) of 'a rare portrait of Shakespeare in the Folger Library in Washington which has been found to have been painted over an earlier portrait of de Vere'.

M. H. Spielmann's 'The Ashbourne Portrait of Shakespeare' (*The Connoisseur*, xxvi (1910), 244–50, and xxvii (1910), 38–42) remains the most reliably detailed discussion, although overtaken by X-rays and Oxfordians. There are several copies; a small but faithfully painted rendering is in the collection of Mr. Charles X. Benck of Yonkers, New York. It is perhaps superfluous to emphasise that, despite all the publicity, the Ashbourne portrait has no standing as a likeness of Shakespeare, but most probably belongs with the other 'supply-portraits' manufactured in the eighteenth century from existing portraits to satisfy the market for new pictures of Shakespeare.

The conservator was still in the process of cleaning the Ashbourne Portrait when I visited his

1 I quote from a printed copy of the letter, pasted on board, which accompanied the portrait when the Folger acquired it.

studio on 25 June 1979. Treatment had already revealed that the date 1611 of the inscription had been altered from 1612, the outline of the original '2' now being visible. Under the inscription, heraldic arms had surfaced. The shield shows what appear to be three rams' heads facing left, in colors of vermillion and gold; above the shield was a helmet surmounted by a griffin, also facing left, clutching a cross. On the band below, the terminal letters 'MORE' could be dimly discerned. Restoration shows that, in repainting, the sitter's forehead has been heightened considerably to provide a suitable casing for the mighty brain within. Michaels himself does not doubt that the portrait was originally painted in 1612.

Subsequent inquiry has pointed to Sir Hugh Hamersley of Pyrton, Oxfordshire, as the original sitter. By trade a haberdasher, Hamersley in 1627 served as Lord Mayor of London, and the next year was dubbed at Whitehall. He died in 1636. His marble monument may be viewed in St. Andrew Undershaft Church, where Stow lies buried. Sir Hugh's armorial bearings included three rams' heads and a crest with 'a demi-griffin segreant or, holding a cross-crosslet fitchée gules'. The motto: 'Honore et amore'. The year of Hamersley's birth, 1565, tallies with the age given in the inscription on the painting. Presumably Hamersley had the arms, which were granted by Camden in 1614, added subsequently.

VIII. The Grafton Portrait

No supposititious Shakespeare portrait in modern times has enjoyed more fortunate sponsorship than the Grafton, unknown prior to 1907; for it has been selected as the frontispiece to a pair of widely read and influential books by respected authorities on Shakespeare, if not on British portraiture. One of these books, John Semple Smart's *Shakespeare: Truth and Tradition* (1928), was, to be sure, published posthumously, but a note informs readers that the author 'greatly admired' the Grafton portrait. In *The Essential Shakespeare* (1932), which boasts the same frontispiece, J. Dover Wilson acknowledges the irresistible hold the painting had on him for almost two decades.

The picture is a small oil, 17¼ by 15½ inches, in a somewhat worm-eaten oak panel. The subject, a young man with large expressive eyes, light moustache, and a shock of dark brown (verging on black) hair that reaches almost to the base of his neck, has on a crimson slashed doublet with a large greenish gauze collar. He wears a gentle expression. At the top, on either side of his head, appears an inscription in raised yellow letters of thickly laid on paint:

Æ SUÆ · 24 1·5·8·8·

The back of the stretcher carries the branded initials 'W+S'.

Dover Wilson calculates that the facial measurements—from chin to lower lip, from lip to end of nose, from nose to lower eyelid, from eyelid to eyebrow, and from eyebrow to top of forehead—tally with Droeshout. The same imposing breadth of forehead distinguishes both heads. But more persuasive than the testimony of the measuring tape is the appeal of 'the wonderful eyes and the oval Shelley-like face'. The ascetic Smart in his bachelor isolation responded to the same appeal; he found in the picture 'his own idea of the youthful Shakespeare, and wished it genuine'. The wish is father of the frontispiece, the choice of which may be seen as a reaction against the stolidity of the Stratford bust; a stolidity that finds its verbal equivalent in the juiceless prose of Lee's magisterial biography. Nevertheless, Wilson was too responsible a scholar to make exaggerated claims of authenticity for the Grafton portrait. 'I do not ask the reader to believe in it', he writes,

> or even to wish to believe in it. All I suggest is that he may find it useful in trying to frame his own image of Shakespeare. It will at any rate help him to forget the Stratford bust. Let him take it, if he will, as a painted cloth or arras, drawn in front of that monstrosity, and symbolising the Essential Poet. . . . We are apt to forget at times, in our preoccupation with Shakespeare the Stratford Institution, Shakespeare the National Bard, or even Shakespeare the world-worshipped dramatic interpreter of mankind, that Shakespeare himself is also 'among the English poets', is with Keats and with Shelley. If my frontispiece reminds even one reader of this, it will not be altogether impertinent.[1]

1 J. Dover Wilson, *The Essential Shakespeare* (Cambridge, 1932), pp. 7–8.

91 THE GRAFTON PORTRAIT. *The John Rylands Library, Manchester.*

It may, Wilson adds, also remind readers that Shakespeare was once young.

Such candour is refreshing in iconographical studies, where special pleading so often masquerades as the disinterested pursuit of truth, and where exceedingly doubtful pictures are touted in monographs with such titles as *An Authenticated Contemporary Portrait of Shakespeare*.[1] The candour, moreover, goes far to explain the persistence of the quest for authentic likenesses to supplement—or, preferably, to supplant—the Folio title-page and the statue in Holy Trinity.

The story of the Grafton portrait is quickly told. It turned up early in this century in the village of Winston-on-Tees between Darlington and Barnard Castle, Durham. There it hung on the walls of a picturesque ivy-covered inn called the Bridgewater Arms, presided over by the Ludgate sisters, daughters of a retired station-master. The portrait had once belonged (so the story went) to a Duke of Grafton, who presented it for undisclosed reasons to a sturdy yeoman in his service. Through collateral descent it passed into the possession of the Ludgates. Their maternal forebears had for five or six generations kept it at an old farmhouse in the village of Grafton, Northamptonshire; a farmhouse owned by the Dukes of Grafton, whose tenants they were. (The family referred to it affectionately as 'Old Matt', after a local character who wore a collar similar to the one in the portrait.) After the former station-master died, his widow took over the licence of the Bridgewater Arms. Thither the picture was removed. When Spielmann began making enquiries about the portrait in 1907, word leaked to the press; on 18 February the *Manchester Guardian* ran a photograph of 'the supposed portrait of Shakespere which has been found in a village inn near Darlington'. There followed the customary overnight sensation.

Reporters interviewed Spielmann, who complained of misquotation. He was able to set the record straight when he published the findings of his inspection in an article in *The Connoisseur* for February 1909. The somewhat harsh effect of the costume, with its obtrusive crosslines and slashings, may (he noted) owe something to the scrubbing administered to the painting with soda and brush by the late Mrs. Ludgate in the laudable interest of hygiene. This was not the only improvement made by the owners. Mr. Ludgate, his daughter cheerfully acknowledged, had branded the initials on, 'remarking that inasmuch as the portrait evidently represented Shakespeare he might as well set it upon record for the guidance of future owners'.

Spielmann thought that some English or Netherlandish follower of Holbein, Bettes, or Stephen painted the portrait; Continental origin could not be ruled out. Thus he entered the Grafton picture 'in that considerable category of genuine portraits which are authentic likenesses of somebody else'.[2] This sceptical appraisal did not prevent a Stockton collector, Mr. Thomas Kay, from buying the painting the same year. (Several times in the preceding century acquaintances of the owners had called the picture to the notice of the National Portrait Gallery, which remained curiously indifferent to the prospect of acquiring it for the nation.) On the eve of the Great War, Kay published an unpretentiously amateurish study, *The Story of the 'Grafton' Portrait of William Shakespeare*. In it he suggested that the picture had been rescued from Grafton House by the Revd. Thomas Bunning when that seat was sacked and plundered during the Civil War; for this interesting hypothesis Kay offered no evidence whatever. When he died in 1914 Kay bequeathed the painting to the John Rylands Library in Manchester. There it is still displayed.

In an exquisitely ineffective article in the John Rylands Library *Bulletin* for July 1945, J. Ernest Jarratt, while making 'no pretension to Shakespearean scholarship' (he thinks Charlotte Stopes was an art critic), suggests that through the influence of the Stanleys, who recognised Shakespeare's genius, 'the Poet might have sat to a painter of ability, and that the Portrait might have reached Northamptonshire'. There is no evidence that the Stanleys thus exerted their influence or that the picture reached Northamptonshire in this way. Nor is there evidence that the picture represents Shakespeare. Even if the inscription is genuine, as Spielmann was inclined to grant, it seems unlikely (*pace* Dr. Hotson) that Shakespeare had achieved sufficient celebrity by 1588 to warrant having his portrait painted. Other twenty-four-year-old youths must have been available

1 The title given by Tracy Kingston to his 1932 monograph on a painting attributed to Karl van Mander (b. 1548), which purportedly shows Shakespeare and Jonson playing chess. Van Mander's Dutch biographer mentions no such picture.

2 Spielmann, 'The "Grafton" and "Sanders" Portraits of Shakespeare', *The Connoisseur*, xxiii (1909), 100.

to have their portraits done. And, while making due allowance for the power of time to transform physiognomy, it is doubtful that the Shakespeare of Droeshout and Janssen could ever have had a nose as thick—especially at the tip—as the one with which the Grafton portrait equips him. Like so many of the attributed portraits, the only claim this one makes is upon romantic fancy. But we must never underestimate the potency of such a claim, which has supported a whole industry of Shakespeare portraiture.

IX. The Ages of Shakespeare

The primary images discussed in the foregoing pages all derive, or presume to derive, from the period in which Shakespeare lived. Later visualisations, allegorical or narrative (the latter flourishing especially in the nineteenth century), complement the biographer's rôle, and illustrate what may be described as the ages of Shakespeare.

These number more than Jaques's seven. George Romney exhibits Shakespeare as a cherubic infant nursed by the muses of tragedy and comedy. Thalia playfully fingers his plump bare bottom as he grasps her flute; Melpomene looks on soberly, her poison bowl standing by unregarded. In another image, this by Richard Westall, the boy Shakespeare lies upon a bank in summer, his imagination thronging with the phantom hosts—Falstaff, old Lear (comforted by Cordelia), Titania, and the rest—who will one day people his plays on a different Bankside. As a young man, although surely past eighteen, he courts Anne Hathaway by the book, presumably in her Wilmcote cottage. She demurely holds a small bunch of flowers. Their thoughts seem far removed from what has been termed antenuptial fornication. Elsewhere we see Shakespeare engrossed in composition, his head lowered to reveal that vast bald crown of genius; his halberd, an instrument of doubtful domestic utility, rests against the wall adjoining his study window. In a playhouse prophetically equipped with curtain and proscenium arch, Shakespeare the actor takes a bow while his enraptured audience flings bouquets. A chain shackles his wrists. What play might this be? Surely not any by Shakespeare; perhaps this obscure drama belongs to the theatre of biographical allegory. Before the assembled Court and Elizabeth seated in state on her throne, her favourite poet improbably recites *Macbeth*. Another image shows Shakespeare declaiming in the bosom of his adoring family. Susanna, Judith, and Hamnet holding his riding crop listen, mutely impressed; illiterate John in a corner looks up from his book, mother from the dishes in the kitchen. Only the faithful dog, outstretched on the carpet with the lute, has yielded to the slumber of indifference. In this illustration Shakespeare's head derives, as do so many others, from Chandos, although this time he wears his gold ring in the right ear. Janssen has set the fashion for the ruff.

The rest is silence, as we see Shakespeare in the grim repose of death. Here the artist's source is the Kesselstadt Death Mask, recovered in 1849 in a broker's shop in Mainz amongst a litter of rags and rubbish.[1] Other images too in this sequence—Shakespeare *en famille*, Shakespeare triumphing in chains (*in Ketten*)—have a Teutonic origin. He has after been, from Schlegel's time onwards, 'unserer Shakespeare'.

The pictures reproduced in this section form part of the Print Collection of the Folger Shakespeare Library.

Opposite:

92 SHAKESPEARE NURSED BY TRAGEDY AND COMEDY. *Art File S527.4, no. 5, pt. 1. Engraved by B[enjamin] Smith after the painting by George Romney (1734–1802), and published by J. and J. Boydell, n.d. Romney reportedly modelled Comedy on Lady Hamilton. His painting inspired this verse encomium:*

When Romney, in his happiest hour, design'd
The Muses fostering young Shakespeares Mind,
Nature surveyed them all with fond regard,
And own'd the Painter worthy of the Bard.

A related Romney canvas, 'The Infant Shakespeare attended by Nature and the Passions', is now owned by the Folger Shakespeare Library. Both pictures were originally exhibited in Boydell's Shakespeare Gallery in Pall Mall.

1 *SL*, 468–70. The mask is in the Darmstadt Museum.

93 THE DREAMS OF THE YOUTHFUL SHAKESPEARE. *Art File S527.4, no. 11, copy 1. Engraved by Augustus Fox after the painting by Richard Westall (1765–1836); published by William Pickering, London, in 1827. Westall was a major exhibitor at Boydell's Shakespeare Gallery.*

94 SHAKESPEARE AND ANNE HATHAWAY. *Art File S527.4, no. 12. Anonymous painting, undated.*

95 SHAKESPEARE COMPOSING. *Art File S527, no. 280. Engraved by A. H. Payne after a painting by Lilburne Hicks (d. 1861) and published by Brain & Payne, London, n.d.*

96 SHAKESPEARE'S TRIUMPH IN KETTEN. *Art File S527.4, no. 25. 'Originalzeichnung von H. Langhammer in Leipzig.' The Folger catalogue lists this item as a woodcut by Artur Langhammer (1854–1901).*

97 SHAKESPEARE BEFORE THE COURT OF QUEEN ELIZABETH RECITING *MACBETH. Art File S527.4, no. 29C.1, pt. 1. 'Engraved for The Eclectic by Perine & Giles, N.Y.', n.d. Artist unknown.*

Opposite:
98 SHAKESPEARE WITH HIS FAMILY AT STRATFORD. *Art File S527.4, no. 31, pt. 2. Coloured lithograph published by F. Sala & Co., Berlin, n.d.; artist unknown. An engraving of this picture for* The Eclectic *identifies the play Shakespeare is reciting as* Hamlet, *but no title appears on the manuscript he holds.*

99 SHAKESPEARE DECEASED. *Art File S527.2, no. 83. One of a series of seven anonymous woodcuts (nos. 81–7) of the Kesselstadt mask.*

6

Shakespeare at the Stationers: 1593-1683

Shakespeare, no bardolater, bestirred himself little to have his writings given the permanence of print. True, his narrative poems *Venus and Adonis* and *The Rape of Lucrece* are exceptions. Despite Shakespeare's self-deprecatory protestations about unpolished or untutored lines, these are the first heirs of his literary—as distinguished from his playwriting—invention. *Venus and Adonis* comes equipped with a title-page motto from Ovid's *Amores*; *Lucrece*, with an argument inspired by Ovid's *Fasti* and Livy's *Historia*. Both boast dedications to the same noble lord. It is the usual destiny of such endeavours to be proofread by the author. Galley proofs, as we know them, did not then exist; customarily a writer perused sheets as they issued from the press in the printing-house or after delivery to his lodgings. 'So, bring me the last proof', Lapet commands his servant in Fletcher's *The Nice Valour*; 'this is corrected'. Erasmus lived with his printer for eight or nine months while his *Adagiorum Chiliades* went through the press. That is an extreme case, but Shakespeare may have corrected his sheets in the Blackfriars shop of his fellow townsman Richard Field. The texts of the poems are remarkably free from error—the best evidence of authorial supervision—although their accuracy may also be attributed to the excellence of Field's work generally. Sometimes the printing process was interrupted for a correction: so in *Lucrece* (l. 50) Shakespeare himself may well have emended *Colatia*, which appears in most copies but is revised to *Colatium* in the Bodley and Yale quartos. The plays are another matter.

Depending upon the status of *The Taming of A Shrew*, either eighteen or nineteen of Shakespeare's plays (including *Pericles*) appeared in quarto editions during his lifetime. They evidence no solicitude for the reader's convenience or author's pride of composition. The texts abound with gross errors that would not have escaped the drowsiest proofreader's eye. None of these editions is equipped with a cast list or divided into acts and scenes. Only *Troilus and Cressida* boasts a prefatory epistle, but this the stationers, not the author, supplied. In this respect, as in others, Jonson provides the age's most striking antithesis. He revised his scripts (in one instance, *Every Man in His Humour*, shifting the scene from Italy to England), composed dedicatory epistles, and gathered together his 'works'—as he had the effrontery to term them—in a sumptuous folio volume, the sheets of which he extensively revised as they went through the press. But if Jonson stands out as an extreme, prefaces, even by journeyman playwrights, are not uncommon. Middleton composed one for *The Roaring Girl*, on which he had collaborated with Dekker; the latter addressed his 'loving, and loved friends and fellowes, the Queenes Majesties servants', in the 1612 quarto of *If This Be Not a Good Play, the Devil Is in It*. Heywood, no élitist, wrote prefaces for *The Rape of Lucrece*, *The Golden Age*, and *The Four Prentices of London*. In his address 'To the Reader' of *The White Devil* Webster bemoaned his unappreciative auditors and praised, as last but not least, 'the right happy and copious industry' of Shakespeare (along with Dekker and Heywood). Shakespeare's industry did not extend so far; he was not one of those playwrights who (in Heywood's phrase) 'used a double sale of their labours, first to the Stage, and after to the Presse'. The Chamberlain's/King's company alone claimed the labours of this dramatist, who found his creative fulfilment in the impermanence of performance.

That most, if not all, of his dramatic output has survived is one of those literary miracles still capable of inspiring awe. Most plays in this period perished. The approximately 180 plays of the professional London troupes published between 1586 and 1616, Shakespeare's adult years, represent (according to one informed estimate) around fifteen to twenty per cent of those acted.

Plays were the property of the companies that paid for them; Heywood in 1633 speaks of certain pieces as being 'still retained in the hands of some Actors, who thinke it against their peculiar profit to have them come in print'. They parted with them when their popularity on the boards had waned, or when they needed ready cash because of plague, official suppression, or other calamities. Or when they were appropriated. In this last category belong the 'diverse stolne, and surreptitious copies, maimed, and deformed by the frauds and stealthes of injurious impostors', to which Heminges and Condell allude in their epistle 'To the great Variety of Readers' prefacing the First Folio.

The plays thus printed in mangled, it is believed reported, texts, are the first editions of *2* and *3 Henry VI*, *Romeo and Juliet*, *Henry V*, *The Merry Wives of Windsor*, *Hamlet*, and *Pericles*. These are the so-called Bad Quartos. Some would add *Richard III* and *King Lear* to this category; also *The Taming of A Shrew*, which others, perhaps still a majority, see as the source play for *The Shrew*. Not all the Good Quartos are that good; *Love's Labour's Lost*, for example, being a borderline case. *Pericles* the Folio editors excluded from their book altogether, but they put in eighteen plays—*Julius Caesar*, *Macbeth*, and *The Tempest* among them—not previously in print.

The story of the publication of Shakespeare's plays is thus one from which the chief protagonist —their creator—stands aloof. It concerns only the editors and stationers and other functionaries who saw them through the press and made them available to the reading public. As this process is an integral aspect of the Shakespearian legacy, we may appropriately give some consideration to the history, organisation and *modus operandi* of the Stationers' Company, the printers and booksellers involved in the production of the Shakespeare quartos and folios, and the Register in which his writings were entered and, over the years, transferred.

I. The Book and the Register

On 4 May 1557, in Catholic Mary's reign, the King and Queen conferred a charter on ninety-seven freemen, duly named, 'of the mistery or art of Stationery of our City of London, and the suburbs of the same'. These stationers now had the right to constitute themselves a corporate body in perpetuity. Nobody—or hardly anybody—might print who could not claim membership of the Company. Exceptions were made for those with special licences under royal letters patent; besides, the universities of Cambridge and Oxford had their own charters. But patents were not all that numerous, Cambridge had not published a book for decades, neither university currently owned a press, and printing at Oxford, although dating from 1478, did not make real headway until after Archbishop Laud's intervention in 1632. London was the effective centre for all publishing in England, with the Charter creating a virtual monopoly.

The Stationers' Company was already of long standing. We hear of it having been 'made a Brotherhood in ye 4th yeare of the raigne of King Henry ye 4th'. That was in 1402–3. Incorporation merely represented another phase in progressive expansion. The term stationer, from medieval Latin *stationarius*, referring to anyone—e.g. a sentry—in a fixed position, is recorded in England in 1262 (cf. *OED*), in London by 1311. It applied to members of the book trade: not, like other guildsmen, those actively engaged in manufacture, but middlemen dealers with fixed stalls. In the days before printing, book production involved several callings. There were the parchminers or parchmenters (i.e. parchment-makers), the scriveners (schismatically subdivided into textwriters and writers of court-letter), the lymners (illuminators), and the bookbinders. Brotherhoods of these skilled craftsmen served the traditional functions of the medieval guild by safeguarding the common interests of workers, as unions do today, and protecting the public (in the fashion of modern consumer groups) from shoddy materials and workmanship. How many guilds participated in book production is uncertain: textwriters and lymners also bound and vended books; while the binders may not have had a separate brotherhood. After 1403 the picture becomes clearer. In that year the Court of Aldermen granted a petition amalgamating 'all the good folks of the trades of text letter, lymenours, and other folks of London, who are wont [also] to bind and sell books'.

That was before printing. In Bruges in 1474 Caxton published *The Recuyell of the Histories of*

Troy, the first book printed in the English language; three years later, books began to issue from the press in his shop in the precincts of Westminster Abbey. The consequent revolution brought mass production, lower prices, and accelerated turnover, new opportunities for capital investment and wholesaling, as well as an increased demand for bookbinders. The trade quickly flourished, with the retail side gravitating to St. Paul's Churchyard. Here dealers set up their stalls and signs, protected by local ordinances from the competition of street-hawkers of books and ballads. To be sure, stalls sprang up in other parts of the metropolis: in Paternoster Row and Barbican, Chancery Lane and St. Dunstan's Churchyard in Fleet Street; even on London Bridge. But Paul's Churchyard attracted by far the most. As early as 1554, some two years before incorporation, the Stationers' Company recognised the importance of the new centre by moving their headquarters from Milk Street, in the parish of St. Mary Magdalen, to Peter's College, towards the western end of Paul's Churchyard on the south side.

The Crown's motive in granting a Charter in 1557 manifests itself in the first sentence, deploring 'seditious and heretical books, rhymes, and treatises, renewing detestable heresies against the sound Catholic doctrine of Holy Mother Church'. Although Henry VIII had publicly worried about 'naughty printed books' as early as 1538, he vetoed the charter debated four years later at the Convocation of Canterbury. By 1557 the time was ripe for incorporation; counter-Reformation needed all the tools it could place at its disposal. For the governance of the Company the Charter established that it might assemble to elect a Master and two Keepers or Wardens. These officers had authority to search the houses or premises of any printer or bookseller in the kingdom, and to confiscate and burn unlicensed books. Only the Goldsmiths and Pewterers had earlier obtained similar rights of search and seizure. The Master and Warden and the *communitas* had, moreover, the right to meet for the establishment of ordinances and statutes for their own self-government. The Charter awarded the Company a seal. Three years later the City made the Stationers a Liveried Company (next in precedence after the Poulterers) of the City of London.

What the Charter neglects is to set forth in detail the shape of the Brotherhood. 'About five years after the grant of their said Charter', we learn from a later petition, the Stationers found their 'former Ordinances . . . somewhat defective', and therefore made 'some alteracions and addicions'. So, by 1562 or thereabouts, the Company's *modus operandi* was established. At the apex of the organisational pyramid were the Master, the Upper Warden, and the Under Warden. They governed with the advice and consent of an executive committee of experienced elders, the Court of Assistants, which had existed before incorporation; for how long is not known. Originally, the Court had some eight to ten members; by 1645 it had grown to twenty-eight. A full court, *plena Curia*, seems to have consisted of the Master, the two Wardens, the Assistants, and the Clerk who kept the records. They met irregularly; more often—usually about once a month—as time wore on. Beneath this élite served the Senior and Junior Renter Wardens, who, although not on the Court, were senior members of the Livery. They had the task of collecting the quarterly subscriptions paid by the freemen. Below them the Yeomanry, called the 'commonalty' in the Charter, drawn from the freemen; then the Brothers who, being mainly aliens, did not (like the Yeomen) have access to promotion; and, inevitably at the bottom, the apprentices, who served terms of seven to nine, sometimes even ten, years.

Mainly through the instrumentality of the Court of Assistants, the Company regulated itself. Some of its responsibilities were no different from those of other guilds, some unique to the Stationers. The Assistants implemented civic ordinances, such as those forbidding shops to keep open on Sundays and saints' days. In time of war or scarcity, or when the Crown levied a subsidy, they administered the tax assessments on individual guildsmen. Apprentices (their number limited) were presented; brethren, freemen, and members of the Livery admitted. The Court meted out fines for breaking the rules: for 'disorderly printing', for failure to observe quality controls—issuing books without covers, for example, or binding primers in flimsy wooden boards, called scabbards—for 'going hawking about the streets', for such breaches of decorum as brawling, using unseemly language, coming late to the hall, coming in a cloak, not coming at all, or leaving before all the ordinances were read. With patriotic self-interest, they worried about aliens. They also controlled 'foreign' printers, that is (to a London citizen) printers of English origin but not free of the City. They listened to trade complaints, and arbitrated disputes between master and man. They saw to it that expenses were met for the annual feast on the Sunday after St. Peter's Day. They guarded the privileges of the monopolists who held exclusive printing rights to certain classes of books: almanacs, psalms in meter and the ABC with the catechism, music books and common-law books and Latin school texts and others. Most important, from our point of view, they registered books for publication.

Registration implies licensing. The Crown, not the Company, devised licensing procedures, which are first set forth in the fifty-first of the *Injunctions Given by the Queen's Majesty. Anno domini. 1559.* Noting the covetousness of printers who, out of greed for gain, publish 'unfruitefull, vayne, and infamous bokes and papers', the Queen commanded that any book—'of what sort, nature, or in what language so ever it be'—must before publication have a licence in writing from either herself or six of her Privy Council, or two of the following: the Archbishops of Canterbury and York, the Bishop of London, the Chancellors of the two universities, and the Bishop and Archdeacon 'of the place where any such shalbe printed'. Of the two licensers, one is always to be the Ordinary, i.e. the judge who in his own right has jurisdiction in ecclesiastical cases; but a Bishop is ordinary in his diocese. The names of the licensers are to be printed at the end of every book. The injunction makes separate reference to 'pamphlettes, playes, and ballettes', as though these comprised an inferior category; but they were subject to the same controls.

The injunction of 1559 was superseded by the Star Chamber decree of 1586, which ordained that no book see print without having been licensed 'according to th[e] order appoynted by the Queenes majesties *Injunctyons*, And been first seen and perused by the Archbishop of CANTERBURY and Bishop of LONDON for the tyme beinge or any one of them'. This decree, in effect politely dismissing the elaborate earlier formulation, has been described as 'the greatest enactment concerning the press in the reigns of Elizabeth or James I'; it established government policy for half a century. That is not to say it was followed literally.

However conscientious, the Archbishop and Bishop could scarcely do all the reading with which the government now charged them. So they deputed the task to their chaplains and secretaries, on the basis of whose recommendations they awarded their *imprimaturs*. Two years later, in 1588, the delegation of authority was formalised by a decree appointing a panel of twelve 'correctors of the press'. Acting in pairs or singly, these reliable 'preachers and others' (episcopal chaplains or prebendaries of St. Paul's, with the odd layman) could by their signatures give 'sufficient warrant' for the entry of a book in the Stationers' Register, and the printing thereof. One of the correctors named was Robert Crowley, vicar of St. Giles's, Cripplegate, and a divine of pronounced Puritan sympathies. The Company, however, had no cause for anxiety about his influence, for Crowley was himself a stationer who had earlier 'perused' a number of books for his colleagues. But he died just after being appointed in the Armada year. No matter; the natural tendency of the guild was to bypass officialdom anyway, and look after their own licensing. 'Before the decree', the then Dean of the Arches, Sir John Lambe, reported around 1636, 'the Master and Wardens licensed all, and . . . when they had any divinity book of much importance they would take the advice of some two or three ministers of this town'. After the decree they turned to Richard Watkins. Elected to the Livery two decades earlier, he had served his two-year term as Renter Warden. This highly successful printer married Katherine Juggs, the daughter of the Queen's Printer, and acquired shares in such profitable patents as those for almanacs, service books, and psalters. After 1591 Watkins was the regular Company licenser.

Such procedural casualness did not go unremarked. In his edifying *Motive to Good Works* of 1593 Philip Stubbes, Puritan anatomiser of abuses, complained of the frustratingly long, sometimes fruitless, wait to have 'a good booke' approved by the ecclesiastical authorities, whereas 'other bookes full of all filthines, scurrilitie, baudry, dissolutenes, cosonage, cony-catching, and the lyke, (which all call for vengeance to heaven) are eyther quickely licensed, or at least easily tollerate, without all denyall or contradiction whatsoever'.

The reins were tightened in 1599. That year, alarmed by the scurrility and lasciviousness of contemporary letters, the Archbishop of Canterbury, acting jointly with the Bishop of London, ordered the burning of certain books, and issued directives for the future reformation of the press. Satires and epigrams they banned altogether, and they commanded 'That noe playes be printed excepte they bee allowed by suche as have aucthorytie'. On 4 June 1599 the condemned books were ceremonially burned in what came to be known as the 'bishops' bonfire'. Even so, the Clerk in Stationers' Hall did not insist upon seeing a licence before entering a book in the Register. However, conditional entries now became more frequent. Thus James Roberts was allowed to enter *Cloth Breeches and Velvet Hose* (a Chamberlain's play) on 27 May 1600 'provided that he is not to putt it in prynte Without further & better Aucthority', and the same Roberts on 7 February 1603 obtained permission to print *Troilus and Cressida* 'when he hath gotten sufficient aucthority for yt'. Around 1607 an arrangement was made whereby the Master of the Revels extended his licensing function from the production to the printing of plays. Between April and October the Master, Edmund Tilney, licensed sixteen plays. At times (as we shall see) provisional registration may have served a blocking function.

It is natural enough to suppose that the *raison d'être* for registration was to ensure copyright, even though the word itself does not come into use until the eighteenth century. (The earliest occurrence cited by the *OED*, Blackstone in 1767, is antedated by Tonson's reference to 'the Proprietors of the Copy-Right' in his 1734 edition of *The Merry Wives of Windsor.*)[1] Copyright, before the Act of 1709, existed for the protection not of the author but of the stationer. In the early days of the Company the latter paid a fee of 1*d.* for every three pages, with a minimum of 4*d.*, to have a book entered in the Register; after 1582 the standard fee became 6*d.* for a book, and 4*d.* for the lesser fry of ballads, broadsides, and the like. A stationer established his proprietary interest in a book by 'presenting it in the Hall' and paying the Clerk his fee; to do so was 'the common and strongest assurance that Stationers have for all their copies'. These contemporary references make the position clear enough.

A complicating factor, however, is that, even if entrance was theoretically obligatory, a sizeable number of books in Shakespeare's day—as many as a third—went unregistered. In some instances at least this benign neglect may have had no more profound motivation than the stationer's desire to save sixpence. He did not necessarily suffer as a result. Take, for example, the bizarrely popular *Mucedorus*: William Jones brought out six editions before it was registered on 17 September 1618. By then Jones had died, and his widow assigned the copyright to another printer. The play was published the same year as 'Printed for John Wright, and . . . to be sold at his Shop at the signe of the Bible without New-gate'. Still, according to Sir Walter Greg, 'So far from copyright being obtained by the mere act of publication, as has sometimes been supposed, unregistered publication might involve both the confiscation of copy and the punishment of the offender'. With *Mucedorus* publication seems to have had no such untoward effects on the stationer, nor did it prevent inheritance of the ownership or its subsequent transfer. Other unregistered plays, among them *The Shoemakers' Holiday*, *Volpone*, and *The White Devil*, were likewise assigned.

Leo Kirschbaum, who made a study of the problem, concluded that custom, as well as law, governed copyright, which had its *de facto* aspect. Another authority suggests that assignment did not depend upon registration, but was 'a private transaction'. This view has not gone unchallenged. The whole question, on which much has been written, is too complex for disentanglement here; the evidence, untidy and incomplete, resists the historian's yearning for a confident solution. C. J. Sisson, however, has illuminatingly brought to bear on the subject records, in the Court of Chancery, of an action of 1616–17 involving an Oxford printer, Barnes, who sued a syndicate of stationers respecting copyright claims in Rider's *Dictionary*. From the testimony Sisson concludes that entry in the Register (with payment of the fee) was not automatic but at the discretion of the stationer, that not too much importance should be attached to the large number of unregistered copies, that printing usually followed on the heels of licensing, and that registration, while less than essential in order to legalise publication, did serve to protect copyright. 'At all points', Sisson writes, 'we are left with full confidence in the emphatic declaration of Stationers of authority in the Company that the sole authentic evidence of ownership of copy rests in entries in the Register'. There, with no confidence whatever that the last word on the subject has been pronounced, we may for present purposes let the matter rest.

The Shakespeare entries in the Register, here reproduced *en bloc* for the first time, chronicle the publishing fortunes of the poems, individual plays, and the four folios from the 1590s to the

1 In the Advertisement, dated 6 September 1734, appended to the text.

Restoration. These entries are scattered through the several volumes of the Register, beginning with that designated B, and covering the years 1576–95. There follow C (1595–1620), D (1620–45), E (1646–56), F (1656–82), and G (1682–1709). The entries furnish information and raise questions.

Sometimes facts about performance, presumably forthcoming from title-pages of the manuscripts, find their way into the entries. *King Lear* was enrolled on 26 November 1607, 'as yt was played before the kinges majestie at Whitehall uppon S[t] Stephans night at Christmas Last by his majesties servantes playinge usually at the globe on the Banksyde'. The same production information appears on the title-page of the 1608 Quarto. More intriguing is the 7 February 1603 entry for *Troilus and Cressida*, 'as yt is acted by my Lord Chamberlens Men'; for the preface to the second issue of the quarto edition, published six years later, speaks of the piece as 'never stal'd with the Stage, never clapper-clawd with the palmes of the vulger', and unsullied by 'the smoaky breath of the multitude'. It is not the only puzzle. *Troilus and Cressida* was entered in the Register a second time by two different stationers, Richard Bonian and Henry Walley, on 28 January 1609, with no reference to assignment. What happened? That the original entrance took place in the presence of the 'Full Court', rather than merely before the Wardens, indicates that some question, maybe related to the 'sufficient aucthoritie' for publication, wanted sorting out. More than half a century ago A. W. Pollard argued that in this and other entries the stationer, acting as the players' agent, was using registration to forestall piracy and to protect the stage run of the plays. Once a piece was printed, anybody could mount it. James Roberts's 1603 entry of *Troilus and Cressida* nevertheless failed to deter Bonian and Walley—this despite the acknowledged opposition of the King's Men, presumably the 'grand possessors' alluded to in the preface. Perhaps re-entry was made possible by the long interval, without publication, after the original entry. Roberts had meanwhile retired, and was probably dead; and the company may have been disinclined to go to special lengths to protect one of their less popular plays.

One or two of Roberts's other entries bear scrutiny in this context. On 22 July 1598 he 'Entred for his copie under the handes of bothe the wardens, a booke of the Marchaunt of Venyce or otherwise called the Jew of Venyce. Provided that yt bee not prynted by the said James Robertes; or anye other whatsoever without lycence first had from the Right honorable the lord Chamberlen'. Clearly the company were depending on their patron to safeguard a valued property. On 4 August, presumably of 1600 (the year is not given), Mr. Roberts had entered to him four other of 'my lord chamberlens mens Plaies':

as yo[w] like yt: / a booke Henry the ffift: / a booke Every man in his humour. / a booke
The commedie of muche A doo about nothinge. / a booke /

After the last item appears the phrase: 'to be staied'. It is interesting that each of the plays is described as 'a booke'—the term used, in theatrical jargon, for the company's official prompt-copy, which would bear as its title, 'The booke of . . . [etc.]'—as, for example, 'The Booke of Sir Thomas Moore'.[1] It is interesting too that, although Roberts registered these four plays, as well as *The Merchant of Venice* and *Troilus and Cressida* and others belonging to the Chamberlain's/King's Men, he never published any of them. He was a bookseller, and also a printer who specialised mainly in almanacs and prognostications; but he had (through marriage) acquired a royal patent for printing all playbills. Hence his connection with the actors.

Had the Chamberlain's Men, as Pollard suggests, used the friendly Roberts to run interference for them, lending him their promptbooks temporarily to demonstrate to the Stationers' Company that the actors were in legal possession, after which he returned the manuscripts? The hypothesis presents problems. Of the four 'staied' plays, two—*Every Man In* and *Much Ado*—were re-registered without conditions a few months later, and published in the same year. The stay did not prevent Thomas Creede from printing a Bad Quarto of *Henry V* for Thomas Millington and John Busby, also in the same year. Of course, if a certain strategy was employed, we need not assume that it invariably succeeded. It is true, however, that other 'staying' entries involved non-dramatic

1 In the Register the term 'booke' does not, however, exclude non-dramatic items such as *Venus and Adonis*.

works, such as Rider's *Dictionary*. It may be that the 8 August notation is not an entry at all, but merely the Clerk's memorandum, and that the staying reference merely signifies that he was waiting for word of the Lord Chamberlain's approbation before proceeding. That is Sisson's view, and has the virtue of simplicity. The Pollard theory suffers the disadvantage of being more elaborate, but accounts for more of the facts, such as Roberts's failure to publish. While powerfully influential for over half a century, it has not, however, gone unchallenged. Andrew S. Cairncross in 1969 revived the older view that Roberts acted in his own interests, not the players'. He was himself the pirate whom the Chamberlain's men sought, through their patron, to block; that Roberts held a monopoly on playbills did not make him the company's agent, but merely gave him opportunities to pick up playbooks on the sly. The subsequent printing of these plays by others was accomplished by a policy of (in Cairncross's phrase) 'evasive transfer', which enabled Roberts seemingly to disassociate himself from their publication while he covertly retained his printing rights. The trouble with secret arrangements is that they are secret, but some of Cairncross's arguments are not without cogency, and he cites pertinent documents—later communications from the Lord Chamberlain to the Stationers—that Pollard overlooked. But like Pollard's reconstruction, or any other from incomplete evidence, Cairncross's is based in large measure on inference. All such reconstructions are, in the last resort, hypothetical. The only certainty is that we have not yet had the last word about these intriguing entries.

A NOTE ON AUTHORITIES

As befits an institution that has figured so prominently in the development of publishing in England, the Stationers, their Company, and its records have themselves inspired numerous publications. Modern scholarly inquiry has its *fons et origo* a century ago in the monumental labours of Edward Arber, who published *A Transcript of the Registers of the Company of Stationers; 1554–1640 A.D.*, in four volumes (1875–77; a fifth volume, devoted to index, appeared separately in 1894). The Great Fire of London destroyed the original Charter of Incorporation in the Company's possession, but Arber prints the Latin text from the enrolments in the Public Record Office, along with his English translation, which I have cited above. He similarly includes the texts of other regulatory documents. E. E. B. Eyre and C. R. Rivington continued transcription of the Register down to the latest entries in 1708 in their three-volume edition in 1913–15. The relevant entries for all dramatic items were re-transcribed, in accordance with more stringent modern standards, by W. W. Greg in *A Bibliography of the English Printed Drama to the Restoration* (1939–59), i. 1–78. Together with E. Boswell, Greg had already edited *Records of the Court of the Stationers' Company, 1576 to 1602, from Register B* (1930), a labour continued by William A. Jackson in *Records of the Court of the Stationers' Company, 1602 to 1640* (1957). In 1962 Greg published *Licensers for the Press, &c. to 1640*, a biographical index garnered mainly from Arber's *Transcript*. These last four works enjoyed the sponsorship of the Bibliographical Society.

Of the special studies I limit myself here to those which I have myself found especially useful or provocative. Cyprian Blagden's *The Stationers' Company: A History, 1403–1959* (1960) fulfils a long-felt need in agreeably readable fashion. Graham Pollard's essays on the brotherhood prior to incorporation, 'The Company of Stationers before 1557' and 'The Early Constitution of the Stationers' Company' (both in *The Library*, 4th Ser., xviii (1937–8), 1–38, 235–60), remain the standard authority on this period. In two pioneering monographs, *Shakespeare Folios and Quartos* (1909) and *Shakespeare's Fight with the Pirates and the Problems of the Transmission of His Text* (1917), A. W. Pollard dealt with publishing conditions in Shakespeare's day, made his celebrated distinction between 'Good' and 'Bad Quartos', and set forth his hypothesis respecting the 'blocking' entries. Although today we know more about some of these matters, it cannot be said that his work has been superseded; all subsequent discussions take their point of departure from Pollard. These include Leo Kirschbaum's controversial *Shakespeare and the Stationers* (Columbus, Ohio, 1955), which deals with stolen and surreptitious copies, and offers a 'conjectural history'—admittedly 'highly hypothetical'—of the relations between Shakespeare's company and the stationers from 1594, when the Chamberlain's Men came into being, until the publication of the First Folio in 1623. In a subsequent paper (to which I have referred) Kirschbaum expresses his views, forcibly as is his wont, on 'The Copyright of Elizabethan Plays' (*The Library*, 5th Ser., xiv (1959), 231–50). 'I have indicated', he allows along the way, 'that one of the things wrong with my *Shakespeare and the Stationers* was a penchant for exactitude.' While the confession has a certain poignance, it perhaps does not place an intolerable strain upon the spirit of *mea culpa*. Drawing upon his matchless knowledge of Elizabethan documentary resources, C. J. Sisson replied to Kirschbaum in 'The Laws of Elizabethan Copyright: the Stationers' View', *The Library*, 5th Ser., xv (1960), 8–20. The article by A. S. Cairncross to which I have alluded is 'Shakespeare and the "Staying Entries"'; it has received insufficient attention, perhaps because it was published somewhat obscurely, in *Shakespeare in the Southwest: Some New Directions*, ed. T. J. Stafford (El Paso, 1969), pp. 80–93.

As one would expect, the Company's rôle is considered in works casting a wider net; of these, E. K. Chambers's wonderfully concise treatment in *William Shakespeare: A Study of Facts and Problems* (1930), i. 128ff., demands special mention. F. P. Wilson saw the significance of Stubbes's grumbling in his *Motive to Good Works*, and passed on the reference to Greg, who mentions it in the masterly Lyell Lectures given at Oxford in 1955, published as *Some Aspects and Problems of London Publishing between 1550 and 1650* (Oxford, 1956). This brief monograph—only a little over a hundred pages—distils expertise acquired over a lifetime, and bears the Greg hallmarks of precision, lucidity, and logical rigour. The several chapters treat decrees and ordinances affecting the Elizabethan book trade, the Stationers' records, licensing, entrance and copyright, imprints and patents, the Master of the Revels as 'corrector' of plays for the press, and the blocking entries.

Correcting of another kind is the subject of Percy Simpson's *Proof-reading in the Sixteenth, Seventeenth and Eighteenth Centuries* (1935). I have found especially useful the first chapter, 'Authors' Proof-reading'.

These are the authorities from whom I have most profited. In my captions I have referred readers to Greg's transcripts for the play entries, and (for non-dramatic items) to Arber or Eyre. For completeness I have included facsimiles of entries for non-canonical plays printed with title-page attributions to Shakespeare or 'W.S.'.

II. Stationers' Register Entries

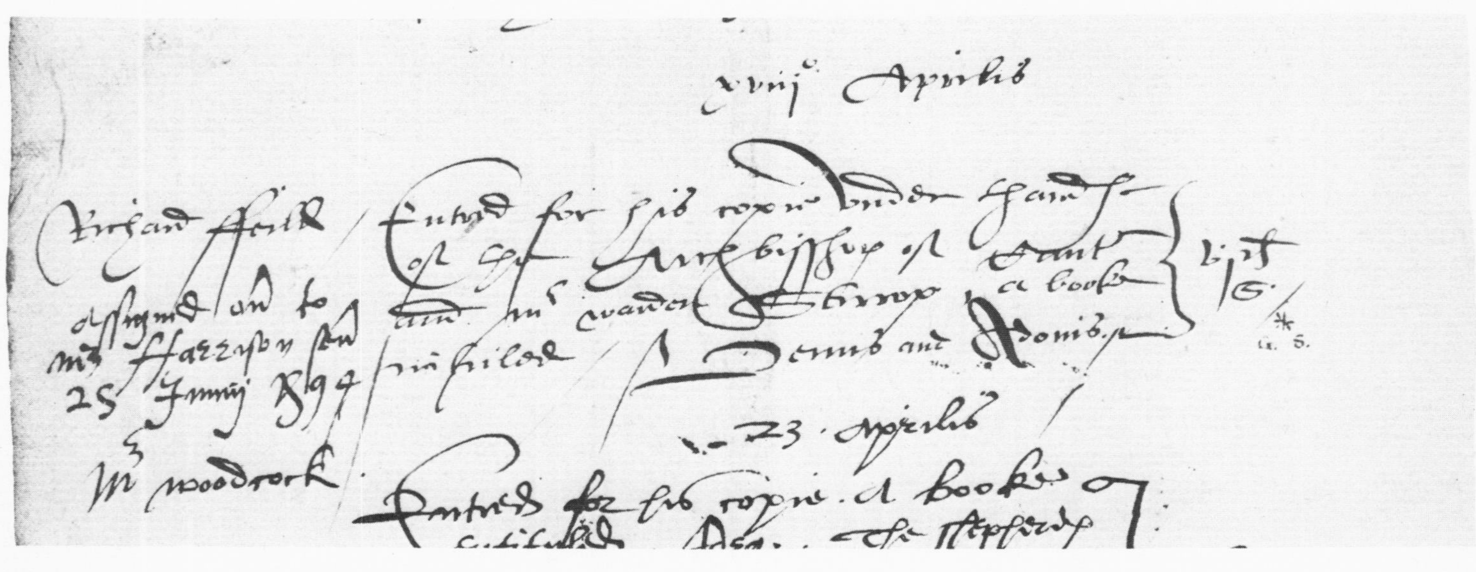

100 18 APRIL 1593/25 JUNE 1594. Venus and Adonis *entered by Richard Field 18 April 1593, and transferred by him to John Harrison, Sr., 25 June 1594. Register B, f. 297ᵛ. Transcript: Arber, ii. 630. See also items 105 and 107 below.*

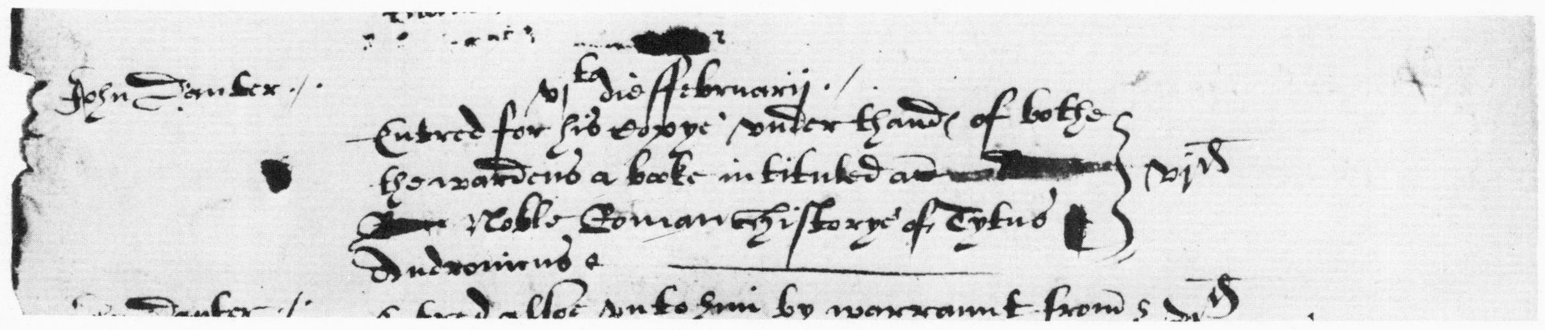

vj^to die ffebruarij ./

John Danter ./ Entred for his Copye vnder thandes of bothe the wardens a booke intituled a Noble Roman Historye of Tytus Andronicus . . . vjd

101 6 FEBRUARY 1594. Titus Andronicus *entered by John Danter. Register B, f. 304v. Transcript: Greg, i. 10.*

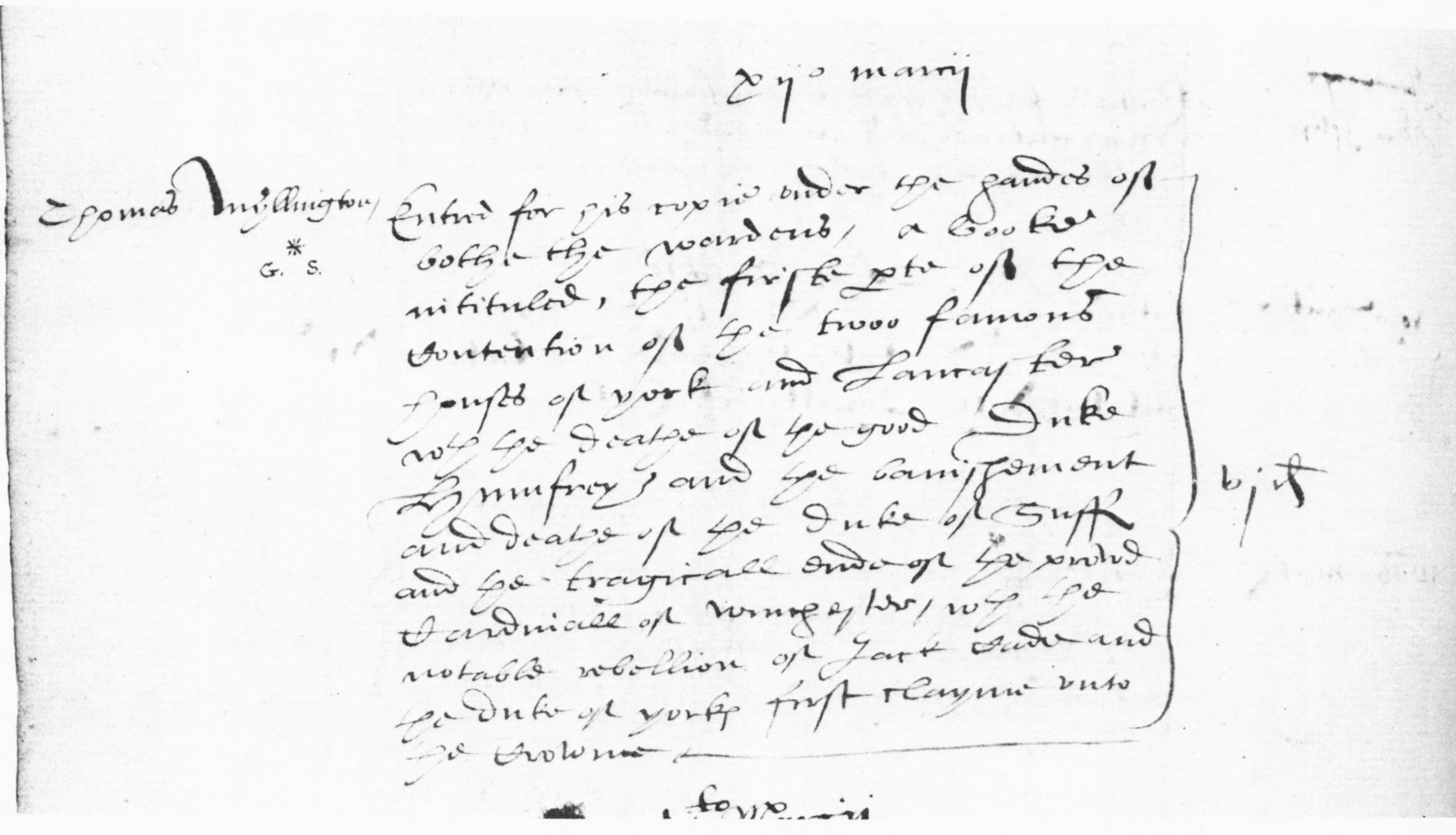

xij^o marcij

Thomas Millington / Entred for his copie vnder the handes of bothe the wardens, a booke intituled, the firste pte of the Contention of the twoo famous houses of york and Lancaster with the deathe of the good Duke Humfrey and the banishement and deathe of the Duke of Suff and the tragicall ende of the proud Cardinall of winchester, with the notable rebellion of Jack Cade and the duke of yorkes first clayme vnto the Crowne . . . vjd

G. * S.

102 12 MARCH 1594. 2 Henry VI *entered by Thomas Millington. Register B, f. 305v. Transcript: Greg, i. 10.*

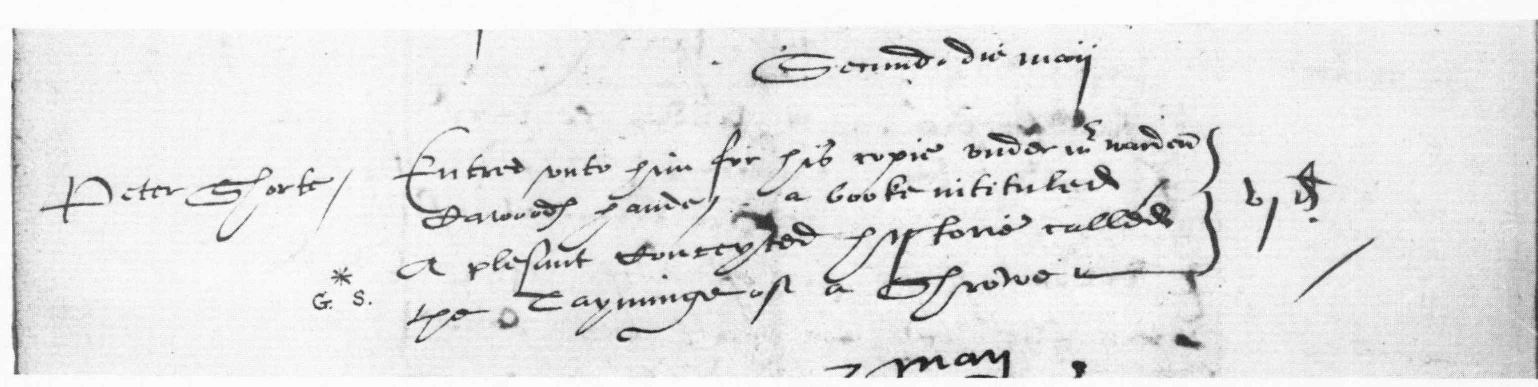

Secundo die maij

Peter Short / Entred vnto him for his copie vnder m^r warden Warcoopes hande, a booke intituled A plesant Conceyted historie called the Tayminge of a Shrowe . . . vjd

G. * S.

103 2 MAY 1594. The Taming of A Shrew *entered by Peter Short. Register B, f. 306v. Transcript: Greg, i. 10.*

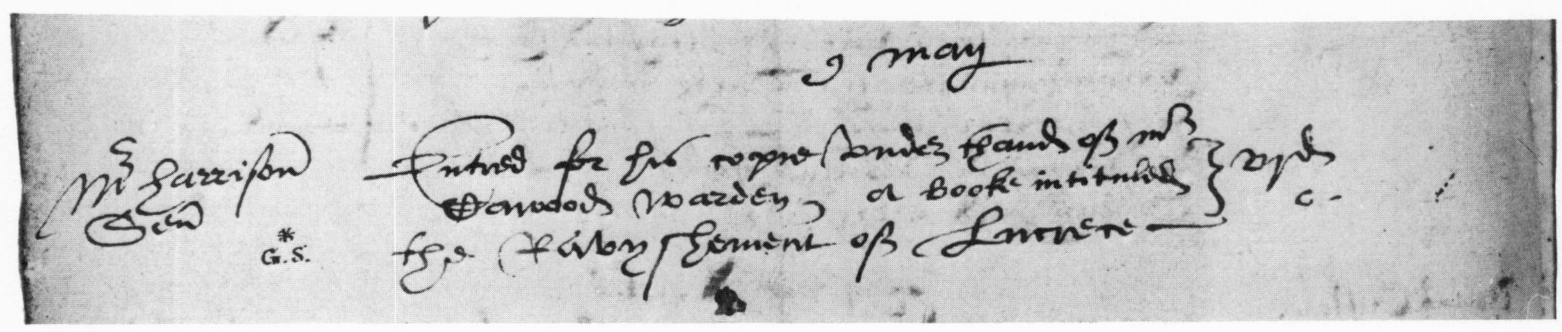
9 may

Mr Harrison Senr — Entred for his copie vnder thand of mr Cawood Warden, a booke intituled the Ravyshement of Lucrece — vjd c

G.S.

104 9 MAY 1594. The Rape of Lucrece *entered by John Harrison, Sr. Register B, f. 306v. Transcript: Arber, ii. 648.*

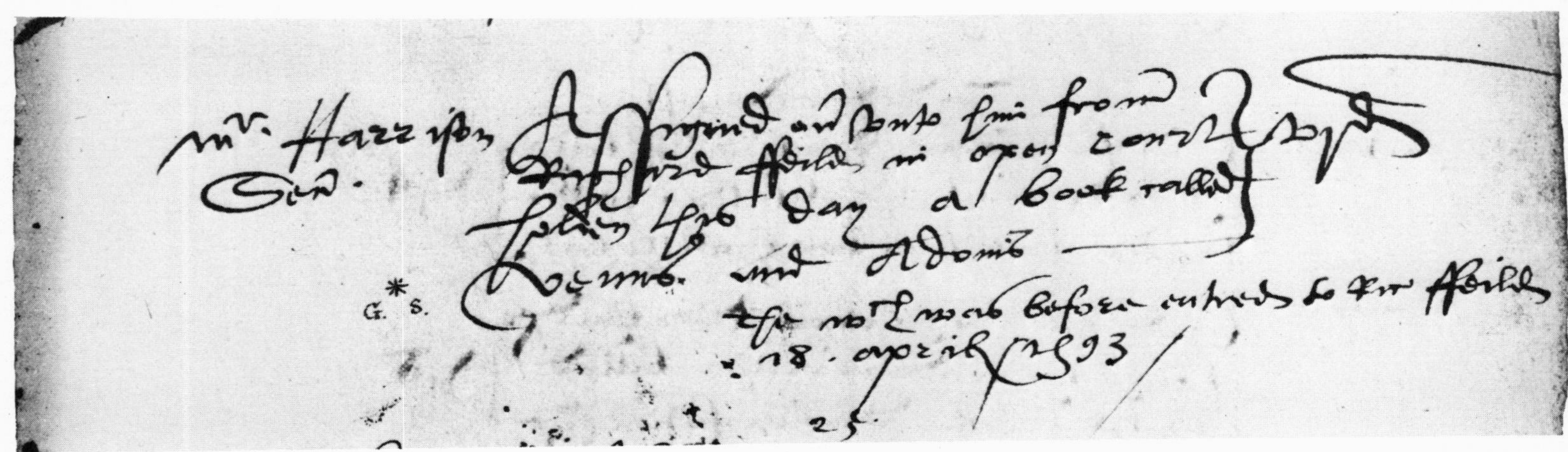
Mr. Harrison Senr. — Assigned ouer vnto him from Richard ffeild in open Court holden this day a book called Venus and Adonis — vjd

G. S. — the which was before entred to Richard ffeild 18 april 1593

105 25 JUNE 1594. Venus and Adonis *transferred by Richard Field to John Harrison, Sr. Register B, f. 310. Transcript: Arber, ii. 655.*

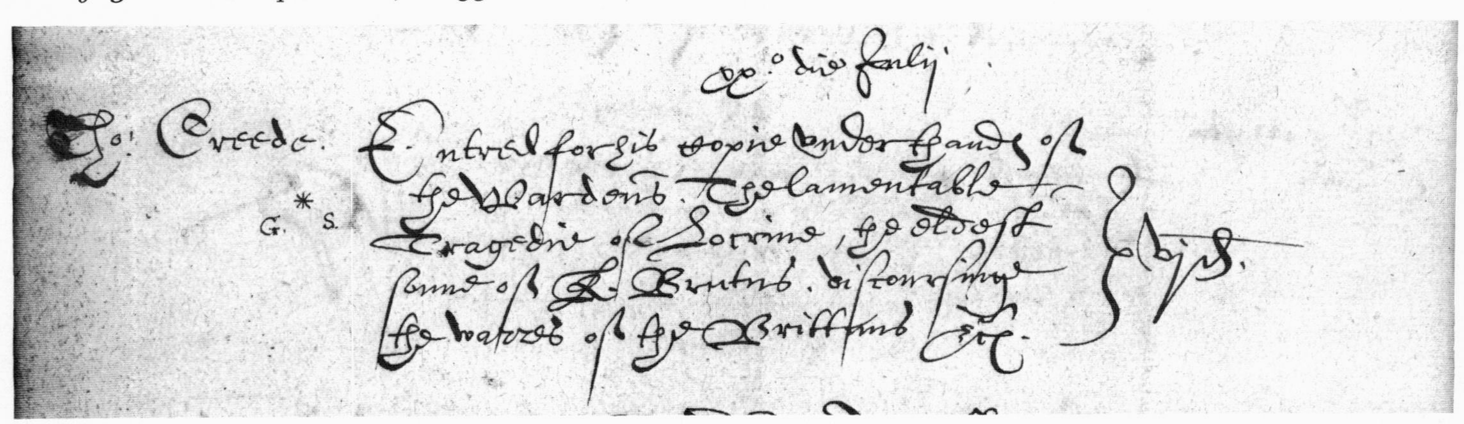
xxo die Julij.

Tho: Creede. — Entred for his copie vnder thandes of the Wardens. The lamentable Tragedie of Locrine, the eldest sonne of K. Brutus, discoursinge the warres of the Brittaines &c. — vjd

G. S.

106 20 JULY 1594. Locrine *entered by Thomas Creede. Register B, f. 310v. Transcript: Greg, i. 12.*

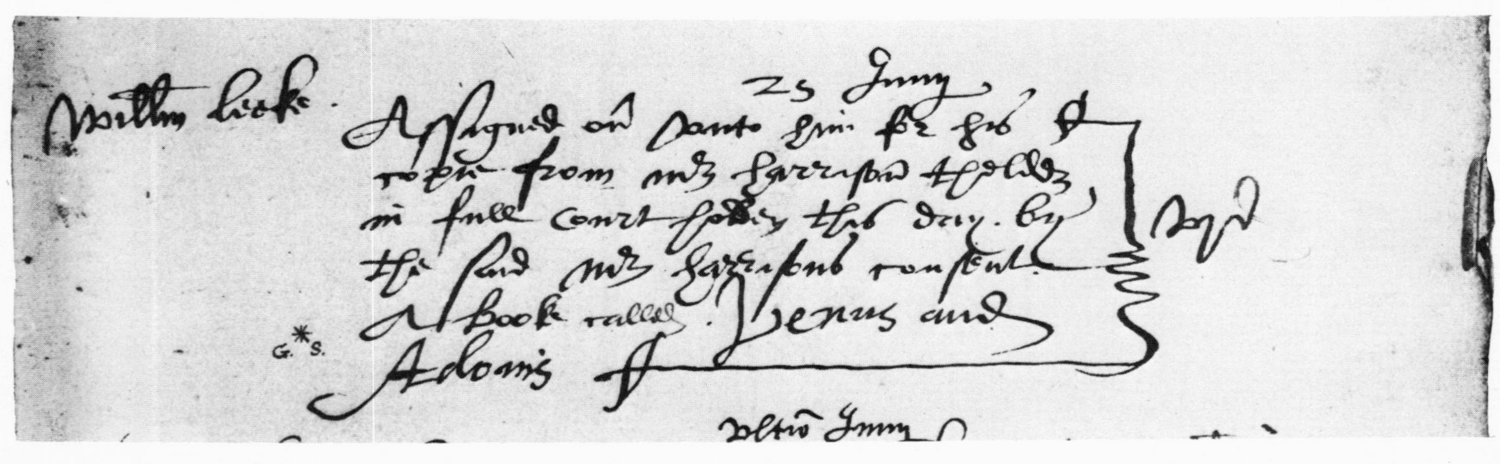
25 Junij

Willm Leake — Assigned ouer vnto him for his copie from mr Harrison thelder in full court holden this day, by the said mr Harrisons consent. A booke called Venus and Adonis — vjd

G. S.

vltimo Junij

107 25 JUNE 1596. Venus and Adonis *transferred from John Harrison, Sr., to William Leake. Register C, f. 11. Transcript: Arber, iii. 65.*

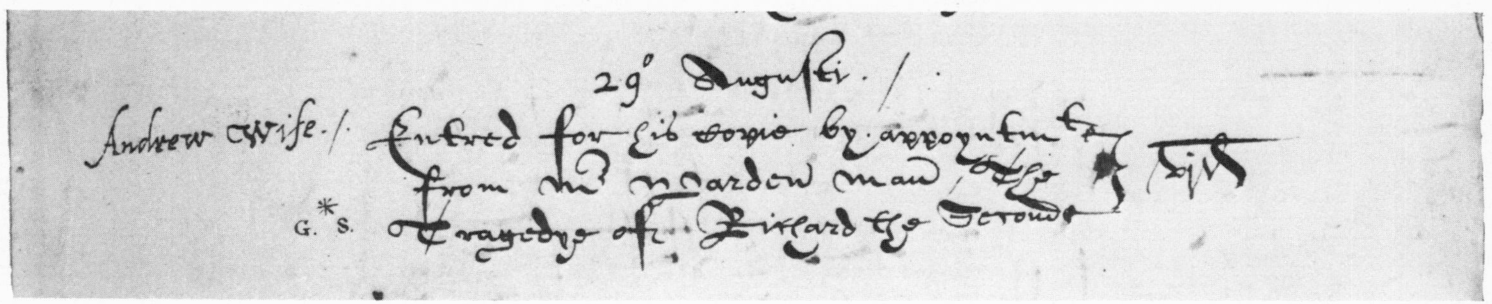

29° Augusti. /

Andrew Wise. / Entred for his copie by appoyntment from m[r] warden man / The Tragedye of Richard the Second — vj[d]

G.*S.

108 29 AUGUST 1597. Richard II *entered by Andrew Wise. Register C, f. 23. Transcript: Greg, i. 13.*

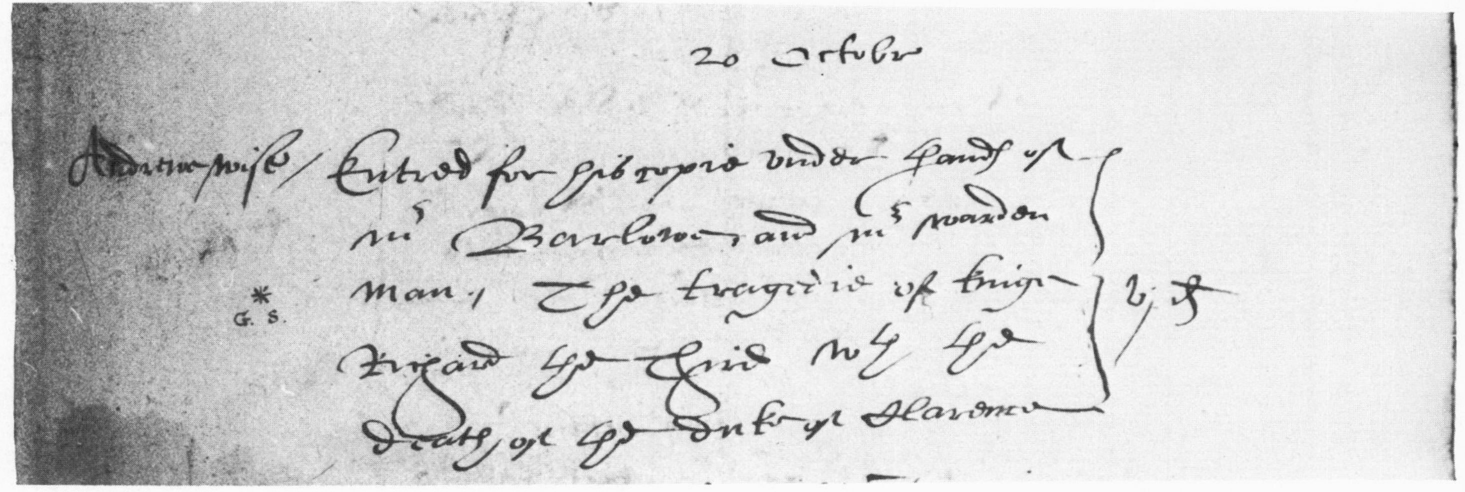

20 Octobr

Andrew wise / Entred for his copie vnder thandes of m[r] Barlowe and m[r] warden man / The tragedie of kinge Richard the Third wth the death of the duke of Clarence — vj[d]

G.*S.

109 20 OCTOBER 1597. Richard III *entered by Andrew Wise. Register C, f. 25. Transcript: Greg, i. 13.*

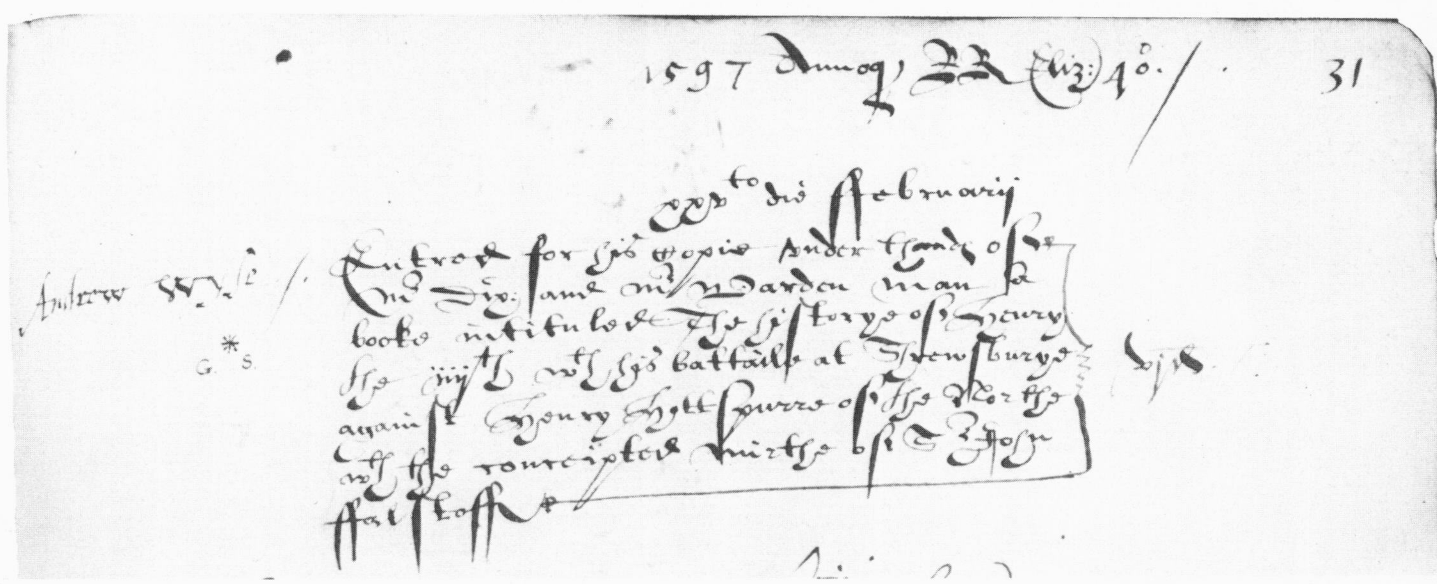

1597 Anno R[egni] R[egin]e Eliz: 40. / 31

xxv[to] die ffebruarij

Andrew Wyse / Entred for his copie vnder thandes of m[r] Dix: and m[r] warden man a booke intituled The historye of Henry the iiij[th] wth his battaile at Shrewsburye against Henry Hottspurre of the Northe wth the conceipted mirthe of Sir John ffalstoff — vj[d]

G.*S.

110 25 FEBRUARY 1598. 1 Henry IV *entered by Andrew Wise. Register C, f. 31. Transcript: Greg, i. 13.*

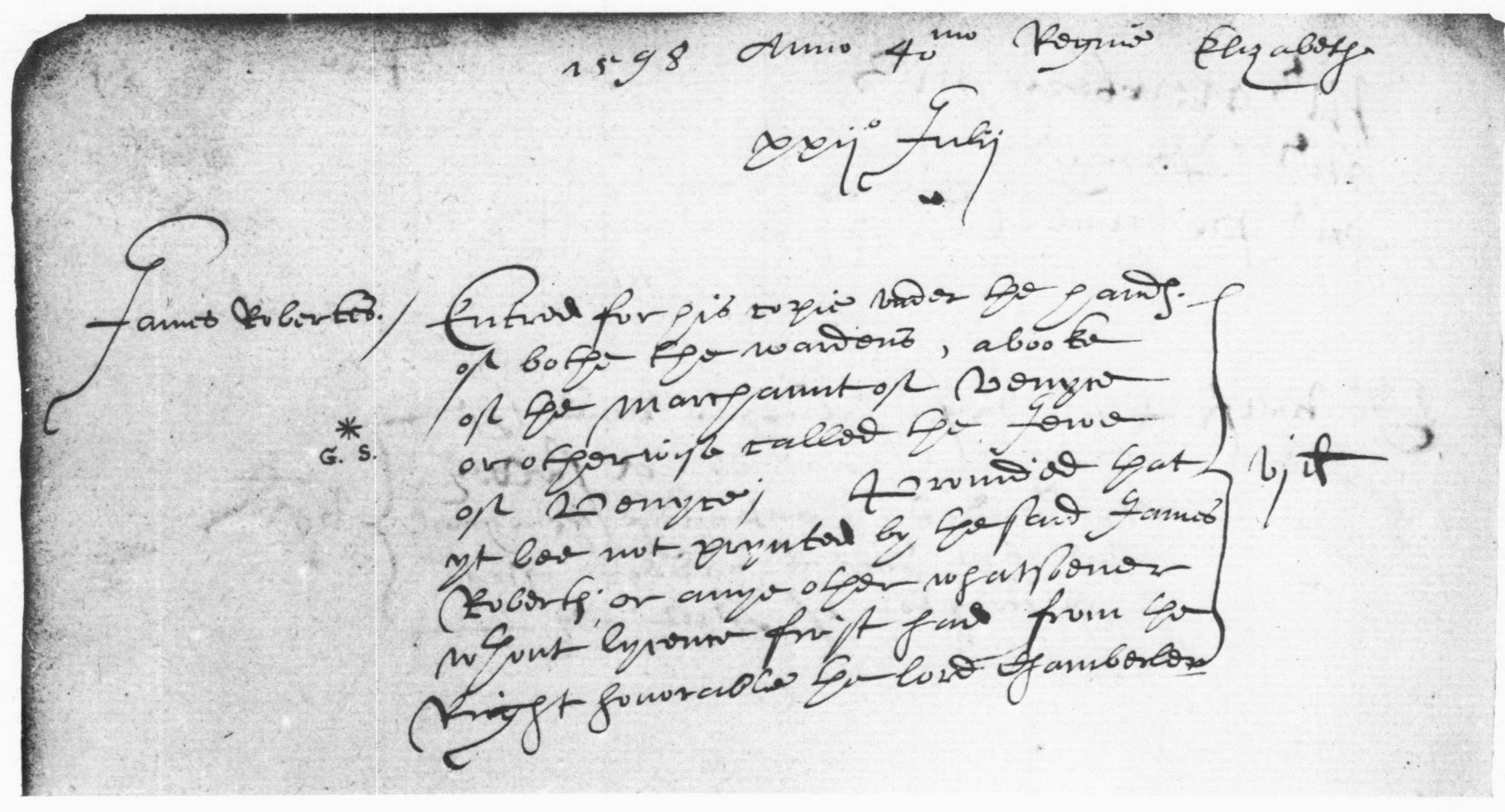
1598 Anno 40mo Regine Elizabeth

xxijo Julij

James Robertes./ Entred for his copie vnder the handes of bothe the wardens, a booke of the Marchaunt of Venyce or otherwise called the Jewe of Venyce, Prouided that yt bee not prynted by the said James Robertes or anye other whatsoeuer without lycence first had from the Right honorable the lord Chamberlen

G. S.

vjd

III 22 JULY 1598. The Merchant of Venice *entered by James Roberts. Register C, f.* 39^v. *Transcript: Greg, i. 13.*

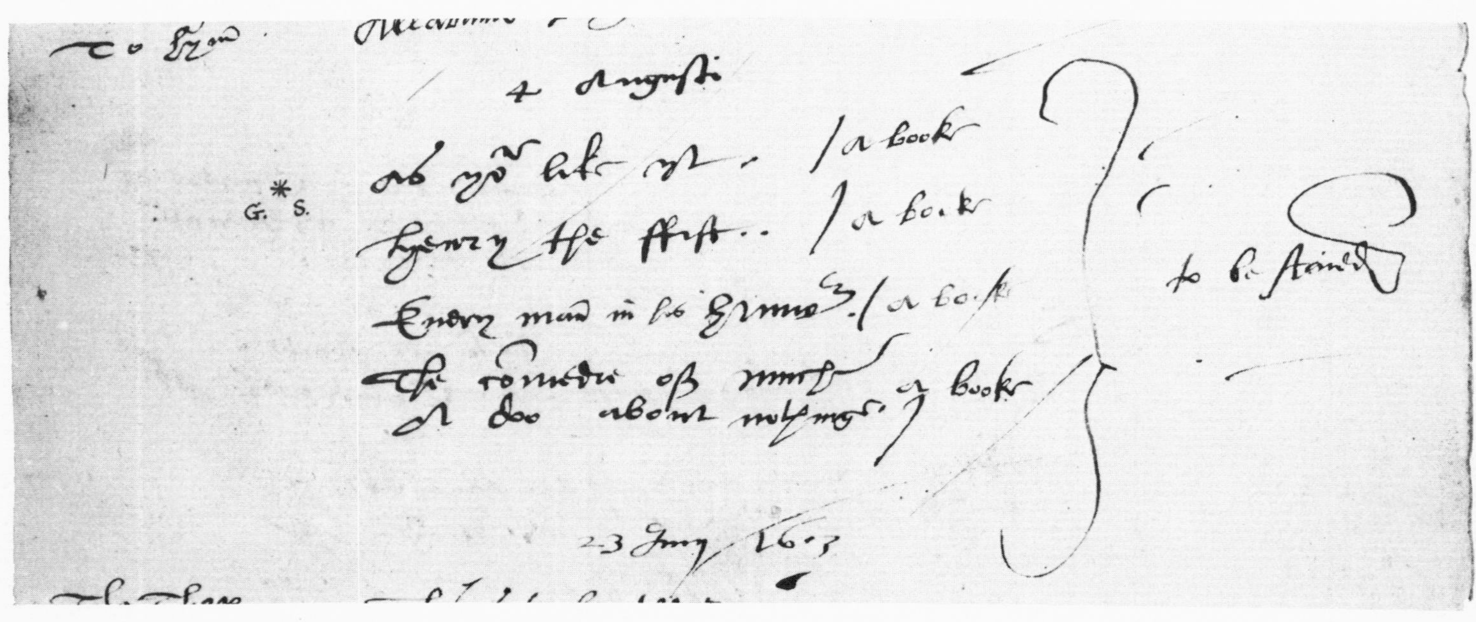
4 Augusti

G. S.

As you like yt / a booke

Henry the ffift / a booke

Every man in his humour / a booke

The commedie of muche A doo about nothinge / a booke

to be staied

23 Juny 1603

II2 4 AUGUST 1600(?). *James Roberts's entry of* As You Like It, Henry V, Much Ado About Nothing (*and* Every Man in His Humour) *'staied'. Register C, fly-leaf. Transcript: Greg, i. 15.*

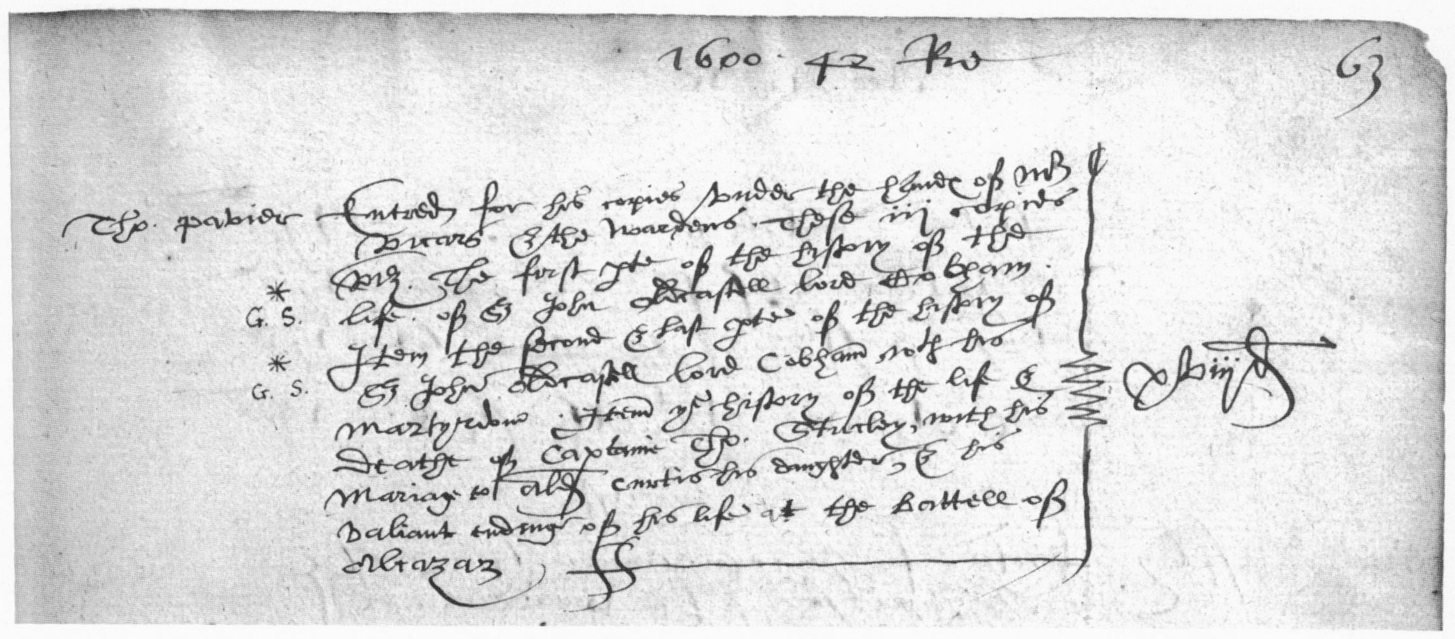

1600 · 42 R 63

Tho. pavier Entred for his copies vnder the handes of mr Vicars and the wardens. These iiij copies viz. The first parte of the history of the life of Sir John Oldcastell lord Cobham. Item the second and last parte of the history of Sir John Oldcastell lord Cobham with his martyrdom. Item the history of the life and deathe of Captaine Tho. Stucley, with his mariage to Alderman Curtes his daughter and his valiant endinge of his life at the battell of Alcazar

G. S. *
G. S. *

xviij d

113 II AUGUST 1600. I Sir John Oldcastle *entered by Thomas Pavier. Register C, f. 63. Transcript: Greg, i. 15. The 1600 Quarto has no title-page attribution, but Pavier's 1619 Quarto (misdated 1600) is ascribed to William Shakespeare.*

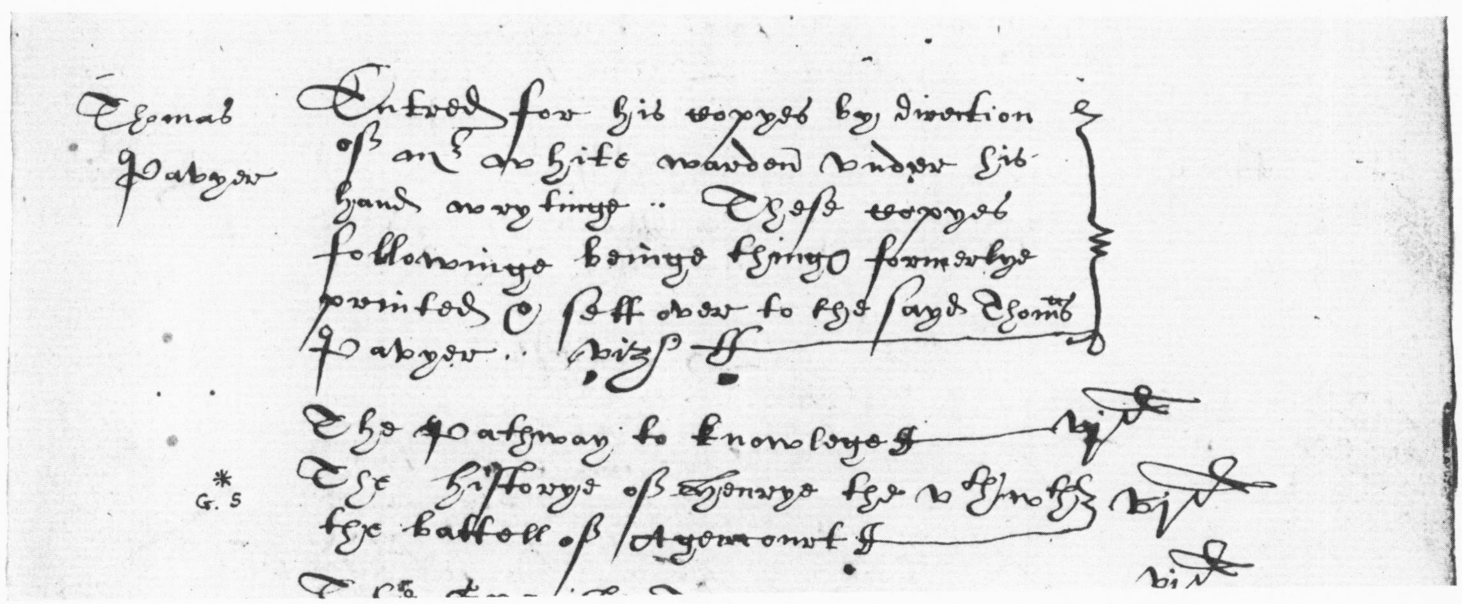

Thomas Payver Entred for his copyes by direction of mr White warden vnder his hand wrytinge. These copyes followinge beinge thinges formerlye printed and sett over to the sayd Thomas Payver. viz.

The Pathway to knowledge vjd

G. S. * The historye of Henrye the Vth with the battell of Agencourt vjd

114 14 AUGUST 1600. Henry V *transferred, as 'formerly printed', to Thomas Pavier. Register C, f. 63. Transcript: Greg, i. 16.*

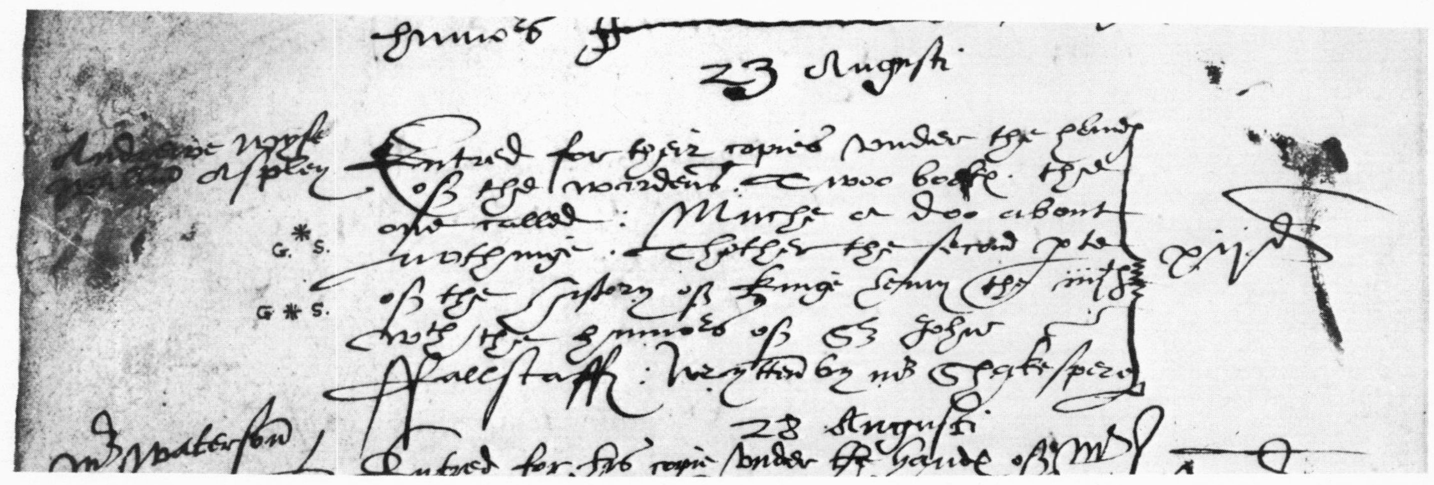

115 23 AUGUST 1600. Much Ado About Nothing *and* 2 Henry IV *entered by Andrew Wise and William Aspley. Register C, f.* 63^{v}. *Transcript: Greg, i. 16.*

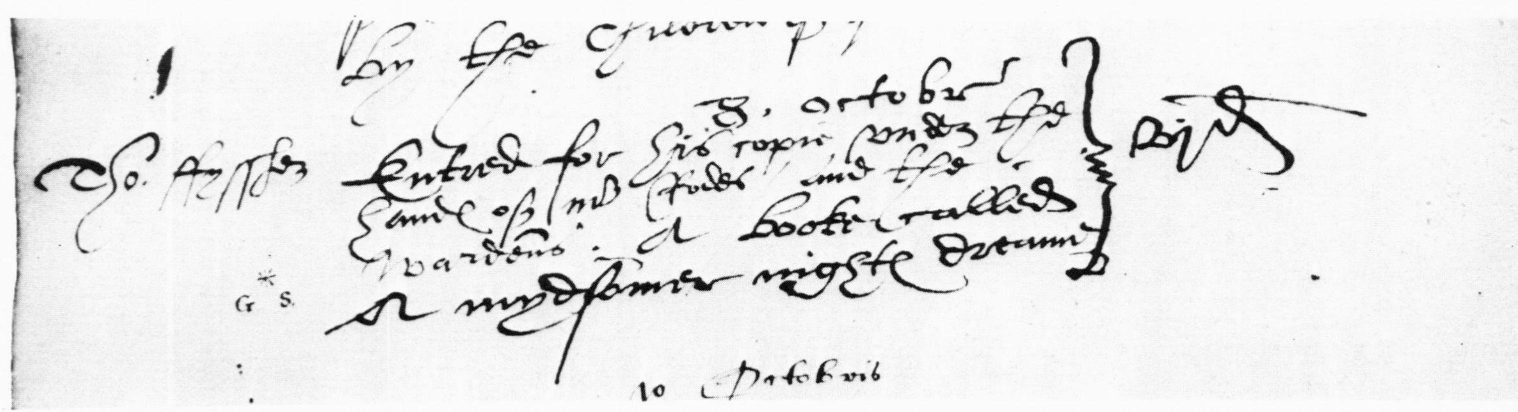

116 8 OCTOBER 1600. A Midsummer-Night's Dream *entered by Thomas Fisher. Register C, f.* 65^{v}. *Transcript: Greg, i. 16.*

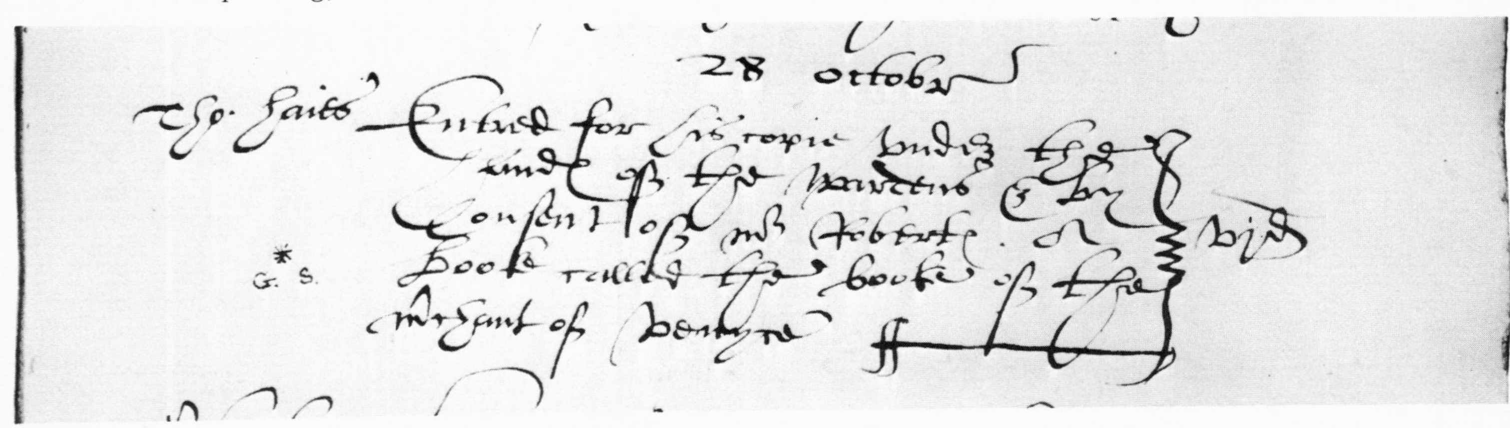

117 28 OCTOBER 1600. The Merchant of Venice *transferred from James Roberts to Thomas Hayes. Register C, f. 66. Transcript: Greg, i. 16.*

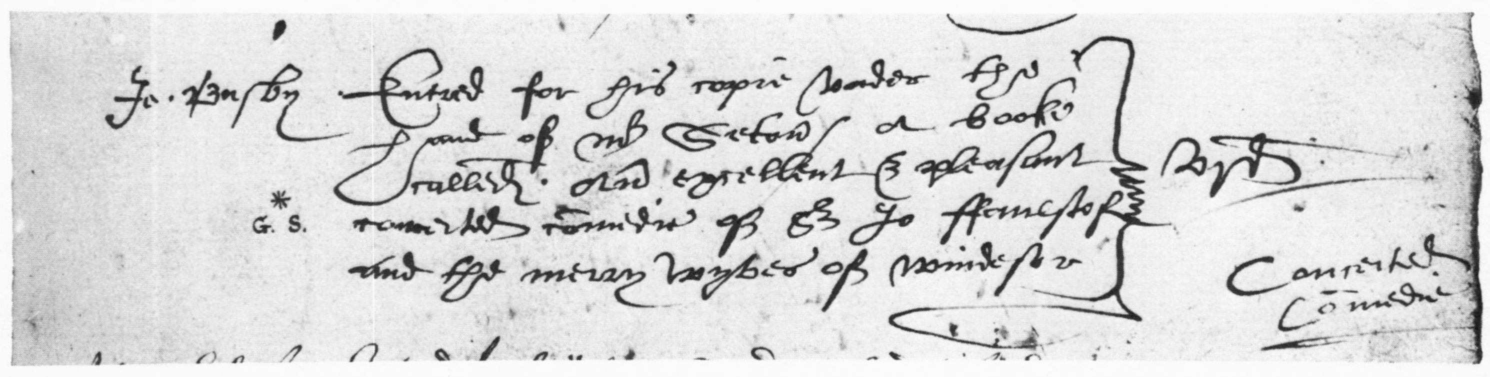

118 18 JANUARY 1602. The Merry Wives of Windsor *entered by John Busby and transferred to Arthur Johnson. Register C, f. 78. Transcript: Greg, i. 18.*

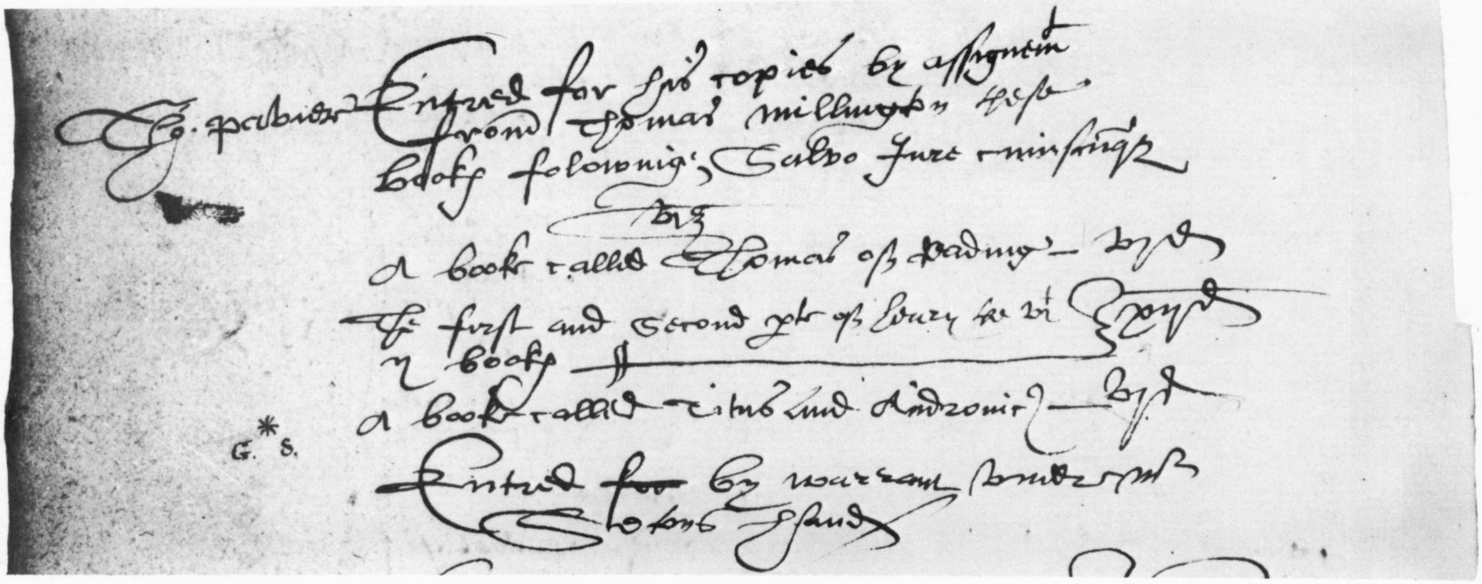

Tho. pavier Entred for his copies by assignement from Thomas millington these bookes folowinge, Saluo Jure cuiuscunque

viz

A booke called Thomas of Reading vjd

The first and Second parte of henry the vjth ij bookes xijd

A booke called Titus and Andronicus vjd

G.*S. Entred by warrant vnder master Setons hand

119 19 APRIL 1602. 1 *and* 2 Henry VI *and* Titus Andronicus *transferred from Thomas Millington to Thomas Pavier. Register C, f. 80v. Transcript: Greg, i. 18.*

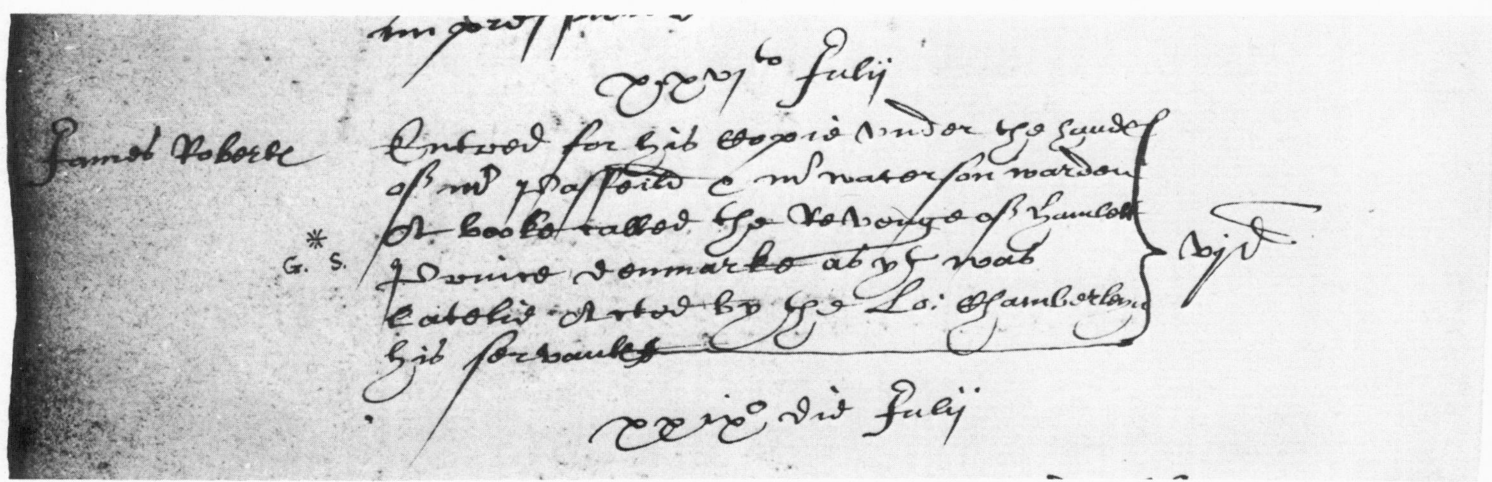

xxvjto Julij

James Robertes Entred for his Copie vnder the handes of master Pasfield and master waterson warden A booke called the Revenge of Hamlett Prince Denmarke as yt was latelie Acted by the Lord Chamberleyne his servantes vjd

G.*S.

xxixo die Julij

120 26 JULY 1602. Hamlet *entered by James Roberts. Register C, f. 84v. Transcript: Greg, i. 18.*

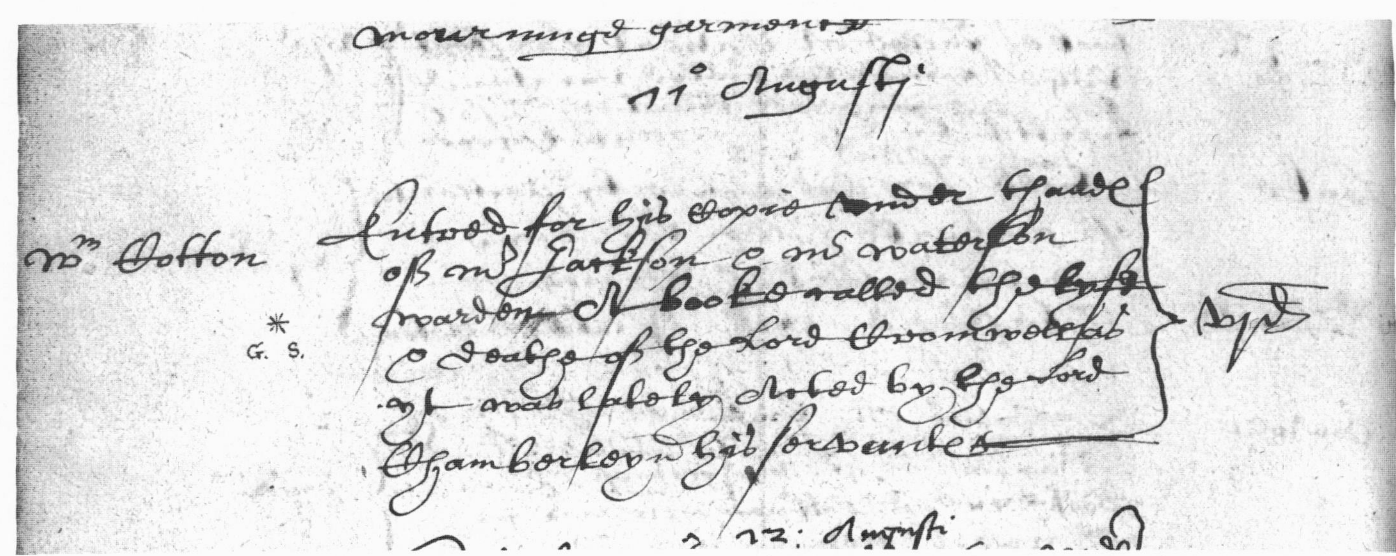

11o Augusti

Wm Cotton Entred for his Copie vnder the handes of master Jackson and master waterson wardens A booke called the lyfe and Deathe of the Lord Cromwell as yt was lately Acted by the Lord Chamberleyn his servantes vjd

G.*S.

121 11 AUGUST 1602. Thomas Lord Cromwell *entered by William Cotton. Register C, f. 85v. Transcript: Greg, i. 18. Printed that year as 'Written by W.S.'.*

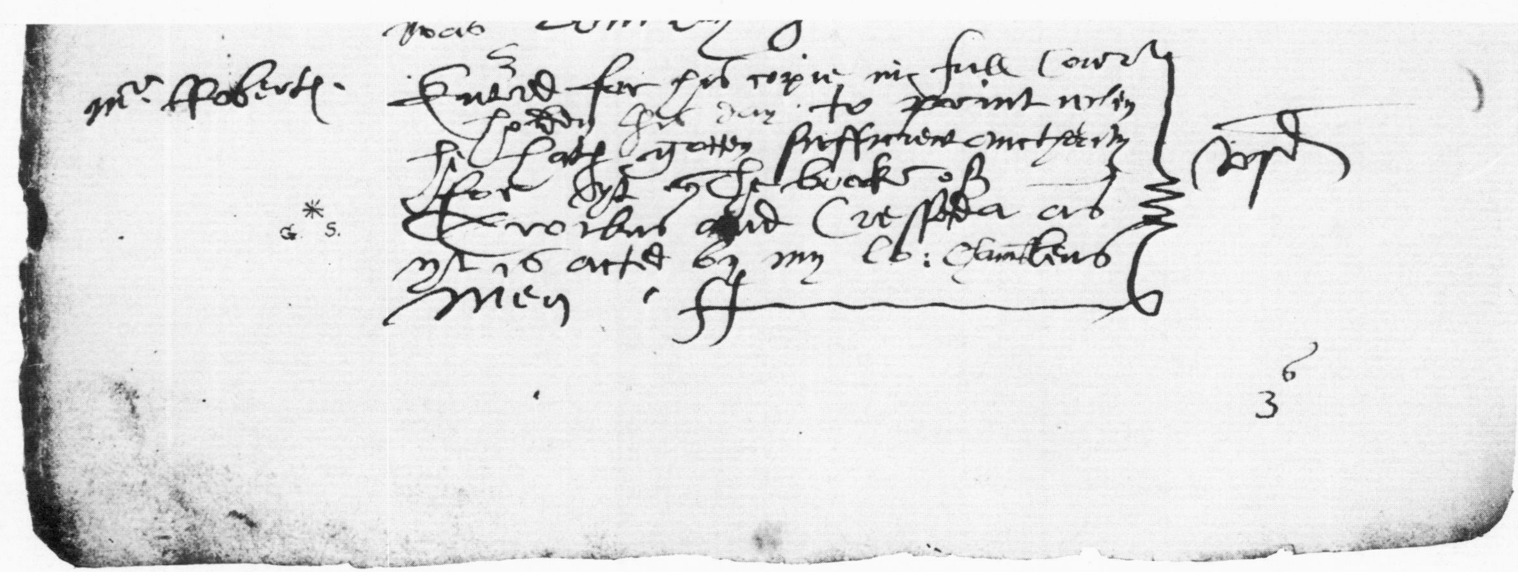

122 7 FEBRUARY 1603. Troilus and Cressida *entered by James Roberts. Register C, f.* 91^{v}. *Transcript: Greg, i. 18.*

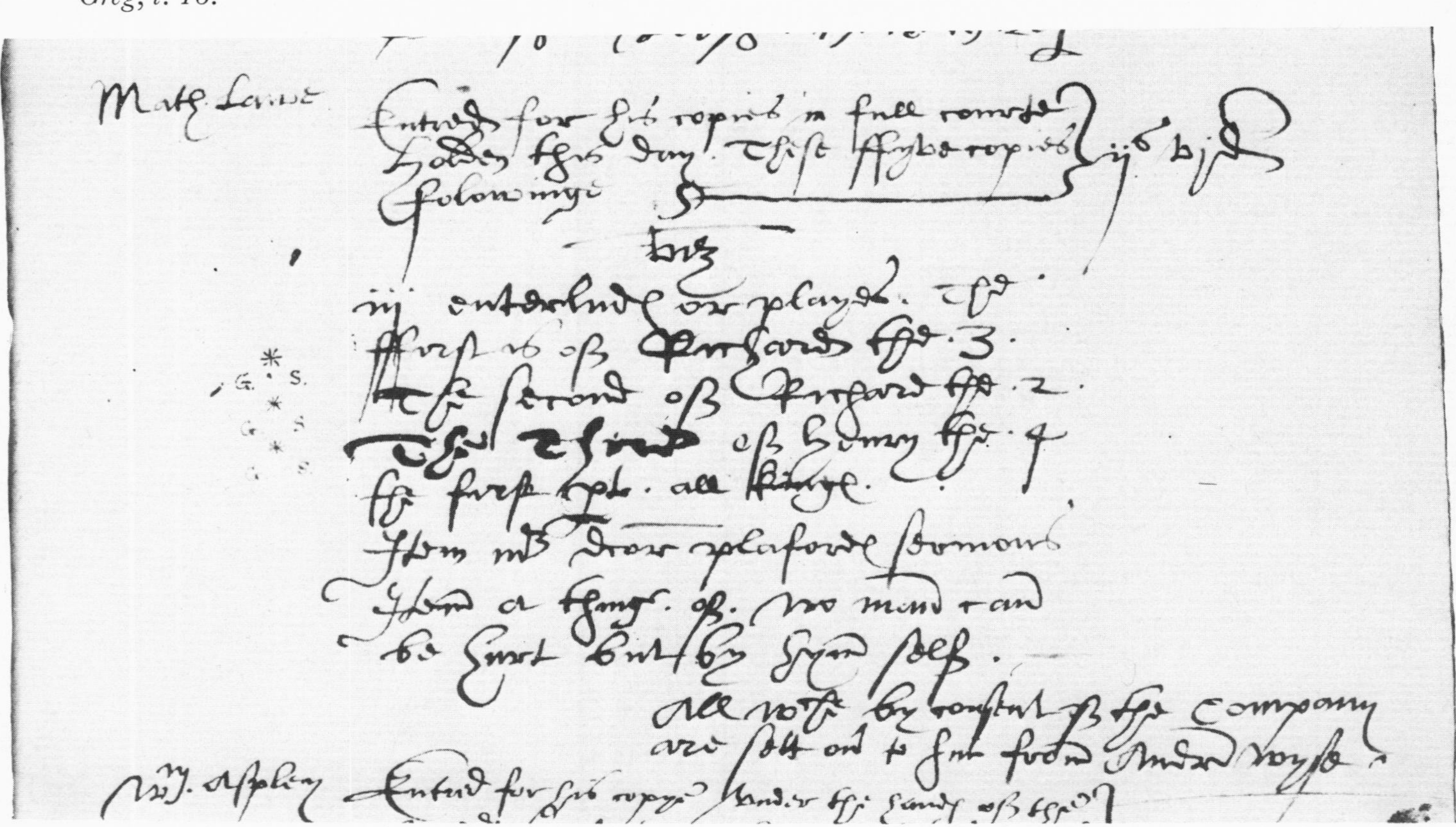

123 25 JUNE 1603. Richard III, Richard II, *and* 1 Henry IV *transferred from Andrew Wise to Matthew Law. Register C, f. 98. Transcript: Greg, i. 18.*

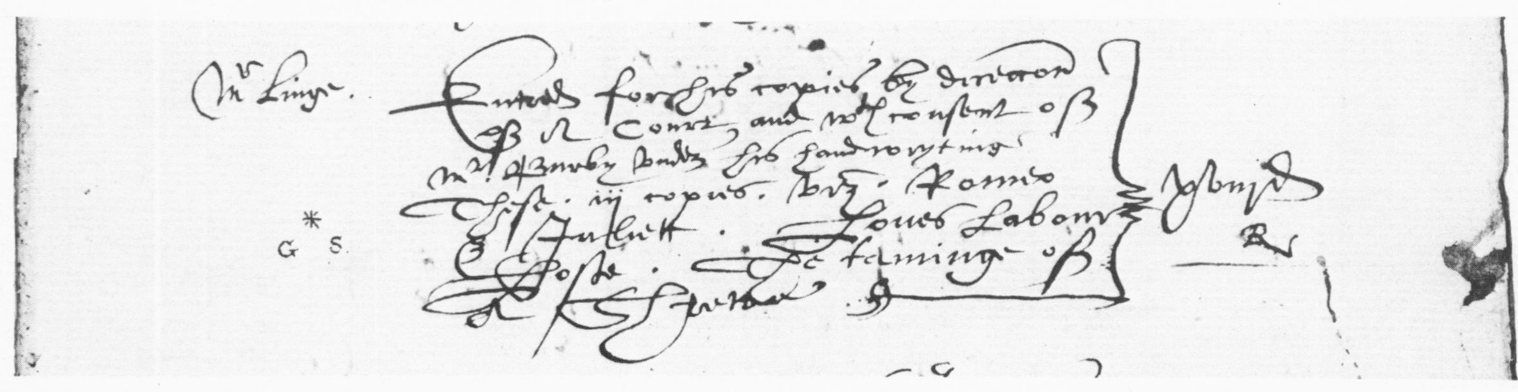

124 22 JANUARY 1607. Romeo and Juliet, Love's Labour's Lost, *and* The Taming of A Shrew *transferred by Cuthbert Burby to Nicholas Ling. Register C, f. 147. Transcript: Greg, i. 22.*

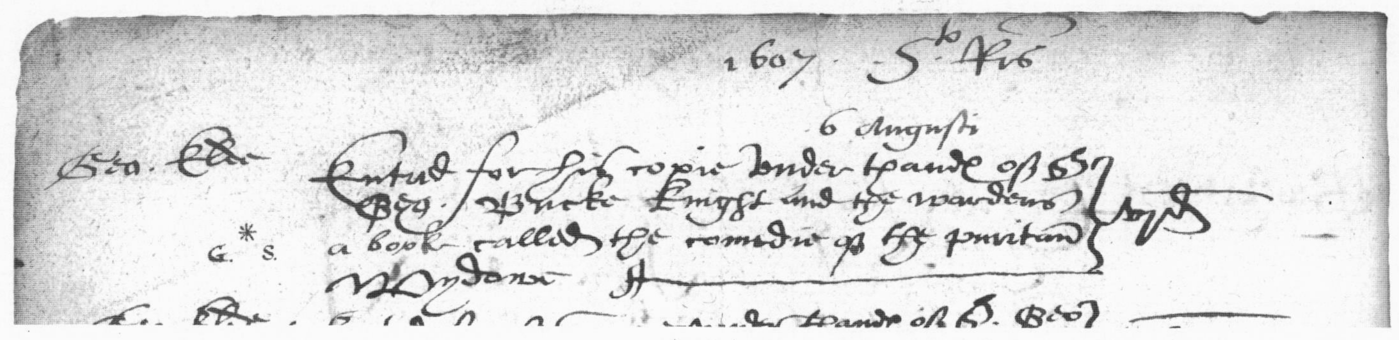

125 6 AUGUST 1607. The Puritan Widow *entered by George Elde. Register C, f. 157ᵛ. Transcript: Greg, i. 23. The play was published that year as* The Puritan, or The Widow of Watling Street, *by 'W.S.'.*

126 19 NOVEMBER 1607. Hamlet, The Taming of A Shrew, Romeo and Juliet, Love's Labour's Lost, *and twelve other books transferred from Nicholas Ling to John Smethwick. Register C, f. 161. Transcript: Arber, iii. 365; Greg, i. 24.*

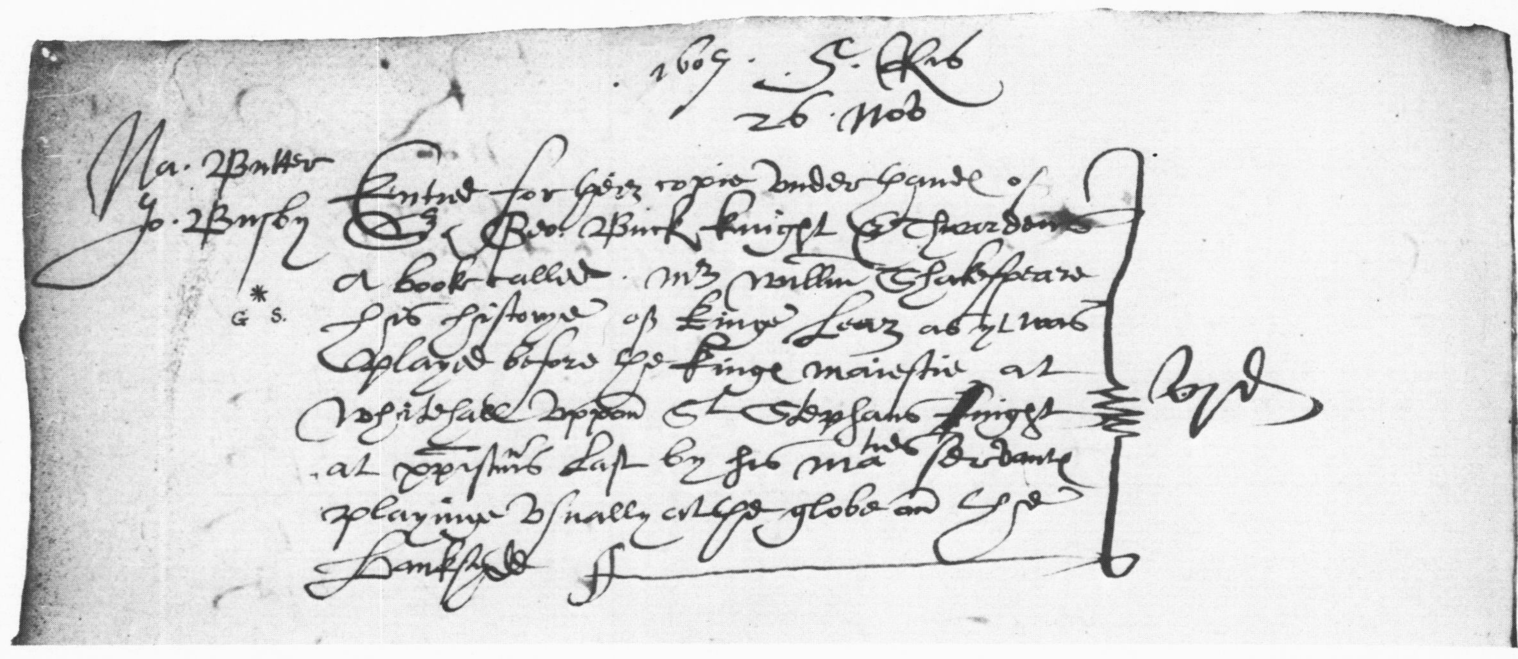

127 26 NOVEMBER 1607. King Lear *entered by Nathaniel Butter and John Busby. Register C, f. 161v. Transcript: Greg, i. 24.*

128 2 MAY 1608. A Yorkshire Tragedy *entered by Thomas Pavier. Register C, f. 167. Transcript: Greg, i. 24. Printed that year as 'Written by W. Shakspeare'.*

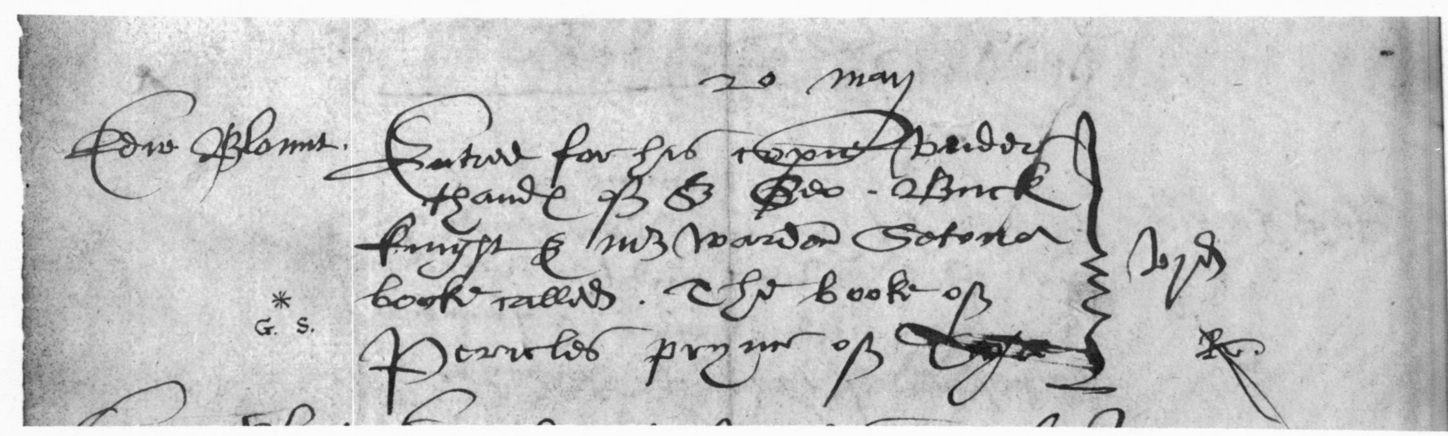

129 20 MAY 1608. Pericles *entered by Edward Blount. Register C, f. 167v. Transcript: Greg, i. 24.*

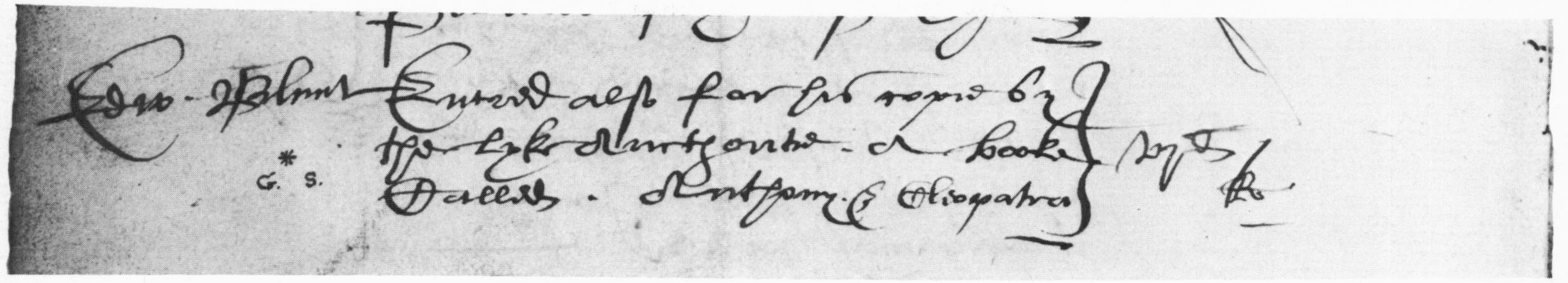

130 20 MAY 1608. Antony and Cleopatra *entered by Edward Blount. Register C, f. 167v. Transcript: Greg, i. 24.*

131 28 JANUARY 1609. Troilus and Cressida *entered by Richard Bonian and Henry Walley. Register C, f. 178v. Transcript: Greg, i. 25.*

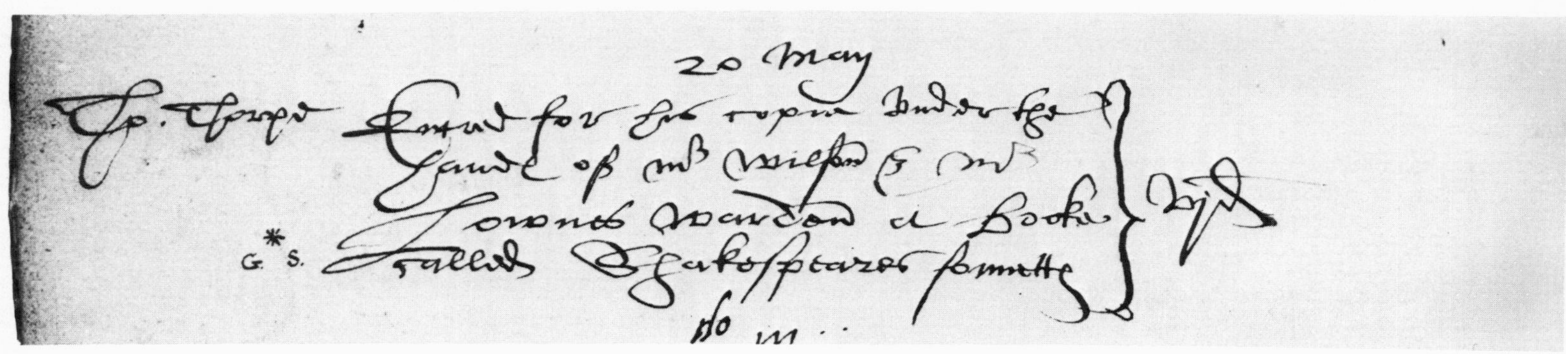

132 20 MAY 1609. *The* Sonnets *entered by Thomas Thorpe. Register C, f. 183v. Transcript: Arber, iii. 410.*

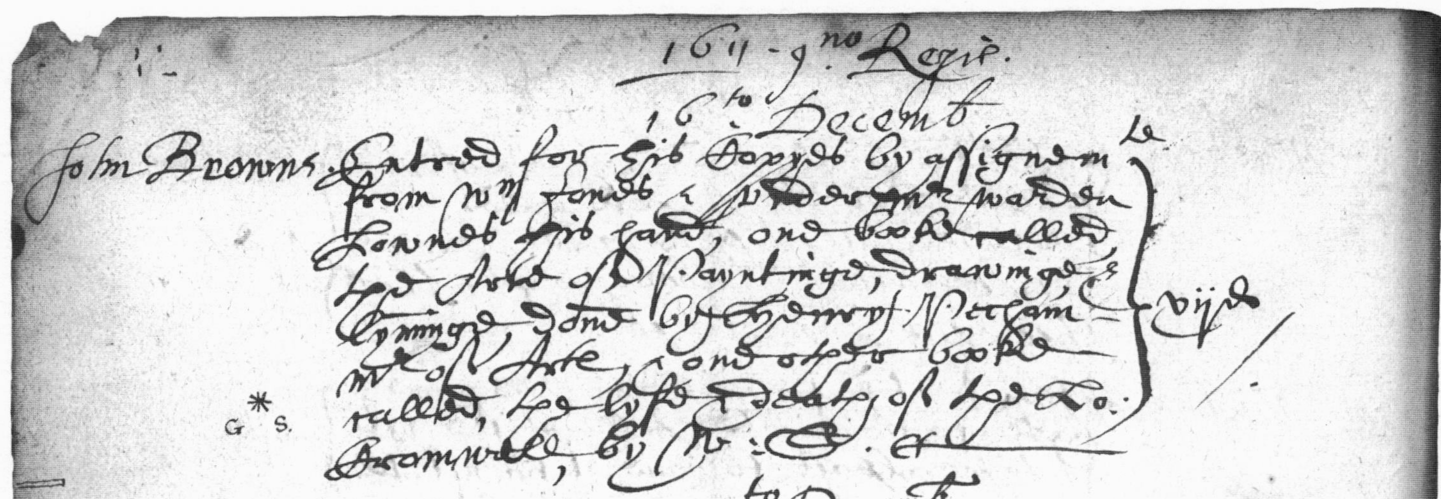

133 16 DECEMBER 1611. Thomas Lord Cromwell *transferred from William Jones to John Browne. Register C, f. 214v. Transcript: Greg, i. 27.*

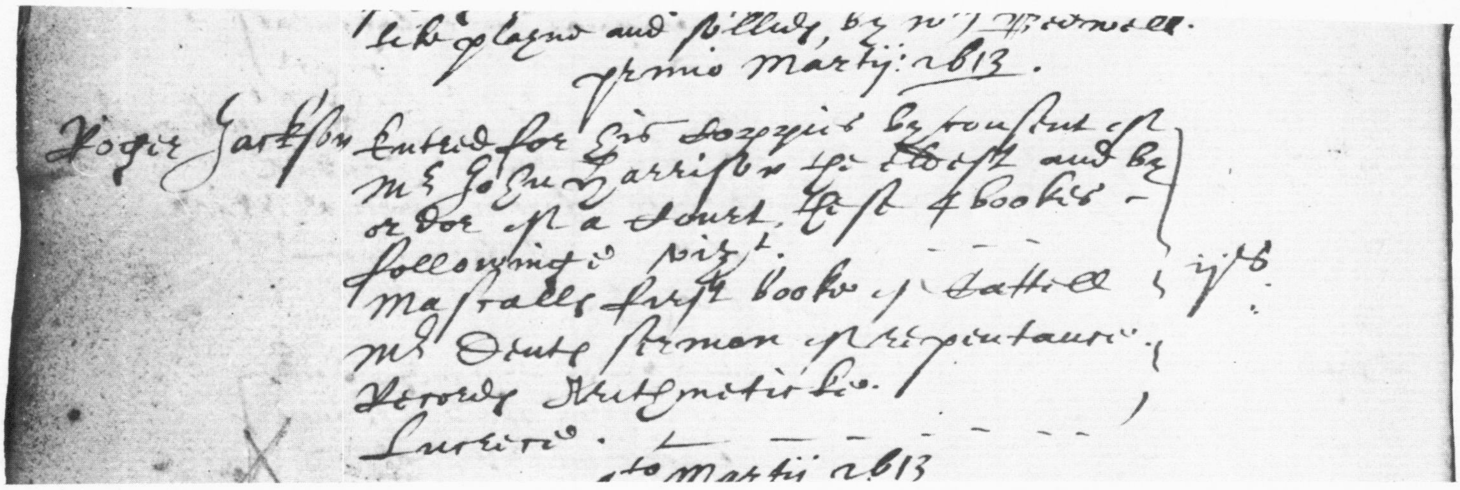

134 1 MARCH 1614. The Rape of Lucrece *transferred from John Harrison to Roger Jackson. Register C, f. 248v. Transcript: Arber, iii. 542.*

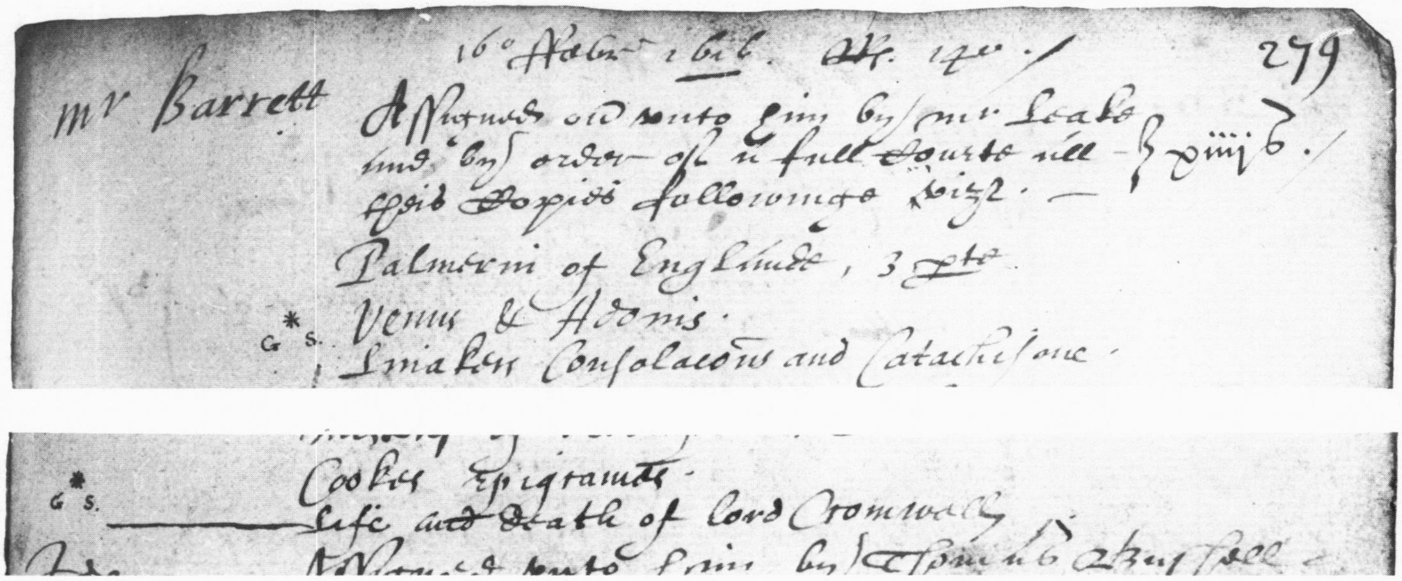

135 16 FEBRUARY 1617. Venus and Adonis *and twenty-nine other books transferred from William Leake to William Barrett. Register C, f. 279. Transcript: Arber, iii. 603.*

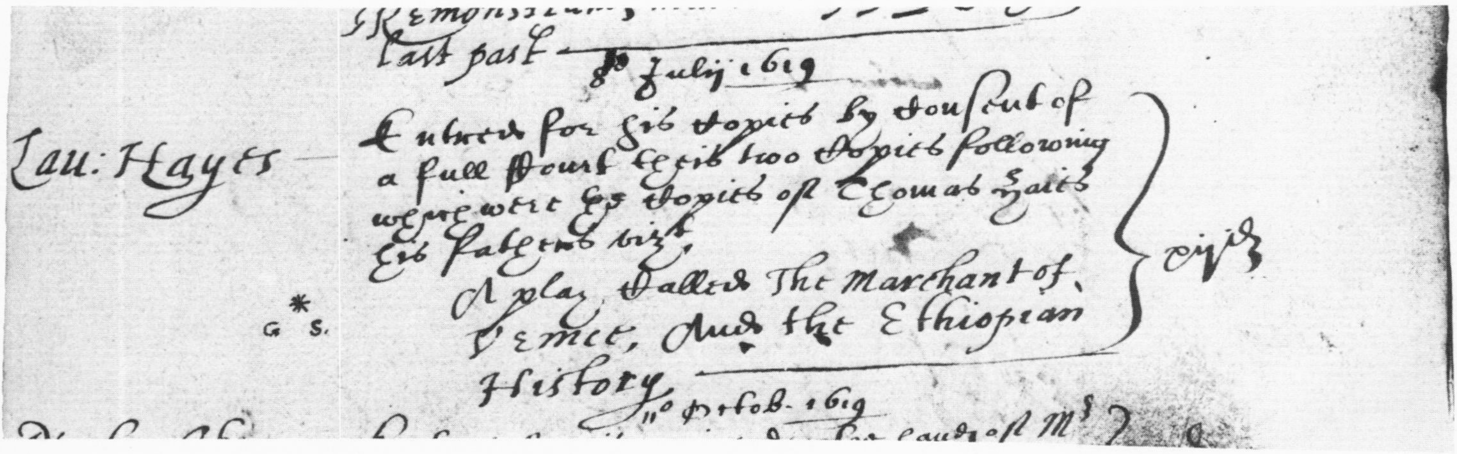

136 8 JULY 1619. The Merchant of Venice *and another book transferred from Thomas Hayes to Laurence Hayes. Register C, f. 303. Transcript: Arber, iii. 651; Greg, i. 31.*

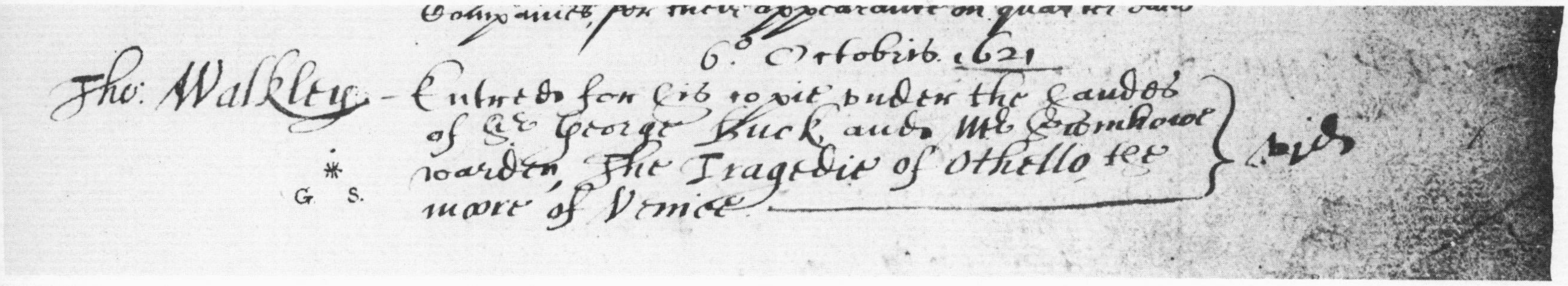

6° Octobris. 1621

Tho: Walkley. Entred for his copie vnder the handes of Sir George Buck and Mr Swinhowe warden, The Tragedie of Othello the moore of Venice. vjd

G * S.

137 6 OCTOBER 1621. Othello *entered by Thomas Walkley. Register D, p. 21. Transcript: Greg, i. 32.*

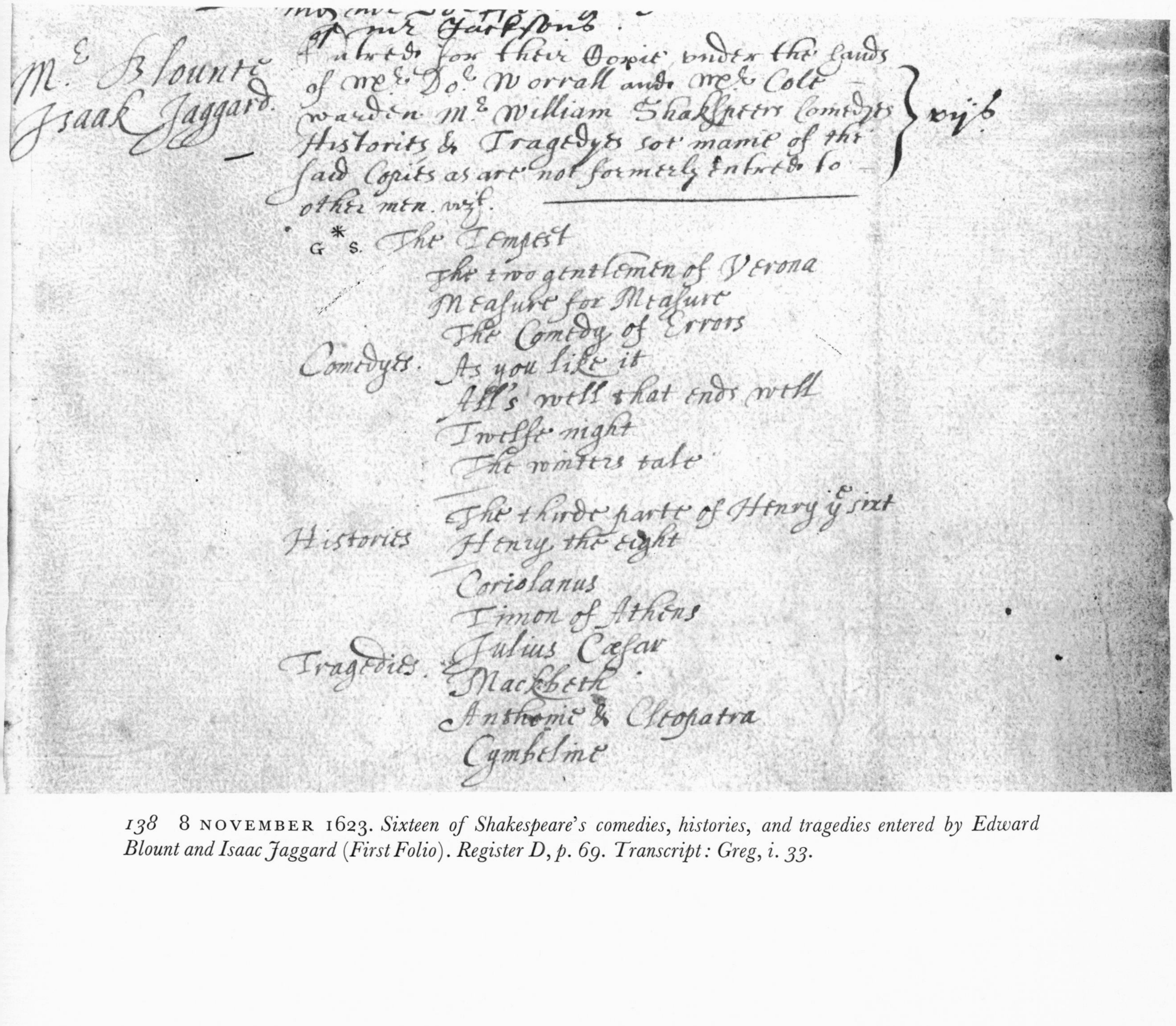

Mr Blounte
Isaak Jaggard.

Entred for their Copie vnder the handes of Mr Doctor Worrall and Mr Cole warden Mr William Shakspeers Comedyes Histories & Tragedyes soe manie of the said Copies as are not formerly entred to other men. vizt. vijs

G * S.

Comedyes.
The Tempest
The two gentlemen of Verona
Measure for Measure
The Comedy of Errors
As you like it
All's well that ends well
Twelfe night
The winters tale

Histories
The thirde parte of Henry ye sixt
Henry the eight

Tragedies.
Coriolanus
Timon of Athens
Julius Caesar
Mackbeth
Anthonie & Cleopatra
Cymbeline

138 8 NOVEMBER 1623. *Sixteen of Shakespeare's comedies, histories, and tragedies entered by Edward Blount and Isaac Jaggard (First Folio). Register D, p. 69. Transcript: Greg, i. 33.*

139 16 JANUARY 1626. The Rape of Lucrece *and twenty-nine other 'Copies' transferred from Roger Jackson's widow to Francis Williams. Register D, pp. 111–12. Transcript: Arber, iv. 149–50.*

140 7 MAY 1626. Venus and Adonis *transferred from John Parker to John Haviland and John Wright. Register D, p. 122. Transcript: Arber, iv. 160.*

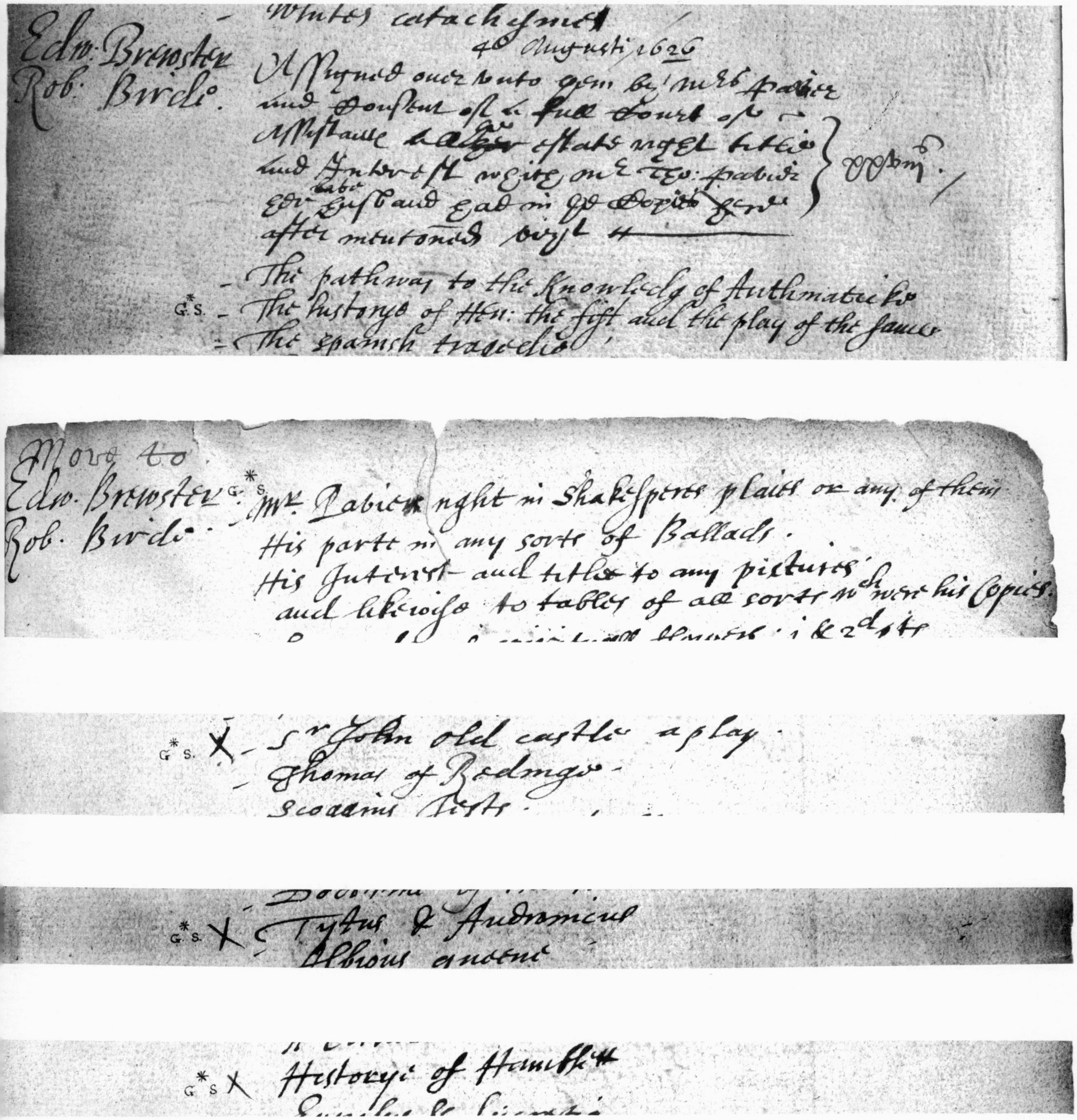

141 4 AUGUST 1626. Henry V, Sir John Oldcastle, '*Titus & Andronicus*', *Thomas Pavier's* '*right in Shakesperes plaies or any of them*', *and fifty-seven other* '*copies*' *transferred by his widow Mary to Edward Brewster and Robert Bird. Register D, pp. 126–8. Transcript: Arber, iv. 164–6; Greg, i. 34–5. The* '*Historye of Hamblett*', *listed among the other items in this entry, is not Shakespeare's play but a translation of Belleforest's* Histoires Tragiques *printed in 1608.*

Tho: Cotes
Rich: Cotes } Assigned over unto them by Dorathye Jaggard widdowe and Consent of a full Court holden this day, All the estate right title and Interest which Isaack Jaggard her late husband had in the Copies following. vizt. } vjs viijd

[illegible]
Their pte in Shackspheere playes. /
[illegible]

142 19 JUNE [OR 19 JUNE–7 JULY] 1627. *Isaac Jaggard's 'parte in Shackspheere playes' transferred by his widow Dorothy to Thomas Cotes and Richard Cotes. Register D, p. 146. Transcript: Greg, i. 35.*

Mr Rich: Hawkins Assigned ov unto him by Thomas Walkley, and Consent of a Court holden this day all the estate right title and Interest which he hath in these Copies following vizt } xviijd

A kinge and no kinge. /
Philaster or love lies a bleeding. /
G.S. Orthello the more of Venice. /

143 I MARCH 1628. Othello *and two other plays transferred from Thomas Walkley to Richard Hawkins. Register D, p. 160. Transcript: Greg, i. 36.*

29 January 1629 193

Mr Meighen Assigned ov unto him by mr Johnson and Consent of Mr Purfoote warden, All the said mr Johnsons estate in the 4 Copies hereafter menconed viz / } ijs

Cupids Whirlegig
Michalmas terme
G.S. The merry wives of Winsor
The Phenix

144 29 JANUARY 1630. The Merry Wives of Windsor *and three other plays transferred from Arthur Johnson to Richard Meighen. Register D, p. 193. Transcript: Greg, i. 37.*

145 29 JUNE 1630. The Rape of Lucrece *and other 'Copies' transferred from Francis Williams to John Harrison. Register D, p. 203. Transcript: Arber, iv. 237.*

146 8 NOVEMBER 1630. Henry V ('*Agincourt*'), '*Titus and Andronicus*', 2 *and* 3 Henry VI ('*Yorke and Lancaster*'), Pericles, *and four other titles transferred from Robert Bird to Richard Cotes. Register D, p. 208. Transcript: Greg, i. 38. The 'Hamblet' is the prose narrative assigned to Brewster and Bird by Pavier's widow in 1626; see item 141.*

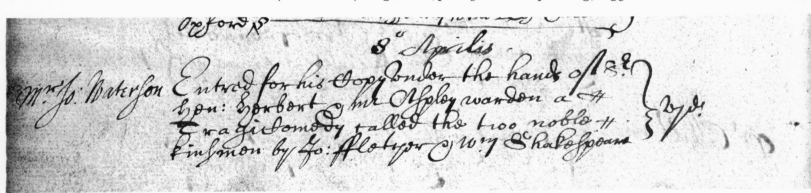

147 16 NOVEMBER 1630. *Sixteen of Shakespeare's comedies, histories, and tragedies transferred from Edward Blount to Robert Allot (Second Folio). Register D, p. 209. Transcript: Greg, i. 39.*

148 8 APRIL 1634. The Two Noble Kinsmen *entered by John Waterson. Register D, p. 290. Transcript: Greg, i. 43. Printed that year as by*

{Mr. John Fletcher, and
Mr. William Shakspeare.} Gent.

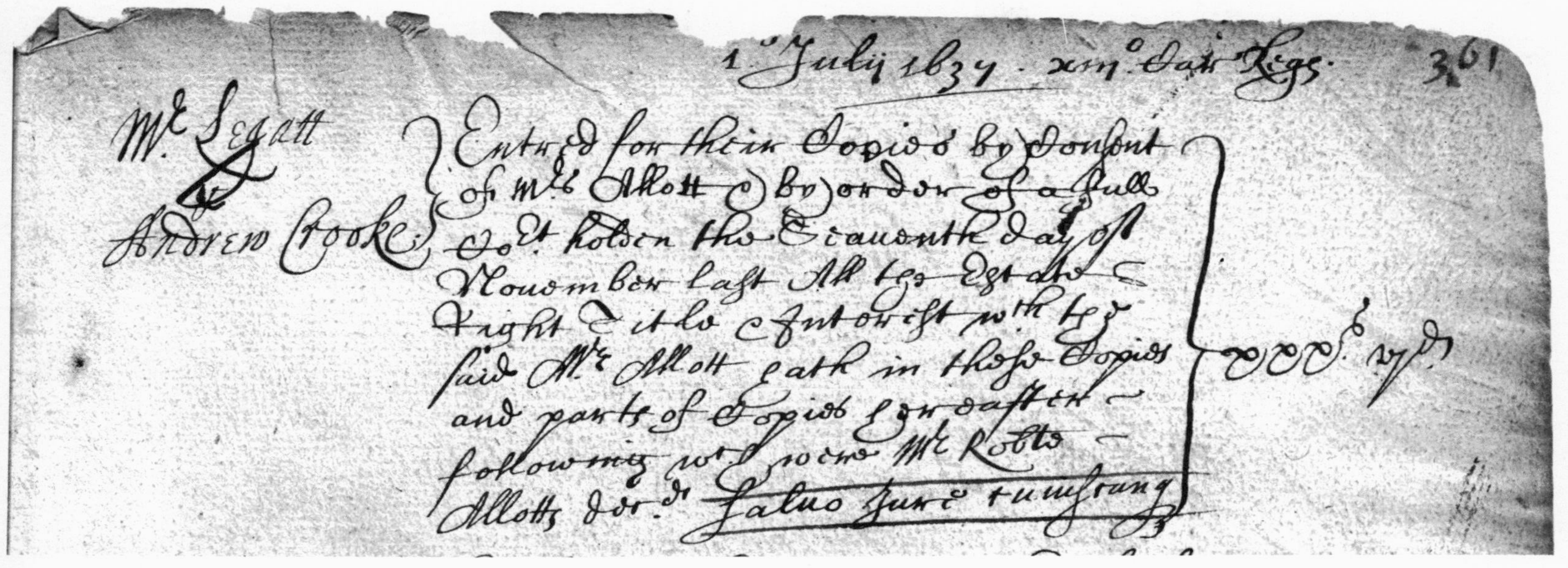

1° July 1637. xiii° Car Regis. 361

Mr Legatt & Andrew Crooke

Entred for their Copies by Consent of Mrs Allott & by order of a full Court holden the Eleaventh day of November last All the Estate Right Title and Interest which the said Mrs Allott hath in those Copies and parts of Copies hereafter following which were Mr Roberts Allotts dec[ease]d Salvo Jure cuiuscunque [illegible]

36. Aristippus

37. Shakespeares workes their Part.

149 1 JULY 1637. *Robert Allot's part in 'Shakespeares workes' and sixty other 'Copies and parts of Copies' transferred by his widow Mary to John Legatt and Andrew Crooke (extracts). Register D, pp. 361–2. Transcript: Arber, iv. 387–8; Greg, i. 46. Allot's widow had to give up her rights in these copies because of her impending marriage to Philip Chetwind, a Clothworker; but Chetwind later successfully challenged the transfer, charging misrepresentation on the part of Legatt and Crooke (Harry Farr, 'Philip Chetwind and the Allott Copyrights',* The Library, *4th Ser., xv (1934), 129–60; Greg, iii. 1116).*

394

29° May 1638. 14° Car Regis.

Mr Mead & Mr Meredith

Entred for their Copies by order of a full Court held the fifth day of June last according to the request of Ursula Hawkins widdow (late wife of Richard Hawkins deceased) then present in Court All these Copies and parts of Copies following which did belong unto her said husband as followeth.

vide page 426. turned over to mr Leake.

[illegible]

Orthello the More of Venice a play.

150 29 MAY 1638. Othello *and twenty-four other titles belonging to Richard Hawkins transferred by his widow Ursula to Robert Mead and Christopher Meredith. Register D, p. 394. Transcript: Arber, iv. 420; Greg, i. 48.*

151 4 SEPTEMBER 1638. Venus and Adonis *and other 'Copies and parts of Copies' entered by John Haviland and John Wright. Register D, p. 405. Transcript: Arber, iv. 431.*

152 25 JANUARY 1639. Othello *and twenty-three other books transferred from Robert Mead and Christopher Meredith to William Leake. Register D, pp. 426–7. Transcript: Arber, iv. 452–3; Greg, i. 49–50.*

153 4 NOVEMBER 1639. '*An Addicion of some excellent Poems to Shakespeares Poems by other gentlemen*' *entered by John Benson, Register D, p. 461. Transcript: Arber, iv. 487.*

154 27 JUNE 1646. *John Wright's 'copies', presumably including* Venus and Adonis, *transferred to Edward Wright. Register E, p. 42. Transcript: Eyre, i. 236.*

(62.

The 31th of October 1646

Mr Moseley. Assigned over unto him by virtue of a Note under the hand & seale of Mr Waterson & both the wardens All the Estate right title & interest wch the said Mr Waterson hath in these Playes following (viz)

The Elder Brother his part
Mounsieur Thomas.
The Noble Kinsman
} by Mr ffletcher

155 31 OCTOBER 1646. The Two Noble Kinsmen *and five other plays transferred by John Waterson to Humphrey Moseley. Register E, p. 62. Transcript: Greg, i. 57.*

Die eodem.

Mr Mosely. Entred also for his Copies the severall Playes following.

The Widdowes Prize: by Mr Wm Samson

The History of Cardenio, by Mr Fletcher. & Shakespeare.

The merry Devill of Edmonton. by Wm: Shakespeare.
Henry ye first, & Hen: ye 2d. by Shakespeare, & Davenport.

156 9 SEPTEMBER 1653. Cardenio (*'by Mr. Fletcher. & Shakespeare'*), The Merry Devil of Edmonton (*'by Wm: Shakespeare'*), Henry I *and* Henry II (*'by Shakespeare*, & Davenport'), *along with thirty-eight other plays, entered by Humphrey Moseley. Register E, pp. 285–6. Transcript: Greg, i. 60–1.*

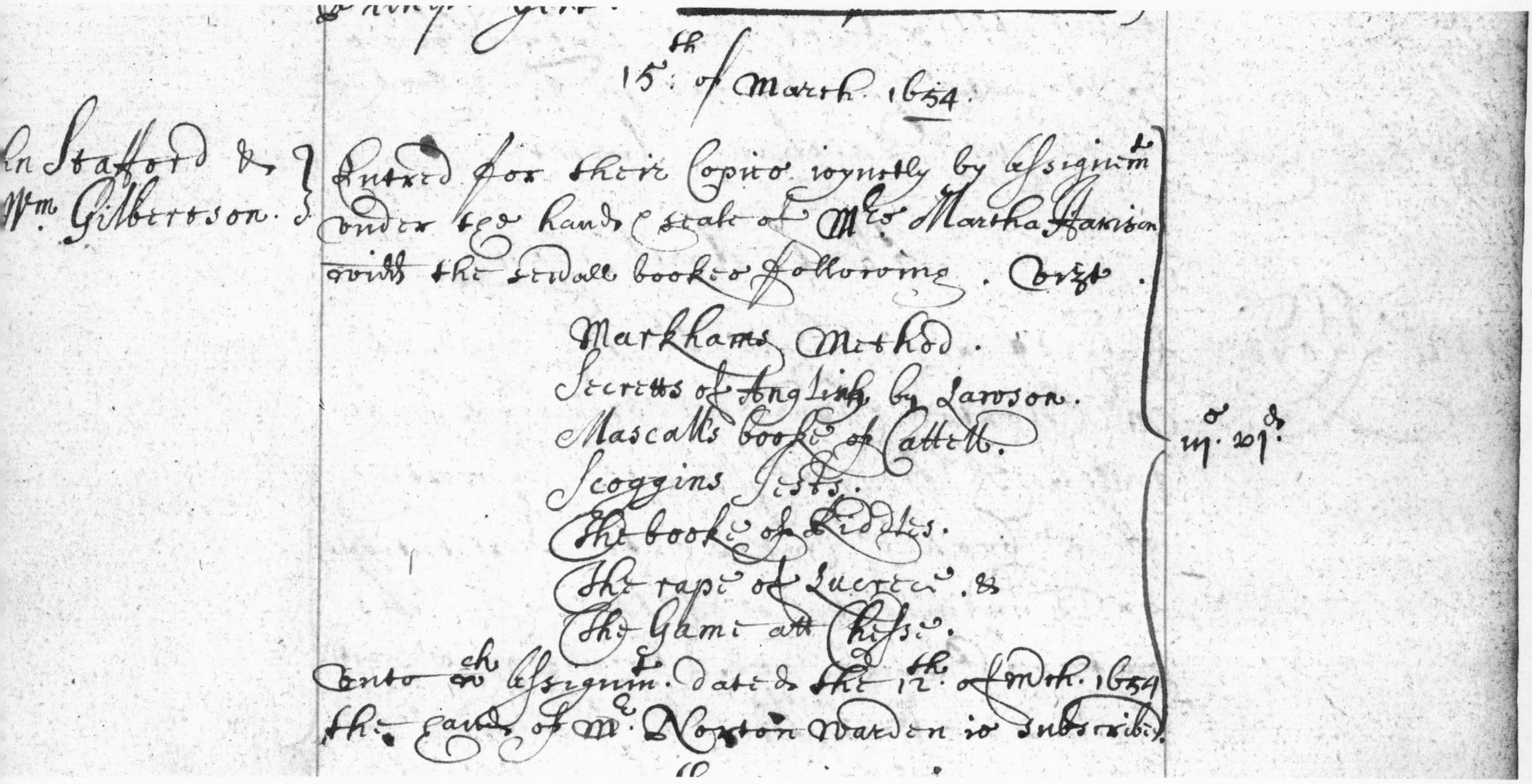
15th: of March. 1654.
[Joh]n Stafford & Wm. Gilbertson.
Entred for their Copies joyntly by Assignmt under the hand & seale of Mrs Martha Harrison with the severall bookes following. Vizt.
Markhams Method.
Secretts of English by Lawson.
Mascall's booke of Cattell.
Scoggins Jests.
The booke of Riddles.
The rape of Lucrece. &
The Game att Chesse.
unto which Assignmt dated the 12th of March. 1654 the hand of Mr Norton Warden is subscribed.
iijs. vjd.

157 15 MARCH 1655. The Rape of Lucrece *and six other 'bookes' transferred from Martha Harrison to John Stafford and William Gilbertson. Register E, p. 337. Transcript: Eyre, i. 468.*

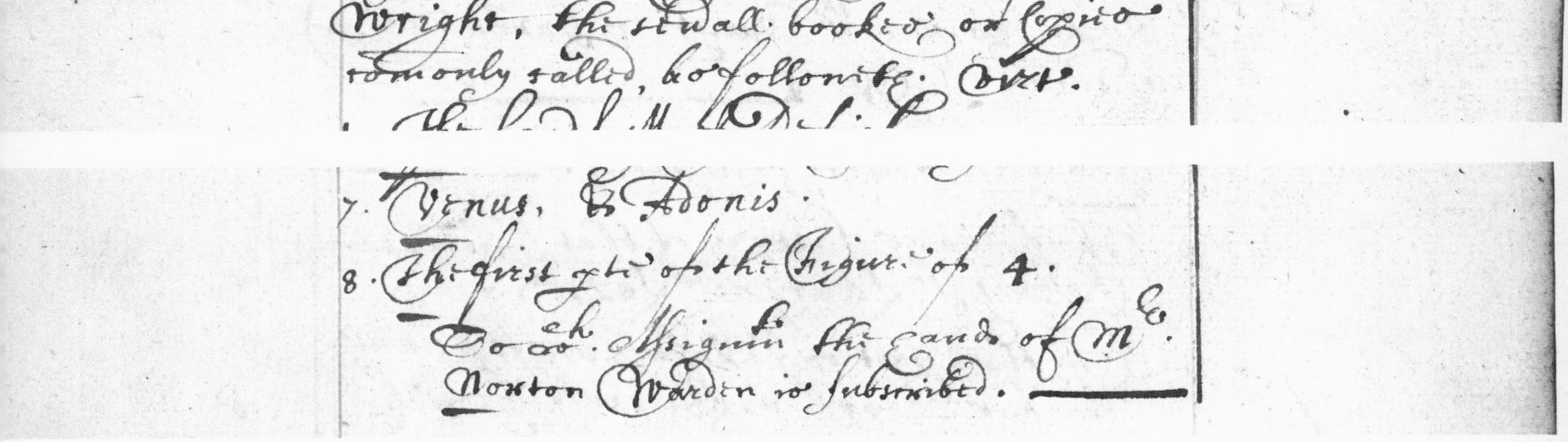
Wm. Gilbertson
Entred for his Copies by vertue of an Assignmt under the hand & seale of Edward Wright, the severall bookes or Copies comonly called, as followeth. Vizt.
7. Venus, & Adonis.
8. The first pte of the Figure of 4.
To which Assignmt the hand of Mr Norton Warden is subscribed.

158 4 APRIL 1655. Venus and Adonis *and seven other 'bookes' transferred from Edward Wright to William Gilbertson. Register E, p. 341. Transcript: Eyre, i. 470.*

17 Octob 1657.

Mr Willm Leake. Entred for his Copie by vertue of an Assignment under the hands & seales of Bridgett Haies widd of Lawrence Haies, & Jane Graisby & by order of a full Cort of Assistants holden the 16 Oct instant the Booke or Copie called The Merchant of Venice a Play written by William Shakspeare Gent To which Assignment the hand of Mr Thomason warden is Subscribed. — — — — vjd

159 17 OCTOBER 1657. The Merchant of Venice *transferred from Bridget Hayes and Jane Graisby to William Leake. Register F, p. 42. Transcript: Greg, i. 65.*

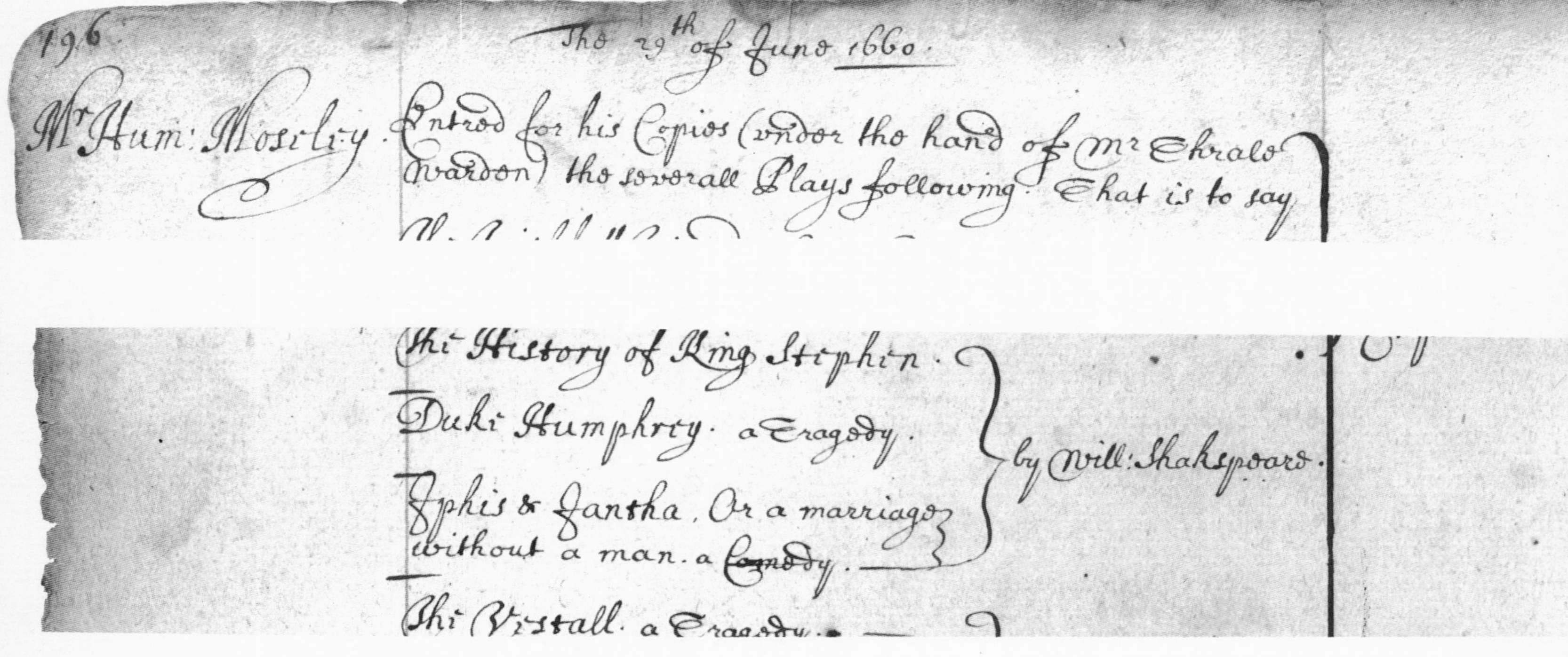
196.

The 29th of June 1660.

Mr Hum: Moseley. Entred for his Copies (under the hand of Mr Thrale warden) the severall Plays following. That is to say

The History of King Stephen.
Duke Humphrey. a Tragedy.
Iphis & Iantha. Or a marriage without a man. a Comedy.
by Will: Shakspeare.

The Vestall. a Tragedy.

160 29 JUNE 1660. King Stephen, Duke Humphrey, and Iphis and Iantha, or A Marriage without a Man, '*by Will: Shakspeare*', *along with twenty-three other plays, entered by Humphrey Moseley. Register F, p. 196. Transcript: Greg, i. 68–9.*

ffl salvo jure cuilibet

Mr Jon Martin &
Mr Hen: Herringman

Eodem die

Entred for their Copies by vertue of an Assignemt under the hand and seale of Andrew Clark Cittizen and Staconer of London Executor of the last will & Testamt of Elianor Coates Widow who was the relict & Executrix of Richard Coates late Cittizen & Staconer of London aforesaid deceased bearing date the 16th day of June last past and by consent of a ffull Court held the 3d day of this instant August all his estate right title interest property claime & demaund of in and to the severall bookes or Copies following vizt. Henry the ffifth / Sr John Oldcastle / Titus & Andronicus / Eureolus & Lucretia / Yorke & Lancaster / Agin-Court / Pericles / Hamlett / Yorkshire Tragedy / The Tempest / The Two Gentlemen of Verona / Measure for Measure / The Comedy of Errors / As you like it / All's well that ends well / Twelfe Night / The Winters Tale / The Third part of Henry the sixth / Henry the Eight / Coriolanus / Timon of Athens / Julius Caesar / Mackbeth / Anthony & Cleopatra / Cymbeline / to wch assignemt the hand of Mr Warden Roycroft is subscribed salvo jure cuilibet

ffl

xijs : vjd :

161 6 AUGUST 1674. *Richard Cotes's rights in twenty-one plays of Shakespeare, and other copies, transferred by Andrew Clark, executor of Cotes's widow Elianor, to John Martin and Henry Herringman. Register F, p. 458. Transcript: Greg, i. 73–4. The entry includes two apocryphal plays,* Sir John Oldcastle *and* A Yorkshire Tragedy. *'Yorke & Lancaster' is 2 and 3* Henry VI; *'Agin-Court' duplicates 'Henry the ffifth'; 'Eureolus and Lucretia' is a romance first printed in 1596; 'Hamlett' is not the play but the prose narrative published in 1608.*

Martin Newton

21th: Augt Anno 1683

Mr: Robt Scott — Entred then for his Bookes or Coppyes by vertue of an Assignmt: under the hand and Seale of Mrs Sarah Martin Relict and Executrx of the last Will and Testamt: of John Martin late Cittizen and Stationer of London deceased her late Husband bearing date the fourteenth day of June Anno Dom 1681 And by order of Court of the Seaventh of Novemr: 1681 These severall Bookes or Coppyes or parts of Bookes or Coppyes hereafter menconed wch: Did formerly belong to the said John Martin decd: Salvo jure cujuscunque viz:

Woodford on the Psalmes, one third.

Shakespeare.

Henry the 5th.
Sr: John Old Castle
Titus Andronicus
Eurialus & Lucretia
} 1/2

162 21 AUGUST 1683. *John Martin's half-interest in twenty-one plays of Shakespeare, 'Sr: John Old Castle', 'Eurialus & Lucretia', 'Hamlett', and 'Yorkesheire Tragedy' (see preceding entry), and his widow Sarah's rights in 335 other copies transferred from her to Robert Scott (extract). Register G, pp. 63–73. Transcript: Greg, i. 75–6.*

Mr. Robert Scott

Yorke and Lancaster - -
Agincourt. - - - -
Pericles. - - - -
Hamlett. - - - -
Yorksheire Tragedy - -
The Tempest. - - -
Gentleman of Verona - -
Measure for Measure. - -
Commedie of Errors. - -
As you like it. - - -
Alls well that ends well - -
Twelve nights. - - - - -
Winters Tale. - - - -
The 3rd part of Hen: 6th - - -
Hen: 8th - - - - - - -
Coriolanus. - - - - - -
Timon of Athens. - - - - -
Julius Cæsar. - - - - - -
Mackbeth. - - - - - -
Anthony and Cleopatra. - -
Cymbelyne. - - - -

} $\frac{1}{2}$

III. Shakespeare's Stationers

Not all of the stationers and printers whose names appear in the Stationers' Register are included in *A Shakespeare Companion* or *The Reader's Encyclopedia of Shakespeare*, or mentioned in Shakespeare biographies. For the convenience of readers without ready access to *A Dictionary of Printers and Booksellers in England, Scotland and Ireland, and of Foreign Printers of English Books 1557–1640* (1910), of which R. B. McKerrow was general editor, or to Henry R. Plomer, *A Dictionary of the Booksellers and Printers who were at work in England, Scotland and Ireland from 1641 to 1667* (1907; reprinted 1968), I have compiled the following biographical notes. Although in print now for over half a century, McKerrow and Plomer remain the basic authorities, along with (it goes without saying) Arber's *Transcript*. Where more recent studies have supplemented or revised our information about individual stationers, I have cited them. Other valuable reference guides are E. Gordon Duff, *A Century of the English Book Trade: Short Notices of all printers, stationers, book-binders, and others connected with it from the issue of the first dated book in 1457 to the incorporation of the Company of Stationers in 1557* (1905); Plomer *et al.*, *A Dictionary of the Printers and Booksellers who were at work in England, Scotland and Ireland from 1668 to 1725* (Oxford, 1922); and McKerrow, *Printers' & Publishers' Devices in England & Scotland 1485–1640* (1913). I hope it will not be taken as any disparagement of my sources if I say that here and there I have been able to correct them.

For the convenience of readers I have expanded coverage to include stationers (usually printers) whose names appear on the title-pages of the plays and poems but not in the Stationers' Register entries. I have used the abbreviation SR for the Register. Citations of first and last entries refer to entrance, not transfer, of copies.

ALLDE, EDWARD. Printer, fl. 1584–1628, at various locations: first in the Poultry; then without Cripplegate; in Aldersgate, over against the Pump (1597); upon Lombard Hill, near Old Fish Street (1604); and near Christ-Church [i.e. Newgate] Street (1615). Son of London printer, John Allde, fl. 1555–c. 1582. Freeman (by patronage) 1584. First SR entry 1 August 1586; last, 24 May 1627. Favoured Roman type and quarto format. In trouble with Company in 1597, again in 1600, for printing unauthorised books, including Catholic polemical writings; but 'he was not, on the whole, by any means a disorderly person' (McKerrow). After his death, probably in 1628, his widow Elizabeth carried on the business. Allde printed mainly ephemeral popular literature, but also Daniel, Dekker, Marlowe and other notable writers. In 1611 he printed Q2 of Robert Chester's *Love's Martyr*, under the title *The Annuals of Great Britain*; this contains added poems by Jonson, Chapman, and others, including Shakespeare's 'The Phoenix and the Turtle'. Allde printed Q3 (1611) of *Titus Andronicus*; possibly also Q1 (1600) of *A Midsummer-Night's Dream.* Source: R. B. McKerrow, 'Edward Allde as a Typical Trade Printer', *The Library*, 4th Ser., x (1929–30), 121–62.

ALLOT, ROBERT (items 147, 149). Bookseller, fl. 1625–35, at Greyhound (1626) and Black Bear in Paul's Churchyard. From Criggleston, West Riding of Yorkshire. Freeman 1625. The next year purchased, from Margaret Hodges, rights in four books, including Sandys's *Travels*; also, from John Budge, forty-one others, mainly theological. Sued in 1632 for delivering damaged copies, late, of Welsh translation of *The Practice of Piety*. Died 1635. His widow Mary transferred all remaining copyrights to John Legatt and Andrew Crooke (q.v.) in 1637; see item 149. Another Robert Allot presumably compiled *Wit's Theatre of the Little World* (1599) and the more familiar *England's Parnassus* (1600). This Allot may have been the stationer's uncle (McKerrow).

ASPLEY, WILLIAM (item 115). Bookseller, fl. 1598–1640, at Tiger's Head and also Parrot in Paul's Churchyard. From Raiston, Cumberland. Apprenticed 1588 to George Bishop, printer and bookseller at Bell in Paul's Churchyard; freeman 1597. First SR entry 5 October 1598; last, 1 September 1616. Published *Eastward Ho*, *Westward Ho*, other plays. Master of Company in 1640, when he died.

BARRETT, WILLIAM (item 135). Bookseller, fl. 1607–24, in Paul's Churchyard at Green Dragon (1608) and Three Pigeons (1614). From Lincolnshire. Apprenticed 1597 to Bonham Norton, a litigious bookseller and printer in Aldersgate Street. Freeman 1605. First SR entry 27 November 1607; last, 12 March 1624. Published Bacon, 1611 translation of *Don Quixote*, travel books, including Coryate's *Crudities* (1611). Died 1624.

BELL, JANE. Bookseller and printer, fl. 1650–9, in east end of Christ-church [i.e. Newgate] Street. She succeeded Moses Bell, presumably her husband, at same address. Printed popular literature, e.g. *Amadis de Gaul* and *Reynard the Fox*, mostly from old type; printed Q3 (1655) of *King Lear*.

BENSON, JOHN (item 153). Bookseller in Chancery Lane (1635–67) and St. Dunstan's Churchyard, Fleet Street (1641). First SR entry 19 January 1635. Published ballads. From 1651 partner with John Playford in publishing music books. Died 1667.

BIRD, ROBERT (items 141, 146). Bookseller, fl. 1621–38, at Bible in St. Lawrence Lane, Cheapside. Freeman 1621. First SR entry 7 February 1623; last, 17 April 1635. Specialised mainly in theology; acquired Philip Birch copyrights 1623. Died 1641.

BLOUNT, EDWARD (items 129, 130, 138, 147). Bookseller, fl. 1594–1632, over against Great North Door of Paul's and at Black Bear (1608) in Paul's Churchyard. Son of London Merchant Taylor. Apprenticed 1578 to William Ponsonby at Bishop's Haed in Paul's Churchyard. Freeman 1588. First SR entry 25 May 1594; last, 17 January 1632. Published Marlowe, Florio's translation of Montaigne, numerous plays. Partner from 1608 with William Barrett (q.v.). Died 1632. Copyrights assigned, 1636, by widow to Andrew Crooke. Source: Sidney Lee, 'An Elizabethan Bookseller', *Bibliographica*, i (1895) 474–98.

BONIAN, or BONION, RICHARD (item 131). Bookseller, fl. 1607–11, at Spread Eagle near North Door of Paul's (1607–10), Red Lion upon London Bridge (1609), and Floure de Luce and Crown in Paul's Churchyard (1611). Father from Hayes, Middlesex. Apprenticed 1598 to Richard Watkins; transferred, after Watkins's death the next year, to Simon Waterson at Crown in Paul's Churchyard. Freeman 1607. First SR entry 18 November 1607; last, 19 February 1611.

BREWSTER, EDWARD (item 141). Bookseller, fl. 1616–47, at Star at west end of Paul's Churchyard (1621–3), Great West Door of Paul's (1624), Bible near North Door of Paul's (1627–34), Bible in Paul's Churchyard (1635), and Bible in Fleet Street (1640–7). Dealt, unsurprisingly, in theology. First SR entry 26 September 1616. Treasurer of Company's English Stock, 1639–47. Died 1647, leaving a son Edward who became Master of Company, 1689–92.

BROWNE, JOHN, SR. (item 133). Bookseller and bookbinder, fl. 1598–1622, at the Bible and other Fleet Street premises. Son of Reading, Berkshire, mercer. Apprenticed 1586 to Ralph Newbery, a Fleet Street bookseller and prominent member of the Company. Freeman 1594. First SR entry 15 April 1598. Owned share in Drayton's *Polyolbion*; published jest books, plays, cookery books, practical manuals, also *No Whipping nor Tripping but a kind friendly Snipping* (1601). Died 1622. His widow Alice the next year assigned Browne's copyrights to John Marriott.

BURBY, CUTHBERT (item 124). Bookseller, fl. 1592–1607, at Poultry by St. Mildred's Church (1592), in Cornhill near Royal Exchange (1601–7), and at Swan in Paul's Churchyard (1602–7). From Ersley, Bedford. Apprenticed 1583 to William Wright, Sr., near French School in Paul's Churchyard. Freeman 1592; Livery 1598. First SR entry 28 April 1592; last, 28 May 1607. Dealt in general literature. Died 1607.

BUSBY, JOHN, SR. (items 118, 127). Bookseller, fl. 1590–1619, in St. Dunstan's Churchyard in Fleet Street. Son of London cordwainer. Apprenticed 1576 to Oliver Wilkes but served term with Andrew Maunsell at Parrot and Brazen Serpent, both in Paul's Churchyard. Freeman 1585. Partner of Arthur Johnson (q.v.). First SR entry 6 October 1590; last, 13 March 1612. With Thomas Millington (q.v.) published pirated *Henry V* (1600). 'He was never more than a second-rate publisher and his reputation is not good' (Greg). Source: W. W. Greg, 'The Two John Busby's', *The Library*, 4th Ser., xxiv (1943), 81–6.

BUTTER, NATHANIEL (item 127). Bookseller, fl. 1604–64, at Pied Bull near St. Austin's Gate in Paul's Churchyard (1608) and in Cursitors Alley (1660). Son of Thomas Butter, bookseller, 1576–90, near St. Austin's Gate. Freeman 1604. First SR entry 4 December 1604. From 1622 published news-sheets in association with Nicholas Bourne, a partnership dissolved in 1639. In latter year Butter assigned his play copyrights to Miles Fletcher. Last SR entry 3 December 1663. Died 1664. Source: Leona Rostenberg, *Literary, Political, Scientific, Religious & Legal Publishing, Printing & Bookselling in England, 1551–1700* (New York, 1965), i. 75–89 et passim.

COTES, RICHARD (items 142, 146, 161). Printer, fl. 1627–52, in Barbican, Aldersgate Street (1635–52). With partner brother Thomas (see next entry) acquired business of Isaac Jaggard when latter died in 1627. After Thomas's death in 1641, became sole owner of printing house and gear upon payment of £100. Appointed, same year, official printer to City of London. Died 1653.

COTES, THOMAS (item 142). Printer in Barbican in Aldersgate Street (1620–41). Freeman 1606. First SR entry 16 November 1630. Partner of brother Richard; see preceding entry. Died 1641, and buried in St. Giles's Church, Cripplegate.

COTTON, WILLIAM (item 121). Bookseller, fl. 1602–9, at Long Shop adjoining Ludgate. Son of Derbyshire husbandman. Apprenticed, 1588, to William Leake, Sr. (q.v.). Freeman 1602. First SR entry 11 August 1602; last, 2 June 1609. Dead by November 1609, when his widow Hannah assigned his copyright in *A Silver Watch Bell* to Clement Knight.

CREEDE, THOMAS (item 106). Printer, fl. 1593–1617, at Catherine Wheel in Thames Street (1593–1600) and Eagle and Child in Old Exchange (1600–17). Freeman, by printer Thomas East, 1578. First SR entry 22 October 1593; last, 13 September 1613. Employed by William Ponsonby, whom McKerrow describes as 'the most important publisher of the Elizabethan period'. Bernard Alsop became Creede's partner in 1616, and succeeded to the business in following year. Besides plays, Creede printed ballads and broadsides. He printed Q1 (1594) of the *Contention* (*2 Henry VI*) and Q1 (1595) of the *True Tragedy* (*3 Henry VI*); Q2 (1598), Q3 (1602), Q4 (1605), and Q5 (1612) of *Richard III*; Q2 (1599) of *Romeo and Juliet*; Q1 (1600) and Q2 (1602) of *Henry V*; Q1 (1602) of *The Merry Wives of Windsor*; also a Shakespeare source play, *The Famous Victories of Henry V* (1598), and the apocryphal *Locrine*, the 1595 Quarto of which bears a title-page ascription to 'W.S.'.

CROOKE, ANDREW (item 149). Bookseller, fl. 1630–74, at Black Bear in Paul's Churchyard, and from 1640 at the nearby Green Dragon. Freeman 1629. Master of Company 1665–6. First SR entry 19 February 1630. Mainly publisher of plays, including Beaumont and Fletcher, and (in partnership with William Cooke) Shirley; also of first authorised edition of Browne's *Religio Medici*. Supplied Scottish booksellers. Died intestate 1674. Source: Allan H. Stevenson, 'Shirley's Publishers: The partnership of Crooke and Cooke', *The Library*, 4th Ser., xxv (1944–5), 140–61, esp. 142–52.

DANTER, JOHN (item 101). Printer, fl. 1589–99, in Duck Lane near Smithfield (1591) and Hosier Lane near Holborn Conduit (1592). Son of Eynsham, Oxford, weaver. Apprenticed 1582 to

John Day, an accomplished printer with premises by St. Paul's; completed apprenticeship with Robert Robinson, a printer of dubious reputation. Freeman 1589. First SR entry 26 August 1591; last, 8 November 1596. Danter, like Robinson, frequently ran foul of the authorities, who once seized his press for printing a Catholic devotional. He turned out poor work. In 1589 Danter entered into partnership with William Hoskins, printer and bookseller, and Henry Chettle, the printer-playwright author of *Kind-Heart's Dream* (see *DL*, 117–19). This partnership lasted until 1592. The title-page of the 1597 first quarto of *Romeo and Juliet*—not entered in SR—contains the assertion, 'Printed by John Danter', and includes Danter's device. He died before 1600.

ELD, or ELDE, GEORGE (item 125). Printer, fl. 1604–24, at Printer's Press in Fleet Lane (1615). Son of Derby carpenter. Apprenticed 1592 to Robert Bolton, London bookseller. Freeman 1600. Married Frances Simpson, widow of master printer, and thus acquired business. Miles Fletcher, who had become his partner, succeeded Eld when the latter died of the plague in 1624. Eld printed *The Revenger's Tragedy* and Stowe's *Annales*, as well as the 1609 Quarto of *Troilus and Cressida*.

FIELD, RICHARD (items 100, 105). Printer, fl. 1579–1624, at Blackfriars and Splayed Eagle in Great Wood Street (from 1615). Born 1561 in Stratford; son of Henry Field, a tanner in Bridge Street who knew John Shakespeare. Apprenticed 1579 to George Bishop, bookseller and printer at Bell in Paul's Churchyard; transferred by Bishop to Thomas Vautrollier, a Huguenot printer in Blackfriars. Married Vautrollier's widow Jacqueline in 1587, thus acquiring business. Master of Company in 1619 and 1622. First SR entry 24 December 1588; last, 14 April 1624. Printed and published Puttenham's *Art of English Poesy* and Harrington's translation of *Orlando Furioso*; printed Spenser and Sidney. Died 1624, leaving estate to a later wife, Jane, and sons Richard and Samuel. The business passed to George Miller, former apprentice, who was joined by Richard Badger of Stratford. Sources: A. E. M. Kirwood, 'Richard Field, Printer, 1589–1624', *The Library*, 4th Ser., xii (1931–2), 1–39; ME, 59–60. See also *DL*, 130–2.

FISHER, THOMAS (item 116). Draper, afterwards bookseller, fl. 1600–2, at White Hart in Fleet Street. Left Drapers to become freeman of Stationers in 1600. First SR entry 8 October 1600; last, 24 October 1601. Published with Matthew Townes, another Fleet Street bookseller, Marston's *Antonio and Mellida* (1602).

GILBERTSON, *alias* DERRICKE, WILLIAM (items 157, 158). Bookseller, fl. 1640–65, at Bible in Giltspur Street, without Newgate, and Bible near Newgate Street. Native of Guildford, Surrey. Gilbertson in April 1655 acquired from Edward Wright copyrights of *King Leir*, Marlowe's *Dr. Faustus*, *Mucedorus*, *The Shoemakers' Holiday*, and many other books, as well as *Venus and Adonis*. Died 1665.

HARRISON, JOHN, SR. (items 100, 104, 105, 107, 134). Printer, fl. 1556–1617, at White Greyhound in Paul's Churchyard and Greyhound in Paternoster Row. Member of Company at time of incorporation, although, because he was not made free until 1556, his name was not on the original list. Livery 1564; three times Warden and three times Master. First SR entry, 1558–9; last, 1 July 1616. Died 1617. Was one of four John Harrisons, all related, in London publishing, 1579–1639.

HARRISON, JOHN, JR. (items 145, 157). Bookseller, fl. 1603–39, at Unicorn in Paternoster Row, 1632. Son of John Harrison, Sr. (q.v.). Freeman by patrimony 1600. First SR entry—if it is by this John Harrison—18 February 1601. Senior Warden 1636; Master 1638.

HAVILAND, JOHN (items 140, 151). Printer, fl. 1613–38, in Old Bailey. Nephew of Thomas Haviland, printer in Aldermanbury, who left John his business in 1619. Freeman 1613. First SR entries on 7 June 1621, of books previously the property of Edward Griffin. Began entering copies in his own name c. 1628. One of twenty master printers appointed by 1637 Star Chamber decree. In partnership with John Wright, Sr. (q.v.), from September 1638.

HAWKINS, RICHARD (items 143, 150). Bookseller, fl. 1613–36, near Sergeant's Inn in Chancery Lane. From Abbey Milton in Dorset. Apprenticed 1604 to Edmund Mattes, bookseller at Hand and Plough in Fleet Street. Freeman 1611. First SR entry 17 December 1612; last, 6 December 1633. Published Beaumont and Fletcher's *Maid's Tragedy* and *A King and No King*; other plays. Copyrights transferred 5–6 June 1637 by widow Ursula.

HAYES, LAURENCE (items 136, 159). Bookseller, fl. 1617–37. Son of Thomas Hayes (see next entry). Freeman 1614. First SR entry 29 April 1617; last, 3 June 1630.

HAYES, THOMAS (items 117, 136). Bookseller, fl. 1600–3, at Green Dragon in Paul's Churchyard· Apprenticed to John Sheppard at Brazen Serpent in Paul's Churchyard; transferred (when Sheppard died in 1580) to William Lownes, whose business address is not known. Freeman 1584; Livery 1602. First SR entry 2 October 1600, for *England's Parnassus*; last, 6 September 1602. Died before 6 February 1604, when his widow (name unknown) assigned copyright of two books to Humphrey Lownes.

HERRINGMAN, HENRY (item 161). Bookseller, fl. 1653–93, at Blue Anchor in Lower Walk of New Exchange. From Carshalton, Surrey. Apprenticed 1644 to Abell Roper, a Fleet Street bookseller. First SR entry 19 September 1653. Sharer in King's Printing House; published Dryden, Cowley, Waller, numerous plays; shop frequented by Pepys. After Humphrey Moseley, most important bookseller of day. Characterised by Arber as first London wholesale publisher in modern sense. Retired after 1693 to Carshalton. Died 1704.

JACKSON, ROGER (items 134, 139). Bookseller, fl. 1601–25, in Fleet Street. Son of Yorkshire yeoman. Apprenticed 1591 to Ralph Newbery, a prominent Fleet Street bookseller. Freeman 1599. First SR entry, with John North (*Greene's Ghost-Haunting Conycatchers*), 3 September 1602. Last entry, 4 December 1623.

JAGGARD, ISAAC (items 138, 142). Printer, fl. 1613–27, in Barbican. Son of William Jaggard (see next entry). Freeman 1613. Took over family business at father's death in 1623. Only SR entry 8 November 1623. After Isaac died in 1627, his widow Dorothy assigned copyrights to Thomas and Richard Cotes (q.v.).

JAGGARD, WILLIAM. Printer and bookseller, fl. 1594–1623, in St. Dunstan's Churchyard in Fleet Street (1594–1608) and Half Eagle and Key in Barbican (1608–23). Son of London barber surgeon. Apprenticed 1584 to Henry Denham, a prominent printer who at one time ran four presses simultaneously. Freeman 1591; Livery 1621. First SR entry 4 March 1595. Bought, c. 1608, printing business of James Roberts (q.v.); became printer to City of London in 1610. Took as apprentice that year John Shakespeare (d. 1646), son of Thomas Shakespeare, a butcher of Warwick. Jaggard offended Thomas Heywood in 1612 (see *DL*, 219–20) and, in 1619, the quarrelsome York Herald Ralph Brooke. In the latter year he embarked with Thomas Pavier (q.v.) and Isaac Jaggard on a scheme to publish a collected edition, in quartos, of a number of Shakespearian and pseudo-Shakespearian plays. Four volumes (including a combined edition of the Bad Quartos of *2* and *3 Henry VI*) had appeared in 1619, when the Lord Chamberlain intervened to have the Stationers' Company prohibit publication without the consent of the King's men. The Jaggards and Pavier proceeded to bring out the remaining five plays, with an attempt to cover the traces by pre-dating them, *Sir John Oldcastle*, *The Merchant of Venice*, and *A Midsummer-Night's Dream* being dated 1600, and *King Lear* 1608. This deceptive gambit did not prevent the editors of the First Folio from engaging the Jaggards as their printers. Last SR entry 23 October 1622. Dead by November 1623, while First Folio printing. Source: Edwin Eliott Willoughby, *A Printer of Shakespeare: The Books and Times of William Jaggard* (1934). See preceding entry.

JOHNSON, ARTHUR (items 118, 144). Bookseller, fl. 1602–30, at Flower de Luce and Crown in Paul's Churchyard (1602–21); afterwards bookseller in Dublin. From Parkhall, Derby. Served two years as apprentice to William Young, draper and bookseller near Great Door of St. Paul's, before transfer in 1594 to Robert Dexter at Brazen Serpent in Paul's Churchyard. Freeman 1601. First SR entry 13 April 1602; last, 12 February 1621. Published general literature. From 1624–30 assigned copies to others. Died 1631.

JONES, WILLIAM (item 133). Bookseller, fl. 1589–1618, at Gun near Holborn Conduit. Son of Northamptonshire yeoman. Apprenticed 1578 to the printer John Judson, an influential stationer. Freeman 1587. First SR entry 13 August 1589; last, 28 June 1618. On 17 September 1618 his widow Sarah transferred her rights in two copies to John Wright (q.v.). Another William Jones was a printer, fl. 1601–26, in Redcross Street. One cannot always tell the two apart, although the latter had Puritan sympathies.

LAW, MATTHEW (item 123). Draper and bookseller, fl. 1595–1624; premises in Paul's Churchyard near Watling Street (1601) and at Fox near St. Austin's Gate in Paul's Churchyard. Translated 1600 from Drapers to Stationers. Several fines for infractions of Company regulations. Held shares in Latin Stock of Stationers. First SR entry 4 September 1600; last, 2 July 1624. Died 1629.

LEAKE, WILLIAM, SR. (items 107, 135, 152, 159). Bookseller, fl. 1592–1618, at Crane (1593); also White Greyhound (1596) and Holy Ghost (1602–18) in Paul's Churchyard. Apprenticed to Francis Coldock (Master of Company in 1591–2 and 1595–6); freeman 1584. First SR entry 17 February 1592; last, 22 October 1618. Livery 1598; Junior Warden 1604 and 1606; Upper Warden 1610 and 1614; Master of Company, 1618. Held shares in Latin and Irish Stocks. Retired to Hereford where he died in 1633. His widow in 1635 assigned remaining copyrights to their son, William Leake, Jr., who carried on the business in Chancery Lane until his death in 1681.

LEGATT, or LEGATE, JOHN (item 149). Printer, fl. 1620–58, in Little Wood Street and in Cambridge. Son of John Legatt, Cambridge printer, 1586–1620. Freeman 1619. First SR entry 12 June 1623. Like his father, he was appointed University printer (1650). After losing his patent through neglect in 1655, Legatt settled permanently in London. He died, 'distempered in his senses', in 1658.

LING, NICHOLAS (items 124, 126). Bookseller, fl. 1580–1607, at various locations: Mermaid in Paul's Churchyard (1580–3); West Door (1584–92), North-west Door (1593–6), and Little West Door (1597) of St. Paul's; and St. Dunstan's Churchyard in Fleet Street (1600–7). Son of Norwich parchmenter. Apprenticed 1570 to Henry Bynneman, printer of Holinshed's *Chronicles*. Freeman 1579. First SR entry 1 June 1582; last, 19 November 1607. Published *England's Parnassus* (1600); edited *Politeuphuia: Wit's Commonwealth* (1597), and probably also *England's Helicon*. Dead by 1610. Source: J. William Hebel, 'Nicholas Ling and *Englands Helicon*', *The Library*, 4th Ser., v (1924–5), 153–60.

MARTIN, JOHN (items 161, 162). Bookseller, fl. 1649–80, at Bell in Paul's Churchyard. Had as partner James Allestry, 'one of the largest capitalists in the trade', and, after the latter's death in 1670, took over from him as Royal Society's bookseller and publisher. Last entry in Term Catalogues, May 1680.

MATHEWES, AUGUSTINE. Printer, fl. 1619–53, in St. Bride's Lane in Fleet Street in the Parsonage House (1620), and Cow Lane near Holborn Circus. Freeman 1615. First SR entry 27 September 1619, for Dekker's *Bellman of London*; last, 6 June 1653. Partner with John White, 1620; printed books for John Norton, Sr. (q.v.). Mathewes was described as a pauper in 1634. The Stationers made over his press to Marmaduke Parsons in 1637, when Mathewes was caught reprinting Dr. Cole's *Holy Table*, but he remained in business until as late as 1653. Mathewes printed Q2 (1630) of *Othello*.

MEAD, ROBERT (items 150, 152). Bookseller (?), fl. 1617–56, at (?) Crane in Paul's Churchyard. Although Mead became a freeman in 1608 after a nine-year apprenticeship to John Standish (publisher of Sir John Davies) and was thrice Master of the Company, no book has come down with his name in the imprint.

MEIGHEN, RICHARD (item 144). Bookseller, fl. 1615–41, under St. Clement's Church in Strand. First SR entry 4 July 1615. Partner, 1641, in publishing law books. Died by 1642.

MEREDITH, CHRISTOPHER (items 150, 152). Bookseller, fl. 1625–53, at Crane in Paul's Churchyard (1629–53). Freeman 1624. First SR entry 3 May 1625. Specialised mainly in theology. Died 1653.

MILLINGTON, THOMAS (items 102, 119). Bookseller, fl. 1593–1603, Under St. Peter's Church in Cornhill. Son of Hampton Gaie, Oxfordshire, husbandman. Apprenticed 1583 to Henry Carre, bookseller dealing mostly in ballads. Freeman 1591. First SR entry 12 March 1594; last, 9 May 1603. Had various partners; published ballads, Chettle's *England's Mourning Garment* (1603). With John Busby, Sr. (q.v.), published pirated *Henry V* (1600).

MOSELEY, HUMPHREY (items 155, 156, 160). Bookseller, fl. 1627–61, at Three Kings (1635) and, from 1638, at Prince's Arms, both in Paul's Churchyard. Son of Thomas Moseley, London cook. Apprenticed 1619 to Matthew Lownes. Freeman 1627; Livery 1633; Junior Warden 1659. Partner, 1627–36, with Nicholas Fussell. Published Milton's *Poems* (1645), Donne, Vaughan, Waller, numerous plays, including (with Humphrey Robinson) 1647 Beaumont and Fletcher Folio. A list of seventy-six books, mostly plays, supplied by Moseley to an unknown customer, and receipted by his servant Nicholas Dixon 4 March 1640, is preserved among the State Papers Domestic, and is printed, with prefatory comment, by Greg, *Bibliography*, iii. 1317–18. Moseley died in 1661. Source: John Curtis Reed, 'Humphrey Moseley, Publisher', *Oxford Bibliographical Society: Proceedings and Papers*, ii (1928), 61–142.

NORTON, JOHN, JR. Printer, fl. 1621–45, location unknown. First SR entry 18 September 1621. Partner of Nicholas Okes, who ran a large established printing business founded by Thomas Judson in 1586; associated with Augustine Mathewes (q.v.) 1624–6. Excluded from 1637 Star Chamber decree listing approved master printers. Printed Q6 (1634) of *Richard II* and Q7 (1632) and Q8 (1639) of *1 Henry IV*.

OKES, NICHOLAS. Printer, fl. 1606–39, near Holborn Bridge (1613) and Foster Lane. Son of London horner. Apprenticed 1596 to William King. Freeman 1603; master printer 1606. First SR entry 6 July 1607; last, 16 May 1636. Succeeded to business founded by Thomas Judson in 1586. Eventually Judson's stock of decorative ornament blocks passed to Okes. After he entered into partnership with John Norton, Jr. (q.v.), they ran two presses. Took son John as partner c. 1627. In trouble for printing Wither's *Motto* in 1621 and (six years later) Cotton's life of Henry III. Excluded from Star Chamber list of approved master printers in 1637 for rôle in reprinting Francis of Sales's suppressed *Introduction to a Devout Life*. Printed quarto editions of (among others) Heywood, Jonson, Marston, Middleton, Webster plays; Q1 (1622) of *Othello*. Source: C. William Miller, 'A London Ornament Stock: 1598–1683', *Studies in Bibliography*, vii (1955), 125–51, esp. 129ff.

PARKER, JOHN (item 140). Bookseller, fl. 1617–48, at Bell and, for many years, Three Pigeons in Paul's Churchyard. Son of Honington, Warwickshire, yeoman. Freeman 1617. First SR entry 1 December 1617. Took over copyrights of William Barrett (q.v.) in 1620. Bought shares in Company's Latin Stock. Warden 1641, 1644, 1645; Master, 1647, 1648. Died 1648.

PAVIER, THOMAS (items 113, 114, 119, 128, 141). Draper, later bookseller, fl. 1600–25, at entrance to and near (Cats and Parrot) Royal Exchange (1604–12) and in Ivy Lane (1623).

Apprenticed to William Barley, draper, bookseller–printer, and early music publisher. Translated from Drapers to Stationers 1600. Livery 1604; Junior Warden 1622. First SR entry 4 August 1600; last, 19 July 1625. Partner with William Jaggard (q.v.) in scheme for collected Shakespeare, 1619. Published ballads, jest-books, news-sheets, etc. Died (of plague?) in 1625.

PURFOOT, THOMAS, JR. Printer, fl. 1591–1640, first at sign of the Lucrece within new rents in Newgate Market, and later over against St. Sepulchre's Church without Newgate. Son of London printer whose name appears in Company's original charter. Apprenticed 1584 to Richard Collins, bookseller. Freeman 1590; master printer 1591; Junior Warden 1629; Senior Warden 1634. First SR entry 30 March 1591; last, 25 May 1633. Partner with father, to whose business he succeeded in 1615. In that year Purfoot was running two presses and printing books for most of the leading London publishers. One of twenty master printers appointed by 1637 Star Chamber decree. Dead by 1640, when his copyrights passed to Richard Lewty, who seems never to have published any of Purfoot's titles. The latter printed Q6 (1622) of *Richard III* and Q6 (1622) of *1 Henry IV*.

ROBERTS, JAMES (items 111, 112, 117, 120, 122). Bookseller and printer, fl. 1569–1607(?), at Love and Death in Fleet Street; also adjoining little Conduit in Cheapside, and in Barbican. Freeman 1564. Dealt in ballads. Married 1593 to widow of John Charlwood, who had patent for printing playbills. First SR entry 1569–70; last, 10 July 1606. Associated, from 1602, with William Jaggard (q.v.). The latter seems to have taken over Roberts's printing house in Barbican by 1607 (Edwin Eliott Willoughby, *A Printer of Shakespeare: The Books and Times of William Jaggard* (1934), p. 74). A number of Roberts's copyrights were transferred to Jaggard in 1615. Died 1618.

SCOTT, ROBERT (item 162). Bookseller, fl. 1661–91, at Prince's Arms in Little Britain. Partner with William Wells, and apparently took over from him when latter died in 1673.

SHEARES, or SHEARS, WILLIAM. Bookseller, fl. 1625–62, in various locations: Paul's Churchyard, Covent Garden, Westminster Hall, etc. Freeman 1623. Suspected of having taken part in printing *Leicester's Commonwealth* (1641), which satirised House of Lords. Died 1662. Sheares printed a number of important works, including Cleveland's *Poems*, Phineas Fletcher's *Sicelides*, and May's translation of Lucan's *Pharsalia*. Printed Q7 (1632) of *1 Henry IV*.

SHORT, PETER (item 103). Printer, fl. 1589–1603, at Star on Bread Street Hill. Freeman by 'redemption' in 1589. Livery 1598. First SR entry (with Richard Yardley) 5 July 1591; last, 31 December 1602. Printed Meres's *Palladis Tamia* (1598) and Foxe's *Acts and Monuments* (1597), which Henry Denham had begun. Died 1603.

SIMMES, VALENTINE. Printer, fl. 1585–1623, at White Swan in Addle Hill, near Baynard's Castle, and at White Friars near the Mulberry Tree (1610). Son of Adderbury, Oxfordshire, shearman. Apprenticed 1576 to Henry Sutton, a London bookseller and retired printer whose name appears in the Company's original charter; transferred to Henry Bynneman, a printer who died in 1583. Freeman 1585. First SR entry 6 December 1594; last, 26 November 1605. Often in trouble for printing books that were objectionable or which belonged to other stationers. Arrested in 1589 for his part as a compositor of forbidden pamphlets for 'second Marprelate' press; in 1599 one of fourteen printers specifically enjoined from printing satires or epigrams. More than once imprisoned. Prohibited from printing by High Commissioners in 1622, but pensioned off by Company. Simmes assigned some of his copyrights to Edward Griffen in 1619. Printed Q2 (1600) of the *Contention* (*2 Henry VI*); Q1 (1597) of *Richard III*; Q3 (1607) of *The Taming of A Shrew* (source or Bad Quarto of *The Shrew*); Q1 (1597), Q2 (1598), and Q3 (1598) of *Richard II*; Q3 (1604) of *1 Henry IV*; the only Quartos (1600) of *2 Henry IV* and *Much Ado About Nothing*; and Q1 (1603) of *Hamlet*. Source: W. Craig Ferguson, *Valentine Simmes: Printer to Drayton, Shakespeare, Chapman, Greene, Dekker, Middleton, Daniel, Jonson, Marlowe, Marston, Heywood, and other Elizabethans* (Charlottesville, 1968).

SMETHWICK, JOHN (item 126). Bookseller, fl. 1597–1640, near Temple Gate and under Dial in St. Dunstan's Churchyard, both in Fleet Street. Apprenticed 1589 to Thomas Newman, bookseller in St. Dunstan's Churchyard. Freeman 1597. First SR entry 6 October 1597; last, 15 February 1630. Although fined more than once, early on, for selling privileged books, he became Junior Warden in 1631, Senior Warden four years later, and, finally, in 1639, Master of Company. Held shares in Latin Stock. For a time in partnership with William Jaggard's nephew John Jaggard, proprietor of Hand and Star in Fleet Street. Died 1641.

STAFFORD, JOHN (item 157). Bookseller, fl. 1637–64, at several locations in or near Fleet Street—Blackhorse Alley, St. Bride's Churchyard, and over against St. Bride's Church—and in Chancery Lane. Possibly apprenticed to Robert Allot (q.v.). Freeman 1637. First SR entry 9 November 1637. Specialised mainly in theology.

STAFFORD, SIMON. Draper and printer, fl. 1596–1626, at several locations: Cornhill, the Cloth Fair, Addle Hill near Carter Lane. Apprenticed to Christopher Barker, Queen's Printer and also draper. Freeman of Drapers' Company. First SR entry 9 February 1596; last, 24 June 1624. Transferred to Stationers' Company; freeman 1599. Printed ballads, sermons, *True Chronicle History of King Leir*, Q2 (1599) of *1 Henry IV*.

STANSBY, WILLIAM. Printer and bookseller, fl. 1597–1639, at Cross Keys at St. Paul's Wharf, Thames Street. Apprenticed 1590 to John Windet, printer at Cross Keys. Freeman 1597. First SR entry 28 April 1597; last, 18 September 1635. Became Windet's partner and took over business when latter died c. 1615. Assigned music books and other copyrights of Thomas Snodham in 1626. Sued in 1635 by George Sandys over payment for latter's translation of Ovid's *Metamorphosis*. Died 1638 or 1639. Printed Q4 (n.d.) of *Hamlet*. Source: R. B. Davis, 'George Sandys *v.* William Stansby: The 1632 Edition of Ovid's *Metamorphosis*', *The Library*, 5th Ser., iii (1948–9), 193–212.

THORPE, THOMAS (item 132). Bookseller, fl. 1603–24. Son of Barnet, Herts, innkeeper. Apprenticed 1584 to the eminent Richard Watkins. Freeman 1594. First SR entry 23 June 1603. Published Marston's *Malcontent* (1604), Jonson's *Sejanus* (1605), and *Volpone* (1607), Chapman's *Biron* (1608), other plays. Although Thorpe's name does not appear on the title-page of Marlowe's translation of Lucan's *First Book*, the copyright of which he owned, he signed the dedication of the 1600 Quarto. On Thorpe's edition of Shakespeare's *Sonnets*, see *DL*, 218–19. Last SR entry 3 November 1624, when Marlowe's *Hero and Leander* assigned by Thorpe and Edward Blount (q.v.) to Samuel Vicars. Died a pauper, c. 1635. Source: Leona Rostenberg, *Literary, Political, Scientific, Religious & Legal Publishing, Printing & Bookselling in England, 1551–1700* (New York, 1965), i. 49–73; to be consulted with caution.

TRUNDELL, or TRUNDLE, JOHN. Bookseller, fl. 1603–36, at sign of Nobody in Barbican (1613). Son of Barnet, Herts, yeoman. Apprenticed 1589 to Ralph Hancock, bookseller over against St. Giles's Church without Cripplegate. Freeman 1597. First SR entry 27 July 1603; last, 18 July 1626. His widow Margaret assigned her copyrights to John Wright, Sr., *et al.* in 1629. Trundell printed plays, ballads, ephemera; for Nicholas Ling (q.v.) he printed Q1 (1603) of *Hamlet*.

WALKLEY, THOMAS (items 137, 143). Bookseller, fl. 1618–58, at Eagle and Child in Britain's Burse, and Flying Horse near York House. Freeman 1618. First SR entry 12 October 1618. In 1620 issued pirated edition of Wither's poems. Accused in 1649 of distributing scandalous communiqués from the late King's exiled sons. Published Denham's *Cooper's Hill* (1642) and Waller's *Poems* (1647). Source: Percy Simpson, 'Walkley's Piracy of Wither's Poems in 1620', *The Library*, 4th Ser., vi (1925–6), 271–7.

WALLEY, HENRY (item 131). Bookseller, fl. c. 1608–55, at Hart's Horn in Foster Lane. Son and grandson of London stationers. Freeman 1608. First SR entry 22 December 1608. Partner, 1608–10, with Richard Bonian (q.v.). Clerk of Company, 1630–40; Master, 1655. Walley was a close friend of the playwright Marston. Source: Philip J. Finkelpearl, 'Henry Walley of the Stationers' Company and John Marston', *The Papers of the Bibliographical Society of America*, lvi (1962), 366–8.

WATERSON, JOHN (items 148, 155). Bookseller, fl. 1620–41(?), at (?) Crown at Cheap Gate in Paul's Churchyard, specialising in plays. Freeman 1620. First SR entry 25 January 1623. Died 1656.

WHITE, EDWARD, SR. Bookseller, fl. 1577–1612, at Gun at Little North Door of Paul's. Son of Bury St. Edmunds, Suffolk, mercer. Apprenticed 1565 to William Lobley, London bookseller and bookbinder. First SR entry 21 January 1577; last, 21 August 1612. Livery 1588. After White's death in 1613, his widow Sarah carried on the business. Their son, Edward Jr., was also a bookseller, fl. 1605–24. White dealt mainly in ballads; he published Q1 (1594), Q2 (1600), and Q3 (1611) of *Titus Andronicus*.

WHITE, WILLIAM. Printer, fl. 1597–1615, at White Horse in Fleet Lane (1588–91) and in Cow Lane near Holborn Conduit. Presented for freedom 1583 by wife of Richard Jugge, whose apprentice White presumably was. Partner of Gabriel Simpson; first SR entry (joint) 13 December 1588. When partnership was dissolved in 1597, took over business of Richard Jones and William Hill in Cow Lane. Last SR entry 5 September 1615. White's son John, freeman 1614, was a partner in his father's business, to which he succeeded. White printed ballads, ephemera, Q2 (1600) of *True Tragedy* (*3 Henry VI*), Q1 (1598) of *Love's Labour's Lost*, Q4 (1608) of *Richard II*, and Q5 (1613) of *1 Henry IV*.

WILLIAMS, FRANCIS (items 139, 145). Bookseller, 1626–30, at Globe, over against Royal Exchange. Freeman 1625. First SR entry 17 May 1626. Published popular literature, including *Scoggin's Jests* and Bretoq's *Fantastics*. Last SR entry 1 March 1628.

WISE (or WYTHES, WITHYS), ANDREW (items 108, 109, 110, 115, 123). Bookseller, fl. 1589–1603, at Angel in Paul's Churchyard. Son of Ollerton Mallyveres, Yorkshire, yeoman. Apprenticed 1580 to Henry Smith, and transferred next year to Thomas Bradshaw, Cambridge stationer, who gave him his freedom in 1589. First SR entry 30 April 1596. Used James Roberts (q.v.) as printer for Nashe's *Christ's Tears over Jerusalem* (1593). Disappears after assignment of copyrights, 25 June 1603, to Matthew Law (q.v.).

WRIGHT, EDWARD (items 154, 158). Bookseller, fl. 1615–55, in London. Brother of John Wright (see next entry). First SR entry 14 December 1624, when with Thomas Pavier, John Wright, and others he seems to have acquired a share in the Company's ballad stock. McKerrow does not include Wright, but provides a cross-reference to Plomer, who does not include him either.

WRIGHT, JOHN, SR. (items 140, 151, 154). Bookseller, fl. 1608–58, at King's Head, Old Bailey. Freeman 1602. Published ballads, chapbooks, some plays, including seven editions of Marlowe's *Dr. Faustus* between 1609 and 1631. Some copies of the 1609 edition of Shakespeare's *Sonnets* have Wright's imprint on the title-page; others, Aspley's (q.v.). Evidently Thorpe employed both booksellers. Wright was in difficulties in 1643 for publishing an anti-Parliament tract, but later became an official printer to the Parliament. With Thomas Bates, published Commonwealth news-sheets, *Mercurius Civicus* and *The True Informer*. Died May 1658.

YOUNG, ROBERT. Printer, fl. 1625–43; whereabouts of his London business unknown. With partners Miles Fletcher (or Flesher) and John Haviland, Young bought up several printing establishments. Involved in printing in Scotland (appointed Royal printer for Scotland in 1632), Ireland (appointed manager of Company's Irish printing office), and Oxford, where he is known to have had a press in 1640. After his death in 1643, his copyrights, numbering 131, were transferred to his son James, a London printer, fl. 1643–53. Robert Young printed Q4 (1637) of *Romeo and Juliet*.

Works Cited

This list brings together references to published and manuscript items from the text, captions, and notes of the present work, as well as citations from its predecessor, *William Shakespeare: A Documentary Life* (1975). Here and there I have included an identifying note for titleless items, and silently made corrections (e.g. Sydney, for Sidney, Race). I have not included the Shakespeare documents themselves. Unless otherwise indicated, the place of publication is London.

ACHESON, ARTHUR. *Mistress Davenant, the Dark Lady of Shakespeare's Sonnets, Demonstrating the Identity of the Dark Lady of the Sonnets, and the Authorship and Satirical Intention of Willobie His Avisa.* 1913.

—. *Shakespeare's Sonnet Story 1592–1598, Restoring the Sonnets Written to the Earl of Southampton to Their Original Books and Correlating Them with Personal Phases of the Plays of the Sonnet Period; with Documentary Evidence Identifying Mistress Davenant as the Dark Lady.* 1922.

ADAMS, JOSEPH QUINCY. *A Life of William Shakespeare.* Boston and New York, 1923.

—. 'A New Signature of Shakespeare?'. *Bulletin of the John Rylands Library*, xxvii (1942–3), 256–9.

—. 'Shakespeare as a Writer of Epitaphs'. *The Manly Anniversary Studies in Language and Literature* (Chicago, 1923), pp. 78–89.

—. *Shakespearean Playhouses: A History of English Theatres from the Beginnings to the Restoration.* Boston and New York, 1917.

AKRIGG, G. P. V. *Shakespeare and the Earl of Southampton.* 1968.

ALEXANDER, PETER. *Shakespeare.* 1964.

—. *Shakespeare's Henry VI and Richard III.* Cambridge, 1929.

ALTON, R. E. Review of A. L. Rowse, *The Casebooks of Simon Forman: Sex and Society in Shakespeare's Age. Notes and Queries*, ccxxiii (1978), 456–7.

ARBER, EDWARD, ED. *A Transcript of the Registers of the Company of Stationers of London: 1554–1640 A. D.* 4 vols. 1875–94. [A fifth volume, devoted to an index, appeared separately in 1894.]

ASHMOLE, ELIAS, AND WILLIAM LILLY. *The Lives of Those Eminent Antiquaries Elias Ashmole, Esquire, and Mr. William Lilly, Written by Themselves; Containing, First, William Lilly's History of His Life and Times, with Notes, by Mr. Ashmole: Secondly, Lilly's Life and Death of Charles I: and Lastly, the Life of Elias Ashmole, Esquire, by Way of Diary.* 1774.

AUBREY, JOHN. *'Brief Lives', Chiefly of Contemporaries, Set Down by John Aubrey, between the Years 1669 & 1696.* Ed. Andrew Clark. 2 vols. Oxford, 1898.

—. *Brief Lives.* Ed. Oliver Lawson Dick. 1949.

AUSTIN, WARREN B. *A Computer-Aided Technique for Stylistic Discrimination: The Authorship of Greene's Groatsworth of Wit.* Washington, D.C., 1969.

—. 'A Supposed Contemporary Allusion to Shakespeare as a Plagiarist'. *Shakespeare Quarterly*, vi (1955), 373–80.

[AVITY, PIERRE d']. *Neuwe Archontologia cosmica, das ist, Beschreibung aller Käyserthumben, Königreichen und Republicken der gantzen Welt . . . wie auch von der alten unnd newen innwohnern gebräuchen . . . Alles auss unverwerfflichen Gründen unnd zeugnussen, vom Anfang biss auff unsere Zeit, das Jahr Christi 1638.* Tr. Johann Ludwig Gottfried. Frankfort am Mayn, 1638.

BALD, R. C. '*The Booke of Sir Thomas More* and Its Problems'. *Shakespeare Survey 2* (Cambridge, 1949), pp. 44–65.

BALDWIN, T. W. *Shakspere's Love's Labor's Won: New Evidence from the Account Books of an Elizabethan Bookseller.* Carbondale, Ill., 1957.

—. *William Shakspere's Petty School.* Urbana, Ill., 1943.

—. *William Shakspere's Small Latine & Lesse Greeke.* 2 vols. Urbana, Ill., 1944.

BARKSTED, WILLIAM. *Mirrha the Mother of Adonis, with Certaine Eclogs by L. M[achin].* 1607.

BARRELL, CHARLES WISNER. 'Identifying "Shakespeare"'. *Scientific American*, clxii (1940), 5–8, 43–5.

BARTHOLOMEUSZ, DENNIS. *Macbeth and the Players.* Cambridge, 1969.

BATESON, F. W. Postscript to Andrew Gurr, "Shakespeare's First Poem: Sonnet 145". *Essays in Criticism*, xxi (1971), 226.

BAYLY, LEWIS. *The Practise of Pietie.* 3rd ed. 1613.

BELLEW, J. C. M. *Shakespere's Home at New Place, Stratford-upon-Avon. Being a History of the 'Great House' Built in the Reign of King Henry VII, by Sir Hugh Clopton, Knight, and Subsequently the Property of William Shakespere, Gent., wherein He Lived and Died.* 1863.

BENTLEY, G. E. *The Jacobean and Caroline Stage.* 7 vols. Oxford, 1941–68.

—. *The Profession of Dramatist in Shakespeare's Time, 1590–1642.* Princeton, 1971.

—. *Shakespeare: A Biographical Handbook.* New Haven, 1961.

—. *Shakespeare and His Theatre.* Lincoln, Neb., 1964.

BERNARD, EDWARD. *Catalogi Librorum Manuscriptorum Angliae et Hiberniae in Unum Collecti, cum Indice Alphabetico.* Oxford, 1697.

BILLINGSLEY, MARTIN. *The Pens Excellencie, or the Secretaries Delight . . . Together with an Insertion of Sondrie Peeces, or Examples, of All ye Usuall Hands of England; as Also an Addition of Certaine Methodicall Observations for Writing, Making of the Pen, Holding the Pen, etc. . . . The Greeke and Hebrewe with Other Peeces Never Yet Extant Are hereunto by the Author Exactlie Adaed.* [1618].

Biographia Britannica: or, The Lives of the Most Eminent Persons Who Have Flourished in Great Britain and Ireland, from the Earliest Ages, down to the Present Times: Collected from the Best Authorities, Both Printed and Manuscript, and Digested in the Manner of Mr. Bayle's Historical and Critical Dictionary. 6 vols. in 7. 1747–66.

BLACKSTONE, SIR WILLIAM. *Commentaries on the Laws of England.* 4 vols. Oxford, 1765–9.

BLAGDEN, CYPRIAN. *The Stationers' Company: A History, 1403–1959.* 1960.

BLOOM, JAMES HARVEY. *Shakespeare's Church, Otherwise the Collegiate Church of the Holy Trinity of Stratford-upon-Avon; an Architectural and Ecclesiastical History of the Fabric and Its Ornaments.* 1902.

BOADEN, JAMES. *An Inquiry into the Authenticity of Various Pictures and Prints, which, from the Decease of the Poet to Our Own Times, Have Been Offered to the Public as Portraits of Shakspeare: Containing a Careful Examination of the Evidence on Which They Claim to be Received; by which the Pretended Portraits Have Been Rejected, the Genuine Confirmed and Established. Illustrated by Accurate and Finished Engravings, by the Ablest Artists, from Such Originals as Were of Indisputable Authority.* 1824.

Bodleian Library. *A Catalogue of the Shakespeare Exhibition Held in the Bodleian Library to Commemorate the Death of Shakespeare, April 23, 1616.* Oxford, 1916.

BOND, EDWARD. *Bingo: Scenes of Money and Death.* 1974.

BOOTH, ABRAHAM. *Een Dienaer der Oost-Indische Compagnie te Londen in 1629.* Ed. A. Merens. 's-Gravenhage, 1942.

BOSWELL, JAMES. *Life of Johnson, together with Journal of a Tour to the Hebrides and Johnson's Diary of a Journey into North Wales.* Ed. George Birkbeck Hill. Rev. L. F. Powell. 6 vols. Oxford, 1934–64. [Vols. 5–6, with revisions by L. F. Powell, first published in 1950; republished in 1964 as 2nd ed., with further revisions.]

[BRAE, A. E.]. *Literary Cookery with Reference to Matter Attributed to Coleridge and Shakespeare. A Letter Addressed to 'The Athenaeum'. With a Postscript Containing Some Remarks upon the Refusal of That Journal to Print It.* 1855.

BRINKWORTH, E. R. C. *Shakespeare and the Bawdy Court of Stratford.* 1972.

[BRINSLEY, JOHN]. *Ludus Literarius: or, The Grammar Schoole; Shewing How to Proceede from the First Entrance into Learning, to the Highest Perfection Required in the Grammar Schooles with Ease, Certainty and Delight Both to Masters and to Schollars; Onely According to Our Common Grammar, and Ordinary Classicall Authours . . . Intended for the Helping of the Younger Sort of Teachers, and of All Schollars, with All Other Desirous of Learning.* 1612.

BRITTON, JOHN. *Remarks on the Monumental Bust of Shakspeare at Stratford-upon-Avon: with Two Wood-Cuts, Representing Front and Profile Views of the Bust.* Chiswick, 1816.

BROOKE, C. F. TUCKER. *Shakespeare of Stratford: A Handbook for Students.* The Yale Shakespeare. New Haven, 1926.

BURGESS, ANTHONY. *Shakespeare.* London and New York, 1970.

BURGESS, J. T. *Historic Warwickshire.* Ed. Joseph Hill. 1876; 2nd ed., 1893.

CAIRNCROSS, A. S. 'Shakespeare and the "Staying Entries"'. *Shakespeare in the Southwest: Some New Directions.* Ed. T. J. Stafford. El Paso, Texas, 1969, pp. 80–93.

C[ALDECOTT], T[HOMAS]. Letter to John Mander, 30 November, 1797. [Pasted as a flyleaf insert to *Shakspeare Papers*, nine previously printed items connected with the Ireland forgeries, bound together in a single volume. The Folger Shakespeare Library; shelfmark: PR 2950. B5 Copy 2. Cage.]

CAMPBELL, JOHN C. *Shakespeare's Legal Acquirements Considered. . . . in a Letter to J. Payne Collier.* 1859.

CAMPBELL, OSCAR JAMES, AND EDWARD G. QUINN, EDS. *The Reader's Encyclopedia of Shakespeare.* New York, 1966.

[CAPELL, EDWARD]. *Notes and Various Readings to Shakespeare, Part the First; Containing, All's Well That Ends Well, Antony and Cleopatra, As You Like It, Comedy of Errors, Coriolanus, Cymbeline, Hamlet, 1 Henry IV, 2 Henry IV, with a General Glossary.* [1774]; [1779]. [Issued previously as a supplementary work to his edition of Shakespeare's plays, 1767–8.]

CARLO BORROMEO, SAINT. *The Contract and Testament, of the Soule.* [St. Omer?], 1638.

CHALMERS, GEORGE. *An Apology for the Believers in the Shakspeare-Papers, Which Were Exhibited in Norfolk-Street.* 1797.

—. *A Supplemental Apology for the Believers in the Shakspeare-Papers: Being a Reply to Mr. Malone's Answer, Which Was Early Announced but Never Published: with a Dedication to George Steevens, F.R.S.S.A., and a Postscript to T. J. Mathias.* 1799.

CHAMBERS, E. K. *The Elizabethan Stage*. 4 vols. Oxford, 1923.
—. 'The First Illustration to "Shakespeare"'. *The Library*, 4th ser., v (1924–5), 326–30.
—. *William Shakespeare: A Study of Facts and Problems*. 2 vols. Oxford, 1930.
CHAMBERS, R. W. 'The Expression of Ideas—Particularly Political Ideas—in the Three Pages, and in Shakespeare'. Alfred Pollard et. al. *Shakespeare's Hand in the Play of Sir Thomas More*. Cambridge, 1923, pp. 142–87.
CHETWOOD, WILLIAM RUFUS. *A General History of the Stage; (More Particularly the Irish Theatre) from Its Origin in Greece down to the Present Time*. Dublin, 1749.
CHUTE, MARCHETTE. *Shakespeare of London*. 1951.
CLARKE, JOHN. *An Essay upon the Education of Youth in Grammar-Schools. In which the Vulgar Method of Teaching Is Examined and a New One Proposed, for the More Easy and Speedy Training up of Youth to the Knowledge of the Learned Languages; together with History, Chronology, Geography, &c.* 1720.
CLAYTON, THOMAS. *The 'Shakespearean' Addition in The Booke of Sir Thomas Moore: Some Aids to Scholarly and Critical Shakespearean Studies*. Shakespeare Studies Monograph Series, I. Ed. J. Leeds Barroll. Dubuque, 1969.
COGHILL, NEVILL. *Shakespeare's Professional Skills*. Cambridge, 1964.
COLLIER, J. PAYNE. *Autobiography*. The Folger Shakespeare Library; shelfmark: MS. M.a.230.
—. *Diary. November 7, 1872–December 11, 1882*. 12 vols. The Folger Shakespeare Library; shelfmark: MS. M.a.29–40.
—. 'Early Manuscript Emendations of Shakespeare's Text'. *The Athenaeum*, no. 1266 (31 January 1852), 142–4; no. 1267 (7 February 1852), 171.
—. 'Early Manuscript Emendations of the Text of Shakspeare'. *The Athenaeum*, no. 1274 (27 March 1852), 355.
COLLIER, J. PAYNE. *Farther Particulars Regarding Shakespeare and His Works*. 1839.
[COLLIER, J. PAYNE]. *A Few Odds and Ends, for Cheerful Friends. A Christmas Gift*. 1870. [The Folger Shakespeare Library copy, shelfmark: PR 4489.C23F5, contains an autograph letter, dated 11 December 1876, to F. W. Cosens.]
COLLIER, J. PAYNE. *The History of English Dramatic Poetry to the Time of Shakespeare: and Annals of the Stage to the Restoration*. 3 vols. 1831; new ed., 1879.
—. 'Manuscript Emendations of Shakespeare's Text'. *The Athenaeum*, no. 1336 (4 June 1853), 677.
—. *Memoirs of Edward Alleyn, Founder of Dulwich College: Including Some New Particulars Respecting Shakespeare, Ben Jonson, Massinger, Marston, Dekker, &c.* Shakespeare Society Publications, no. 1. 1841.
—. *Memoirs of the Principal Actors in the Plays of Shakespeare*. Shakespeare Society Publications, no. 32. 1846.
—. *Mr. J. Payne Collier's Reply to Mr. N. E. S. A. Hamilton's 'Inquiry' into the Imputed Shakespeare Forgeries*. 1860.
—. 'The New Fact Regarding Shakespeare and His Wife, Contained in the Will of Thomas Whittington'. *The Shakespeare Society's Papers*, iii (1847), 127–30.
—. *New Facts Regarding the Life of Shakespeare. In a Letter to Thomas Amyot, Esq., F.R.S., Treasurer of the Society of Antiquaries, from J. Payne Collier, F.S.A.* 1835.
—. *New Particulars Regarding the Works of Shakespeare. In a Letter to the Rev. A. Dyce . . . from J. Payne Collier, F.S.A.* 1836.
—. *Notes and Emendations to the Text of Shakespeare's Plays, from Early Manuscript Corrections in a Copy of the Folio, 1632, in the Possession of J. Payne Collier . . . Forming a Supplemental Volume to the Works of Shakespeare by the Same Editor*. 1853. [First issued by the Shakespeare Society, but afterwards withdrawn from the Society's list, and published in 1853.]
—. *Reasons for a New Edition of Shakespeare's Works, Containing Notices of the Defects of Former Impressions, and Pointing out the Lately Acquired Means of Illustrating the Plays, Poems, and Biography of the Poet*. 1841.
—. 'Shakespearian Discovery'. *The Times*, 7 July 1859, p. 9.
—. 'Shakespearian Discovery'. *The Times*, 19 July 1859, p. 12. [Misdated 20 July 1859 by Ingleby in *A Complete View of the Shakspere Controversy*.]
COLLINS, ARTHUR. *Letters and Memorials of State, . . . Written and Collected by Sir Henry Sydney, . . . Sir Philip Sydney, . . . Sir Robert Sydney, &c.* 2 vols. 1746.
COLMAN, GEORGE. *Prose on Several Occasions; Accompanied with Some Pieces in Verse*. 3 vols. 1787.
CORY, WILLIAM J. *Extracts from the Letters and Journals of William Cory*. Ed. Francis Warre Cornish. Oxford, 1897.
CUNNINGHAM, PETER, ED. *Extracts from the Accounts of the Revels at Court, in the Reigns of Queen Elizabeth and King James I, from the Original Office Books of the Masters and Yeomen*. Shakespeare Society Publications. 1842.
DARLINGTON, IDA. *Bankside*. Gen. eds. Sir Howard Roberts and Walter H. Godfrey. *Survey of London*. Vol. 22, 1950.
DARLINGTON, IDA, and JAMES HOWGEGO. *Printed Maps of London, circa 1553–1850*. 1964.
DAVIES, JOHN. *The Complete Works*. Ed. Alexander B. Grosart. 2 vols. 1876.
—. *Microcosmos; the Discovery of the Little World*. Oxford, 1603.
[DAVIES, JOHN]. *The Scourge of Folly. Consisting of Satyricall Epigramms and Others in Honor of Many Noble and Worthy Persons of Our Land*. 1611.

DAVIS, RICHARD BEALE. 'George Sandys *v.* William Stansby: The 1632 Edition of Ovid's *Metamorphosis*'. *The Library*, 5th ser., iii (1948–9), 193–212.

DAWSON, GILES E. 'Authenticity and Attribution of Written Matter'. *English Institute Annual, 1942* (New York, 1943), pp. 77–100.

—. Correspondence, 'Art Provenance—Shakespeare: The Felton Portrait'. The Folger Shakespeare Library.

—. 'John Payne Collier's Great Forgery'. *Studies in Bibliography*, xxiv (1971), 1–26.

DAWSON, GILES E., and LAETITIA KENNEDY-SKIPTON. *Elizabethan Handwriting 1500–1650: A Manual.* New York, 1966.

DAWSON, GILES E. 'Theobald, *table/babbled*, and *Sir Thomas More*'. *Times Literary Supplement*, 22 April 1977, p. 484.

DE BEAU CHESNE, JOHN, and JOHN BAILDON. *A Booke Containing Divers Sortes of Hands, as Well the English as French Secretarie.* 1571.

DEELMAN, CHRISTIAN. *The Great Shakespeare Jubilee.* London and New York, 1964.

The Defence of Conny-Catching or A Confutation of Those Two Injurious Pamphlets Published by R. G. Against the Practitioners of Many Nimble-Witted and Mysticall Sciences. By Cuthbert Cunny-Catcher. 1592.

DE GROOT, JOHN HENRY. *The Shakespeares and 'The Old Faith'.* New York, 1946.

DE LUNA, BARBARA N. *The Queen Declined: An Interpretation of Willobie His Avisa.* Oxford, 1970.

DENNIS, JOHN. *The Comical Gallant: or The Amours of Sir John Falstaffe. A Comedy. As It Is Acted at the Theatre Royal in Drury-Lane. By His Majesty's Servants. By Mr. Dennis. To Which Is Added, a Large Account of the Taste in Poetry, and Causes of the Degeneracy of It.* 1702.

[DENNIS, JOHN]. *The Person of Quality's Answer to Mr. Collier's Letter, Being a Disswasive from the Play-House.* 1704.

'Did Shakespeare Pen the "Million-Dollar Dot"?'. *Christian Science Monitor, Eastern Edition*, 30 July 1971, pp.1–2.

'A Document Concerning Shakespeare's Garden'. *The Huntington Library Bulletin*, no. 1 (1931), 199–201.

[DOWDALL, JOHN]. *Traditionary Anecdotes of Shakespeare. Collected in Warwickshire, in the Year MDCXCIII. Now First Published from the Original Manuscript.* 1838.

DOWDEN, EDWARD. *Shakspere: A Critical Study of His Mind and Art.* 1875.

DOWELL, STEPHEN. *A History of Taxation and Taxes in England from the Earliest Times to the Present Day.* 4 vols. 1884; 2nd ed. rev. and altered, 1888.

[DOWNES, JOHN]. *Roscius Anglicanus, or An Historical Review of the Stage: After It Had Been Suppres'd by Means of the Late Unhappy Civil War, Begun in 1641, till the Time of King Charles the IIs. Restoration in May 1660. Giving an Account of Its Rise Again . . . The Names of the Principal Actors and Actresses . . .With the Names of the Most Taking Plays . . . from 1660, to 1706.* 1708.

DRAYTON, MICHAEL. *Poly-Olbion, or a Chorographical Description of Great Britaine.* [1612].

DRYDEN, JOHN. *Works.* Gen. eds. Edward Niles Hooker and H. T. Swedenberg, Jr. 10 vols. Berkeley and London, 1956–76.

DUFF, E. GORDON. *A Century of the English Book Trade. Short Notices of All Printers, Stationers, Book-Binders, and Others Connected with It from the Issue of the First Dated Book in 1457 to the Incorporation of the Company of Stationers in 1557.* The Bibliographical Society. 1905.

DUGDALE, SIR WILLIAM. *The Antiquities of Warwickshire Illustrated: From Records, Leiger-Books, Manuscripts, Charters, Evidences, Tombes, and Armes: Beautified with Maps, Prospects and Portraictures.* 1656.

—. *The Life, Diary, and Correspondence of Sir William Dugdale, Knight, Sometime Garter Principal King of Arms. With an Appendix, Containing an Account of His Published Works, an Index to his Manuscript Collections, Copies of Monumental Inscriptions to the Memory of the Dugdale Family, and Heraldic Grants and Pedigrees.* Ed. William Hamper. 1827.

DYCE, ALEXANDER. *Strictures on Mr. Collier's New Edition of Shakespeare, 1858.* 1859.

EAGLE, RODERICK L. 'Travels of a "Shakspere" Signature'. *The Daily Telegraph*, 24 August 1971, p. 12.

[EARLE, JOHN]. *Micro-Cosmographie. Or, a Peece of the World Discovered; in Essayes and Characters. Newly Composed for the Northerne Parts of This Kingdome.* 1628.

ECCLES, AUDREY. 'Running of the Reins'. *Times Literary Supplement*, 17 May 1974, p. 527.

ECCLES, MARK. Review of E. R. C. Brinkworth, *Shakespeare and the Bawdy Court of Stratford. Modern Language Review*, lxix (1974), 373–4.

—. *Shakespeare in Warwickshire.* Madison, Wisc., 1961.

EDMOND, MARY. 'Pembroke's Men'. *Review of English Studies*, n.s., xxv (1974), 129–36.

—. 'Simon Forman's Vade-Mecum'. *The Book Collector*, xxvi (1977), 44–60.

ELIOT, JOHN. *The Survay or Topographical Description of France: With a New Mappe . . . for the Surveying of Every . . . Country, Cittye, Fortresse, River, Mountaine, and Forrest.* 1592; 2nd. ed. 1593.

ELIZABETH I, QUEEN. *Injunctions Geven by the Queenes Majestie. Anno Domini. 1559.* [1559?].

ELLRODT, ROBERT. 'Self-Consciousness in Montaigne and Shakespeare'. *Shakespeare Survey 28* (Cambridge, 1975), pp. 37–50.

ELTON, CHARLES ISAAC. *William Shakespeare: His Family and Friends.* Ed. A. Hamilton Thompson. London and New York, 1904.

ELYOT, THOMAS. *The Boke Named the Governour.* 1531.

ENGLAND, MARTHA WINBURN. *Garrick's Jubilee.* Columbus, 1964.

EVANS, N. E. *Shakespeare in the Public Records.* Public Record Office Handbooks, no. 5. 1964.

EYRE, G. E. B., and C. R. RIVINGTON. *A Transcript of the Registers of the Worshipful Company of Stationers: From 1640–1708 A.D.* 3 vols. 1913–14.

FAIRFAX-LUCY, ALICE. *Charlecote and the Lucys: The Chronicle of an English Family.* 1958.

FARR, HARRY. 'Philip Chetwind and the Allott Copyrights'. *The Library*, 4th ser., xv (1934–5), 129–60.

FERGUSON, W. CRAIG. *Valentine Simmes: Printer to Drayton, Shakespeare, Chapman, Greene, Dekker, Middleton, Daniel, Jonson, Marlowe, Marston, Heywood, and Other Elizabethans.* Bibliographical Society of the University of Virginia. Charlottesville, 1968.

FERNE, SIR JOHN. *The Blazon of Gentrie: Devided into Two Parts. The First Named The Glorie of Generositie. The Second, Lacyes Nobilitie. Comprehending Discourses of Armes and of Gentry. Wherein Is Treated of the Beginning, Parts, and Degrees of Gentlenesse, with Her Lawes: Of the Bearing, and Blazon of Cote-Armors: Of the Lawes of Armes, and of Combats.* 1586.

FINKELPEARL, PHILIP J. 'Henry Walley of the Stationers' Company and John Marston'. *The Papers of the Bibliographical Society of America*, lvi (1962), 366–8.

FISHER, SIDNEY. *The Theatre, the Curtain & the Globe.* Montreal, 1964.

FORREST, H. E. *The Old Houses of Stratford-upon-Avon.* [1925].

FOX, LEVI. *Anne Hathaway's Cottage: A Pictorial Guide.* A 'Wensum Series Colour Book'. Norwich, 1963.

—. *The Borough Town of Stratford-upon-Avon.* Stratford-upon-Avon, 1953.

—. 'An Early Copy of Shakespeare's Will'. *Shakespeare Survey 4* (Cambridge, 1951), pp. 69–77.

—. 'The Heritage of Shakespeare's Birthplace'. *Shakespeare Survey 1* (Cambridge, 1948), pp. 79–88.

—. *The Shakespearian Properties.* Norwich, [1964?].

FREEMAN, ARTHUR. 'Notes on the Text of "2 Henry VI", and the "Upstart Crow"', *Notes and Queries*, ccxiii (1968), 128–30.

FRENCH, G. R. *Shakspeareana Genealogica. Part I. Identification of the Dramatis Personae in Shakspeare's Historical Plays: from K. John to K. Henry VIII. Notes on Characters in Macbeth and Hamlet. Persons and Places Belonging to Warwickshire, Alluded to in Several Plays. Part II. The Shakspeare and Arden Families, and Their Connections: With Tables of Descent.* 1869.

FRIEND, GEORGE M. 'A Possible Portrait of Anne Hathaway'. *Philobiblon*, ix (1972), 44–51.

FRIPP, EDGAR I. *Master Richard Quyny, Bailiff of Stratford-upon-Avon and Friend of William Shakespeare.* 1924.

—. *Shakespeare, Man and Artist.* 2 vols. 1938.

—. *Shakespeare Studies, Biographical and Literary.* 1930.

FRYE, ROLAND MUSHAT. *Shakespeare and Christian Doctrine.* Princeton, 1963.

FULLER, THOMAS. *The Church-History of Britain; from the Birth of Jesus Christ, untill the Year M.DC.XLVIII.* 1655.

—. *The History of the Worthies of England.* 1662.

—. *The Holy State.* Cambridge, 1642. [In five books; book five has a special title page, *The Profane State.*]

FULLOM, S. W. *History of William Shakespeare, Player and Poet, with New Facts and Traditions.* 1862.

GAEDERTZ, KARL THEODOR. *Zur Kenntnis der altenglischen Bühne, nebst andern Beiträgen zur Shakespeare-Litteratur. Mit der ersten authentischen innern ansicht des Schwan-theaters in London und Nachbildung von Lucas Cranachs Pyramus und Thisbe.* Bremen, 1888.

GEORGE, MARY DOROTHY. *Catalogue of Political and Personal Satires preserved in the Department of Prints and Drawings in the British Museum.* Vol. vii, 1793–1800. 1942.

Gesta Grayorum; or, The History of the High and Mighty Prince Henry, Prince of Purpoole, Anno Domini 1594. Ed. Desmond Bland. English Reprint Series, no. 22. Liverpool, 1968.

GIUSEPPI, M. S. 'The Exchequer Documents Relative to Shakespeare's Residence in Southwark'. *Transactions of the London and Middlesex Archaeological Society*, n.s., v (1929), 281–8.

GRAY, JOSEPH WILLIAM. *Shakespeare's Marriage, His Departure from Stratford and Other Incidents in His Life.* 1905.

The Great Frost; Cold Doings in London. 1608.

GREBANIER, BERNARD. *The Great Shakespeare Forgery: A New Look at the Career of William Henry Ireland.* 1966.

GREENE, JOSEPH. *Correspondence of the Reverend Joseph Greene, Parson, Schoolmaster, and Antiquary, 1712–1790.* Ed. Levi Fox. Great Britain Historical Manuscripts Commission. Dugdale Society Publications, vol. 23. 1965.

GREENE, ROBERT. *The Plays & Poems.* Ed. J. Churton Collins. 2 vols. Oxford, 1905.

—. *Greenes Groats-Worth of Witte, Bought with a Million of Repentance. Describing the Follie of Youth, the Falshood of Makeshifte Flatterers, the Miserie of the Negligent, and Mischiefes of Deceiving Courtezans. Written before His Death and Published at His Dyeing Request.* 1592.

—. *Greenes Never Too Late. Or, a Powder of Experience Sent to All Youthfull Gentlemen.* 2 pts. 1590.

GREENE, THOMAS. *A Poets Vision, and a Princes Glorie.* 1603.

Greenes Newes Both from Heaven and Hell 1593 and Greenes Funeralls 1594. Ed. R. B. McKerrow. 1911.

GREENWOOD, SIR GRANVILLE GEORGE. *Is There a Shakespeare Problem? With a Reply to Mr. J. M. Robertson and Mr. Andrew Lang.* 1916.

GREG, W. W. *A Bibliography of the English Printed Drama to the Restoration.* The Bibliographical Society. 4 vols. Oxford, 1939–59.
—. *The Shakespeare First Folio: Its Bibliographical and Textual History.* Oxford, 1955.
—. *Some Aspects and Problems of London Publishing between 1550 and 1650.* Oxford, 1956.
—. 'The Two John Busby's'. *The Library*, 4th ser., xxiv (1943), 81–6.
GREG, W. W., and E. BOSWELL, eds. *Records of the Court of the Stationers' Company, 1576 to 1602, from Register B.* The Bibliographical Society. 1930.
Grolier Club, New York. *Catalogue of an Exhibition Illustrative of the Text of Shakespeare's Plays as Published in Edited Editions; Together with a Large Collection of Engraved Portraits of the Poet.* New York, 1916.
[GUILPIN, EDWARD]. *Skialetheia or, A Shadowe of Truth, in Certaine Epigrams and Satyres.* 1598.
GURR, ANDREW. 'Shakespeare's First Poem: Sonnet 145'. *Essays in Criticism*, xxi (1971), 221–6.
HAAKER, ANNE. 'The Plague, the Theater, and the Poet'. *Renaissance Drama*, n.s., i (Evanston, 1968), pp. 283–306.
HALES, JOHN W. 'London Residences of Shakspeare'. *The Athenaeum*, no. 3987, 26 March 1904, 401–2.
HALL, EDGAR VINE. *Testamentary Papers.* Vols. i and ii, 1933; vol. iii, 1937.
HALL, JOHN. *Select Observations on English Bodies: or, Cures Both Empericall and Historicall, Performed upon Very Eminent Persons in Desperate Diseases.* Trans. James Cooke. 1657.
HALLIDAY, FRANK. *A Shakespeare Companion, 1564–1964.* 1952; rev. ed. 1964.
HALLIWELL-PHILLIPPS, JAMES ORCHARD. *A Calendar of the Shakespearean Rarities, Drawings and Engravings, Preserved at Hollingbury Copse, Near Brighton.* 1887; 2nd ed. Ernest E. Baker, 1891. [Books prior to 1874 are under the name of James Orchard Halliwell.]
—. *A Descriptive Calendar of the Ancient Manuscripts and Records in the Possession of the Corporation of Stratford-upon-Avon; Including Notices of Shakespeare and His Family, and of Several Persons Connected with the Poet.* 1863.
—. *A Facsimile of the Deed of Bargain and Sale of Shakespeare's Blackfriars Estate, That Which Was Conveyed to the Poet and Trustees on March the 10th, 1613; from the Original Indenture, Which Was Shortly Afterwards Enrolled in the Court of Chancery, and Is Now Preserved at Hollingbury Copse, Brighton.* Brighton, 1884.
—. *A Fragment of Mr. J. O. Halliwell's 'Illustrations of the Life of Shakespeare'.* 1874.
—. *An Historical Account of the New Place, Stratford-upon-Avon, the Last Residence of Shakespeare.* 1864.
—. *Illustrations of the Life of Shakespeare in a Discursive Series of Essays on a Variety of Subjects Connected with the Personal and Literary History of the Great Dramatist.* 1874.
—. Letter to J. Payne Collier dated 18 December 1847. The Folger Shakespeare Library; shelfmark: MS. Y.c.1207 (1–2).
—. Letter to William Grose dated 28 July 1886. The Folger Shakespeare Library; shelfmark: MS. Y.c.1225 (1).
—. *The Life of William Shakespeare. Including Many Particulars Respecting the Poet and His Family Never before Published.* 1848.
—. *Observations on Some of the Manuscript Emendations of the Text of Shakespeare, and Are They Copyright?* 1853.
—. *Observations on the Shaksperian Forgeries at Bridgewater House; Illustrative of a Facsimile of the Spurious Letter of H.S.* 1853.
—. *On the Character of Sir John Falstaff, as Originally Exhibited by Shakespeare in the Two Parts of King Henry IV.* 1841.
—. *Outlines of the Life of Shakespeare.* 2 vols. 1881; 7th ed., 1887.
—. *Shakespeare's Grave. Notes on Traditions That Were Current at Stratford-on-Avon, in the Latter Part of the Seventeenth Century, Now First Printed from the Original Manuscript Preserved in the Bodleian Library.* Brighton, 1884.
—. 'A Shakespearian Discovery'. *The Athenaeum*, no. 1905, 30 April 1864, 612–13.
—. *Shakespearian Facsimiles; a Collection of Curious Documents, Plans, Signatures, &c., Illustrative of the Biography of Shakespeare and the History of His Family, from the Originals Chiefly Preserved at Stratford-on-Avon.* 1863.
HAMER, DOUGLAS. Review of S. Schoenbaum, *Shakespeare's Lives* (1970). *Review of English Studies*, n.s., xxii (1971), 482–5.
HAMILTON, N. E. S. A. *An Inquiry into the Genuineness of the Manuscript Corrections in Mr. J. Payne Collier's Annotated Shakspere, Folio, 1632; and of Certain Shaksperian Documents Likewise Published by Mr. Collier.* 1860.
[HANDS, A. C.]. *A Short History of Stratford-on-Avon Written in Ballad Form by an Old Warwickshire Boy.* Stratford-on-Avon, 1926.
HANLEY, HUGH A. 'Shakespeare's Family in Stratford Records'. *Times Literary Supplement*, 21 May 1964, p. 441.
HARBAGE, ALFRED. *Shakespeare and the Rival Traditions.* New York, 1952.
HARDING, EDWARD. See *Shakespeare Illustrated.*
HARRISON, G. B. *Shakespeare under Elizabeth.* New York, 1933.
HARRISON, WILLIAM. 'The Description of England'. Raphael Holinshed. *The First and Second Volumes of Chronicles.* Vol. i, 1587, pp. 131–250.
HART, ALFRED. *Shakespeare and the Homilies, and Other Pieces of Research into the Elizabethan Drama.* Melbourne, 1934.

HARVEY, GABRIEL. *Foure Letters, and Certaine Sonnets: Especially Touching Robert Greene, and Other Parties, by Him Abused: but Incidently of Divers Excellent Persons, and Some Matters of Note.* 1592.
HAYES, JOHN. 'Claude de Jongh'. *The Burlington Magazine*, xcviii (1956), 3–11.
HAYS, MICHAEL L. 'Shakespeare's Hand in *Sir Thomas More:* Some Aspects of the Paleographic Argument'. *Shakespeare Studies*, viii (New York, 1975), pp. 241–53.
HEARNE, THOMAS. *Remarks and Collections of Thomas Hearne.* Ed. C. E. Doble. Oxford Historical Society, vol. ii. Oxford, 1886.
HEBEL, J. WILLIAM. 'Nicholas Ling and *Englands Helicon*'. *The Library*, 4th ser., v (1924–5), 153–60.
HENSLOWE, PHILIP. *The Diary of Philip Henslowe, from 1591 to 1609.* Ed. J. Payne Collier. Shakespeare Society Publications, no. 28. 1845.
—. *Diary.* Ed. R. A. Foakes and R. T. Rickert. Cambridge, 1961.
—. *The Henslowe Papers.* 2 vols. 1977.
HENTZNER, PAUL. *Paul Hentzner's Travels in England, During the Reign of Queen Elizabeth, Translated by Horace, Late Earl of Orford, and First Printed by Him at Strawberry Hill: to Which Is Now Added, Sir Robert Naunton's Fragmenta Regalia; or, Observations on Queen Elizabeth's Times and Favourites; with Portraits and Views.* Trans. Richard Bentley. 1797.
HEYLYN, PETER. *Miypoxosmos. A Little Description of the Great World.* 1621; rev. ed. Oxford, 1625.
HEYWOOD, THOMAS. *An Apology for Actors. Containing Three Briefe Treatises. 1. Their Antiquity. 2. Their Ancient Dignity. 3. The True Use of Their Quality.* 1612.
HIND, ARTHUR M. *Engraving in England in the Sixteenth & Seventeenth Centuries: A Descriptive Catalogue with Introductions.* Completed by Margery Corbett and Michael Norton. 3 vols. Cambridge, 1952–64.
—. *Wenceslaus Hollar and His Views of London and Windsor in the Seventeenth Century.* 1922.
HINMAN, CHARLTON. *The Printing and Proof-Reading of the First Folio of Shakespeare.* 2 vols. Oxford, 1963.
HODGES, C. WALTER. *The Globe Restored: A Study of the Elizabethan Theatre.* 1953; 2nd ed. London and New York, 1968.
—. *Shakespeare's Second Globe: The Missing Monument.* 1973.
HOLINSHED, RAPHAEL. *The Firste Volume of the Chronicles of England, Scotlande, and Irelande.* 1577.
HOLLAR, WENCESLAUS. *Long Bird's-Eye View of London from Bankside.* London and Antwerp, 1647.
HOTSON, LESLIE. 'A Great Shakespeare Discovery'. *The Atlantic Monthly*, cxlviii (1931), 419–36.
—. *Mr. W. H.* 1964.
—. *Shakespeare Versus Shallow.* London and Boston, 1931.
—. *Shakespeare's Sonnets Dated, and Other Essays.* London and New York, 1949.
—. '"This Wooden O": Shakespeare's Curtain Theatre Identified'. *The Times*, 26 March 1954, pp. 7, 14.
HOWELL, JAMES. *Londinopolis; an Historicall Discourse; or, Perlustration of the City of London, the Imperial Chamber, and Chief Emporium of Great Britain: Whereunto Is Added Another of the City of Westminster, with the Courts of Justice, Antiquities, and New Buildings Thereunto Belonging.* 1657.
HUBER, R. A. 'On Looking over Shakespeare's "Secretarie"'. *Stratford Papers on Shakespeare, 1960.* Ed. B. A. W. Jackson. Toronto, 1961, pp. 52–70.
HUNTER, JOSEPH. *New Illustrations of the Life, Studies, and Writings of Shakespeare. Supplementary to All the Editions.* 2 vols. 1845.
INGLEBY, C. M. *A Complete View of the Shakspere Controversy, Concerning the Authenticity and Genuineness of Manuscript Matter Affecting the Works and Biography of Shakspere, Pub. by Mr. J. Payne Collier as the Fruits of His Researches.* 1861.
—, ed. *Shakespeare and the Enclosure of Common Fields at Welcombe, Being a Fragment of the Private Diary of Thomas Greene, Town Clerk of Stratford-upon-Avon, 1614–1617.* Birmingham, 1885.
—. *Shakespeare; the Man and the Book: Being a Collection of Occasional Papers on the Bard and His Writings.* 2 vols. 1877–81.
—. *Shakespeare's Centurie of Prayse; Being Materials for a History of Opinion on Shakespeare and His Works, A. D. 1591–1693.* Ed. Lucy Toulmin Smith. New Shakspere Society Publications, ser. iv: Shakspere Allusion-Books, no. 2. 1879.
—. *The Shakspeare Fabrications, or the MS. Notes of the Perkins Folio Shown to Be of Recent Origin. With an Appendix on the Authorship of the Ireland Forgeries.* 1859.
INGRAM, WILLIAM. 'The Playhouse at Newington Butts: A New Proposal'. *Shakespeare Quarterly*, xxi (1970), 385–98.
IRELAND, SAMUEL. *An Investigation of Mr. Malone's Claim to the Character of Scholar, or Critic, Being an Examination of His Inquiry into the Authenticity of the Shakspeare Manuscripts, &c.* n.d. [1797?].
—. Letter to G. Charles George dated 26 June 1797. Transcript included in a grangerized version of William Ireland, *Miscellaneous Papers and Legal Instruments under the Hand and Seal of William Shakespeare.* 1796. The Folger Shakespeare Library; shelfmark: MS. S.b.119.
—. *Mr. Ireland's Vindication of His Conduct, Respecting the Publication of the Supposed Shakspeare MSS., Being a Preface or Introduction to a Reply to the Critical Labors of Mr. Malone, in His 'Enquiry into the Authenticity of Certain Papers, &c. &c.'.* 1796.
—. Obituary. *The Gentleman's Magazine*, 2nd ser., lxx, pt. ii (1800), 901–2.

—. *A Picturesque Tour through Holland, Brabant, and Part of France; Made in the Autumn of 1789*. 2 vols. 1790.

—. *Picturesque Views on the Upper, or Warwickshire Avon, from Its Source at Naseby to Its Junction with the Severn at Tewkesbury: With Observations on the Public Buildings, and Other Works of Art in Its Vicinity*. 1795. [Copy annotated by Edmond Malone, in British Library: shelfmark C.182.aaF.].

IRELAND, WILLIAM-HENRY. *An Authentic Account of the Shaksperian Manuscripts, &c.* 1796.

[IRELAND, WILLIAM-HENRY]. *Chalcographimania; or, The Portrait-Collector and Printseller's Chronicle, with Infatuations of Every Description*. By Satiricus Sculptor, esq. 1814.

—. *The Confessions of William-Henry Ireland, Containing the Particulars of His Fabrication of the Shakspeare Manuscripts; together with Anecdotes and Opinions . . . of Many Distinguished Persons in the Literary, Political, and Theatrical World*. 1805.

—. *Full and Explanatory Account of the Shakesperian Forgery*. Unpublished manuscript in the Hyde Collection at Four Oaks Farm in New Jersey.

[IRELAND, WILLIAM-HENRY]. *Miscellaneous Papers and Legal Instruments under the Hand and Seal of William Shakespeare: Including the Tragedy of King Lear and a Small Fragment of Hamlet, from the Original MSS. in the Possession of Samuel Ireland, of Norfolk Street*. 1796. [A grangerized copy in the Folger Shakespeare Library, shelfmark: MS. S.b.119, contains a transcript of Samuel Ireland's letter, dated 26 June 1797, to G. Charles George.]

[IRELAND, WILLIAM-HENRY]. *Vortigern, an Historical Tragedy, in Five Acts; Represented at the Theatre Royal, Drury Lane. And Henry the Second, an Historical Drama. Supposed to be Written by the Author of Vortigern*. [1799].

IRVING, WASHINGTON. 'Stratford-on-Avon'. *Rip Van Winkle, and Other Sketches*. New York, 1882, pp. 154–79.

JACKSON, WILLIAM A., ed. *Records of the Court of the Stationers' Company 1602 to 1640*. Bibliographical Society Publications for the years 1955 and 1956. 1957.

JAGGARD, WILLIAM. *Shakespeare Bibliography: a Dictionary of Every Known Issue of the Writings of Our National Poet and of Recorded Opinion thereon in the English Language*. Stratford-upon-Avon, 1911.

JAMES, HENRY. 'In Warwickshire'. *English Hours*. 1905.

JAMES, RICHARD. *The Poems, etc., of Richard James, B.D. (1592–1638)*. Ed. Alexander B. Grosart. 1880.

JARRATT, J. ERNEST. 'The Grafton Portrait'. *Bulletin of the John Rylands Library*, xxix (1945–6), 225–9.

JENKINS, HAROLD. 'A Supplement to Sir Walter Greg's Edition of *Sir Thomas More*'. Malone Society Collections, vol. 6. 1961 (1962), pp. 177–92.

JENKINSON, HILARY. 'Elizabethan Handwritings: A Preliminary Sketch'. *The Library*, 4th ser., iii (1922–3), 1–34.

[JENNENS, CHARLES]. *The Tragedy of King Lear, as Lately Published, Vindicated from the Abuse of the Critical Reviewers*. 1772.

JOHNSON, DAVID J. *Southwark and the City*. 1969.

JONSON, BEN. *Workes*. 1616; 1640.

—. *Ben Jonson*. Eds. C. H. Herford and Percy and Evelyn Simpson. 11 vols. Oxford, 1925–52.

JORDAN, JOHN. *Original Collections on Shakespeare & Stratford-on-Avon, by John Jordan, the Stratford Poet*. Ed. James O. Halliwell[-Phillipps]. 1864.

—. *Welcombe Hills, near Stratford upon Avon, a Poem, Historical and Descriptive*. 1777.

JOSEPH, HARRIET. *Shakespeare's Son-in-Law: John Hall, Man and Physician*. Hamden, Conn., 1964. [With a facsimile of the 2nd ed. of Hall's *Select Observations on English Bodies*.]

KAY, THOMAS. *The Story of the 'Grafton' Portrait of William Shakespeare . . . with an Account of the Sack and Destruction of the Manor House of Grafton Regis by the Parliamentary Forces on Christmas Eve, 1643*. 1914 [i.e. 1915].

KINGMAN, TRACY. *An Authenticated Contemporary Portrait of Shakespeare*. New York, 1932.

KIRSCHBAUM, LEO. 'The Copyright of Elizabethan Plays'. *The Library*, 5th ser., xiv (1959), 231–50.

—. *Shakespeare and the Stationers*. Columbus, Ohio, 1955.

KIRWOOD, A. E. M. 'Richard Field, Printer, 1589–1624'. *The Library*, 4th ser., xii (1931–2), 1–39.

KNIGHT, W. NICHOLAS. 'The Seventh Shakespeare Signature'. *The Shakespeare Newsletter*, xxi, (1971), 25.

—. *Shakespeare's Hidden Life: Shakespeare at the Law, 1585–1595*. New York, 1973.

LAMBARDE, WILLIAM. *Archaionomia*. 1568. [The doubtful Shakespeare signature is on the title-page of the copy of *Archaionomia* owned by the Folger Shakespeare Library; shelfmark: MS. V.a.230]

[LANEHAM, ROBERT]. *A Letter: whearin, Part of the Entertainment untoo the Queenȝ Majesty, at Killingwoorth Castl, in Warwik Sheer in this Soomerȝ Progress 1575 Iȝ Signified, from a Freend Officer Attendant in the Coourt untoo Hiȝ Freend a Citizen and Merchant of London*. [1575].

LANGBAINE, GERARD. *The Lives and Characters of the English Dramatick Poets. Also an Exact Account of All the Plays That Were Ever Yet Printed in the English Tongue*. Ed. Charles Gildon. 1699.

LATHAM, JOHN. *Facts and Opinions Concerning Diabetes*. 1811.

LAVIN, J. A. 'Shakespeare and the Second Blackfriars'. *Elizabethan Theatre III*. Ed. David Galloway. Toronto, 1973, pp. 66–81.

LAW, ERNEST. *Shakespeare as a Groom of the Chamber*. 1910.

LEE, SIDNEY. 'A Discovery about Shakespeare'. *The Times*, 27 December 1905, p. 9.

—. 'An Elizabethan Bookseller'. *Bibliographica*, i (1895), 474–98.
—. *A Life of William Shakespeare*. 1898; new ed. 1915; 4th ed. of rev. version, 1925.
—. *Stratford-on-Avon from the Earliest Times to the Death of Shakespeare*. 1885; new ed., Philadelphia, 1904.
LEISHMAN, J. B., ed. *The Three Parnassus Plays (1598–1601)*. 1949.
LELAND, JOHN. *The Itinerary of John Leland in or about the Years 1535–1543. Parts I–II*. Ed. Lucy Toulmin Smith. 5 vols. 1907–10.
LEVIN, RICHARD. 'The King James Version of *Measure for Measure*'. *Clio*, iii (1974), 129–63.
LEWIS, B. ROLAND. *The Shakespeare Documents: Facsimiles, Transliterations, Translations & Commentary*. 2 vols. Stanford and London, 1940.
LEWIS, C. S. *English Literature in the Sixteenth Century, Excluding Drama*. Oxford History of English Literature, vol. 3. Oxford, 1954.
[LILY, WILLIAM]. *A Shorte Introduction of Grammar Generally to Be Used: Compiled . . . for . . . Those That Intende to Attaine the Knowledge of the Latine Tongue*. 1549; 1566–7.
'Literary Gossip'. *The Athenaeum*, no. 2280 (8 July 1871), 51–2. [The first paragraph of the column is the report of a note from Halliwell-Phillipps to *The Athenaeum* stating that Shakespeare attended on the Spanish ambassador at Somerset House in August, 1604.]
'Literary Notes and News'. *The Westminster Gazette*, xxiv (31 October 1904), p. 4. [Andrew Clark's extracts from the Plume MSS. communicated by F. S. Furnivall.]
LOMAS, S. C., ed. *Calendar of the Manuscripts of the Marquis of Bath, Preserved at Longleat, Wiltshire*. Vol. 2. Dublin, 1907.
London and Its Environs Described. Containing an Account of Whatever Is Most Remarkable for Grandeur, Elegance, Curiosity or Use, in the City and in the Country Twenty Miles Around It. Comprehending Also Whatever Is Most Material in the History and Antiquities of This Great Metropolis. Decorated and Illustrated with a Great Number of Views in Perspective, Engraved from Original Drawings, Taken on Purpose for This Work. Together with a Plan of London, a Map of Its Environs, and Several Other Useful Cuts. 6 vols. 1761.
LUCY, MARY ELIZABETH. *Biography of the Lucy Family of Charlecote Park, in the County of Warwick*. 1862.
LUTHER, MARTIN. *Dris Martini Lutheri Colloquia Mensalia: or, Dr. Martin Luther's Divine Discourses at His Table, . . . Collected First Together by Dr. Antonius Lauterbach*. Tr. Henrie Bell. 1652.
MACHYN, HENRY. *The Diary of Henry Machyn, Citizen and Merchant-Taylor of London, from A. D. 1550 to A. D. 1563*. Ed. John Gough Nichols. Camden Society Publications, no. 42. 1848.
MCKERROW, R. B. 'Edward Allde as a Typical Trade Printer'. *The Library*, 4th ser., x (1929–30), 121–62.
—. *Printers' & Publishers' Devices in England & Scotland 1485–1640*. The Bibliographical Society, no. 16. 1913.
MCKERROW, R. B., et al. *A Dictionary of Printers and Booksellers in England, Scotland and Ireland, and of Foreign Printers of English Books, 1557–1640*. The Bibliographical Society. 1910.
MCMANAWAY, JAMES G. 'John Shakespeare's "Spiritual Testament"'. *Shakespeare Quarterly*, xviii (1967), 197–205. Rpt. *Studies in Shakespeare, Bibliography, and Theater*. Eds. Richard Hosley, Arthur C. Kirsch, and John W. Velz. New York, 1969, pp. 293–304.
—. 'Little Crown Street, Westminster'. *Notes and Queries*, clxxvii (1939), 478.
MADAN, FALCONER. 'Two Lost Causes and What May Be Said in Defence of Them'. *The Library*, 3rd ser., ix (1918), 89–105.
MADDEN, SIR FREDERIC. *Observations on an Autograph of Shakspere, and the Orthography of His Name*. 1838.
MAIR, JOHN. *The Fourth Forger: William Ireland and the Shakespeare Papers*. 1938.
MALONE, EDMOND. *An Inquiry into the Authenticity of Certain Miscellaneous Papers and Legal Instruments, Published Dec. 24, MDCCXCV. and Attributed to Shakspeare, Queen Elizabeth, and Henry, Earl of Southampton: Illustrated by Fac-similes of the Genuine Hand-Writing of That Nobleman, and of Her Majesty; a New Fac-simile of the Hand-Writing of Shakspeare, Never before Exhibited; and Other Authentick Documents: in a Letter Addressed to the Right Hon. James, Earl of Charlemont*. 1796.
—. Letter to Bishop Percy dated 21 September 1793. *The Correspondence of Thomas Percy & Edmond Malone*. Ed. Arthur Tillotson. *The Percy Letters*. Gen. eds. David Nichol Smith and Cleanth Brooks. 7 vols. 1944–77. Vol. 1, Baton Rouge, 1944, pp. 58–61.
—. *The Life of William Shakspeare, by the Late Edmond Malone. And an Essay on the Phraseology and Metre of the Poet and His Contemporaries, by James Boswell*. 1821.
—. *Original Letters from Edmund Malone, the Editor of Shakespeare, to John Jordan, the Poet, Now First Printed from the Autograph Manuscripts Preserved at Stratford-Upon-Avon*. Ed. J. O. Halliwell[-Phillipps.] 1864.
—. *Supplement to the Edition of Shakspeare's Plays Published in 1778, by Samuel Johnson and George Steevens. Containing Additional Observations by Several of the Former Commentators: to which Are Subjoined the Genuine Poems of the Same Author, and Seven Plays That Have Been Ascribed to Him*. 2 vols. 1780.
MANNINGHAM, JOHN. *Diary of John Manningham, of the Middle Temple, and of Bradbourne, Kent, Barrister-at-Law, 1602–1603*. Ed. John Bruce. The Camden Society. 1868.
MARCHAM, FRANK, ed. *William Shakespeare and His Daughter Susannah*. 1931.
MARDER, LOUIS. Editorial comment following W. Nicholas Knight, 'The Seventh Shakespeare Signature'. *The Shakespeare Newsletter*, xxi (1971), 25.
MARTIN, E. M. 'Shakespeare in a Seventeenth Century Manuscript'. *English Review*, li (1930), 484–9.

MATHEW, FRANK. *An Image of Shakespeare.* 1922.

MEHEW, ERNEST. 'Running of the Reins'. *Times Literary Supplement*, 3 May 1974, p. 477.

MELLON, PAUL. *English Drawings and Watercolors, 1550–1850, in the Collection of Mr. and Mrs. Paul Mellon.* New York, 1972.

MERES, FRANCIS. *Palladis Tamia. Wits Treasury Being the Second Part of Wits Common Wealth.* 1598.

—. *Francis Meres's Treatise, 'Poetrie': A Critical Edition.* Ed. Don Cameron Allen. Urbana, Ill., 1933.

—. *Palladis Tamia (1598).* Ed. Don Cameron Allen. Scholars' Facsimiles and Reprints. New York, 1938.

MILLER, C. WILLIAM. 'A London Ornament Stock: 1598–1683'. *Studies in Bibliography*, vii (1955), 125–51.

MILWARD, PETER. *Shakespeare's Religious Background.* London and Bloomington, 1973.

Minutes and Accounts of the Corporation of Stratford-upon-Avon and Other Records, 1553–1620. Eds. Richard Savage and Edgar I. Fripp. Dugdale Society Publications, vols. i, iii, v, x. Oxford, 1921–9.

MORGAN, F. C. 'Honorificabilitudinitatibus'. *Notes and Queries*, ccxxiii (1978), 445.

MORGAN, PAUL. '"Our Will Shakespeare" and Lope de Vega: An Unrecorded Contemporary Document'. *Shakespeare Survey 16* (Cambridge, 1963), pp. 118–20.

MUIR, KENNETH. *Shakespeare the Professional, and Related Studies.* London and Totowa, New Jersey, 1973.

MUNRO, JOHN, ed. *The Shakspere Allusion-Book: A Collection of Allusions to Shakspere from 1591 to 1700 . . . Originally Compiled by C. M. Ingleby, Miss L. Toulmin Smith, and by Dr. F. J. Furnivall, with the Assistance of the New Shakspere Society: and Now Re-Edited, Revised, and Re-Arranged, with an Introduction.* 2 vols. London and New York, 1909; 1932.

NASH, JOSEPH. *The Mansions of England in the Olden Time.* 4 vols. 1839–49.

NASHE, THOMAS. *Works.* Ed. Ronald B. McKerrow; rev. F. P. Wilson. 5 vols. Oxford, 1958.

NETHERCOT, ARTHUR H. *Sir William D'Avenant, Poet Laureate and Playwright-Manager.* Chicago, 1938.

'A New Shakspeare Autograph'. *The Athenaeum*, no. 1944 (28 January 1865), 126–7.

NICHOLS, JOHN. *The Progresses, and Public Processions, of Queen Elizabeth. Among Which Are Interspersed Other Solemnities, Public Expenditures, and Remarkable Events, During the Reign of That Illustrious Princess.* Society of Antiquaries of London. 3 vols. 1788–1805.

NICHOLS, YVONNE. 'Bradford Rudge—Artist'. *Bedfordshire Magazine*, xvi, 123 (1977), 101–6.

NOBLE, RICHMOND. *Shakespeare's Biblical Knowledge and Use of the Book of Common Prayer, as Exemplified in the Plays of the First Folio.* Society for Promoting Christian Knowledge. London and New York, 1935.

NORDEN, JOHN. *Speculum Britanniae. The First Parte an Historicall, & Chorographicall Discription of Middlesex . . . with Direction Spedelie to Finde Anie Place Desired in the Mappe & the Distance betwene Place and Place without Compasses.* 1593.

NORRIS, J. PARKER. *The Portraits of Shakespeare.* Philadelphia, 1885.

NOSWORTHY, J. M. '*Macbeth* at the Globe'. *The Library*, 5th ser., ii (1947–8), 108–18.

—. *Shakespeare's Occasional Plays: Their Origin and Transmission.* London and New York, 1965.

'A Note on the Swan Theatre Drawing'. *Shakespeare Survey 1* (Cambridge, 1948), pp. 23–4.

NOWELL, ALEXANDER. *A Catechisme, or First Instruction and Learning of Christian Religion.* Tr. T. Norton. 1570.

—. *Catechismus Parvus Pueris Primum Latinè qui Ediscatur, Proponendus in Scholis. Latinè & Graèce.* 1573.

ORDISH, T. FAIRMAN. *Shakespeare's London: A Commentary on Shakespeare's Life and Work in London.* 1897; new ed. 1904.

[PARSONS, ROBERT]. *The Third Part of a Treatise Intituled of Three Conversions of England. Conteyninge an Examen of the Calendar or Catalogue of Protestant Saintes, Martyrs and Confessors, Divised by John Fox, and Prefixed before His Huge Volume of Actes and Monuments: With a Paralell or Comparison therof to the Catholike Roman Calendar and Saintes therin Conteyned.* [St. Omer] 1604.

PAUL, HENRY N. *The Royal Play of Macbeth: When, Why, and How It Was Written by Shakespeare.* New York, 1950.

PECK, FRANCIS. 'Explanatory or Critical Notes on Divers Passages of *Shakespeare's* Plays'. *New Memoirs of the Life and Poetical Works of Mr. John Milton.* 1740, pp. 222–54.

[PERCY, BISHOP THOMAS], ed. *Reliques of Ancient English Poetry; Consisting of Old Heroic Ballads, Songs, and Other Pieces of Our Earlier Poets, (Chiefly of the Lyric Kind.) Together with Some Few of Later Date.* 3 vols. 1765.

PHILLIPPS, THOMAS. 'A New Notice of Shakespeare'. *Archaeologia*, xxxii (1847), 444–5.

PHILLIPS, SIR RICHARD. 'Shakspeariana'. *Monthly Magazine and British Register*, xlv (1818), 1–8.

PIPER, DAVID. *O Sweet Mr. Shakespeare, I'll Have His Picture.* 1964.

PLOMER, HENRY R. *A Dictionary of the Booksellers and Printers Who Were at Work in England, Scotland and Ireland from 1641 to 1667.* The Bibliographical Society. 1907; rpt. 1968.

—et al. *A Dictionary of the Printers and Booksellers Who Were at Work in England, Scotland and Ireland from 1668 to 1725.* Ed. Arundell Esdaile. The Bibliographical Society. Oxford, 1922.

POLLARD, A. W. *Shakespeare Folios and Quartos: A Study in the Bibliography of Shakespeare's Plays, 1594–1685.* 1909.

—. *Shakespeare's Fight with the Pirates and the Problems of the Transmission of His Text.* 1917.

POLLARD, A. W., et al. *Shakespeare's Hand in the Play of Sir Thomas More: Papers by Alfred W. Pollard, W. W. Greg, E. Maunde Thompson, J. Dover Wilson and R. W. Chambers, with the Text of the Ill May Day Scenes.* Cambridge, 1923.

POLLARD, GRAHAM. 'The Company of Stationers before 1557'. *The Library*, 4th ser., xviii (1937–8), 1–38.
—. 'The Early Constitution of the Stationers' Company'. *The Library*, 4th ser., xviii (1937–8), 235–60.
POPE, ALEXANDER. *Imitations of Horace, with An Epistle to Dr. Arbuthnot and the Epilogue to the Satires*. Ed. John Butt. The Twickenham Pope, vol. 4. 2nd ed., London and New Haven, 1953.
PRICE, HEREWARD T. 'Shakespeare's Classical Scholarship'. *Review of English Studies*, n.s., ix (1958), 54–5.
QUARLES, FRANCIS. *Emblemes*. 1635.
—. *Hieroglyphikes of the Life of Man*. 1638.
RACE, SYDNEY. 'Manningham's Diary: The Case for Re-examination'. *Notes and Queries*, cxcix (1954), 380–83.
—. 'Simon Forman's "Bocke of Plaies" Examined'. *Notes and Queries*, cciii (1958), 9–14.
RALLI, AUGUSTUS. *A History of Shakespearian Criticism*. 2 vols. 1932.
RAMSEY, PAUL. 'Shakespeare and *Sir Thomas More* Revisited: or, a Mounty on the Trail'. *Papers of the Bibliographical Society of America*, lxx (1976), 333–46.
RAVENSCROFT, EDWARD. *Titus Andronicus, or The Rape of Lavinia. Acted at the Theatre Royall, a Tragedy, Alter'd from Mr. Shakespears Works*. 1687.
RAYMONT, HENRY. '"Shakspere": New Findings'. *The New York Times*, 19 August 1971, p. 40.
[REDFORD, JOHN]. *The Marriage of Wit and Wisdom, an Ancient Interlude. To Which Are Added Illustrations of Shakespeare and the Early English Drama*. Ed. J. O. Halliwell[-Phillipps]. The Shakespeare Society. 1846.
REED, JOHN CURTIS. 'Humphrey Mosely, Publisher'. *Oxford Bibliographical Society: Proceedings and Papers*, ii (1928), 61–142.
REESE, M. M. *Shakespeare: His World & His Work*. London and New York, 1953.
The Registers of Stratford-on-Avon, in the County of Warwick. Ed. Richard Savage. Parish Register Society. 3 vols. 1897–1905.
Review of A. Wivell, *An Inquiry into the History, Authenticity, and Characteristics of the Shakspeare Portraits, &c. The London Literary Gazette; and Journal of Belles Lettres, Arts, Sciences, &c.*, no. 546 (7 July 1827), 435–6.
RICHARDSON, WILLIAM. 'Shakspeare'. *The European Magazine, and London Review*, xxvi (1794), 277–82.
RINGLER, WILLIAM A., JR. 'Spenser, Shakespeare, Honor, and Worship'. *Renaissance News*, xiv (1961), 159–61.
[ROBERTS, JOHN]. *An Answer to Mr. Pope's Preface to Shakespear. In a Letter to a Friend. Being a Vindication of the Old Actors Who Were the Publishers and Performers of That Author's Plays. Whereby the Errors of Their Edition Are Further Accounted for, and Some Memoirs of Shakespear and Stage-History of His Time Are Inserted, Which Were Never before Collected and Publish'd*. By a Stroling Player. 1729.
ROCQUE, JEAN. *A Plan of the Cities of London and Westminster and Borough of Southwark, with the Contiguous Buildings, from an Actual Survey Taken by John Rocque and Engraved by John Pine*. 1746.
ROSTENBERG, LEONA. *Literary, Political, Scientific, Religious & Legal Publishing, Printing & Bookselling in England, 1551–1700: Twelve Studies*. Burt Franklin Bibliography and Reference Series, no. 56. 2 vols. New York, 1965.
ROSENBERG, MARVIN. *The Masks of Macbeth*. Berkeley, 1978.
ROWAN, D. F. 'The "Swan" Revisited'. *Research Opportunities in Renaissance Drama*, x (1967), 33–48.
ROWLANDS, SAMUEL. *The Melancholie Knight*. 1615.
ROWSE, A. L. *The England of Elizabeth: The Structure of Society*. His *The Elizabethan Age*, vol. 1. London and New York, 1950.
—. *The English Spirit: Essays in Literature and History*. 1944; rev. ed. 1966. [The first edition has the title *The English Spirit: History and Literature*.]
—. 'Secrets of Shakespeare's Landlady'. *The Times*, 23 April 1973, p. 6.
—. 'Shakespeare and Emilia'. *Times Literary Supplement*, 26 April 1974, p. 447.
—. *Shakespeare the Man*. 1973.
—. *Shakespeare's Southampton, Patron of Virginia*. 1965.
—. *Simon Forman: Sex and Society in Shakespeare's Age*. 1974.
—. *The Tower of London in the History of England*. New York, 1972.
—. *William Shakespeare: A Biography*. London and New York, 1963.
[RYAN, RICHARD]. *Dramatic Table Talk; or Scenes, Situations, & Adventures, Serious & Comic, in Theatrical History & Biography*. 3 vols. 1825.
RYE, WILLIAM BRENCHLEY, tr. and ed. *England as Seen by Foreigners in the Days of Elizabeth and James the First. Comprising Translations of the Journals of the Two Dukes of Wirtemberg in 1592 and 1610; Both Illustrative of Shakespeare. With Extracts from the Travels of Foreign Princes and Others, Copious Notes, an Introduction, and Etchings*. 1865.
RYMER, THOMAS. 'Pro Laurentio Fletcher & Willielmo Shakespeare & Aliis'. *Foedera, Conventiones, Literae, et Cujuscunque Generis Acta Publica, inter Regis Angliae, et Alios Quosvis Imperatores, Reges, Pontifices, Principes, vel Communitates, ab Inuente Saeculo Duodecimo, viz. ab Anno 1101, ad Nostra Usque Tempora, Habita aut Tractata; ex Autographis, infra Secretiores Archivorum Regiorum Thesaurarias, per Multa Saecula Reconditis, Fideliter Exscripta*. 17 vols. 1704–1717. Vol. xvi, 1715, p. 505. [Vol. xvi is misdated 1615; vol. xvii is misdated 1617; vols. xvii–xx (1726–1735) comprise a supplement covering the years 1625–1654.]

SANFORD, JOHN. *Apollinis et Musarum Euktika Eidyllia*. Oxford, [1592?]

SAVAGE, RICHARD. 'Shakspeare in Stratford: A New Residence'. *The Athenaeum*, no. 4218, 29 August 1908, 250.

SCHANZER, ERNEST. 'Thomas Platter's Observations on the Elizabethan Stage'. *Notes and Queries*, cci (1956), 465–7.

SCHOECK, R. J. Review of W. Nicholas Knight, *Shakespeare's Hidden Life: Shakespeare at the Law 1585–1595*. *Shakespeare Quarterly*, xxvi (1975), 305–7.

SCHOENBAUM, S. *Internal Evidence and Elizabethan Dramatic Authorship: An Essay in Literary History and Method*. Evanston, Ill., and London, 1966.

—. 'A New Vertue Shakespeare Portrait'. *Shakespeare Quarterly*, xxviii (1977), 85–6.

—. 'Running of the Reins'. *Times Literary Supplement*, 24 May 1974, p. 559.

—. 'Shakespeare and Jonson: Fact and Myth'. *Elizabethan Theatre II*. Ed. David Galloway. Toronto, 1970, pp. 1–19.

—. *Shakespeare's Lives*. Oxford and New York, 1970.

—. *William Shakespeare: A Documentary Life*. Oxford, 1975.

SCOTT, SIR WALTER. *Journal*. Ed. W. E. K. Anderson. Oxford, 1972.

—. *Kenilworth: A Romance*. 3 vols. 1821.

SCOTT-GILES, C. W. *Shakespeare's Heraldry*. London and New York, 1950.

SCOULOUDI, IRENE. *Panoramic Views of London, 1600–66, with Some Later Adaptations: An Annotated List*. 1953.

SCRAGG, LEAH. 'Macbeth on Horseback'. *Shakespeare Survey 26* (Cambridge, 1973), pp. 81–8.

SHAKESPEARE, WILLIAM. *Comedies, Histories & Tragedies*. 1623; 1632; 1663; 1685.

—. *Works*. Ed. Nicholas Rowe. 6 vols. 1709.

—. *Works, Volume the Seventh. Containing Venus & Adonis. Tarquin & Lucrece and His Miscellany Poems*. Ed. Charles Gildon. 1710 [i.e. 1709].

—. *Works*. Ed. Alexander Pope. 6 vols. 1725.

—. *Works*. Ed. Lewis Theobald. 7 vols. 1733; 3rd ed., 1752.

—. *Plays*. Ed. Samuel Johnson. 8 vols. 1765.

—. *Works*. Ed. Edward Capell. 10 vols. [1767–8].

—. *Works*. Ed. Sir Thomas Hanmer. 6 vols. 1744; 2nd ed., 1771.

—. *Plays*. Eds. Samuel Johnson and George Steevens. 10 vols. 1773; 2nd ed., 10 vols. 1778; 4th ed., 15 vols. 1793; 5th ed., rev. Isaac Reed, 21 vols. 1803. [1778 ed. contains a two volume *Supplement* by Malone.]

—. *Dramatic Works*. Ed. Samuel Ayscough. 3 vols. 1790.

—. *Plays and Poems*. Ed. Edmond Malone. 10 vols. 1790.

—. *Plays and Poems*. Eds. Edmond Malone and James Boswell. 21 vols. 1821.

—. *Dramatic Works*. Ed. Thomas Campbell. 1838.

—. *Works*. Ed. J. Payne Collier. 8 vols. 1842–4. [Collier's *The Life of William Shakespeare* is included in vol. i, 1844]; 2nd ed.: *Comedies, Histories, Tragedies, and Poems*. 6 vols. 1858.

—. *Works*. Ed. J. O. Halliwell[-Phillipps]. 16 vols. 1853–65.

—. *Works*. Ed. Alexander Dyce. 6 vols. 1857.

—. *Works*. Ed. Richard Grant White. 12 vols. Boston, 1865.

—. *Complete Works*. Ed. C. J. Sisson. 1954.

—. *The First Folio of Shakespeare*. Intro. Charlton Hinman. The Norton Facsimile. New York, 1968.

—. *Complete Works*. Ed. Hardin Craig; rev. David Bevington. Glenview, Ill., 1973.

—. *The Riverside Shakespeare*. Ed. G. Blakemore Evans et al. Boston, 1974.

—. *All's Well That Ends Well*. Ed. G. K. Hunter. New Arden Shakespeare. 1959.

—. 'Deposition in the Belott-Mountjoy Suit'. Transcribed in *Shakespeare Survey 3* (Cambridge, 1950), p. 13.

—. *The First Part of King Henry VI*. Ed. Andrew S. Cairncross. New Arden Shakespeare. 1962.

—. *The Second Part of King Henry VI*. Ed. J. Dover Wilson. The New Shakespeare. Cambridge, 1952.

—. *M. William Shak-speare: His True Chronicle Historie of the Life and Death of King Lear and His Three Daughters*. 1608.

—. *King Lear. A Tragedy*. Ed. Charles Jennens. 1770. [An excerpt from *Five Plays: Lear, Hamlet, Macbeth, Othello, Julius Caesar*. 2 vols. 1770–74.]

—. *The Tragedie of Macbeth*. Ed. Mark Harvey Liddell. The Elizabethan Shakspere Series, vol. i. New York, 1903.

—. *Macbeth*. Ed. Joseph Quincy Adams. Cambridge, Mass., 1931.

—. *The Merry Wives of Windsor*. Ed. J. Tonson. 1734.

—. *The Merry Wives of Windsor*. Ed. H. J. Oliver. New Arden Shakespeare. 1971.

—. *A Midsummer-Night's Dream*. Ed. Stanley Wells. New Penguin Shakespeare. Harmondsworth, 1967.

—. *Poems*. Pirated ed. by John Benson. 1640.

—. *A Collection of Poems*. Printed for Bernard Lintot. [1709?].

—. *The Poems: Venus and Adonis, Lucrece, The Passionate Pilgrim, The Phoenix and the Turtle, A Lover's Complaint*. Ed. Hyder Edward Rollins. New Variorum Edition, vol. 22. London and Philadelphia, 1938.

—. *Lucrece*. 1594.

—. *The Rape of Lucrece, Committed by Tarquin the Sixt; and the Remarkable Judgments That Befel Him for It. Whereunto Is Annexed, The Banishment of Tarquin: or, The Reward of Lust.* By J. Quarles. 1655.
—. *Sonnets.* 1609.
—. *Sonnets.* Ed. Hyder Edward Rollins. New Variorum Edition, vols. 24, 25. 2 vols. London and Philadelphia, 1944.
—. *Titus Andronicus.* Ed. J. Dover Wilson. The New Shakespeare. Cambridge, 1948. [See Edward Ravenscroft, *Titus Andronicus*, for the 1687 adaptation.]
—. *The Historie of Troylus and Cresseida.* 1609.
Shakespeare Illustrated, by an assemblage of Portraits & Views, appropriated to the Whole Suite, of our Authors Historical Dramas; to which are added Portraits of Actors, Editors, &c. 1793.
Shakespeare's England: An Account of the Life & Manners of His Age. 2 vols. Oxford, 1916.
SHAPIRO, I. A. 'The Bankside Theatres: Early Engravings'. *Shakespeare Survey 1* (Cambridge, 1948), pp. 25–37.
—. 'The "Mermaid Club"'. *Modern Language Review*, xlv (1950), 6–17.
—. 'An Original Drawing of the Globe Theatre'. *Shakespeare Survey 2* (Cambridge, 1949), pp. 21–3.
[SHIELS, ROBERT]. *The Lives of the Poets of Great Britain and Ireland, to the Time of Dean Swift. Compiled from Ample Materials Scattered in a Variety of Books, and Especially from the MS. Notes of the Late Ingenious Mr. Coxeter and Others, Collected for this Design.* Rev. Theophilus Cibber. 5 vols. 1753.
A Short-Title Catalogue of Books Printed in England, Scotland, & Ireland and of English Books Printed Abroad, 1475–1640. Comp. A. W. Pollard and G. R. Redgrave. 1926.
SIMPSON, FRANK. 'New Place: The Only Representation of Shakespeare's House, from an Unpublished Manuscript'. *Shakespeare Survey 5* (Cambridge, 1952), pp. 55–7.
SIMPSON, PERCY. 'The Play of "Sir Thomas More" and Shakespeare's Hand in It'. *The Library*, 3rd ser., viii (1917), 79–96.
—. *Proof-Reading in the Sixteenth, Seventeenth and Eighteenth Centuries.* Oxford Books on Bibliography. 1935.
—. 'Walkley's Piracy of Wither's Poems in 1620'. *The Library*, 4th ser., vi (1925–6), 271–7.
SIMPSON, RICHARD. 'Are There Any Extant MSS. in Shakespeare's Handwriting?'. *Notes and Queries*, 4th ser., viii (1871), 1–3.
SIMS, RICHARD. 'Shakspeare Documents'. *The Athenaeum*, no. 3042, 13 February 1886, 241.
SINGER, SAMUEL WELLER. *The Text of Shakespeare Vindicated from the Interpolations and Corruptions Advocated by John Payne Collier, Esq., in His Notes and Emendations.* 1853.
Sir Thomas More. A Play; Now First Printed. Ed. Alexander Dyce. Shakespeare Society Publications, no. 23. 1844.
The Book of Sir Thomas Moore. Ed. J. S. Farmer. Tudor Facsimile Texts. 1910.
The Book of Sir Thomas More. Ed. W. W. Greg. Malone Society Reprints. 1911. [The 1961 lithographic reprint contains Harold Jenkins, 'A Supplement to Sir Walter Greg's Edition of *Sir Thomas More*'.]
SISSON, CHARLES J. 'The Laws of Elizabethan Copyright: The Stationers' View'. *The Library*, 5th ser., xv (1960), 8–20.
—. 'Studies in the Life and Environment of Shakespeare Since 1900'. *Shakespeare Survey 3* (Cambridge, 1950), pp. 1–12.
SMART, JOHN SEMPLE. *Shakespeare: Truth and Tradition.* 1928.
—. 'Shakespeare's Italian Names'. *Modern Language Review*, xi (1916), 339.
SMITH, LOGAN PEARSALL, ed. *The Life and Letters of Sir Henry Wotton.* 2 vols. Oxford, 1907.
SPEAIGHT, ROBERT. *Shakespeare: The Man and His Achievement.* London and New York, 1977.
SPEDDING, JAMES. *Reviews and Discussions, Literary, Political, and Historical, Not Relating to Bacon.* 1879.
SPENCE, JOSEPH. *Observations, Anecdotes, and Characters of Books and Men, Collected from Conversation.* Ed. James M. Osborn. 2 vols. New ed., 1966.
SPENCER, T. J. B. 'Ben Jonson on His Beloved, The Author Mr. William Shakespeare'. *Elizabethan Theatre IV.* Ed. G. R. Hibbard. Toronto, 1974, pp. 22–40.
SPIELMANN, M. H. 'The Ashbourne Portrait of Shakespeare'. *The Connoisseur*, xxvi (1910), 244–50; xxvii (1910), 38–42.
—. 'The "Grafton" and "Sanders" Portraits of Shakespeare'. *The Connoisseur*, xxiii (1909), 97–102.
—. 'The Janssen, or Somerset, Portrait of Shakespeare'. *The Connoisseur*, xxiv (1909), 230–7; xxvi (1910), 105–10; xxviii (1910), 151–8.
—. *The Portraits of Shakespeare.* Stratford-upon-Avon, 1907. [Also included in the Stratford Town Shakespeare, vol. x, pp. 373–98.]
—. 'Shakespeare's Portraiture'. *Studies in the First Folio Written for the Shakespeare Association in Celebration of the First Folio Tercentenary and Read at Meetings of the Association Held at King's College, University of London, May–June, 1923, by M. H. Spielmann, J. D. Wilson, et al.* 1924, pp. 1–52.
—. *The Title-Page of the First Folio of Shakespeare's Plays: A Comparative Study of the Droeshout Portrait and the Stratford Monument.* 1924.
STAMP, A. E. *The Disputed Revels Accounts Reproduced in Collotype Facsimile, with a Paper Read before the Shakespeare Association.* The Shakespeare Association. 1930.

[STEEVENS, GEORGE]. 'Answer to a Letter in the *Gazetteer*, &c. Relative to the New Edition of *Shakespeare's King Lear*. To the Printer of the *Gazetteer*, Jan. 8 1771'. *The Critical Review: or, Annals of Literature*, xxxi (1771), 82–4.

[STEEVENS, GEORGE]. 'The Authenticity of the New Found Portrait of Shakspeare Asserted'. *The European Magazine, and London Review*, xxvi (1794), 388–90.

[STEEVENS, GEORGE]. 'King *Lear*. A Tragedy. By *William Shakespeare*; Collated with the Old and New Editions'. *The Critical Review: or, Annals of Literature*, xxx (1770), 436–9.

[STEEVENS, GEORGE]. *Shakspeare*. [1794]. [Account of a supposed portrait of Shakespeare signed by William Richardson, printseller, but written by Steevens.]

STEPHENSON, H. T. *Shakespeare's London*. New York and Westminster, Eng., 1905.

STEVENSON, ALLAN H. 'Shirley's Publishers: The Partnership of Crooke and Cooke'. *The Library*, 4th ser., xxv (1944–5), 140–61.

STEVENSON, DAVID LLOYD. 'The Historical Dimension in *Measure for Measure*: The Role of James I in the Play'. Appendix to *The Achievement of Shakespeare's Measure for Measure*. Ithaca, New York, 1966, pp. 134–66.

STOCHHOLM, JOHANNE M. *Garrick's Folly: The Shakespeare Jubilee of 1769 at Stratford and Drury Lane*. New York, 1964.

STOPES, CHARLOTTE CARMICHAEL. '"Shakespeare of the Court": Roger, Thomas, John, William'. *The Athenaeum*, no. 4298, 12 March 1910, 319–20.

—. *Shakespeare's Environment*. 1914.

—. *The True Story of the Stratford Bust: A Contemporary Likeness of Shakespeare*. 1904.

STOW, JOHN. *A Survey of London*. Ed. C. L. Kingsford. 2 vols. Oxford, 1908.

—. *A Survey of the Cities of London and Westminster: Containing the Original, Antiquity, Increase, Modern Estate and Government of Those Cities. Written at First in the Year MDXCVIII. . . . Now Lastly, Cor., Improved, and Very Much Enl.: and . . . Brought Down from the Year 1633 . . . to the Present Time; by John Strype. . . . To Which Is Prefixed, the Life of the Author, Writ by the Editor*. 2 vols. 1720.

STRONG, ROY. *Tudor & Jacobean Portraits*. 2 vols. 1969.

STUBBES, PHILLIP. *A Motive to Good Workes. Or Rather, to True Christianitie Indeede. Wherein by the Waie is Shewed, How Farre Wee Are behinde, not onely our Fore-Fathers in Good Workes, but also Many Other Creatures in the Endes of Our Creation: with the Difference betwixt the Pretenced Good Workes of the Antichristian Papist, and the Good Workes of the Christian Protestant*. 1593.

STYLES, PHILIP. 'Borough of Stratford-upon-Avon'. *The Victoria History of the County of Warwick*. Gen. ed. I. F. Salzman. Vol. iii, *Barlichway Hundred*, 1945, pp. 221–82.

SWINBURNE, HENRY. *A Briefe Treatise of Testaments and Last Willes, Very Profitable to be Understoode of All the Subjects of This Realme of England*. 1590.

TANNENBAUM, SAMUEL A. 'A Portrait of Anne Hathaway?' *Shakespeare Association Bulletin*, xvii (1942), 112.

—. *Problems in Shakspere's Penmanship, Including a Study of the Poet's Will*. New York, 1927.

—. *Shakspere Forgeries in the Revels Accounts*. New York, 1928.

—. *Shaksperian Scraps and Other Elizabethan Fragments*. New York, 1933.

TARLTON, RICHARD. *Tarltons Newes out of Purgatorie: Onelye Such a Jest as His Jigge, Fit for Gentlemen to Laugh at an Houre, &c*. By Robin Goodfellow. 1590.

TATE, VERNON D. 'Preliminary Report on the Examination of a Signature Appearing on the Title-Page of "Apxaionomia, Sive de Priscis Anglorum Legibus Libri, Sermone Anglico", London 1568'. The Folger Shakespeare Library: Correspondence Files (1931–47).

TAYLOR, GEORGE C. 'The Date of Edward Capell's *Notes and Various Readings to Shakespeare, Volume II*'. *Review of English Studies*, v (1929), 317–19.

TAYLOR, JOHN. *All The Works of John Taylor the Water-Poet. Beeing Sixty and Three in Number. Collected into One Volume by the Author: With Sundry New Additions, Corrected, Revised, and Newly Imprinted*. 1630. [Not a complete ed. of the author's works.]

—. *Taylor on Thame Isis: or The Description of the Two Famous Rivers of Thame and Isis, Who Being Conjoyned or Combined Together, Are Called Thamisis, or Thames*. 1632.

—. *The Fearefull Summer: or, Londons Calamitie, the Countries Discourtesie, and Both Their Miserie*. 1625; rev. ed. 1636.

TAYLOR, RUPERT. 'Shakespeare's Cousin, Thomas Greene, and His Kin: Possible Light on the Shakespeare Family Background'. *PMLA*, lx (1945), 81–94.

THIRSK, JOAN. *Tudor Enclosures*. Historical Association General Series, no. 41. 1959.

THOMPSON, SIR EDWARD MAUNDE. 'Handwriting'. *Shakespeare's England*. Oxford, 1916, vol. i, pp. 284–310.

—. 'The Handwriting of the Three Pages Attributed to Shakespeare Compared with His Signatures'. *Shakespeare's Hand in the Play of Sir Thomas More*. Eds. A. W. Pollard, et. al. Cambridge, 1923, pp. 57–112.

—. *Shakespeare's Handwriting*. Oxford, 1916.

—. 'Shakespeare's Handwriting'. *Times Literary Supplement*, 12 June 1919, p. 325.

—. 'Two Pretended Autographs of Shakespeare'. *The Library*, 3rd ser., viii (1917), 193–217.

THOMS, WILLIAM J., ed. *Anecdotes and Traditions, Illustrative of Early English History and Literature, Derived from MS. Sources*. The Camden Society. 1839.

—. *Three Notelets on Shakespeare.* 1865.

THURSTON, HERBERT, S. J. 'A Controverted Shakespeare Document'. *The Dublin Review*, clxxiii (1923), 161–76.

TUCKER, STEPHEN. *The Assignment of Arms to Shakespere and Arden, 1596–1599.* 1884.

[TYRWHITT, THOMAS]. *Observations and Conjectures upon Some Passages of Shakespeare.* 1766.

UNDERHILL, ARTHUR. 'Law'. *Shakespeare's England.* Oxford, 1916, vol. i, pp. 381–412.

VER HUELL, A. *Jacobus Houbraken et son Oeuvre.* Arnhem, 1875.

VERTUE, GEORGE. *Note Books.* Walpole Society Annual, vols. xviii, xx, xxii, xxiv, xxvi, xxix, xxx. 7 vols. Oxford, 1930–55.

WALDO, T. R. Review of Warren B. Austin, *A Computer-Aided Technique for Stylistic Discrimination: The Authorship of Greene's Groatsworth of Wit. Computers and the Humanities*, vii (1972–3), 109–10.

WALLACE, C. W. *The First London Theatre: Materials for a History.* Nebraska *University Studies*, vol. xiii, nos. 1, 2, 3. 1913.

—. 'New Shakespeare Discoveries: Shakespeare as a Man among Men'. *Harper's Monthly Magazine*, cxx (1910), 489–510.

—. '*Shakespeare and His London Associates as Revealed in Recently Discovered Documents.* Nebraska *University Studies*, vol. x, no. 4. 1910.

—. 'Shakspere's Money Interest in the Globe Theatre'. *The Century Magazine*, lxxx (1910), 500–512.

WARD, JOHN. *Diary, Extending from 1648 to 1679. From the Original MSS. Preserved in the Library of the Medical Society of London.* Ed. Charles Severn, M. D., Registrar to the Medical Society of London. 1839.

WARNICKE, RETHA M. *William Lambarde, Elizabethan Antiquary, 1536–1601.* 1973.

WELLS, STANLEY. 'The Dark Lady'. *Times Literary Supplement*, 11 May 1973, p. 528.

WEST, WILLIAM. *The First Part of Simboleography. Which May Be Termed the Art, or Description, of Instruments and Presidents . . . And Now Newly Augmented with Divers Presidents Touching Marchants Affaires.* 1610–11; 1615.

WHELER, ROBERT BELL. *Collectanea de Stratford.* Shakespeare Birthplace Trust Records Office; shelfmark: MS. ER 1/8.

—. *A Guide to Stratford-upon-Avon.* Stratford-upon-Avon, 1814.

—. *History and Antiquities of Stratford-upon-Avon: Comprising a Description of the Collegiate Church, the Life of Shakespeare, and Copies of Several Documents Relating to Him and His Family, Never before Printed; with a Biographical Sketch of Other Eminent Characters, Natives of, or Who Have Resided in Stratford. To Which Is Added, a Particular Account of the Jubilee, Celebrated at Stratford, in Honour of Our Immortal Bard.* Stratford-upon-Avon, 1806.

—. 'Memorials of Literary Characters, No. xv. Shakspeare's Marriage License Bond'. *The Gentleman's Magazine*, n.s., vi (1836), 266–8.

—. 'Tomb of Shakespeare: His Birth-Place &c'. *The Gentleman's Magazine, and Historical Chronicle*, 2nd ser., lxxxv (1815), 389–91.

WHINNEY, MARGARET. *Sculpture in Britain, 1530 — 1830.* The Pelican History of Art. Harmondsworth and Baltimore, 1964.

W[HITE], T[HOMAS]. *A Sermon Preached at Pawles Crosse on Sunday the Thirde of November 1577. in the Time of the Plague.* 1578.

WHITEBROOK, J. C. 'Some Fresh Shakespearean Facts'. *Notes and Queries*, clxii (1932), 93–5.

WIDMANN, R. L. Review of Warren B. Austin, *A Computer-Aided Technique for Stylistic Discrimination: The Authorship of* '*Greene's Groatsworth of Wit*'. *Shakespeare Quarterly*, xxiii (1972), 214–15.

WILKINS, GEORGE. *The Miseries of Inforst Marige.* 1607.

—. *The Painful Adventures of Pericles Prince of Tyre. Being the True History of the Play of Pericles, as It Was Lately Presented by John Gower.* 1608.

'William Henry Ireland'. *Willis's Current Notes*, v (1885), 98.

WILLIAMS, IOLO A. 'Hollar: A Discovery'. *The Connoisseur*, xcii (1933), 318–21.

WILLOBY, HENRY. *Willobie his Avisa. Or The True Picture of a Modest Maid.* 1594.

WILLOUGHBY, EDWIN ELIOTT. *A Printer of Shakespeare: The Books and Times of William Jaggard.* 1934.

WILSON, F. P. *The Plague in Shakespeare's London.* Oxford, 1927.

—. 'Shakespeare's Reading'. *Shakespeare Survey 3* (Cambridge, 1950), pp. 14–21.

WILSON, J. DOVER. *The Essential Shakespeare: A Biographical Adventure.* Cambridge, 1932.

—. 'Malone and the Upstart Crow'. *Shakespeare Survey 4* (Cambridge, 1951), pp. 56–68.

—. '"Titus Andronicus" on the Stage in 1595'. *Shakespeare Survey 1* (Cambridge, 1948), pp. 17–22.

WILSON, J. DOVER, and R. W. HUNT. 'The Authenticity of Simon Forman's *Bocke of Plaies*'. *Review of English Studies*, xxiii (1947), 193–200.

WIVELL, ABRAHAM. *An Historical Account of the Monumental Bust of William Shakespeare in . . . the Church at Stratford-upon-Avon.* 1827.

—. *An Inquiry into the History, Authenticity, & Characteristics of the Shakspeare Portraits, in Which the Criticisms of Malone, Steevens, Boaden, & Others, Are Examined, Confirmed, or Refuted. Embracing the Felton, the Chandos, the Duke of Somerset's Pictures, the Droeshout Print, and an Exposé of the Spurious Pictures and Prints.* 1827.

—. *An Inquiry into the History, Authenticity, and Characteristics of the Shakspere Portraits; Embracing Martin Droe-*

shout's Engraving, the Chandos Picture, the Janssen, and Others of That Period; together with the Stratford Monument, Roubiliac's, and the One in Westminster Abbey. 1848.

WOLF, EDWIN, the second, and JOHN F. FLEMING. *Rosenbach: A Biography*. Cleveland and New York, 1960.

WOOD, D. T. B. 'The Revels Books: The Writer of the "Malone Scrap".' *Review of English Studies*, i (1925), 72–4.

[WRIGHT, JAMES]. *Historia Histrionica: an Historical Account of the English Stage, Shewing the Ancient Use, Improvement, and Perfection, of Dramatick Representations, in This Nation. In a Dialogue, of Plays and Players*. 1699.

WRIGHT, THOMAS, ED. *Queen Elizabeth and Her Times; A Series of Original Letters, Selected from the Inedited Private Correspondence of the Lord Treasurer Burghley, the Earl of Leicester, the Secretaries Walsingham and Smith, Sir Christopher Hatton, and Most of the Distinguished Persons of the Period*. 2 vols. 1838.

YEATMAN, JOHN PYM. *'Is William Shakspere's Will Holographic?' With Some Remarks upon the Recent Action for Libel of Pym Yeatman v. 'The Saturday Review', Respecting 'The Gentle Shakspere'*. Lewes, 1901.

A Yorkshire Tragedy. Not So New as Lamentable and True. Acted by His Majesties Players at the Globe. Written by W. Shakspeare. 1608.

YOUNG, JOHN. 'Is There a New Bard in the House?'. *The Times*, 25 May 1977, p. 16.

Index

Note: *Titles in this index have been modernized. Italicised citations refer to the page numbers of captions.*

Rear endpaper:

EDWARD RUDGE (?), RIVER AVON AT STRATFORD, C. 1830. *This watercolour is preserved in a small quarto notebook, measuring 13.5 by 20.5 cm, deposited by the Bedford Archaeological Society in the County Record Office in Bedford; shelfmark: X69/12. The notebook of thirty-two pages contains—besides watercolours—pencil sketches and some partly completed pictures. One watercolour shows the Stratford Guild Chapel; another, the Guild Chapel and school.*

Edward Rudge was art master at Rugby School. The entry for his marriage in Coventry in 1810 describes him as an artist of Snitterfield. He died in Dunchurch, Warwickshire, in 1841, aged fifty-one. His son Bradford, one of eight children, was also an artist. The latter attended Rugby and later migrated to Bedford, where he became drawing master to the Commercial School. Presumably he took with him some of his father's sketchbooks, which he seems to have reused. Father and son occasionally exhibited in Royal Academy showings in London. It is sometimes difficult to tell the two apart, but the Warwickshire subject matter, some obliterated writing inside the front cover of the notebook and slight differences of style point to Edward Rudge as the artist who made the watercolour here reproduced. An informative short essay is Yvonne Nichols, 'Bradford Rudge—Artist', Bedfordshire Magazine, *xvi, 123 (1977), 101–6.*